Praise for the Book

"What a rich devotional! Scripture—beribboned with trenchant questions, goading insights, and invitations to sit, to pray, to write. Invitations to read Zora Neale Hurston and W. H. Auden. Yes, please!"
— Lauren F. Winner, author of *Wearing God*

"Offering excerpts from the biblical text and the Connections commentary series, questions for deeper reflection, lectio divina, and space for personal reflection and thoughts, *Everyday Connections* provides a rich and essential resource to strengthen and support your spiritual and devotional practice."
— Song-Mi Suzie Park, Associate Professor of Old Testament,
Austin Presbyterian Theological Seminary

"Given the richness of this devotional companion to the Connections commentary, I can't imagine it sitting on your shelf unused! Designed with simplicity yet filled with depth, it is a resource that will help you engage Scripture and life both more fully and more joyfully. The flexibility built into its use—individually, in small groups, and in relation to worship—gives this guide longevity well beyond a particular lectionary year."
— Marjorie Thompson, author of *Soul Feast*

"In days of great tumult and stress, the guided meditations on Scripture and the prompts to prayer collected in *Everyday Connections* are a welcome balm and generous call to heed God's voice in the everyday life of those of us who yearn to follow Jesus. In days of joy and hope, this same book invites believers to praise a God whose word shows us the way of faithfulness and whose grace is ever abounding."
— Eric D. Barreto, Frederick and Margaret L.
Weyerhaeuser Associate Professor of New Testament,
Princeton Theological Seminary

D1569051

"*Everyday Connections* leads readers through the spiritual practice of centering our heads and hearts in faithful reflection and connection. It resources the writings of the Bible as well as the broader spiritual and intellectual resources of the Christian tradition, inviting us to link Christian wisdom, images, and teachings to the lived experiences of our communities and the communities of others. I commend this resource to pastors, chaplains, laypeople, and teachers engaged in the hermeneutical task of rendering biblical texts meaningful for our contemporary realities. If you seek to cultivate fresh engagement with the Bible, communities, the Christian lectionary calendar, and the self and to have fresh voices accompany you along the way, this resource can guide you in that endeavor."

— Shively T. J. Smith, Assistant Professor of New Testament,
Boston University

Everyday Connections

Everyday Connections

*Reflections and
Practices for Year C*

Edited by Heidi Haverkamp

WESTMINSTER
JOHN KNOX PRESS
LOUISVILLE • KENTUCKY

First Edition
Published by Westminster John Knox Press
Louisville, Kentucky

21 22 23 24 25 26 27 28 29 30—10 9 8 7 6 5 4 3 2 1

Unless otherwise indicated, Scripture quotations are from the New Revised Standard Version of the Bible, copyright © 1989 by the Division of Christian Education of the National Council of the Churches of Christ in the U.S.A., and are used by permission. Scripture quotations marked TEV are from the *Good News Bible—Old Testament:* Copyright © American Bible Society 1976; *New Testament:* Copyright© American Bible Society 1966, 1971, 1976.

Excerpt from *Blood Letters* by Lian Xi copyright © 2018. Reprinted by permission of Basic Books, an imprint of Hachette Book Group, Inc.

Book design by Allison Taylor
Cover design by Allison Taylor

Library of Congress Cataloging-in-Publication Data
Names: Haverkamp, Heidi, editor.
Title: Everyday connections : reflections and practices for Year C / edited by Heidi Haverkamp.
Description: First edition. | Louisville, Kentucky : Westminster John Knox Press, 2021. |
  Series: Connections: A Lectionary Commentary for Preaching and Worship | Includes
  index. | Summary: "This beautifully bound volume provides a full fifty-two weeks of
  devotional prompts based on the Revised Common Lectionary for Year C, drawing from
  the insightful Bible commentaries in the Connections series"—Provided by publisher.
Identifiers: LCCN 2021021819 (print) | LCCN 2021021820 (ebook) |
  ISBN 9780664264529 | ISBN 9781646982059 (ebook)
Subjects: LCSH: Common lectionary (1992). Year C—Prayers and devotions. | Church year—
  Prayers and devotions. | LCGFT: Devotional literature.
Classification: LCC BV30 .E94 2021 (print) | LCC BV30 (ebook) | DDC 263/.9—dc23
LC record available at https://lccn.loc.gov/2021021819
LC ebook record available at https://lccn.loc.gov/2021021820

Most Westminster John Knox Press books are available at special quantity discounts when purchased in bulk by corporations, organizations, and special-interest groups. For more information, please e-mail SpecialSales@wjkbooks.com.

Contents

A Note from the Publisher

This devotional resource is part of the series Connections: A Lectionary Commentary for Preaching and Worship. Connections embodies two complementary convictions about the study of Scripture. First, to best understand an individual passage of Scripture, we should put it in conversation with the rest of the Bible. Second, since all truth is God's truth, we should bring as many "lenses" as possible to the study of Scripture, drawn from as many sources as we can find. The essential idea of Connections is that biblical texts display their power most fully when they are allowed to interact with a number of contexts, that is, when many connections are made between a biblical text and realities outside that text. Like the two poles of a battery, when the pole of the biblical text is connected to a different pole (another aspect of Scripture or a dimension of life outside Scripture), creative sparks fly and energy surges from pole to pole.

Based on the Revised Common Lectionary (RCL), which has wide ecumenical use, Connections offers hundreds of essays on the full array of biblical passages in the three-year cycle. Two major interpretive essays, called Commentary 1 and Commentary 2, address every scriptural reading in the RCL. Commentary 1 explores connections between a lectionary reading and other texts and themes within Scripture, and Commentary 2 makes connections between the lectionary texts and themes in the larger culture outside of Scripture. These essays have been written by pastors, biblical scholars, theologians, and others.

During the seasons of the Christian year (Advent through Epiphany and Lent through Pentecost), the RCL provides three readings and a psalm or canticle for each Sunday and feast day: (1) a first reading, usually from the Old Testament; (2) a psalm or canticle, chosen to respond to the first reading; (3) a second reading, usually from one of the New Testament epistles; and (4) a Gospel reading. The first and second readings are chosen as complements to the Gospel reading for the day.

During the time between Pentecost and Advent, the RCL includes an additional first reading for every Sunday. There is the usual complementary reading, chosen in relation to the Gospel reading, but there is also a "semicontinuous" reading. These semicontinuous first readings move through the books of the Old Testament more or less continuously in narrative sequence, offering the stories of the patriarchs (Year A), the kings of Israel (Year B), and the prophets (Year C). Connections covers both the complementary and the semicontinuous readings.

Because not all lectionary days are used in a given year, depending on how the calendar falls, you may not need some of the readings here until a subsequent lectionary cycle. Check the official RCL website at http://lectionary.library.vanderbilt.edu for a list of readings for the current year.

We want to thank the many talented individuals who made Connections possible: our general editors, Joel B. Green, Thomas G. Long, Luke A. Powery, Cynthia L. Rigby, and Carolyn J. Sharp; Psalms editor Kimberly Bracken Long and sidebar editors Bo Adams and Rachel Toombs; the esteemed members of our editorial board; our superb slate of writers; and our indefatigable project manager Joan Murchison. Finally, our sincere thanks to the administration, faculty, and staff of Austin Presbyterian Theological Seminary, our institutional partner in producing Connections.

We are deeply grateful to Heidi Haverkamp for her exhaustive editorial and creative work developing Everyday Connections for the spiritual enrichment of every Christian who desires to delve deeply into Scripture. This insightful volume pairs weekly texts and reflections with prompts, prayers, and practices to spark connections between the Bible and everyday life as well as nurture one's own connection with the Divine.

Westminster John Knox Press

How to Use This Book

In this book, you will find a panoply of modes and methods for reflection on the Sunday readings of the Revised Common Lectionary, Year C. Some are serious, some are playful, some are personal, some are relational, some are pastoral, some are prophetic, some are practical, some are poetic; all are centered in Christ's radical call and love for us. Whether you want to deepen your prayer life, your grasp of Scripture, your small-group discussions, your sermon preparation, or some other aspect of your Christian life and relationship with God, I hope you will discover in these pages a wide variety of resources, information, ideas, questions, and spiritual practices to support you.

Your conversation partners for each week's reflections are excerpts from the Connections preaching and worship commentary series, also published by Westminster John Knox Press. The series is a treasure trove of background and insights, with essays on each Scripture passage written by Bible scholars, theologians, and pastors. They are easy to read but offer significant historical and linguistic information, theological reflection, connections across the biblical text, and connections from the text to social and cultural realities in our world. Choosing a single excerpt from so many of these essays was incredibly challenging. There are great riches to be found in the full commentaries, for those seeking more.

There are many ways Everyday Connections can guide and strengthen your Christian life, leadership, and community, depending on what works best for you, your group, or your congregation in any given week:

- Personal reflection: use for prayer, study, meditation, and journaling
- Sermon or worship preparation: explore ideas, get inspired, and prepare to preach or plan worship
- Small groups: see the appendix for a suggested format to use Everyday Connections as a curriculum or study text
- Teaching: study and reflect as you prepare to teach a Bible study or class of any age
- Meetings: use an excerpt as an opening meditation or discussion for staff or committee meetings

- Beyond church: use on visits to individuals or groups in a hospital, assisted living facility, prison, or other social agency, or as part of a mission trip, retreat, or conference

Here are some other suggestions to get the most from this devotional:

Use alongside a Bible. Since this book offers only short excerpts from Scripture for the sake of length, reading the full passage in your Bible will expand your perspective.

Choose what to study. Each week of reflections offers multiple options and ideas for engagement with the texts. Focus on whatever is speaking to you that day. Or, over time, you may discover certain exercises or modules work best for you. Do not feel that you need to interact with every single entry, every single week.

Choose what order. Reflections have been laid out in a certain order, but you can use them in any order you like.

Choose what frequency. You may want to use this book every day, studying one or two entries at a time, or just once or twice a week, studying several or most of a week's entries at once.

The material for each week is divided into these sections:

1. **A Scripture Overview.** On the first page of each week, a selection of verses excerpted from that week's readings gives you a sense of what to expect. (Excerpts from psalms and canticles are omitted in the season after Pentecost in order to accommodate excerpts from the two Old Testament tracks.) Then, a shortened form of **Lectio Divina**, Latin for "holy reading," is suggested, as a way to begin to reflect on the week's Scriptures: choose a phrase or a few words that speak to you, then listen in prayer or meditation for what God might be saying to you through those words. Benedictine monks have prayed in this way for centuries.

2. **Themes from This Week's Writers.** Two themes, drawn from the week's commentary essays, are suggested for study, reflection, or sermon preparation. Brief quotes from the essays that support the theme are provided. See if the commentators' words inspire you or other connections emerge for you. A **Spiritual Practice** associated with the themes or liturgical season is also suggested. The practice

can be done on your own, as a family, with a friend or prayer partner, or as a small-group activity, and on any day of the week.

3. **First Reading, Canticle, Second Reading, and Gospel.** A deeper dive into four of the week's readings (five for Palm/Passion Sunday and six for Easter Sunday) includes a verse or two of Scripture, an excerpt from a commentary essay, some reflection questions, and a brief prayer. These reflections will invite you to make connections that (usually) go in different directions from the two themes. You could read one each day, read them all at once, or pick just one or two to read, depending on the week.

4. **Weekend Reflections.** Choose a way to wrap up the week's study and Scripture connections, perhaps on the day you are sitting down to write a sermon or plan worship. First, a **Further Connection** is offered: a quote from a source outside of Scripture and the commentary essays, which may speak to you in a new way or deepen a connection you have made with a theme or reading already that week. Full sources and citations for these quotes are available in the appendix. **Making the Connections** invites you to consider one of four questions (repeated each week) to focus your reflections and connections from the readings to a conclusion, sermon, or final theme for the week. **My Connections** provides extra space to write your own notes.

5. **Sabbath Day.** These exercises are meant to be done on a day you consider the end of the week or a day off. The **Scripture of Assurance** is meant to offer solace—and sometimes a little humor—to a weary soul. The **Weekly Examen** is adapted from the daily examen of Ignatius of Loyola. It can be done on your own, as a family, with a friend or prayer partner, or in a small group.

Again, choose what speaks to you; do not feel you need to engage every single section. The options in this book were designed to be used in different combinations to suit the needs of different readers, contexts, and schedules.

A few sections use slightly different formats:

Christmas Week. For this busy holiday time, a single week of reflections draws on the Scriptures from both Christmas and the Sunday after Christmas, since many of the readings and themes overlap and complement one another.

Weekday Holy Days. Five significant holy days always or usually fall on weekdays: Epiphany, Ash Wednesday, Holy Thursday, Good Friday, and Ascension of the Lord. Each has a separate, shortened entry (appearing before the start of the week leading up to the following Sunday) that includes Scripture quotes, excerpts from the commentary essays, a reflection question, and a prayer.

All Saints'. There is a full week of entries for All Saints' Day (November 1) or All Saints' Sunday (the first Sunday following November 1). Note that your congregation may celebrate Proper 26 or Proper 27 instead, depending on whether All Saints' is commemorated in your tradition or perhaps celebrated on November 1, proper, rather than the Sunday following.

May God bless you richly as you explore, study, connect, and pray your way through the pages of this book and God's Word as it is proclaimed in the lectionary cycle of Year C.

Heidi Haverkamp

Everyday
Connections

The Week Leading Up to the
First Sunday of Advent

Jeremiah 33:14–16

The days are surely coming, says the LORD, when I will fulfill the promise I made to the house of Israel and the house of Judah. (v. 14)

Psalm 25:1–10

To you, O LORD, I lift up my soul.
O my God, in you I trust;
    do not let me be put to shame;
    do not let my enemies exult over me. (vv. 1–2)

1 Thessalonians 3:9–13

Now may our God and Father himself and our Lord Jesus direct our way to you. And may the Lord make you increase and abound in love for one another and for all, just as we abound in love for you. (vv. 11–12)

Luke 21:25–36

"People will faint from fear and foreboding of what is coming upon the world, for the powers of the heavens will be shaken. Then they will see 'the Son of Man coming in a cloud' with power and great glory." (vv. 26–27)

LECTIO DIVINA

Underline a word or phrase that especially grabs your attention. Pray from that word or phrase and ask God to help you connect to its particular invitation for you this week.

Themes from This Week's Writers

THEME 1: *Waiting*

Psalm 25:1–10

The psalmist waits in trust as long as necessary. His waiting is not passive. To "untwist" his life, the psalmist must relearn and humbly replace his feet in God's ways.

KIMBERLY L. CLAYTON

1 Thessalonians 3:9–13

At the root of Paul's eschatological vision—however soon or delayed the redemptive completion of all things may be—is this claim: God holds the future, and God is pulling us, even now, toward that future.

THEODORE J. WARDLAW

Luke 21:25–36

This is a Jesus-shaped present in which we follow his own life of expectation and trust, and his own faith and hope in God. Just as he waited on God, so too we enter his waiting bound up in his work. He is with us in the waiting and in the work, sharing in our challenges but offering us strength.

WILLIE JAMES JENNINGS

THEME 2: *Is There Good News in Apocalypse?*

Luke 21:25–36

The good news stands even when everything else falls. . . . For those who trust God and whose trust of God is mirrored in their own faithfulness, the coming of the end is not a calamity to be feared but redemption to be welcomed.

JOEL B. GREEN

Jeremiah 33:14–16

The vision of a future beyond the contemporary horizon, therefore, calls the people of God to look beyond the present moment, with its violence, disintegration, and failed leadership, to the restorative end toward which the Lord is moving, and so to orient faith and decision making within the context of God's ultimate power and purposes, rather than the clamoring demands of a paralyzed present.

L. DANIEL HAWK

1 Thessalonians 3:9–13

Christ has indeed come and brought us the gift of transformed life—abundant life now and the promise of life eternal—yet the transformation is not complete.

CYNTHIA M. CAMPBELL

WHAT IS THE HOLY SPIRIT SAYING TO YOU THIS WEEK?

_____

_____

_____

_____

_____

A SPIRITUAL PRACTICE FOR THIS WEEK

Pray or read by the light of your Advent wreath this week. If you do not have one, simply light any candle and attach a sticky note or other label that says, "Hope."

First Reading

Jeremiah 33:14–16

In those days and at that time I will cause a righteous Branch to spring up for David; and he shall execute justice and righteousness in the land. In those days Judah will be saved and Jerusalem will live in safety. (vv. 15–16a)

REFLECTION

Early church theologians spoke of God's kingdom as *autobasileia*, a "self-kingdom"—a kingdom in Jesus Christ himself. God's righteousness and justice are found in Christ, as well as salvation and safety. This makes it possible for us to live in God's reign here and now. We can live in the freedom of serving God and receive the blessings of God's presence with us in Christ. This sustains us and launches us into participating in God's kingdom in Christ every day!

DONALD K. MCKIM

RESPONSE

Without a sense of safety, a sense of freedom may be impossible. What does it mean to you to live in safety? How is spiritual safety different from physical safety? What safety and what freedom is God offering you in Christ right now?

PRAYER

O Jesus Christ, no matter what is happening around me, teach me to find safety and freedom in you. Amen.

Canticle

Psalm 25:1–10

Do not let those who wait for you be put to shame;
> let them be ashamed who are wantonly treacherous.

Make me to know your ways, O LORD;
> teach me your paths.
Lead me in your truth, and teach me,
> for you are the God of my salvation;
> for you I wait all day long. (vv. 3–5)

REFLECTION

We are not without hope, because we are not without God.

The psalmist waits in trust (v. 2) as long as necessary (v. 5). His waiting is not passive. To "untwist" his life, the psalmist must relearn and humbly re-place his feet in God's ways (v. 4). No matter how off-target we become, God's paths remain open, cleared by truth (v. 5) and marked by steadfast love and faithfulness at every turn (v. 10).

KIMBERLY L. CLAYTON

RESPONSE

We usually think of waiting as a purely passive activity, rather than as a time to learn, relearn, take steps, or ask for help. The psalmist thinks differently. This Advent, what could an active waiting for the birth of Jesus look like or change in your life?

PRAYER

God of truth, for you I wait all day long, and in you I trust. Lead me and teach me your paths. Amen.

Second Reading

1 Thessalonians 3:9–13

And may the Lord make you increase and abound in love for one another and for all, just as we abound in love for you. And may he so strengthen your hearts in holiness that you may be blameless before our God and Father at the coming of our Lord Jesus with all his saints. (vv. 12–13)

REFLECTION

The love that creates this community is not simply for the sake of the in-group. The prayer is that they (we) will abound in love "for all." This Christian community is to show love, compassion, care, and respect not only to one another but also to those who have rejected them. Christian life is not a closed loop or zero-sum game. The beloved community is one that "abounds" and overflows with love, a place where the door is always open and there is always room for more.

CYNTHIA M. CAMPBELL

RESPONSE

Sometimes, we long for what C. S. Lewis calls "the delicious sense of secret intimacy." Community, without hospitality to outsiders, is just an in-group. Consider likely "closed loops" in your own life and communities. How might Christ be calling you to more hospitality? Even to those who have rejected you?

PRAYER

Lord Jesus, increase my love and teach me hospitality, even for those who have rejected me. Amen.

Gospel

Luke 21:25–36

"Heaven and earth will pass away, but my words will not pass away." (v. 33)

REFLECTION

God's direction orients us in faith, not in fear toward our world. Even the cataclysmic events (as suggested in vv. 25–26), involving both the environment and nations, should not disorient us but turn us toward God, who has not and will not abandon this world. . . . The words of Jesus outline the order of discipleship inside a politics of reading the signs of the times: see what is happening and continue to do the work.

WILLIE JAMES JENNINGS

RESPONSE

Meditate on holding fast to faith and the Word of God in the midst of destructive forces, whatever those may be in your life right now. What images emerge in your heart and mind? Draw, doodle, or write a poem based on these images.

PRAYER

Almighty and everlasting God, even though the heavens and earth will pass away, you will not abandon me or your people. Amen.

Weekend Reflections

FURTHER CONNECTION

There have been many attempts, in recent years, to soften the message of Advent . . . new names for the candles of the Four Seasons of Advent have been proposed along the lines of Peace, Joy, Love, and Hope. This presents quite a contrast with the medieval Advent themes of death, judgment, heaven and hell—in that order! As we have seen, hope is a very meager concept if it is not measured against the malevolence and godlessness of the forces that assail creation and its creatures every day in this "present evil age" (Gal. 1:4).

FLEMING RUTLEDGE (1937–), *ADVENT: THE ONCE
AND FUTURE COMING OF JESUS CHRIST*

MAKING THE CONNECTIONS

Choose one or two questions for reflection:

1. What connections have you noticed between this week's texts and other passages in Scripture?

2. What connections have you made between this week's texts and the world beyond Scripture?

3. Does either of this week's two commentary themes speak especially to your life or the life of the world around you right now?

4. What is God saying to your congregation in particular through this week's readings and commentaries?

MY CONNECTIONS

_____

_____

_____

_____

_____

Sabbath Day

SCRIPTURE OF ASSURANCE

> Give ear to my words, O Lord;
>   give heed to my sighing.
> Listen to the sound of my cry,
>   my King and my God,
>   for to you I pray.
> O Lord, in the morning you hear my voice;
>   in the morning I plead my case to you, and watch.
>   (Psalm 5:1–3)

WEEKLY EXAMEN

- Take a quiet moment, seek out God's presence, and pray for the guidance of the Spirit.

- Consider the past week; recall specific moments and feelings that stand out to you.

- Choose one moment or feeling for deeper examination, thanksgiving, or repentance.

- Let go, breathe deeply, and invite Christ's love to surround and fill you in preparation for the week ahead.

- End with the Lord's Prayer.

The Week Leading Up to the
Second Sunday of Advent

Malachi 3:1–4

See, I am sending my messenger to prepare the way before me, and the Lord whom you seek will suddenly come to his temple. The messenger of the covenant in whom you delight—indeed, he is coming, says the LORD of hosts. (v. 1)

Luke 1:68–79

"By the tender mercy of our God,
    the dawn from on high will break upon us,
to give light to those who sit in darkness and in the shadow of death,
    to guide our feet into the way of peace." (vv. 78–79)

Philippians 1:3–11

And this is my prayer, that your love may overflow more and more with knowledge and full insight to help you to determine what is best, so that in the day of Christ you may be pure and blameless, having produced the harvest of righteousness that comes through Jesus Christ for the glory and praise of God. (vv. 9–11)

Luke 3:1–6

During the high priesthood of Annas and Caiaphas, the word of God came to John son of Zechariah in the wilderness. (v. 2)

LECTIO DIVINA

Underline a word or phrase that especially grabs your attention. Pray from that word or phrase and ask God to help you connect to its particular invitation for you this week.

Themes from This Week's Writers

THEME 1: *Hope*

Malachi 3:1–4

In the end, of course, what sustains the church, and all human beings touched by God's grace, lies beyond the words of judgment, in the faithfulness with which God shall complete the loving work of creation.

ALAN GREGORY

Philippians 1:3–11

For Paul, the second coming of Christ is a day in which all of God's promises will be fulfilled, God's people will be redeemed, and resurrection life will reconcile all to one another and to God (see Rom. 8:18–25). It is precisely the anticipation of that "day" that fuels the joy that pours out of his letter to the Philippians.

CYNTHIA M. CAMPBELL

Luke 3:1–6

We live in its hope, yet are always edging toward frustration as we wait for a world filled with the sight, sound, and knowledge of God and shaped in the divine rule.

WILLIE JAMES JENNINGS

THEME 2: *Repentance*

Malachi 3:1–4

In what ways have we contributed to social and economic conditions about which we so easily become upset—even angry? It is far too easy to blame others (and historically, this has often fallen on foreigners, migrants, and the weak). The prophets often turn the mirror on ourselves. Who, indeed, can "endure the day"?

DANIEL L. SMITH-CHRISTOPHER

Luke 1:68–79

Although [John the Baptist] appears in the wilderness, he has his eye on the temple and the empire itself. . . . Against these earthly and corrupt powers John, son of Zechariah, appears, preparing the Lord's way of light and peace (Luke 1:79).

KIMBERLY L. CLAYTON

Luke 3:1–6

This is fully consistent with the way Luke describes this central aspect of John's ministry: it is a "baptism of repentance," that is, a repentance-baptism. This realignment of hearts and lives in relation to God's agenda is the means by which God's people "prepare the way of the Lord" and "make his paths straight."

JOEL B. GREEN

WHAT IS THE HOLY SPIRIT SAYING TO YOU THIS WEEK?

_____

_____

_____

_____

_____

A SPIRITUAL PRACTICE FOR THIS WEEK

Pray or read by the light of your Advent wreath this week. If you do not have one, simply light any candle and attach a sticky note or other label that says, "Peace."

First Reading

Malachi 3:1–4

But who can endure the day of his coming, and who can stand when he appears?

For he is like a refiner's fire and like fullers' soap; he will sit as a refiner and purifier of silver, and he will purify the descendants of Levi and refine them like gold and silver, until they present offerings to the LORD in righteousness. (vv. 2–3)

REFLECTION

The church, therefore, must seek the strange blessing in the words of God's judgment, listening intently to this word that purifies and never flatters. When Christians accept God's calling, it is good news for the world, because the church, when it is willing to bear God's refining, represents the glory of humanity as it exists in God's desire. In the end, of course, what sustains the church, and all human beings touched by God's grace, lies beyond the words of judgment, in the faithfulness with which God shall complete the loving work of creation.

ALAN GREGORY

RESPONSE

In what ways are you or your congregation being refined by God's fire or washed with strong soap in this season? What hardships are you experiencing? What hope do you feel? What does "the glory of humanity as it exists in God's desire" look like, as it is being revealed in you?

PRAYER

O God, you are sending your messenger to prepare the way for us. Purify and refine us, for your love's sake. Amen.

Canticle

Luke 1:68–79

"And you, child, will be called the prophet of the Most High;
  for you will go before the Lord to prepare his ways,
to give knowledge of salvation to his people
  by the forgiveness of their sins." (vv. 76–77)

REFLECTION

Zechariah, the proud papa, acknowledges the divine differential in his canticle: He begins by praising of the God of Israel who "raised up a mighty Savior" (Luke 1:69) and lingers there for eight verses. Only after the Messiah is lifted up does Zechariah turn his attention to his own child for four verses. As "the prophet of the Most High," John will go before the Lord, preparing the way, giving knowledge of salvation by forgiveness of sins (Luke 1:76–79).

KIMBERLY L. CLAYTON

RESPONSE

Listen to Zechariah's words, and imagine that he is saying them about you. How does it make you feel? What phrases especially stand out to you? Then consider, like Zechariah, "the divine differential": what you are called to do versus what can only be done by the Messiah.

PRAYER

Merciful God, give light to us who sit in darkness and the shadow of death, and guide our feet into the way of peace. Amen.

Second Reading

Philippians 1:3–11

I thank my God every time I remember you, constantly praying with joy in every one of my prayers for all of you, because of your sharing in the gospel from the first day until now. I am confident of this, that the one who began a good work among you will bring it to completion by the day of Jesus Christ. (vv. 3–6)

REFLECTION

There are moments when, in the midst of utter ordinariness, something breaks through; seen with the eyes of faith, that which is rudimentary is suddenly transformed into something holy. Sometimes people of faith are fortunate enough to see all of it, even themselves, with the eyesight of God; the only fitting response to it all is a great, unimaginable gratitude.

THEODORE J. WARDLAW

RESPONSE

When have you seen the ordinary transformed into something holy recently? What does it mean, do you think, to see with the "eyesight of God"? What would it mean to see yourself this way? Your neighborhood? Your faith community?

PRAYER

Jesus Christ, may our love overflow more and more, remembering one another in joy and prayer. Amen.

Gospel

Luke 3:1–6

He went into all the region around the Jordan, proclaiming a baptism of repentance for the forgiveness of sins, as it is written in the book of the words of the prophet Isaiah,

> "The voice of one crying out in the wilderness:
> 'Prepare the way of the Lord,
>   make his paths straight.'" (vv. 3–4)

REFLECTION

We therefore recognize that the repentance John proclaims is marked by baptism but it is not a one-time event. It refers to a continuing journey on an obstructed path requiring ongoing roadwork. God's people begin the conversionary journey with baptism, but baptism is not so much the arrival at one's destination as it is the beginning of a journey.

JOEL B. GREEN

RESPONSE

Have you ever thought about Advent as a season for conversion? It is a season for new beginnings and repentance, as John the Baptist reminds us. What sort of conversion are you longing for in the baptismal journey of your life right now?

PRAYER

Show me, O God, how to walk in your paths and prepare the way, that all may know the salvation of your love. Amen.

Weekend Reflections

FURTHER CONNECTION

It is so easy to be hopeful in the daytime when you can see the things you wish on. But it was night, it stayed night. Night was striding across nothingness with the whole round world in his hands. . . . They sat in company with the others in other shanties, their eyes straining against cruel walls and their souls asking if He meant to measure their puny might against His. They seemed to be staring at the dark, but their eyes were watching God.

ZORA NEALE HURSTON (1891–1960), *THEIR EYES WERE WATCHING GOD*

MAKING THE CONNECTIONS

Choose one or two questions for reflection:

1. What connections have you noticed between this week's texts and other passages in Scripture?

2. What connections have you made between this week's texts and the world beyond Scripture?

3. Does either of this week's two commentary themes speak especially to your life or the life of the world around you right now?

4. What is God saying to your congregation in particular through this week's readings and commentaries?

_____

_____

_____

_____

_____

_____

Sabbath Day

SCRIPTURE OF ASSURANCE

Answer me, O LORD, answer me, so that this people may know that you, O LORD, are God, and that you have turned their hearts back. (1 Kings 18:37)

WEEKLY EXAMEN

- Take a quiet moment, seek out God's presence, and pray for the guidance of the Spirit.

- Consider the past week; recall specific moments and feelings that stand out to you.

- Choose one moment or feeling for deeper examination, thanksgiving, or repentance.

- Let go, breathe deeply, and invite Christ's love to surround and fill you in preparation for the week ahead.

- End with the Lord's Prayer.

The Week Leading Up to the
Third Sunday of Advent

Zephaniah 3:14–20

Sing aloud, O daughter Zion;
    shout, O Israel!
Rejoice and exult with all your heart,
    O daughter Jerusalem! (v. 14)

Isaiah 12:2–6

Sing praises to the LORD, for he has done gloriously;
    let this be known in all the earth.
Shout aloud and sing for joy, O royal Zion,
    for great in your midst is the Holy One of Israel. (vv. 5–6)

Philippians 4:4–7

Rejoice in the Lord always; again I will say, Rejoice. Let your gentleness be known to everyone. The Lord is near. (vv. 4–5)

Luke 3:7–18

"His winnowing fork is in his hand, to clear his threshing floor and to gather the wheat into his granary; but the chaff he will burn with unquenchable fire."

So, with many other exhortations, [John] proclaimed the good news to the people. (vv. 17–18)

LECTIO DIVINA

Underline a word or phrase that especially grabs your attention. Pray from that word or phrase and ask God to help you connect to its particular invitation for you this week.

Themes from This Week's Writers

THEME 1: *Joy*

Zephaniah 3:14–20

God's blessing, therefore, takes burdened men and women, despised and spurned by their neighbors, and brings them joyfully into the common life (3:19). No longer will a constant shadow of fear and threat dampen all celebration. The penurious, the refugee, and all who dread what the next month may bring shall breathe freely as God rejoices over them.

ALAN GREGORY

Isaiah 12:2–6

In both Zephaniah 3:14–20 and Isaiah 12:2–6, fear is replaced by trust and joy. Imperatives of praise pile up: Sing! Shout! Sing for joy!

Isaiah 12:2–6 is the sustained doxology of people who, despite their present condition of suffering and fear, know that death will not have the last word, because God controls the narrative.

KIMBERLY L. CLAYTON

Philippians 4:4–7

Paul is thinking here of something much deeper than happiness or a sunny outlook or a "put on a happy face" form of denial. He *knows* that he is in prison; he knows that there are challenges for this community of believers both within and without. Nevertheless Paul has found in the gospel the source of deepest joy. Christ's self-emptying has become Paul's abundance.

CYNTHIA M. CAMPBELL

THEME 2: *Reconciliation*

Zephaniah 3:14–20

It takes genuine strength to be actually concerned about transformation of enemies.

DANIEL L. SMITH-CHRISTOPHER

Luke 3:7–18

Though John does not address this wider range of persons in their day-to-day circumstances, the prophet has begun to map the patterns of thinking, feeling, believing, and behaving that deserve the label "fruits worthy of repentance." These patterns reflect "the way of the Lord," who restores God's people, and they reach into the routine matters of life.

JOEL B. GREEN

Luke 3:7–18

John draws them toward a life that shows profound care and concern for their sisters and brothers. Clothes and food, the very things that speak of intimacy and life, must be shared. To show repentance involves, first, a sharing of the staples of life with anyone in need.

WILLIE JAMES JENNINGS

WHAT IS THE HOLY SPIRIT SAYING TO YOU THIS WEEK?

_____

_____

_____

_____

_____

A SPIRITUAL PRACTICE FOR THIS WEEK

Pray or read by the light of your Advent wreath this week. If you do not have one, simply light any candle and attach a sticky note or other label that says, "Joy."

First Reading

Zephaniah 3:14–20

At that time I will bring you home,
    at the time when I gather you;
for I will make you renowned and praised
    among all the peoples of the earth,
when I restore your fortunes
    before your eyes, says the Lord. (v. 20)

REFLECTION

What is the kind of behavior that we can exhibit in the world—a behavior clearly based on our love for God—that would so deeply impress the nations of the world (even, perhaps *especially*, nations with whom we are angry!) that we are "renowned and praised" as a result? Surely it is not how effective we are at punishing enemies, but how effective we are at *impressing* enemies toward changed relationships. Such positive changes would indeed be "renowned and praised."

DANIEL L. SMITH-CHRISTOPHER

RESPONSE

Make a list of nations, groups, or people that you consider to be enemies. What would it look like to love them toward a transformed relationship? Choose one, and make a list of ways you might do this, in practical terms, with God's help. How crazy does this feel?

PRAYER

Gather and bring me home, O God, that I might live from love, even for my enemies. Amen.

Canticle

Isaiah 12:2–6

Surely God is my salvation;
    I will trust, and will not be afraid,
for the LORD GOD is my strength and my might;
    he has become my salvation.

With joy you will draw water from the wells of salvation. (vv. 2–3)

REFLECTION

The Hebrew word for salvation, rarely used in the first thirty-nine chapters of Isaiah, appears three times in this brief passage. The prophet knows that God can and indeed will save the people from ultimate destruction. This repetitive use of "salvation" closes this unit of Isaiah, whose name means, "The Lord is Salvation."
    God forgives and saves.

KIMBERLY L. CLAYTON

RESPONSE

Isaiah interweaves words of salvation with words of joy. Could there be a relationship between feeling joy and believing in grace? Consider things that bring you joy, and reflect on how those things may manifest God's salvation now and in the life to come.

PRAYER

Lord God, you have become our salvation, in this world and the next. Teach me to trust and not to be afraid. Amen.

Second Reading

Philippians 4:4–7

Rejoice in the Lord always; again I will say, Rejoice. Let your gentleness be known to everyone. The Lord is near. Do not worry about anything, but in everything by prayer and supplication with thanksgiving let your requests be made known to God. And the peace of God, which surpasses all understanding, will guard your hearts and your minds in Christ Jesus. (vv. 4–7)

REFLECTION

Christians are urged to get gentle or generous with each other and also with the world around them. This is not an ethic of "niceness," but rather a new way of life made possible by Christ's presence.

. . . However, it seems much more likely that Paul sees the immediacy of Christ's presence as what makes Christian life possible. Because God in Christ is with us, we are able to have "the mind of Christ" among us and live at peace with each other.

CYNTHIA M. CAMPBELL

RESPONSE

What does it mean that Christ's presence makes the Christian way of life possible, rather than our own efforts or "niceness"? Today, strive to let your gentleness be known to all you meet; try to lean on Christ rather than your own will or efforts.

PRAYER

Teach me, God, to rejoice in you always, that your peace may guard my heart and my mind. Amen.

Gospel

Luke 3:7–18

And the crowds asked [John the Baptist], "What then should we do?" In reply he said to them, "Whoever has two coats must share with anyone who has none; and whoever has food must do likewise." Even tax collectors came to be baptized, and they asked him, "Teacher, what should we do?" He said to them, "Collect no more than the amount prescribed for you." Soldiers also asked him, "And we, what should we do?" He said to them, "Do not extort money from anyone by threats or false accusation, and be satisfied with your wages." (vv. 10–14)

REFLECTION

They do not ask, "What can we do, given the nature of our positions?" or "What is possible, given the constraints within which we operate?" Such questions would be reasonable but not born of repentance and the new age John announces. The life of repentance reverses the order of possibility. When it comes to our life and work, the life of repentance demands that we ask what *must* be done for the sake of God before we ask what *can* be done, given structural constraints.

WILLIE JAMES JENNINGS

RESPONSE

Imagine yourself on the shores of the Jordan with John. When asked, "What then should we do?" what do you think his particular answer might be to you or a group you are part of? What does a life of repentance demand right now, despite other constraints?

PRAYER

God of grace, what shall I do? Show me how to bear fruits worthy of repentance. Amen.

Weekend Reflections

FURTHER CONNECTION

Twinkle lights are the perfect metaphor for joy. Joy is not a constant. It comes to us in moments—often ordinary moments. Sometimes we miss out on the bursts of joy because we're too busy chasing down extraordinary moments. Other times we're so afraid of the dark that we don't dare let ourselves enjoy the light. A joyful life is not a floodlight of joy. That would eventually become unbearable. I believe a joyful life is made up of joyful moments gracefully strung together by trust, gratitude, inspiration, and faith.

BRENÉ BROWN (1965–), *THE GIFTS OF IMPERFECTION*

MAKING THE CONNECTIONS

Choose one or two questions for reflection:

1. What connections have you noticed between this week's texts and other passages in Scripture?

2. What connections have you made between this week's texts and the world beyond Scripture?

3. Does either of this week's two commentary themes speak especially to your life or the life of the world around you right now?

4. What is God saying to your congregation in particular through this week's readings and commentaries?

_____

_____

_____

_____

_____

_____

Sabbath Day

SCRIPTURE OF ASSURANCE

You then, my child, be strong in the grace that is in Christ Jesus; and what you have heard from me through many witnesses entrust to faithful people who will be able to teach others as well. (2 Timothy 2:1–2)

WEEKLY EXAMEN

- Take a quiet moment, seek out God's presence, and pray for the guidance of the Spirit.

- Consider the past week; recall specific moments and feelings that stand out to you.

- Choose one moment or feeling for deeper examination, thanksgiving, or repentance.

- Let go, breathe deeply, and invite Christ's love to surround and fill you in preparation for the week ahead.

- End with the Lord's Prayer.

The Week Leading Up to the
Fourth Sunday of Advent

Micah 5:2–5a

But you, O Bethlehem of Ephrathah,
who are one of the little clans of Judah,
from you shall come forth for me
one who is to rule in Israel. (v. 2a)

Luke 1:46b–55

And Mary said,
"My soul magnifies the Lord,
and my spirit rejoices in God my Savior,
for he has looked with favor on the lowliness of his servant."
(vv. 46–48a)

Hebrews 10:5–10

And it is by God's will that we have been sanctified through the offering of
the body of Jesus Christ once for all. (v. 10)

Luke 1:39–45 (46–55)

When Elizabeth heard Mary's greeting, the child leaped in her womb. And
Elizabeth was filled with the Holy Spirit and exclaimed with a loud cry,
"Blessed are you among women, and blessed is the fruit of your womb. And
why has this happened to me, that the mother of my Lord comes to me?"
(vv. 41–43)

LECTIO DIVINA

Underline a word or phrase that especially grabs your attention. Pray
from that word or phrase and ask God to help you connect to its
particular invitation for you this week.

Themes from This Week's Writers

THEME 1: *Love, Not Law*

Micah 5:2–5a

Jesus is likely seen not merely as a descendant from, but actually *as a corrective to*, the violent and flawed David in the spirit of Micah's call for change. . . . Mary was right—this *is* a revolutionary change (Luke 1:52–54). We, like Micah, long for change from a stubborn pattern of human leadership that sets sister against sister, brother against brother.

DANIEL L. SMITH-CHRISTOPHER

Luke 1:46b–55

The reversals declared by Mary (Luke 1:51–53) are framed within God's mercy (1:50 and 1:54). God's mercy and God's justice are never separated; therefore the mercy and the reversals interpret each other.

KIMBERLY L. CLAYTON

Hebrews 10:5–10

Therefore, even though the ritual sacrifices "are offered according to the law," they cannot be pleasing to God, because they cannot fully, finally cleanse. The author echoes this in 10:14 . . . as testimony spoken (*eirēkenai*) by the Holy Spirit (10:15–17) culminating with "where there is forgiveness . . . there is no longer any offering for sin" (10:18).

STEVEN J. KRAFTCHICK

THEME 2: *God Does the Unexpected*

Micah 5:2–5a

Micah's announcement of the ruler who is to come from Bethlehem, "who [is] one of the little clans of Judah," rejects these limits in the name of the God who is not part of the cosmic order, who does not conform to the inevitabilities, and who judges the powers feared or imagined by men and women. The prophet speaks, therefore, of a new beginning, a ruler unlike those the people expect or to whom they resign themselves, one whose faithful leadership is inspired by God.

ALAN GREGORY

Hebrews 10:5–10

Second, if Jesus "abolishes the first in order to establish the second" (Heb. 10:9), he is not replacing sacrifice with something else, but fulfilling the previous sacrifices with the sacrificial offering of his own body. This is not Jewish sacrifice versus Christian obedience, but a scriptural (*Israel's* Scriptures, to be sure) affirmation of the obedient sacrifice of one Jew named Jesus.

AMY PEELER

Luke 1:39–45 (46–55)

If these two women are a prototype of church, they certainly embody how improbable and how subversive the church can be. They make quite a pair: a postmenopausal woman and a middle-school-age girl, both impossibly pregnant.

PAUL SIMPSON DUKE

WHAT IS THE HOLY SPIRIT SAYING TO YOU THIS WEEK?

_____

_____

_____

_____

_____

A SPIRITUAL PRACTICE FOR THIS WEEK

Pray or read by the light of your Advent wreath this week. If you do not have one, simply light any candle and attach a sticky note or other label that says, "Love."

First Reading

Micah 5:2–5a

And he shall stand and feed his flock in the strength of the LORD,
in the majesty of the name of the LORD his God.
And they shall live secure, for now he shall be great
to the ends of the earth. (v. 4)

REFLECTION

The prophet Isaiah . . . survived the Assyrian onslaught in the walled
bastions of Jerusalem and could afford comforting words to the
Davidic king. Micah, on the other hand, a prophet from the devastated
villages between the coast and Jerusalem, endured the horrific Assyrian
destruction on Sennacherib's march to Jerusalem. Micah clearly was
furious and, like so many others who have suffered, based his hope on
a change, not on stability. The great Israeli human-rights activist Uri
Avnery is fond of saying, "When you are on the top, you love stability.
When you are on the bottom, you want change!"

DANIEL L. SMITH-CHRISTOPHER

RESPONSE

Are you more like Isaiah or Micah—do you long more for stability or
for change? In what ways? What kind of messiah or savior do you want
Jesus to be? How does your class or social position play a role in this, do
you think?

PRAYER

Almighty God, feed me as one of your flock and lead me to return to
you, that I may know you are the one of peace. Amen.

Canticle

Luke 1:46b–55

"He has brought down the powerful from their thrones,
  and lifted up the lowly;
he has filled the hungry with good things,
  and sent the rich away empty." (vv. 52–53)

REFLECTION

This theme of reversal, so prominent in Luke, is stated at the outset. The context only underscores the content of Mary's proclamation: it is uttered from a little Judean hill-country house, not from the temple in Jerusalem. It is announced by two women with no status, not by the learned official clergy. It anticipates a child who cannot yet live outside his mother's womb, so tiny and fragile is he; yet he will grow and—like his older cousin—become "strong in spirit" (Luke 1:80), the Savior of the world.

KIMBERLY L. CLAYTON

RESPONSE

What strikes you most about God's reversal of power and proclamation in Luke 1? How does this story speak to your own community or your own life right now? What is God turning upside down and backward?

PRAYER

O God, you are raising up the lowly and bringing down the mighty; help me to join in your saving work, and to praise and magnify your name. Amen.

Second Reading

Hebrews 10:5–10

When he said above, "You have neither desired nor taken pleasure in sacrifices and offerings and burnt offerings and sin offerings" (these are offered according to the law), then he added, "See, I have come to do your will." He abolishes the first in order to establish the second. (vv. 8–9)

REFLECTION

If a congregant wrestles with unworthiness before God, this passage, like many in Hebrews, clearly affirms the effectiveness and sufficiency of God's work in Christ. God's will, recorded long before in the psalm and enacted when the Son came, is that Christ makes humans whole and eternally holy. No matter how one might feel, it is good and right to hear the proclamation of one's true holiness in Christ. This is the power of God to rescue humanity, and that stirs gratefulness in those who have been sanctified by his offering.

AMY PEELER

RESPONSE

What feelings of unworthiness have you been wrestling with lately? What does it mean to hear that sacrifices and offerings are not required by God? What does it mean to you, this week, to be made worthy and holy, not because of law, but because of love?

PRAYER

Loving God, I have come to do your will. Make me holy through your offering of the body and birth of your Son, Jesus Christ. Amen.

Gospel

Luke 1:39–45 (46–55)

In those days Mary set out and went with haste to a Judean town in the hill country, where she entered the house of Zechariah and greeted Elizabeth. (vv. 39–40)

REFLECTION

The visitation is the first gathering of the community of Jesus. It invites us to recall how much we need each other, to draw fresh courage from each other, and to celebrate all that we share as bearers of the promise together.

If these two women are a prototype of church, they certainly embody how improbable and how subversive the church can be.

PAUL SIMPSON DUKE

RESPONSE

Would you say your congregation or community gathers in the same spirit of this meeting of Mary and Elizabeth? How do you need and draw courage from one another? How do you bear God's promise together? How are you a subversive, celebrating, improbable community of Jesus?

PRAYER

Holy Spirit, visit me with your presence and lead me among my kin and community, that we may be filled with true expectation at the coming of Jesus. Amen.

Weekend Reflections

Del Verbo divino
la Virgen preñada
viene de camino:
¡si le dais posada!

The Virgin, pregnant,
with the Word of God
is coming down the road:
if only you would give her shelter!

JOHN OF THE CROSS (1542–91), "DEL VERBO DIVINO"

MAKING THE CONNECTIONS

Choose one or two questions for reflection:

1. What connections have you noticed between this week's texts and other passages in Scripture?

2. What connections have you made between this week's texts and the world beyond Scripture?

3. Does either of this week's two commentary themes speak especially to your life or the life of the world around you right now?

4. What is God saying to your congregation in particular through this week's readings and commentaries?

MY CONNECTIONS

_____

_____

_____

_____

_____

_____

Sabbath Day

SCRIPTURE OF ASSURANCE

> Come and hear, all you who fear God,
> and I will tell what he has done for me. (Psalm 66:16)

WEEKLY EXAMEN

- Take a quiet moment, seek out God's presence, and pray for the guidance of the Spirit.

- Consider the past week; recall specific moments and feelings that stand out to you.

- Choose one moment or feeling for deeper examination, thanksgiving, or repentance.

- Let go, breathe deeply, and invite Christ's love to surround and fill you in preparation for the week ahead.

- End with the Lord's Prayer.

Christmas Week

Christmas Eve, Christmas Day, and First Sunday after Christmas Day

Isaiah 9:2–7

The people who walked in darkness
    have seen a great light;
those who lived in a land of deep darkness—
    on them light has shined. (v. 2)

Luke 2:1–14

And she gave birth to her firstborn son and wrapped him in bands of cloth, and laid him in a manger, because there was no place for them in the inn. (v. 7)

John 1:1–14

In the beginning was the Word, and the Word was with God, and the Word was God. He was in the beginning with God. All things came into being through him, and without him not one thing came into being. What has come into being in him was life, and the life was the light of all people. The light shines in the darkness, and the darkness did not overcome it. (vv. 1–5)

Luke 2:41–52

When the festival was ended and they started to return, the boy Jesus stayed behind in Jerusalem, but his parents did not know it. (v. 43)

LECTIO DIVINA

Underline a word or phrase that especially grabs your attention. Pray from that word or phrase and ask God to help you connect to its particular invitation for you this week.

Themes from This Week's Writers

THEME 1: *The Word Became Flesh*

John 1:1–14

Not only did God create "all things" through the Word, but God sent the Word into the world as flesh to live in the midst of the human family, so that we might behold the glory of Jesus.

RONALD J. ALLEN

Hebrews 1:1–4 (5–12)

He, the Son, is cocreator with God of all the worlds and at the same time is the heir of everything created. Not only that: he is the spitting image of God, reflecting precisely the glory of God. Said in another way, he is "the exact imprint of God's very being," God's full nature, and by his speech "he sustains all things by" the means of "his powerful word."

JOHN C. HOLBERT

Luke 2:41–52

Luke's candid acknowledgment that Jesus matured as a person can indeed catch us off guard. That Jesus "grew in wisdom" suggests both a Christology that confesses Jesus' full humanity and an anthropology that confesses that we, like him, are called to "grow in wisdom."

MICHAEL L. LINDVALL

THEME 2: *Light in the Darkness*

Isaiah 9:2–7

The good news proclaimed by Isaiah is that God will not abandon God's people to the darkness; God is at work to overcome death and to bring wisdom, peace, justice, and righteousness, in ways as hidden and seemingly as weak as a newborn child.

THOMAS G. LONG

Luke 2:1–14 (15–20)

The light shines in darkness. . . . The sky erupts with it. For Mary, one angel was required, and so too for Zechariah—but for the shepherds, a sky full! From the beginning of time, the heavens were telling the glory of God, yet never with words (Ps. 19:1–3); now the words can be heard at last. What the heavens have always been singing is, "Glory to God, and on earth peace!"

PAUL SIMPSON DUKE

Isaiah 62:6–12

Unlike our Christmas purchases, God's gifts last forever. A glorious procession of all tribes and nations streams into Jerusalem; the watchers posted on its walls rejoice. With exaltation, they greet those passing through the gates as holy people, redeemed by God. Jerusalem is desired, "a city not forsaken." God gives the gift of relationship. How wonderful it is to belong!

JULIE FAITH PARKER

WHAT IS THE HOLY SPIRIT SAYING TO YOU THIS WEEK?

_____

_____

_____

_____

_____

A SPIRITUAL PRACTICE FOR THIS WEEK

"To you, a child is born!" Take time to savor the good news of Christmas by practicing something that delights, whether listening to music, taking a winter walk, or doing any activity that will truly preach _Immanuel, God with us_ to your spirit.

Christmas Prophecy

Isaiah 9:2–7

For the yoke of their burden,
  and the bar across their shoulders,
  the rod of their oppressor,
  you have broken as on the day of Midian. (v. 4)

REFLECTION

Isaiah's voice on Christmas Eve reminds us that God's salvation is not merely a spiritual victory to be serenaded with a lullaby. The Christ child took on the power of death, and this birth signals the time when the tools of war and injustice—the guns, the boots, the unjust laws, the oppressor's rod—will be consumed by the fire of God's great victory.

THOMAS G. LONG

RESPONSE

Make a list of whatever tools of war and injustice have been making headlines this week. Pray for the victims they have hurt. Consider burning the list, putting it through a shredder, or flushing it down a toilet, and believe that the "zeal of the LORD of hosts will do this."

PRAYER

Mighty God, those who walked in darkness have seen a great light. Give me zeal for the work of justice and righteousness in the name of the child who will be born for us. Amen.

Epistle for Christmas

Titus 2:11–14

He it is who gave himself for us that he might redeem us from all iniquity and purify for himself a people of his own who are zealous for good deeds. (v. 14)

REFLECTION

Titus 2 . . . proclaims the ineffable good news that salvation has come, but, as is fitting for a true *Christian* celebration of Christmas, it is not sentimental. It recognizes the cost of that salvation for God, that the Savior Jesus Christ gave himself to rescue us. It also acknowledges the life of discipleship demanded of those who enjoy this salvation, which is to grow in the zeal for good works. It tells the gathered congregation: we know where we have come from, what we need to work on, and where we are going.

AMY PEELER

RESPONSE

How do you think Christians get lost in the sentimental at Christmas? How do you see the shadow of the cross across the manger this year? How might Christ be calling you to "grow in the zeal for good works"?

PRAYER

Redeemer Christ, your grace has appeared, and you give yourself for us. Make us all a people of your own, zealous for good deeds. Amen.

Christmas Gospel

John 1:1–14

And the Word became flesh and lived among us, and we have seen his glory, the glory as of a father's only son, full of grace and truth. (v. 14)

REFLECTION

The truer understanding of the incarnation . . . is that God is with us always, that God is forever proximate, always and everywhere as near to us as our own breath. The incarnation of Jesus Christ . . . is the definitive expression of the great unfolding of the divine presence that *always was, always is, and always shall be* with us. The incarnation means that God is not "up there" or "back then." Rather, God is in the proximate; God is to be encountered in that which is close at hand; God is to be glimpsed in the ordinary.

MICHAEL L. LINDVALL

RESPONSE

The incarnation is both a glorious and very ordinary thing. God is in our midst, not just in ancient Judea, but here and now. How do you observe this in your own community and everyday life? How could you be surprised today at the ordinary presence of God, close at hand?

PRAYER

Holy Word, your true light is coming into the world. Help me to see your glory, full of grace and truth. Amen.

Sunday Gospel

Luke 2:41–52

[Jesus] said to them, "Why were you searching for me? Did you not know that I must be in my Father's house?" (v. 49)

REFLECTION

By staying behind, Jesus interrupted the lives of his parents. They intended to return home, but they had to interrupt their trip to return to Jesus. . . . Jesus' invitation to the realm of God interrupted the lives of many others in the Gospel and Acts. For Luke, the ministry of Jesus is the model for the apostles and the church. How might we interrupt our lives, as Jesus did, by staying behind (so to speak) to be in the Parent's house, or to be about the Parent's business (the realm of God)?

RONALD J. ALLEN

RESPONSE

How might you, like Jesus, interrupt your life this week to linger in God's house or "be about the Parent's business"? We often consider interruptions to be jarring or unwelcome; what could be life-giving or joyful in this season of your life?

PRAYER

Jesus, I am searching for you. Bring me to your Parent's house and into your wisdom. Amen.

Weekend Reflections

FURTHER CONNECTION

How could the Eternal do a temporal act,
The Infinite become a finite fact?
Nothing can save us that is possible:
We who must die demand a miracle.

W. H. AUDEN (1907–73), FOR THE TIME BEING: A CHRISTMAS ORATORIO

MAKING THE CONNECTIONS

Choose one or two questions for reflection:

1. What connections have you noticed between this week's texts and other passages in Scripture?

2. What connections have you made between this week's texts and the world beyond Scripture?

3. Does either of this week's two commentary themes speak especially to your life or the life of the world around you right now?

4. What is God saying to your congregation in particular through this week's readings and commentaries?

MY CONNECTIONS

_____

_____

_____

_____

_____

_____

Sabbath Day

SCRIPTURE OF ASSURANCE

The grace of the Lord Jesus Christ be with your spirit. (Philippians 4:23)

WEEKLY EXAMEN

- Take a quiet moment, seek out God's presence, and pray for the guidance of the Spirit.

- Consider the past week; recall specific moments and feelings that stand out to you.

- Choose one moment or feeling for deeper examination, thanksgiving, or repentance.

- Let go, breathe deeply, and invite Christ's love to surround and fill you in preparation for the week ahead.

- End with the Lord's Prayer.

The Week Leading Up to the
Second Sunday after Christmas Day

Jeremiah 31:7–14

Hear the word of the LORD, O nations,
    and declare it in the coastlands far away;
say, "He who scattered Israel will gather him,
    and will keep him as a shepherd a flock." (v. 10)

Psalm 147:12–20

He sends out his command to the earth;
    his word runs swiftly.
He gives snow like wool;
    he scatters frost like ashes. (vv. 15–16)

Ephesians 1:3–14

He destined us for adoption as his children through Jesus Christ, according to the good pleasure of his will, to the praise of his glorious grace that he freely bestowed on us in the Beloved. (vv. 5–6)

John 1:(1–9) 10–18

No one has ever seen God. It is God the only Son, who is close to the Father's heart, who has made him known. (v. 18)

LECTIO DIVINA

Underline a word or phrase that especially grabs your attention. Pray from that word or phrase and ask God to help you connect to its particular invitation for you this week.

Themes from This Week's Writers

THEME 1: *Our Dwelling Place Is in Christ*

Jeremiah 31:7–14

As people who come from a long line of sojourners, we must always be people who help others find their way home. The story in Jeremiah reminds us that our ancestors knew the pain of the wilderness and exile.

MELISSA BROWNING

Ephesians 1:3–14

Being destined by God for adoption as God's children is neither fictive nor imaginary. Rather, being brought into God's family through Jesus Christ is an extraordinary demonstration of God's love and grace for us all, and at the same time normative and a sign of God's covenantal love.

RODGER Y. NISHIOKA

John 1:(1–9) 10–18

Jesus replaces the mode of divine presence invoked in Exodus and Ezekiel. . . . The Word travels with the church through wilderness and exile in a way similar to God traveling with Israel.

RONALD J. ALLEN

THEME 2: *A New Cosmic Order*

Psalm 147:12–20

In this season, we offer praise to God because God continues to order and reorder the world through the person and work of Jesus Christ.

JOEL MARCUS LEMON

Ephesians 1:3–14

The church is far more than the vessel of this great mystery; it itself is a crucial part of the revelation of God, because it is itself the "fullness" of Christ and hence shares in Christ's cosmic status. The church is the locus of a new humanity and of a cosmic peace (2:15–16).

JOHN C. HOLBERT

John 1:(1–9) 10–18

Our postmodern world is often profoundly skeptical about any overarching order or meaning to the universe. It is often equally incredulous of claims that "light" really is overcoming—and finally shall overcome—the forces of "darkness."

MICHAEL L. LINDVALL

WHAT IS THE HOLY SPIRIT SAYING TO YOU THIS WEEK?

_____

_____

_____

_____

_____

A SPIRITUAL PRACTICE FOR THIS WEEK

One evening this week, step outside and look at the place where you live. Take a photo or stand there a while. Imagine what it would be like to be forced to leave and never return. Pray for refugees; consider making a financial gift to a charity that advocates for them.

First Reading

Jeremiah 31:7–14

See, I am going to bring them from the land of the north,
and gather them from the farthest parts of the earth,
among them the blind and the lame,
those with child and those in labor, together;
a great company, they shall return here. (v. 8)

REFLECTION

We come from wandering people whom God pulled together to
create a great community. While we rejoice that we serve a God who
has turned our weeping into dancing, we must also do God's work
by welcoming others into this kin-dom celebration. Our work in this
world is to share God's great joy, to be agents of transformation who
proclaim the good news of the gospel—that all God's children are
welcomed home.

MELISSA BROWNING

RESPONSE

Remember a time of wandering in your own life, whether physical
or spiritual. What did you learn? What could it mean to think of your
church as a community of wanderers? How might you or your church,
in this time and place, be called to welcome other wanderers home?

PRAYER

O God, you have pitched your tent near to me and called me home
to you. Amen.

Canticle

Psalm 147:12–20

He hurls down hail like crumbs—
  who can stand before his cold?
He sends out his word, and melts them;
  he makes his wind blow, and the waters flow.
He declares his word to Jacob,
  his statutes and ordinances to Israel. (vv. 17–19)

REFLECTION

In the context of the Christmas season, we can appreciate the various ways that the "word of God" appears in both Psalm 147 and Jeremiah 31. For the psalmist, God's word is the divine order that is apparent in God's control of nature (Ps. 147:15, 18). The psalmist also understands God's word as the law (Ps. 147:19–20). The law gives the community a mode of living that will promote God's order—right relationships among the people.

JOEL MARCUS LEMON

RESPONSE

The psalmist believes that God's order prevails in our world. This can be hard to believe as modern people. How might divine order in all things be different from divine control? How could reading "his word" in the psalm as Jesus (the Word) deepen this meaning for you further?

PRAYER

God, teach me to live in relationships of love and justice, even at the center of the storm. Amen.

Second Reading

Ephesians 1:3–14

With all wisdom and insight he has made known to us the mystery of his will, according to his good pleasure that he set forth in Christ, as a plan for the fullness of time, to gather up all things in him, things in heaven and things on earth. (vv. 8b–10)

REFLECTION

On this second Sunday after the celebration of Christmas Day, the colossal role of the Church (and all churches) in the plan of God may be equally celebrated as God's gift to us, the heirs of Christ in the world. . . . Though the larger Christmas crowds have disappeared from many of our sanctuaries, Ephesians reminds us that the Church remains as the living embodiment of Christ in the world, and as such continues to have eternal significance in the plan of God.

JOHN C. HOLBERT

RESPONSE

Make a list of ways your church or community has been a gift of God to you. Make a list of ways it has been disappointing. How easy or hard is it to see your community as truly a "living embodiment of Christ in the world"?

PRAYER

God, you have bestowed your grace upon us and adopted us, your church, as your own in Christ. Give me and my community courage and confidence to continue as your family in the world. Amen.

Gospel

John 1:(1–9) 10–18

There was a man sent from God, whose name was John. He came as a witness to testify to the light, so that all might believe through him. He himself was not the light, but he came to testify to the light. (vv. 6–8)

REFLECTION

Ours is a world of Facebook "likes" and selfie-sticks, a world of entitlement, rights, and quests for personal power. Even more daunting is the fact that even religion, even church, even ministry, can become all about *me*. . . . John's gracious movement away from the center, his pointing away from self to the one who is the center, is the very liberating movement we are called to make ourselves: to step out of the spotlight, to point toward the *logos*, and confess with the Baptist: "It is not about me."

MICHAEL L. LINDVALL

RESPONSE

How do you relate to Lindvall's suggestion that too much of a focus on our self can become burdensome? What kind of movements might you make in your life to point more toward Christ and away from the self, in ways that feel liberating and joyful?

PRAYER

O God, no one has ever seen you, but you have made yourself known in the light of Christ. May that light shine in me toward others, not for myself, but for you. Amen.

Weekend Reflections

FURTHER CONNECTION

All around worlds are dying out, new worlds are being born; all around life is dying but life is being born. The fruit ripens on the trees, while the roots are silently at work in the darkness of the earth against a time when there shall be new leaves, fresh blossoms, green fruit. Such is the growing edge! It is the one more thing to try when all else has failed, the upward reach of life. It is the incentive to carry on. Therefore, I will light the candle of hope this Christmas, that must burn all year long.

HOWARD THURMAN (1899–1981), *THE INWARD JOURNEY*

MAKING THE CONNECTIONS

Choose one or two questions for reflection:

1. What connections have you noticed between this week's texts and other passages in Scripture?

2. What connections have you made between this week's texts and the world beyond Scripture?

3. Does either of this week's two commentary themes speak especially to your life or the life of the world around you right now?

4. What is God saying to your congregation in particular through this week's readings and commentaries?

MY CONNECTIONS

_____

_____

_____

_____

_____

Sabbath Day

SCRIPTURE OF ASSURANCE

So it depends not on human will or exertion, but on God who shows mercy. (Romans 9:16)

WEEKLY EXAMEN

- Take a quiet moment, seek out God's presence, and pray for the guidance of the Spirit.

- Consider the past week; recall specific moments and feelings that stand out to you.

- Choose one moment or feeling for deeper examination, thanksgiving, or repentance.

- Let go, breathe deeply, and invite Christ's love to surround and fill you in preparation for the week ahead.

- End with the Lord's Prayer.

Epiphany of the Lord

Isaiah 60:1–6

Then you shall see and be radiant;
  your heart shall thrill and rejoice,
because the abundance of the sea shall be brought to you,
  the wealth of the nations shall come to you. (v. 5)

Psalm 72:1–7, 10–14

Give the king your justice, O God,
  and your righteousness to a king's son.
May he judge your people with righteousness,
  and your poor with justice. (vv. 1–2)

Ephesians 3:1–12

In former generations this mystery was not made known to humankind, as it has now been revealed to his holy apostles and prophets by the Spirit: that is, the Gentiles have become fellow heirs, members of the same body, and sharers in the promise in Christ Jesus through the gospel. (vv. 5–6)

Matthew 2:1–12

When they saw that the star had stopped, they were overwhelmed with joy. On entering the house, they saw the child with Mary his mother; and they knelt down and paid him homage. Then, opening their treasure chests, they offered him gifts of gold, frankincense, and myrrh. (vv. 10–11)

Isaiah 60:1–6

The nations of the earth make a grand procession to the city, praising the God of Israel and bringing the very best gifts they have, gifts so fine they are fitting to be placed on the altar in the house of God—camels, gold, frankincense, rams, and more (60:5–7).

Isaiah asks us to "lift up your eyes and look" (60:4), and when we do, we will see this new community of God shining in surprising places.

THOMAS G. LONG

Psalm 72:1–7, 10–14

In Jesus Christ, we see the king who finally enacts God's justice, whose power extends throughout the entire world. Jesus illuminates the darkness. He draws the nations together. He causes the world to rejoice.

JOEL MARCUS LEMON

Ephesians 3:1–12

Paul describes a unilateral movement, taking the gospel to the Gentiles, and there are likely Christians who continue to understand mission this way. However, the language of mission and outreach is also shifting to describe an experience of finding the light of Christ in the world rather than taking it there. Christians involved in outreach regularly describe learning from and growing through these experiences, indicating a dynamic movement between church and the world, rather than a unilateral movement from church to world.

ELLEN OTT MARSHALL

Matthew 2:1–12

The first people to recognize the arrival of "the king of the Jews" are outsiders. . . . Guided by signs in the night sky, their astrological wisdom makes them appear suspicious—and maybe dangerous—because of the Old Testament's prohibitions of divination and augury (e.g., Deut. 18:9–14). No one else in this Gospel resembles the magi; their amazing cameo suggests that God finds ways to attract others—or that others discover ways of finding God.

MATTHEW L. SKINNER

RESPONSE

Reflect on a time when you felt like an outsider at church or in a small group. Did this experience reveal something about Christ you might not otherwise have known? What could people we consider suspicious or dangerous teach us about Christ? What is an example from your own context?

PRAYER

God, you welcome all to know Jesus from many paths and places. Help me to see that no one is an outsider to your gospel. Amen.

The Week Leading Up to the
Baptism of the Lord

Isaiah 43:1–7

But now thus says the LORD,
he who created you, O Jacob,
he who formed you, O Israel:
Do not fear, for I have redeemed you;
I have called you by name, you are mine. (v. 1)

Psalm 29

The voice of the LORD is over the waters;
the God of glory thunders,
the LORD, over mighty waters.
The voice of the LORD is powerful;
the voice of the LORD is full of majesty. (vv. 3–4)

Acts 8:14–17

Now when the apostles at Jerusalem heard that Samaria had accepted the word of God, they sent Peter and John to them. The two went down and prayed for them that they might receive the Holy Spirit. (vv. 14–15)

Luke 3:15–17, 21–22

As the people were filled with expectation, and all were questioning in their hearts concerning John, whether he might be the Messiah, John answered all of them by saying, "I baptize you with water; but one who is more powerful than I is coming; I am not worthy to untie the thong of his sandals. He will baptize you with the Holy Spirit and fire." (vv. 15–16)

LECTIO DIVINA

Underline a word or phrase that especially grabs your attention. Pray from that word or phrase and ask God to help you connect to its particular invitation for you this week.

Themes from This Week's Writers

THEME 1: *A New Identity in Christ*

Isaiah 43:1–7

It is important to note that this action of restoration is initiated by God and not by the people. Redemption occurs not because Israel has suddenly come to its senses. It springs rather from the character of God. God is creator, and God will create again. The salvation of the people comes not because they love God, but because God loves them.

THOMAS G. LONG

Acts 8:14–17

Philip baptized the Samaritans "in the name of the Lord Jesus." The phrase "in the name of" appears nowhere in the LXX[1] and seldom anywhere else. Acts uses it to distinguish the church's baptism from all others, including John the Baptist's. John's baptism was about repentance and forgiveness (Luke 3:3), but for Luke, baptism "in the name of Lord Jesus" is more.

JERRY L. SUMNEY

Luke 3:15–17, 21–22

Jesus therefore does not commence his ministry until first he is told again who he is, to whom he belongs. His ministry thus exists as a prolonged expression of his identity as God's chosen and sent agent. We might say similar things about Jesus' followers, including ourselves.

MATTHEW L. SKINNER

---

1. LXX is the traditional abbreviation for the *Septuagint*, the earliest extant Greek translation of the Old Testament from Hebrew.

Isaiah 43:1–7

"Do not fear" is "easier said than done." Regardless of assurances from strong, supportive sources, none of us lives free from fear. Fears come in all sorts of shapes and sizes, and abstract assurances are cold comfort. . . . [Isaiah] speaks of passing through the waters and walking through fire—not around or away from, but through what are legitimate occasions of genuine fear.

DAVID J. SCHLAFER

Acts 8:14–17

Recalling the context of persecution and vision surrounding this baptism narrative, we are also prompted to reflect on the fears that obstruct our openness to the other. This story is filled with courageous people who take tremendous risks for their faith. How does our faith call and equip us to risk relationship or change?

ELLEN OTT MARSHALL

Luke 3:15–17, 21–22

John's protests integrated the political and the spiritual in ways that move some contemporary Christians to march against injustices in our own day. For some of us, publicly and communally questioning political power when it fails to serve the "least of these" is indeed a spiritual act of commitment.

EMERSON B. POWERY

WHAT IS THE HOLY SPIRIT SAYING TO YOU THIS WEEK?

_____

_____

_____

_____

_____

A SPIRITUAL PRACTICE FOR THIS WEEK

Fill a small container—a cup, glass, bowl, or jar—with water, and use it as a focus as you reflect on this week's readings. First, dip your fingers in the water and touch your forehead or make the sign of the cross and give thanks for your baptism.

First Reading

Isaiah 43:1–7

When you pass through the waters, I will be with you;
    and through the rivers, they shall not overwhelm you;
when you walk through fire you shall not be burned,
    and the flame shall not consume you. (v. 2)

REFLECTION

The fire and water of our fears can be negotiated if we are accompanied by someone who knows and names us. As Isaiah sees it, the God who creates, forms, and redeems, honors, and loves them, not only knows the names of all the chosen; God bestows the divine name upon them. . . .

On this day, it is worth noting that he who went through fire and water for us began his ministry in a baptism of blessing—being named as cherished by the One from whom he came.

DAVID J. SCHLAFER

RESPONSE

Name some fears that are present for you this week. Name some individuals and communities who are also going through a time of fear. Offer these fears and names in prayer, knowing God knows, cherishes, and names us all, too.

PRAYER

Jesus, you are with me as I pass through the waters and the fire. In you, I shall not be overwhelmed or consumed. Amen.

Canticle

The Lord sits enthroned over the flood;
the Lord sits enthroned as king forever.
May the Lord give strength to his people!
May the Lord bless his people with peace! (vv. 10–11)

REFLECTION

While the scene presented is chaotic, it unfolds at the voice of the
Lord, reminding us that God is in control of that which seems to be
uncontrollable and that God's sovereignty is proclaimed through nature.
While in our preaching we may not typically use the same type of
language, we can express and understand God to be the celebrated one
who keeps us from being overwhelmed, the one who is enthroned over
the metaphoric floods of our lives.

KHALIA J. WILLIAMS

RESPONSE

What does "the flood" feel like in your life today? How might you
envision God enthroned over that flood? How can God help keep you
from feeling overwhelmed today?

PRAYER

O God, your voice calls out over the waters. Give me strength, and bless
your people with peace. Amen.

Second Reading

Acts 8:14–17

Then Peter and John laid their hands on them, and they received the Holy Spirit. (v. 17)

REFLECTION

John and Peter pray over the Samaritans and lay their hands on them. . . . This passage also encourages us to reflect more generally on the power of ritual in community formation. . . .

Studies on engaged Buddhist and Christian prayer practices for peace note an encouraging correspondence between forms of compassion meditation and an openness to engaging the other in the work of peace building. Forms of meditation strengthen our capacity to remain open and receptive to one who is different and historically perceived as enemy.

ELLEN OTT MARSHALL

RESPONSE

Are there rituals in your church that include a laying on of hands? What about elsewhere in your community? In your experience, do rites like these, of compassion or healing touch, grow a sense of community or peace building? How?

PRAYER

Holy Spirit, gather me with your people and, through our hands, spread your peace and your gospel. Amen.

Gospel

Luke 3:15–17, 21–22

Now when all the people were baptized, and when Jesus also had been baptized and was praying, the heaven was opened, and the Holy Spirit descended upon him in bodily form like a dove. And a voice came from heaven, "You are my Son, the Beloved; with you I am well pleased." (vv. 21–22)

REFLECTION

> More than an act of baptism as a symbolic act of joining the community, an act that others should emulate, Luke's baptism narrative more likely emphasizes the disclosure of Jesus' identity from God. The open space implies an accessible opportunity between that which separates the heavenly from the earthly. . . . This baptism is God's identity marker, not John's.
>
> EMERSON B. POWERY

RESPONSE

> Imagine standing in a body of water that is special to you. Then, imagine hearing: "You are my Child, the Beloved; with you I am well pleased." What do God's words speak to in your life right now? What does it mean to you that baptism is God's identity marker, not yours?

PRAYER

> O God, I am your child, your beloved. Baptize me with your fire and burn off my chaff that I may serve your people. Amen.

Weekend Reflections

You know the one thing I love most about the Baptism of our Lord text is not just that God the Father says "This is my son, the beloved with whom I am well pleased," but that God says this—before Jesus had really done anything. . . . As far as we know Jesus hadn't even done anything yet and he was called beloved. The one in whom the Father was well pleased. That's God for you. And I mean that literally. That is God FOR YOU.

NADIA BOLZ-WEBER (1969–), JANUARY 2014 SERMON

MAKING THE CONNECTIONS

Choose one or two questions for reflection:

1. What connections have you noticed between this week's texts and other passages in Scripture?

2. What connections have you made between this week's texts and the world beyond Scripture?

3. Does either of this week's two commentary themes speak especially to your life or the life of the world around you right now?

4. What is God saying to your congregation in particular through this week's readings and commentaries?

_____

_____

_____

_____

_____

_____

Sabbath Day

SCRIPTURE OF ASSURANCE

> The Lord God has given me
>   the tongue of a teacher,
> that I may know how to sustain
>   the weary with a word.
> Morning by morning he wakens—
>   wakens my ear
> to listen as those who are taught. (Isaiah 50:4)

WEEKLY EXAMEN

- Take a quiet moment, seek out God's presence, and pray for the guidance of the Spirit.

- Consider the past week; recall specific moments and feelings that stand out to you.

- Choose one moment or feeling for deeper examination, thanksgiving, or repentance.

- Let go, breathe deeply, and invite Christ's love to surround and fill you in preparation for the week ahead.

- End with the Lord's Prayer.

The Week Leading Up to the
Second Sunday after the Epiphany

Isaiah 62:1–5

For as a young man marries a young woman,
    so shall your builder marry you,
and as the bridegroom rejoices over the bride,
    so shall your God rejoice over you. (v. 5)

Psalm 36:5–10

How precious is your steadfast love, O God!
    All people may take refuge in the shadow of your wings.
They feast on the abundance of your house,
    and you give them drink from the river of your delights. (vv. 7–8)

1 Corinthians 12:1–11

All these [gifts] are activated by one and the same Spirit, who allots to each one individually just as the Spirit chooses. (v. 11)

John 2:1–11

The steward called the bridegroom and said to him, "Everyone serves the good wine first, and then the inferior wine after the guests have become drunk. But you have kept the good wine until now." Jesus did this, the first of his signs, in Cana of Galilee, and revealed his glory; and his disciples believed in him. (vv. 9b–11)

LECTIO DIVINA

Underline a word or phrase that especially grabs your attention. Pray from that word or phrase and ask God to help you connect to its particular invitation for you this week.

Themes from This Week's Writers

THEME 1: *God's Abundance*

Isaiah 62:1–5

Isaiah's point is not to reinforce the pattern of patriarchal obedience. Instead, Isaiah points to the amazing perspective of a caring God through all times and spaces. He casts this thought into a metaphor valid for his own days. God is provider who is in charge of life-giving food, and God's people need to be fed.

KLAUS-PETER ADAM

1 Corinthians 12:1–11

It makes no sense for a particular Christian to boast of possessing a certain spiritual gift, for that gift was given *by* another and intended *for* the whole community.

In this way, the spiritual gifts are similar to the wine at the wedding in Cana (John 2:1–11). . . . Jesus clearly intends that the hosts to whom he has given wine will, in turn, give wine to the rest of the gathered community. How odd it would seem if the hosts shut the party down in order to save the fine wine for themselves!

SHANNON CRAIGO-SNELL

John 2:1–11

In this story, the chief steward is undoubtedly desperate; he needs wine. Imagine his delight when he samples the new stuff that the servants have brought and discovers its quality. Imagine the servants' relief or amusement when they see that Jesus has done more than save the wedding with a merely passable beverage. This wine bursts with flavor— it has a joyful body, with hints of amazement and a finish of enduring fulfillment.

MATTHEW L. SKINNER

1 Corinthians 12:1–11

Preachers in the season of Epiphany could easily spend the whole sermon on what has not changed over the past two thousand years. The No. 1 issue that has literally caused the church to divide is mistaking the manifestation of Christ's presence in the world as cause for one group of believers to consider themselves better than, more holy than, more saved than the rest.

CYNTHIA A. JARVIS

Psalm 36:5–10

God loves God's people and allows for a much deeper experience of God. We are offered the blessed privilege of encountering the very nature of God as sustainer, redeemer, nurturer, and savior. This personal encounter is seen through the psalmist's complete trust in God's immeasurable and unfailing love.

KHALIA J. WILLIAMS

John 2:1–11

Jesus performs the first of his signs and apparently by doing so brings about belief and reveals his glory.

The season of Epiphany is about revelation, a time shortly after the excitement of the arrival of God's Son, Jesus. So what difference does God's revelation make during this season, a season full of promise and chaos, full of joy and sorrow?

EMERSON B. POWERY

WHAT IS THE HOLY SPIRIT SAYING TO YOU THIS WEEK?

_____

_____

_____

_____

_____

A SPIRITUAL PRACTICE FOR THIS WEEK

Each day this week, ask God to help you find the "party" in that day!
Commemorate the feast of Cana: wear fun clothes, try fun foods or
beverages, and celebrate in ways that seem right for you. Learn from
Jesus' miracle of generosity and indulgence.

First Reading

You shall no more be termed Forsaken,
    and your land shall no more be termed Desolate;
but you shall be called My Delight Is in Her,
    and your land Married;
for the LORD delights in you,
    and your land shall be married. (v. 4)

REFLECTION

God's history with God's people is told as a variant of the narrative of
the ever-dutiful, ever-loving, ever-forgiving, and ever-patient lover.
    . . . The patriarchal groom-and-bride metaphor, despite the
dissonances it creates for contemporary hearers, is meant to portray
God in a way that reassures the Israelites they will be provided for and
protected. God is not portrayed as a domineering husband, but as a
compassionate spouse who attends to the needs of God's beloved.

KLAUS-PETER ADAM

RESPONSE

What is it like to imagine God as your ideal spouse or lover? For
instance: that God delights in you, notices your needs, has compassion
for you, and loves you for who you are. Is this weird? How could it be
reassuring and sustaining?

PRAYER

God, I am never forsaken or alone because you rejoice in me, delight in
me, and love me for who I am. Amen.

Canticle

Psalm 36:5–10

Your steadfast love, O Lord, extends to the heavens,
  your faithfulness to the clouds.
Your righteousness is like the mighty mountains,
  your judgments are like the great deep;
  you save humans and animals alike, O Lord. (vv. 5–6)

REFLECTION

Humanity and all creation are dependent upon God's providential care. Even the host of the wedding at Cana (John 2:1–11) unwittingly depended upon divine intervention to provide hospitality for his guests. The psalmist emphasizes this dependence on God's saving help through images of shelter (v. 7b), food and drink (v. 8), and God as the very source of life (v. 9). Everything that sustains life comes from God; therefore, every living thing is dependent upon God.

KHALIA J. WILLIAMS

RESPONSE

How do you see God's abundance at work in your life? Do you feel as though your life is dependent on God? What, for you, is the balance between believing that "God will provide" and "I will provide"?

PRAYER

God, your righteousness is like mountains under my feet and your faithfulness like clouds above my head. Thank you for sustaining my life. Amen.

Second Reading

1 Corinthians 12:1–11

Now there are varieties of gifts, but the same Spirit; and there are varieties of services, but the same Lord; and there are varieties of activities, but it is the same God who activates all of them in everyone. To each is given the manifestation of the Spirit for the common good. (vv. 4–7)

REFLECTION

In the season of Epiphany, Paul's words encourage reflection on the relational nature of spiritual gifts, as they flow between God and the community. He portrays a kind of holy regifting. We receive gifts in order to give them to others. What are we regifting? What changes if we remember that we are go-betweens, living in-between?

SHANNON CRAIGO-SNELL

RESPONSE

We often think of our talents and interests as personal rather than something God has given us to help the common good. Make a list of some of your favorite talents and interests and next to each, reflect on how these gifts can be a holy regifting — relational and not just individual.

PRAYER

Holy Spirit, giver of all spiritual gifts, activate yourself in me so that I manifest your love and power for the common good. Amen.

Gospel

John 2:1–11

His mother said to the servants, "Do whatever he tells you." Now standing there were six stone water jars for the Jewish rites of purification, each holding twenty or thirty gallons. Jesus said to them, "Fill the jars with water." And they filled them up to the brim. (vv. 5–7)

REFLECTION

> When Jesus produces the equivalent of six hundred to nine hundred bottles of fine wine, we can linger for a while over extravagance. . . .
> John's Jesus expresses little interest in remaining hidden or counseling moderation; he promises a life lived abundantly (10:10). Christians, therefore, should refuse to rely on dour methods of assessing our ministry's proper limits. We cannot do everything, but limited time, energy, and resources should not make us stingy in our dispositions toward God and neighbors.
>
> MATTHEW L. SKINNER

RESPONSE

> Where is the tension in your life between a theology of generosity and a tendency to overwork? In what ways are you extravagant? How do you tend to be dour or stingy? In what life-giving way might God be inviting you to grow?

PRAYER

> Jesus, fill me to the brim with the best wine of your gospel that I may overflow with grace for others. Amen.

Weekend Reflections

FURTHER CONNECTION

Water is needed to live, but wine expresses the abundance of the banquet and the joy of the celebration. It is a wedding feast lacking wine; the newlyweds are embarrassed by this. Imagine finishing a wedding feast drinking tea; it would be an embarrassment. Wine is necessary for the celebration.

POPE FRANCIS (1936–), "THE FIRST SIGN OF MERCY,"
SERMON GIVEN JUNE 8, 2016

MAKING THE CONNECTIONS

Choose one or two questions for reflection:

1. What connections have you noticed between this week's texts and other passages in Scripture?

2. What connections have you made between this week's texts and the world beyond Scripture?

3. Does either of this week's two commentary themes speak especially to your life or the life of the world around you right now?

4. What is God saying to your congregation in particular through this week's readings and commentaries?

MY CONNECTIONS

_____

_____

_____

_____

_____

_____

Sabbath Day

SCRIPTURE OF ASSURANCE

No longer drink only water, but take a little wine for the sake of your stomach and your frequent ailments. (1 Timothy 5:23)

WEEKLY EXAMEN

- Take a quiet moment, seek out God's presence, and pray for the guidance of the Spirit.

- Consider the past week; recall specific moments and feelings that stand out to you.

- Choose one moment or feeling for deeper examination, thanksgiving, or repentance.

- Let go, breathe deeply, and invite Christ's love to surround and fill you in preparation for the week ahead.

- End with the Lord's Prayer.

The Week Leading Up to the
Third Sunday
after the Epiphany

Nehemiah 8:1–3, 5–6, 8–10

And Ezra opened the book in the sight of all the people, for he was standing above all the people; and when he opened it, all the people stood up. (v. 5)

Psalm 19

The law of the LORD is perfect,
  reviving the soul;
the decrees of the LORD are sure,
  making wise the simple;
the precepts of the LORD are right,
  rejoicing the heart;
the commandment of the LORD is clear,
  enlightening the eyes. (vv. 7–8)

1 Corinthians 12:12–31a

For just as the body is one and has many members, and all the members of the body, though many, are one body, so it is with Christ. For in the one Spirit we were all baptized into one body—Jews or Greeks, slaves or free—and we were all made to drink of one Spirit. (vv. 12–13)

Luke 4:14–21

"The Spirit of the Lord is upon me,
  because he has anointed me
  to bring good news to the poor.

He has sent me to proclaim release to the captives
and recovery of sight to the blind,
to let the oppressed go free,
to proclaim the year of the Lord's favor." (vv. 18–19)

LECTIO DIVINA

Underline a word or phrase that especially grabs your attention. Pray
from that word or phrase and ask God to help you connect to its
particular invitation for you this week.

Themes from This Week's Writers

THEME 1: *One Body in Christ*

Nehemiah 8:1–3, 5–6, 8–10

A great work cannot be accomplished by self-defined individuals without a common vision. God's people reject the limiting labels either as the remnant who remained around Jerusalem or as leaders who were faithful in far-off exile. Instead, only as one community united in faithfulness can their God-given mission be achieved.

GLEN BELL

1 Corinthians 12:12–31a

As it is, as we are held together in him, the suffering of one causes all to suffer; when one is honored, all rejoice. This is not our own doing, even when we actually manage to behave as God's redeemed! Like the gifts mentioned at the beginning of this chapter, our interrelatedness in our diversity, our identity in our interrelatedness, is in Christ.

CYNTHIA A. JARVIS

Luke 4:14–21

It takes a village—or a body of varying members and ministries, as Paul says in the reading from 1 Corinthians 12—to continue this work. Animated by the Spirit, the church, the body of Christ, has a huge mission, as well as the personnel, resources, skills, and energy to work hard to change the world. Everyone has a contribution to make to this mission.

WARREN CARTER

THEME 2: *Good News to the Poor*

Nehemiah 8:1–3, 5–6, 8–10

We gather the community together, not to tell them statistics about how terrible their neighborhood is, but to spark a catalyst of change by asking them to celebrate the things they love about their home.

. . . The people who were hopeless suddenly see things differently, when they realize that they do not have to wait on outside help, but they can work together to transform their community now. When we learn to celebrate the gifts that God has given, "the joy of the Lord" can be our strength to create change.

MELISSA BROWNING

1 Corinthians 12:12–31a

[Jesus] spent his days teaching, serving, and healing others, as well as rejecting injustice and subverting social structures of domination. By naming the collective body of the church the body *of Christ*, Paul enjoins the church to imitate Jesus in all of these ways.

SHANNON CRAIGO-SNELL

Luke 4:14–21

Note that the first word spoken by the public Jesus in Luke's Gospel, other than the reading of Isaiah, is "today"—not yesterday, not tomorrow, not someday. . . . This today continues throughout Jesus' ministry. Now is always the time to release the captives, to give sight to the blind, to free the oppressed, to proclaim the year of the Lord's favor.

BLAIR R. MONIE

WHAT IS THE HOLY SPIRIT SAYING TO YOU THIS WEEK?

_____

_____

_____

_____

_____

Read aloud any of this week's Scriptures—to a person, a pet, or an empty room—and truly feel and believe the gospel of those words, like Nehemiah or Jesus. What do you notice? How does the Spirit move through the proclaimed, spoken word?

First Reading

Nehemiah 8:1–3, 5–6, 8–10

Then he said to them, "Go your way, eat the fat and drink sweet wine and send portions of them to those for whom nothing is prepared, for this day is holy to our LORD; and do not be grieved, for the joy of the LORD is your strength." (v. 10)

REFLECTION

The people's custom during this ritual reading of Scripture was to weep and cry, but . . . they were told to make the day holy through their eating, drinking, and rejoicing.

The commandment we find here might strike us as odd. This is a fractured community with deep and abiding problems. Yet rather than be overwhelmed with the problems, the people are told to build community by throwing a party. There is no need to stay for a town-hall meeting and lament the issues that divide them. They need to celebrate!

MELISSA BROWNING

RESPONSE

A church leadership guru once said: "We make our best decisions when we're having fun." Serious problems can make us serious, which can stiffen our creativity and relationships. How can you bring some fun and celebration into the serious problem-solving in your life or congregation this week?

PRAYER

O God, teach me to truly celebrate, to eat and drink good things, that your joy may be my strength. Amen.

Canticle

Psalm 19

The ordinances of the LORD are true
    and righteous altogether.
More to be desired are they than gold,
    even much fine gold;
sweeter also than honey,
    and drippings of the honeycomb. (vv. 9b–10)

REFLECTION

The psalmist is suggesting the law of the Lord is more than one can ask
for, and should be sought after. . . . This is the law the psalmist praises.
Just as Ezra in Nehemiah 8 encourages the people to hear the word of
the Lord with joy and not grief, the psalmist celebrates God's law with
great joy and admiration.

However, the psalmist does not simply praise God's law for its ability
to appeal to humanity; instead, the psalmist praises God's law for its
ability to transform the one who keeps the law.

KHALIA J. WILLIAMS

RESPONSE

Most people do not like being told what to do, but laws, values,
and order help form us in integrity and compassion. Make a list of
some of your favorite laws and commandments, religious or secular.
How do they bring you joy? Are they transforming you and your
community? How?

PRAYER

O God, transform me in your law that my soul may be revived and my
eyes enlightened. Amen.

Second Reading

1 Corinthians 12:12–31a

Now you are the body of Christ and individually members of it. . . . Are all apostles? Are all prophets? Are all teachers? Do all work miracles? Do all possess gifts of healing? Do all speak in tongues? Do all interpret? But strive for the greater gifts. (vv. 27, 29–31a)

REFLECTION

Paul concludes . . . by returning to the things that need doing in the church and the people set apart to do them. . . . One is not more important than the other; all need the others to be who they are and to do what they do. Each must strive together for the greater gifts of the one Spirit, gifts that thus far have coincided with the particular tasks they have been given to do. All these gifts are useless without the greatest gift the church has been given in Jesus Christ: the gift of love.

CYNTHIA A. JARVIS

RESPONSE

Paul reminds us how difficult it is to live as a diverse community, that we can find unity only in Christ and with love. What are some ways your church or community struggles with diversity of gifts and people? How could a greater emphasis on love than skills be lived out in your context?

PRAYER

Loving Christ, in you are the greatest gifts and in the Holy Spirit we are all baptized into one body. Amen.

Gospel

Luke 4:14–21

And [Jesus] rolled up the scroll, gave it back to the attendant, and sat down. The eyes of all in the synagogue were fixed on him. Then he began to say to them, "Today this scripture has been fulfilled in your hearing." (vv. 20–21)

REFLECTION

The time of divine action is always now. This today continues throughout Jesus' ministry. Now is always the time to release the captives, to give sight to the blind, to free the oppressed, to proclaim the year of the Lord's favor. . . .

. . . Too often, the prophetic word is followed by those who will answer, "Tomorrow"—or simply, "Wait." History is full of examples of how people of faith have been tragically slow to embrace the cries of the prophets or the opportunities to "do justice, love kindness, and walk humbly with God" (Mic. 6:8).

BLAIR R. MONIE

RESPONSE

What is an issue that, today, you feel society or your community has been slow to address? Where and for what has there been too much waiting? What could you do, today, to propel some movement toward action, change, and justice?

PRAYER

God, this is the year of your favor. Teach me how to do justice, love kindness, and walk humbly with you, now and into the future. Amen.

Weekend Reflections

FURTHER CONNECTION

We begin our day by seeing Christ in the consecrated bread, and throughout the day we continue to see Him in the torn bodies of our poor. We pray, that is, through our work, performing it with Jesus, for Jesus, and upon Jesus. The poor are our prayer. They carry God in them.

TERESA OF CALCUTTA (1910–97), *THE LOVE OF CHRIST:
SPIRITUAL COUNSELS*

MAKING THE CONNECTIONS

Choose one or two questions for reflection:

1. What connections have you noticed between this week's texts and other passages in Scripture?

2. What connections have you made between this week's texts and the world beyond Scripture?

3. Does either of this week's two commentary themes speak especially to your life or the life of the world around you right now?

4. What is God saying to your congregation in particular through this week's readings and commentaries?

_____

_____

_____

_____

_____

_____

Sabbath Day

SCRIPTURE OF ASSURANCE

The LORD is my light and my salvation;
whom shall I fear?
The LORD is the stronghold of my life;
of whom shall I be afraid? (Psalm 27:1)

WEEKLY EXAMEN

- Take a quiet moment, seek out God's presence, and pray for the guidance of the Spirit.

- Consider the past week; recall specific moments and feelings that stand out to you.

- Choose one moment or feeling for deeper examination, thanksgiving, or repentance.

- Let go, breathe deeply, and invite Christ's love to surround and fill you in preparation for the week ahead.

- End with the Lord's Prayer.

The Week Leading Up to the
Fourth Sunday
after the Epiphany

Jeremiah 1:4–10

Before I formed you in the womb I knew you,
  and before you were born I consecrated you;
I appointed you a prophet to the nations. (v. 5)

Psalm 71:1–6

In you, O LORD, I take refuge;
  let me never be put to shame.
In your righteousness deliver me and rescue me;
  incline your ear to me and save me. (vv. 1–2)

1 Corinthians 13:1–13

And if I have prophetic powers, and understand all mysteries and all knowledge, and if I have all faith, so as to remove mountains, but do not have love, I am nothing. (v. 2)

Luke 4:21–30

[Jesus] said to them, "Doubtless you will quote to me this proverb, 'Doctor, cure yourself!' And you will say, 'Do here also in your hometown the things that we have heard you did at Capernaum.'" And he said, "Truly I tell you, no prophet is accepted in the prophet's hometown." (vv. 23–24)

LECTIO DIVINA

Underline a word or phrase that especially grabs your attention. Pray from that word or phrase and ask God to help you connect to its particular invitation for you this week.

Themes from This Week's Writers

THEME 1: *Called to Be Prophets*

Jeremiah 1:4–10

The revelation that Jeremiah was appointed a prophet while in
the womb, along with his protest to the revelation, establishes the
framework for understanding Jeremiah's compulsion to prophesy and
his protests against the Lord (15:10–21; 20:7–18); the prophetic word is
etched in his DNA.

L. DANIEL HAWK

Jeremiah 1:4–10

Jeremiah himself was "only a boy," but the call of God came to him.
We realize this when we recall that even the "greats" in the Bible were
ordinary persons whom God used in extraordinary ways. The same is
true for the disciples of Jesus; they were used by God, but not because of
anything within themselves that earned them this privilege.

DONALD K. MCKIM

Luke 4:21–30

They have heard [Jesus] cite two examples of prophets who shared God's
favor with Gentiles but not with Israel, suggesting—staggeringly—that
God's favor had been withheld from Israel. These factors suggest that
the hometown folks express not anger at having to share God's favor
but anger that Jesus seems to exclude Nazareth from it. The townsfolk
rightly protest their exclusion from God's loving actions.

WARREN CARTER

THEME 2: *The Greatest of These Is Love*

1 Corinthians 13:1–13

While Christians should be confident in the power of the Spirit given to
us, we must also be humble and discerning, aware that our prophecies

are partial, our knowledge incomplete, and our vision dim. Whatever spiritual gifts we may boast of, or even generously offer to the common good, are fleeting. What remains is love.

SHANNON CRAIGO-SNELL

1 Corinthians 13:1–13

Paul knows you just cannot say what love is without saying Jesus! He knows only Christ can make unconditional lovers out of otherwise selfish human beings. He knows this because Christ has done this for him. Hence he offers no definition but, instead, turns the Corinthians to the one who alone is love.

CYNTHIA A. JARVIS

Luke 4:21–30

The people were "filled with rage" because Jesus proclaimed a grace that was wider and more generous than they were. Grace is more difficult to really embrace than we often assume. We are happy when the "right" people are forgiven, accepted, or healed, but we're not so sure that we want those things extended to people outside our favored circles, or that we want to extend that grace ourselves.

BLAIR R. MONIE

WHAT IS THE HOLY SPIRIT SAYING TO YOU THIS WEEK?

_____

_____

_____

_____

_____

First Corinthians 13 is read at many weddings. This week, find a distinctly different place to study and pray with this passage, hearing its words speak to other stages and places in life: a coffee shop, a parking lot, a hospital lobby, or another place that suggests itself to you.

First Reading

Jeremiah 1:4–10

But the LORD said to me,
"Do not say, 'I am only a boy';
for you shall go to all to whom I send you,
and you shall speak whatever I command you.
Do not be afraid of them,
for I am with you to deliver you,
says the LORD." (vv. 7–8)

REFLECTION

The initiative in our salvation and in our callings and ministries is God's. The promises we receive from God are grounded in God's call, God's taking us as we are, and God's calling us into who God wants us to be as God's people engaged in mission and ministry.

God takes the initiative in calling us and continuing to be with us. We need not be afraid, for God is with us to rescue and deliver.

DONALD K. MCKIM

RESPONSE

How much responsibility for your salvation, calling, and ministry do you put on yourself? What would it mean for your life if you truly believed that God takes you as you are? That God calls you and equips you to serve? That God will deliver you?

PRAYER

God, you have searched me out and known me. Here I am; send me. Amen.

Canticle

Psalm 71:1–6

Rescue me, O my God, from the hand of the wicked,
    from the grasp of the unjust and cruel.
For you, O Lord, are my hope,
    my trust, O LORD, from my youth. (vv. 4–5)

REFLECTION

Considered as a response, today's psalm of lament can be heard as an appropriate reply to Jeremiah's call narrative. The call to be a prophet implies both intimacy with God and a resulting confrontational relationship with the world. The one who is appointed to "pluck up and to pull down, to destroy and to overthrow, to build and to plant" (Jer. 1:10) is likely to need a "rock of refuge" behind which to hide, or a rescuer ready to "incline [an] ear" (Ps. 71:2).

RHODORA E. BEATON

RESPONSE

What do you need to lament this week? Have any of your prophecies been rejected? What or who has been unjust or cruel? Read this psalm aloud today with your life this week in mind, trusting in God's refuge for you.

PRAYER

In you, O God, I take refuge. Deliver me and rescue me. Amen.

Second Reading

1 Corinthians 13:1–13

Love never ends. But as for prophecies, they will come to an end; as for tongues, they will cease; as for knowledge, it will come to an end. For we know only in part, and we prophesy only in part; but when the complete comes, the partial will come to an end. (vv. 8–10)

REFLECTION

Even though a person can have the outward appearance of knowing God theologically, receiving God's word prophetically, working God's works miraculously, and saying the unsayable, if that one is puffed up with knowledge or self-important about her or his faith, then there can be no witness to the One who in love emptied himself.

CYNTHIA A. JARVIS

RESPONSE

Make a list of the spiritual gifts and churchy virtues you possess and are often proud of. Reflect on what Paul means when he says all these will come to an end. Or, what does it mean to you that "love never ends," at this point in your life?

PRAYER

O God, without your love, I am nothing. Now I know only in part; later I will know fully, even as I have been fully known. Amen.

Gospel

Luke 4:21–30

When they heard this, all in the synagogue were filled with rage. They got up, drove [Jesus] out of the town, and led him to the brow of the hill on which their town was built, so that they might hurl him off the cliff. But he passed through the midst of them and went on his way. (vv. 28–30)

REFLECTION

This is a passage full of the themes of "us" versus "them." Jesus, you did it for them, so why not us? . . .

The people of Nazareth who gathered on the Sabbath that day in the synagogue may not have been wealthy or powerful, but many thought of themselves as God's people in terms of privilege in the negative sense of favoritism. That led them to resent a grace that was extended to others and, ironically, kept them from joyously receiving grace themselves, when it was so publicly announced.

BLAIR R. MONIE

RESPONSE

What is a recent grace someone else has received that you have resented? Sometimes, we wish the grace God gave us was more like the grace God seems to give to others. What is a grace you long for? What would it be like to ask God to grant this to you?

PRAYER

O God, teach me to believe in grace not only for myself, but for all. Amen.

Weekend Reflections

FURTHER CONNECTION

The beginning of love is the will to let those we love be perfectly themselves, the resolution not to twist them to fit our own image. If in loving them we do not love what they are, but only their potential likeness to ourselves, then we do not love them: we only love the reflection of ourselves we find in them.

THOMAS MERTON (1915–68), NO MAN IS AN ISLAND

MAKING THE CONNECTIONS

Choose one or two questions for reflection:

1. What connections have you noticed between this week's texts and other passages in Scripture?

2. What connections have you made between this week's texts and the world beyond Scripture?

3. Does either of this week's two commentary themes speak especially to your life or the life of the world around you right now?

4. What is God saying to your congregation in particular through this week's readings and commentaries?

_____

_____

_____

_____

_____

_____

Sabbath Day

SCRIPTURE OF ASSURANCE

For just as the sufferings of Christ are abundant for us, so also our consolation is abundant through Christ. (2 Corinthians 1:5)

WEEKLY EXAMEN

- Take a quiet moment, seek out God's presence, and pray for the guidance of the Spirit.

- Consider the past week; recall specific moments and feelings that stand out to you.

- Choose one moment or feeling for deeper examination, thanksgiving, or repentance.

- Let go, breathe deeply, and invite Christ's love to surround and fill you in preparation for the week ahead.

- End with the Lord's Prayer.

The Week Leading Up to the
Fifth Sunday
after the Epiphany

Isaiah 6:1–8 (9–13)

Then I heard the voice of the Lord saying, "Whom shall I send, and who will go for us?" And I said, "Here am I; send me!" (v. 8)

Psalm 138

The LORD will fulfill his purpose for me;
  your steadfast love, O LORD, endures forever.
Do not forsake the work of your hands. (v. 8)

1 Corinthians 15:1–11

For I handed on to you as of first importance what I in turn had received: that Christ died for our sins in accordance with the scriptures, and that he was buried, and that he was raised on the third day in accordance with the scriptures. (vv. 3–4)

Luke 5:1–11

When [Jesus] had finished speaking, he said to Simon, "Put out into the deep water and let down your nets for a catch." Simon answered, "Master, we have worked all night long but have caught nothing. Yet if you say so, I will let down the nets." (vv. 4–5)

LECTIO DIVINA

Underline a word or phrase that especially grabs your attention. Pray from that word or phrase and ask God to help you connect to its particular invitation for you this week.

Themes from This Week's Writers

THEME 1: *Awe and Fear of the Lord*

Isaiah 6:1–8 (9–13)

While God is not directly described, the text makes clear that God is massive (just the edges of the divine robe fill the temple, v. 1b) and served by fantastic beings: six-winged seraphim that proclaim the holiness and glory of God (vv. 2–3) to such an extent that the very building shakes (v. 4). Isaiah is rightly overcome—even terrified—by what he sees, which is an altogether proper response in the face of the holy God (cf. Exod. 3:5–6).

BRENT A. STRAWN

Psalm 138

The psalm's dual emphasis on thanksgiving as well as "trouble" and "the wrath of [one's] enemies" (Ps. 138:7) make it an especially appropriate response both to Isaiah's experience of exuberance in the presence of God and concern ("how long, O Lord," Isa. 6:11) in light of God's message of judgment.

RHODORA E. BEATON

Luke 5:1–11

Peter falls down before Jesus (as others do in the Gospel who seek or experience God's power manifested through him, 8:41; 17:16). Peter begs Jesus to leave him, and names himself "a sinful man" (5:8). The latter is not a moral confession of a sinful life; it expresses awe in the presence of a manifestation of Jesus' identity as agent of God's rule/empire.

WARREN CARTER

1 Corinthians 15:1–11

Though we may have trouble feeling that Christ is present in the darkness, the *givenness* of Jesus' story and the *givenness* of the Scriptures are nonetheless here and true. They are given for us, and they make us who we are. We do not have to produce ourselves as the people of God. We are the ones who are being produced by the story and by the flesh of Jesus who is risen from the dead.

BETH FELKER JONES

1 Corinthians 15:1–11

In spite of his previous behavior as persecutor of the church and the unlikely late appearance of the risen Christ to Paul, his apostleship is just as real and valid as that of other apostles.

Paul responded to God's grace of his birth (calling) as an apostle by working "harder than any of them [other apostles]," although it was grace that energized his efforts ("the grace of God that is with me," v. 10).

MARK ABBOTT

Luke 5:1–11

Luke often stresses Jesus' ministry to the outsider and the sinner: "Those who are well have no need of a physician, but those who are sick" (5:31). Simon's reply to Jesus exhibits a paradox that Martin Luther would have recognized: those who see their need of grace are in the best position to find it.

BLAIR R. MONIE

WHAT IS THE HOLY SPIRIT SAYING TO YOU THIS WEEK?

_____

_____

_____

_____

_____

A SPIRITUAL PRACTICE FOR THIS WEEK

With a sense of fun and grace for whatever your drawing skills may be, attempt to draw the scene described in Isaiah 6:1–8. Have fun. Try to include all the details the prophet describes. What do you notice about the passage that you had not before?

First Reading

Isaiah 6:1–8 (9–13)

I saw the Lord sitting on a throne, high and lofty; and the hem of his robe filled the temple. Seraphs were in attendance above him; each had six wings: with two they covered their faces, and with two they covered their feet, and with two they flew. (vv. 1b–2)

REFLECTION

We move through the elements of worship—toward what end? We can manufacture neither the grandeur nor the intimacy that Isaiah encountered in the temple, yet his vision invites us to consider the invisible reality toward which all our hymns, prayers, and sermons point: the dazzling, devastating presence of a holy God.

Isaiah's experience of God's presence was shockingly direct. Our own personal and congregational experiences may feel less so, but the seraphs tell the truth: "the whole earth is full of [God's] glory."

STACEY SIMPSON DUKE

RESPONSE

What is *glory*? How much of a feeling of glory do you encounter in Sunday worship at your present church? What does it mean to you in your own experiences of the holy? Does a church need a sense of glory to thrive?

PRAYER

Holy, holy, holy are you, O Lord of hosts; the whole earth is full of your glory. Touch my mouth that I may speak of your love and call to all people. Amen.

Canticle

Psalm 138

I bow down toward your holy temple
    and give thanks to your name for your steadfast love and your
        faithfulness;
    for you have exalted your name and your word
    above everything.
On the day I called, you answered me,
    you increased my strength of soul. (vv. 2–3)

REFLECTION

When the psalmist bows down toward God's holy temple, the modern
worshiper, hearing these readings in the liturgical context, can picture
the heavenly court above the temple. . . . What human would not,
as the psalmist does, bow down (Ps. 138:2) toward the God whose
voice is at the center of this image of the heavenly court? . . . The
psalm and prophetic reading together suggest the possibility of human
participation in the heavenly liturgy: "before the gods I sing your praise"
(Ps. 138:1).

RHODORA E. BEATON

RESPONSE

The awe and glory surrounding our God, whether in a temple or in the
world, is not meant to keep us at a distance; we are meant to participate.
How do you distance yourself from God's glory? How do you feel drawn
to and part of God's glory?

PRAYER

O God, your glory and beauty are great, and so is your love, which
endures forever. Hide me in the shadow of your wings and help me to
give thanks with my whole heart. Amen.

Second Reading

1 Corinthians 15:1–11

Last of all, as to one untimely born, he appeared also to me. For I am the least of the apostles, unfit to be called an apostle, because I persecuted the church of God. But by the grace of God I am what I am, and his grace toward me has not been in vain. (vv. 8–10a)

REFLECTION

Paul's dramatic encounter with the risen Christ on the road to Damascus and Isaiah's vision of the Lord on the throne resonate strongly with one another. Isaiah the prophet answered the Lord's call, "Whom shall I send, and who will go for us?"; Paul became apostle to the Gentiles. Luke 5 gives the account of another apostolic call, as Jesus tells Simon Peter, "From now on you will be catching people" (Luke 5:10). In both Isaiah and Luke, personal encounter with God leads to missional engagement and is not an end in itself.

MARK ABBOTT

RESPONSE

Reflect on how a personal encounter with God, dramatic or subtle, led you to change your life or answer God's call. What does it mean to you that an encounter like this should not be an end in itself? How do you feel called by God in this season of your life?

PRAYER

O God, show me how to hold firmly to your message and welcome the ways you appear to me today and in the days to come. It is by your grace that I am what I am. Amen.

Gospel

Luke 5:1–11

But when Simon Peter saw it, he fell down at Jesus' knees, saying, "Go away from me, Lord, for I am a sinful man!" For he and all who were with him were amazed at the catch of fish that they had taken; and so also were James and John, sons of Zebedee, who were partners with Simon. Then Jesus said to Simon, "Do not be afraid; from now on you will be catching people." (vv. 8–10)

REFLECTION

Peter begs Jesus to leave him, and names himself "a sinful man" (5:8). The latter is not a moral confession of a sinful life; it expresses awe in the presence of a manifestation of Jesus' identity as agent of God's rule/empire. This response of awe is repeated in verses 9–10. Peter's amazement is shared by "all who were with him" (employees) and his business partners, James and John, who also become followers (6:14). A miraculous display of power produces insight into and commitment to God's working (also 5:25–26; 7:16).

WARREN CARTER

RESPONSE

Have you ever felt, like Peter or Isaiah, unworthy or sinful because of awe in the presence of God or Christ? What does "awe" mean to you in this season of your Christian life? How can awe give us "insight into and commitment to God's working," do you think?

PRAYER

Jesus, show me how to not be afraid or ashamed, but to trust and listen to your word and your love, that I may cast my nets into the deep water. Amen.

Weekend Reflections

FURTHER CONNECTION

Earth's crammed with heaven,
And every common bush afire with God,
But only he who sees takes off his shoes;
The rest sit round and pluck blackberries.

ELIZABETH BARRETT BROWNING (1806–61), *FROM AURORA LEIGH*

MAKING THE CONNECTIONS

Choose one or two questions for reflection:

1. What connections have you noticed between this week's texts and other passages in Scripture?

2. What connections have you made between this week's texts and the world beyond Scripture?

3. Does either of this week's two commentary themes speak especially to your life or the life of the world around you right now?

4. What is God saying to your congregation in particular through this week's readings and commentaries?

MY CONNECTIONS

_____

_____

_____

_____

_____

_____

Sabbath Day

SCRIPTURE OF ASSURANCE

> We ponder your steadfast love, O God,
>> in the midst of your temple.
> Your name, O God, like your praise,
>> reaches to the ends of the earth. (Psalm 48:9–10)

WEEKLY EXAMEN

- Take a quiet moment, seek out God's presence, and pray for the guidance of the Spirit.

- Consider the past week; recall specific moments and feelings that stand out to you.

- Choose one moment or feeling for deeper examination, thanksgiving, or repentance.

- Let go, breathe deeply, and invite Christ's love to surround and fill you in preparation for the week ahead.

- End with the Lord's Prayer.

The Week Leading Up to the
Sixth Sunday
after the Epiphany

Jeremiah 17:5–10

Thus says the LORD:
Cursed are those who trust in mere mortals
  and make mere flesh their strength,
  whose hearts turn away from the LORD. (v. 5)

Psalm 1

Happy are those
  who do not follow the advice of the wicked,
or take the path that sinners tread,
  or sit in the seat of scoffers;
but their delight is in the law of the LORD,
  and on his law they meditate day and night. (vv. 1–2)

1 Corinthians 15:12–20

We are even found to be misrepresenting God, because we testified of God that he raised Christ—whom he did not raise if it is true that the dead are not raised. (v. 15)

Luke 6:17–26

Then he looked up at his disciples and said:
  "Blessed are you who are poor,
    for yours is the kingdom of God.
  "Blessed are you who are hungry now,
    for you will be filled." (vv. 20–21)

Underline a word or phrase that especially grabs your attention. Pray from that word or phrase and ask God to help you connect to its particular invitation for you this week.

Themes from This Week's Writers

THEME 1: *What Is Happiness? What Is Blessedness?*

Jeremiah 17:5–10

The contrasting blessedness of those who trust in the Lord takes the extreme in the opposite direction. This person is like a tree planted in a place where water is always available, enabling it to extend the roots that provide stability and nourishment, and so to produce luxuriant foliage and continuous fruit.

L. DANIEL HAWK

Psalm 1

Psalm 1 offers a worldview that suggests happiness and prosperity are to be found through prayer, meditation, and the law of the Lord. . . . The "two paths" motif is common in the Wisdom literature, as is the idea that those who follow the way of God will be sustained by God. It may be important to remember that the book of Job, also classified as Wisdom literature, calls this worldview into question.

RHODORA E. BEATON

Luke 6:17–26

Jesus challenges appearances by associating blessing and warning with a call to discipleship. Who is blessed and who is woeful are to be determined by how one waits on God and whether one serves the Son of Man.

WES AVRAM

THEME 2: *Salvation for Souls and Bodies*

1 Corinthians 15:12–20

Gnosticism hoped for escape from this world and this flesh. Resurrection hope is for the redemption of this world and this flesh.

. . . Our new Gnosticisms have been stripped of the metaphysical and religious baggage of the ancient forms, but they retain and perhaps even heighten the hierarchical dualism that despises bodies and material creation.

BETH FELKER JONES

1 Corinthians 15:12–20

Paul does not see value in trusting in Christ without the hope of resurrection. This implies not only that present Christian existence is sustained by the resurrection hope, but that the vision of new life with God becomes the ground for present living. Just as the future vision shapes our present living, so what we do in our bodily existence now matters for our future.

MARK ABBOTT

Luke 6:17–26

We are called to feed the poor, comfort the afflicted, house the homeless. . . . Giving money is good, giving of your time and presence is even better. We are to be God's instruments in transforming their woes into blessings.

ROBERT F. DARDEN

WHAT IS THE HOLY SPIRIT SAYING TO YOU THIS WEEK?

_____

_____

_____

_____

_____

Make a list of some things that make you happy. Then, a list of things that make you feel deeply, truly happy. Then, a list of things you believe make God deeply, truly happy. What is the overlap in these lists? Where is there conflict? What else do you notice?

First Reading

Jeremiah 17:5–10

They shall be like a tree planted by water,
  sending out its roots by the stream.
It shall not fear when heat comes,
  and its leaves shall stay green;
in the year of drought it is not anxious,
  and it does not cease to bear fruit. (v. 8)

REFLECTION

Trusting in the Lord means a renewing source of nourishment is always
available. Even in the midst of the drought—when all else seems
hopeless and a tree in itself may appear helpless—its roots receive
needed nurture from the stream that gives life to the tree. The "invisible"
resources sustain, even when, to all outward appearances, disaster seems
imminent. The "leaves shall stay green"; the actions of the human heart
that trusts in God will continue vitally, in ways pleasing to God, because
the heart trusts in the living Lord.

DONALD K. MCKIM

RESPONSE

What was a time when, through a time of drought, you were able to
keep your roots planted in God's stream? Recall also a time when you
struggled to do so. What did you learn, looking back? How are your
roots doing this week?

PRAYER

God, test my mind and search my heart. Help me to trust in you, to not
turn away, and to send my roots into your stream. Amen.

Canticle

Psalm 1

Happy are those
    who do not follow the advice of the wicked.
. . . .
They are like trees
    planted by streams of water,
which yield their fruit in its season,
    and their leaves do not wither.
In all that they do, they prosper. (vv. 1a, 3)

REFLECTION

While Psalm 1 presents the matter of happiness as a straightforward choice for God and against the "wicked," the remaining psalms demonstrate that the path to happiness is not as clear-cut as one might hope; injustice, cruelty, and abandonment can stand in the way. As the first reading from Jeremiah suggests, sometimes even the human heart can become a source of unhappiness. . . . The Gospel reading for today picks up on this question, as Jesus preaches in the Beatitudes an inverted understanding of happiness and blessing.

RHODORA E. BEATON

RESPONSE

Have you ever experienced happiness as the result of a "straightforward choice for God" and refusal of the wicked? Have you ever tried these things and felt miserable anyway? Were there obstacles, like injustice or cruelty, that got in the way? What does happiness look like for you this week?

PRAYER

O God, your law is my delight. Help me not to follow the advice of the wicked or a path of sin, but to walk and grow strong in you. Amen.

Second Reading

1 Corinthians 15:12–20

Now if Christ is proclaimed as raised from the dead, how can some of you say there is no resurrection of the dead? If there is no resurrection of the dead, then Christ has not been raised; and if Christ has not been raised, then our proclamation has been in vain and your faith has been in vain. (vv. 12–14)

REFLECTION

There is comfort here for those who have been told they are worthless, for those who have believed they are beyond redemption. God does not want to destroy us. God wants to redeem us. At the same time, we need transformation. There is comfort here for "the dead," for all of us who groan against our mortality, for that very mortality is being transformed and overcome. There is comfort here for all of us who long for change, who battle some habit or pain that seems intransigent.

BETH FELKER JONES

RESPONSE

How have you been longing for transformation or "groaning against mortality" in this season of your life? What do you need to hear, this week, in the news that Christ has been raised from the dead, that God is transforming our mortality, that there is life beyond this one?

PRAYER

Jesus Christ, you have been raised from the dead. Teach me to live in hope and resurrection, and to give myself to transformation. I believe; help my unbelief. Amen.

Gospel

Luke 6:17–26

"Blessed are you who are hungry now,
  for you will be filled.
"Blessed are you who weep now,
  for you will laugh.

. . . .

"Woe to you who are full now,
  for you will be hungry.
"Woe to you who are laughing now,
  for you will mourn and weep." (vv. 21, 25)

REFLECTION

The poor and hungry who gathered around Jesus during the Sermon on the Plain are still with us. . . .

. . . He told them to take heart, rejoice, and know that if they had been excluded, hated, reviled, and defamed as they earnestly sought to follow the Son of Man, their reward would be great. Looking at these words in one way, it was—and is—a message to the oppressed, not the oppressor.

At the same time, Jesus was and is speaking to the rich Christian today, reaching across time and gender and race and geography and beyond.

ROBERT F. DARDEN

RESPONSE

Are you hungry? Or full? Are you poor? Or rich? Are you weeping? Or laughing? How do you feel, hearing Jesus speak to you in these words? What is God calling you to consider or do?

PRAYER

Jesus, you came down among your people and taught them. Teach me, through woes and blessings, to live with justice and seek you above all things. Amen.

Weekend Reflections

Lord, make me an instrument of your peace; where there is hatred, let me sow love; where there is injury, pardon; where there is discord, union; where there is doubt, faith; where there is despair, hope; where there is darkness, light; and where there is sadness, joy. O Divine Master, grant that I may not so much seek to be consoled, as to console; to be understood, as to understand; to be loved, as to love; for it is in giving that we receive, it is in pardoning that we are pardoned, and it is in dying that we are born to eternal life. Amen.

FRANCIS OF ASSISI (1182–1226), TRADITIONALLY ATTRIBUTED

MAKING THE CONNECTIONS

Choose one or two questions for reflection:

1. What connections have you noticed between this week's texts and other passages in Scripture?

2. What connections have you made between this week's texts and the world beyond Scripture?

3. Does either of this week's two commentary themes speak especially to your life or the life of the world around you right now?

4. What is God saying to your congregation in particular through this week's readings and commentaries?

_____

_____

_____

_____

_____

Sabbath Day

SCRIPTURE OF ASSURANCE

> For the LORD takes pleasure in his people;
> he adorns the humble with victory.
> Let the faithful exult in glory;
> let them sing for joy on their couches. (Psalm 149:4–5)

WEEKLY EXAMEN

- Take a quiet moment, seek out God's presence, and pray for the guidance of the Spirit.

- Consider the past week; recall specific moments and feelings that stand out to you.

- Choose one moment or feeling for deeper examination, thanksgiving, or repentance.

- Let go, breathe deeply, and invite Christ's love to surround and fill you in preparation for the week ahead.

- End with the Lord's Prayer.

The Week Leading Up to the
Seventh Sunday
after the Epiphany

Genesis 45:3–11, 15

He said, "I am your brother, Joseph, whom you sold into Egypt. And now do not be distressed, or angry with yourselves, because you sold me here; for God sent me before you to preserve life." (vv. 4b–5)

Psalm 37:1–11, 39–40

Refrain from anger, and forsake wrath.
 Do not fret—it leads only to evil.
For the wicked shall be cut off,
 but those who wait for the LORD shall inherit the land. (vv. 8–9)

1 Corinthians 15:35–38, 42–50

So it is with the resurrection of the dead. What is sown is perishable, what is raised is imperishable. It is sown in dishonor, it is raised in glory. It is sown in weakness, it is raised in power. (vv. 42–43)

Luke 6:27–38

"But I say to you that listen, Love your enemies, do good to those who hate you, bless those who curse you, pray for those who abuse you." (vv. 27–28)

LECTIO DIVINA

Underline a word or phrase that especially grabs your attention. Pray from that word or phrase and ask God to help you connect to its particular invitation for you this week.

Themes from This Week's Writers

THEME 1: *Forgiveness and Loving Our Enemies*

Genesis 45:3–11, 15

[Joseph's] theological understanding transforms his suffering, so that, instead of passing on that suffering through retaliation, he can forgive.

STACEY SIMPSON DUKE

Genesis 45:3–11, 15

Reconciliation will not happen in the space of a verse, or a day, or even many years. The one tasked with forgiveness will need virtue and prudence—often hard won—and a good dose of divine assistance . . . like Joseph.

BRENT A. STRAWN

Luke 6:27–38

[Christian life] asks us to sacrifice our long-cherished sense of aggrievement toward our enemies, rendering them in the process not enemies at all, but fellow sinners forgiven by God.

ROBERT F. DARDEN

THEME 2: *Resurrection and Mercy Are of the Body, Not Just the Soul*

1 Corinthians 15:35–38, 42–50

After all, if the body is something humans inhabit for the time being but discard at death, why should what someone does with it matter? . . . Christ died to redeem us as whole human beings.

JAMES C. MILLER

1 Corinthians 15:35–38, 42–50

Many of us today still cannot overcome the limitations of an imagination shaped by a culture filled with dualisms that split reality between the known physical world and an unknown spiritual world.

MARÍA TERESA DÁVILA

Luke 6:27–38

The woes that immediately precede it are directed to well-fed, highly regarded, socially powerful, personally secure people. . . . The call is not to give things up, but to love, to regard others with mercy, and to sacrifice one's comfort on their behalf.

WES AVRAM

WHAT IS THE HOLY SPIRIT SAYING TO YOU THIS WEEK?

_____

_____

_____

_____

_____

A SPIRITUAL PRACTICE FOR THIS WEEK

Choose an enemy to pray for this week. Write their name on a piece of paper and place it somewhere you will see it regularly. You might use this prayer: "May they have enough. May they love and be loved. May they know and be known by God."

First Reading

Genesis 45:3–11, 15

And he kissed all his brothers and wept upon them; and after that his brothers talked with him. (v. 15)

REFLECTION

The dysfunction in Joseph's family runs back generations, as we see in the many stories of dishonesty, manipulation, sibling rivalry, and other bad behavior. . . . Joseph disrupts the old family pattern. In the episodes leading up to this text, he has toyed with his brothers, and cruelly so, but now he makes a choice that changes everything: he forgives them. Even within a family system loaded with manipulation, jealousy, and fear, a single person within the system has the power to transform relationships, and even the system itself, through an unexpected act of reconciliation.

STACEY SIMPSON DUKE

RESPONSE

What long-standing pattern of hurt or dysfunction may be at work in your family or other context? How do Joseph's actions remind you of your own experiences or choices? What would it mean for you to move toward a place of forgiveness, like Joseph?

PRAYER

O God, you gave Joseph honor and humility, so that he could save his family and his people. Teach me also to forgive and to seek reconciliation. Amen.

Canticle

Psalm 37:1–11, 39–40

Commit your way to the LORD;
   trust in him, and he will act.
He will make your vindication shine like the light,
   and the justice of your cause like the noonday. (vv. 5–6)

REFLECTION

Patience, patience, patience. That's the drumbeat of this psalm. . . .
   Confidence is the colleague of patience, and so this psalm affirms
and assures that God will act to make things right, granting fulfillment
to the seeker, extending care to the righteous, and lifting the lowly. God
"will give you the desires of your heart" (v. 4). God "will make your
vindication shine like the light, and the justice of your cause like the
noonday" (v. 6). Just wait. Just be patient.

JOHN W. WURSTER

RESPONSE

The psalmist is certain that God will make things right if we trust and
wait. Western culture focuses on individual effort and the will as forces of
change. How do you see the push and pull of these two in your own life?

PRAYER

O God, you invite me to be still, to take delight in you, and to trust
you. Help me not to worry or to get angry, but to wait for you. Amen.

Second Reading

1 Corinthians 15:35–38, 42–50

It is sown a physical body, it is raised a spiritual body. If there is a physical body, there is also a spiritual body. (v. 44)

REFLECTION

Paul speaks of the preresurrected body and the resurrected body, using phrases that are difficult to translate. The NRSV's "physical body" and "spiritual body" can be misleading, since they suggest a dualism between the physical and spiritual that is foreign to Paul. Paul never speaks of the soul's being resurrected, as if resurrection leaves the body behind. Rather, Paul's overall point is that a continuity exists between a preresurrection *body* and a resurrected *body*. To get from one state to another requires transformation, but human existence never ceases to be bodily. Humans do not *have* bodies; they exist as bodies.

JAMES C. MILLER

RESPONSE

What evidence do you have from your own life that your spiritual body and physical body are intertwined? Reflect on what this mystery might mean, in both this world and the next: that "human existence never ceases to be bodily."

PRAYER

O God, you have given me a body that is perishable, like a seed; even so, help me to trust that, at the end, my life will be changed, not ended. Amen.

Gospel

Luke 6:27–38

"But love your enemies, do good, and lend, expecting nothing in return. Your reward will be great, and you will be children of the Most High; for he is kind to the ungrateful and the wicked. Be merciful, just as your Father is merciful." (vv. 35–36)

REFLECTION

Jesus' words force us to deliberate on the *ongoing* revelation of Christ. This continued outpouring of wisdom tosses previous beliefs and tenets into disarray. Like so many of the words of Jesus, they operate on multiple levels. Jesus dares listeners in verses 27–31 to compare ourselves not with the heroes and prophets of the Old Testament, but with the sinners and beggars of *our* day. Verses 32–38 then take it a step further. We are told to love the unlovable, no questions asked—even if we ourselves are the hardest persons to love and forgive.

ROBERT F. DARDEN

RESPONSE

Loving our enemies or the unlovable is not just (or even mostly) for their sake, but for us, for God, and for the world. Gandhi and Dr. Martin Luther King Jr. taught this, too. Who is hardest for you to love? Is it hard to love yourself? How are these two connected?

PRAYER

Loving God, you are merciful and kind. Teach me how to love my neighbor, even my enemy, and to do good, expecting nothing in return. Amen.

Weekend Reflections

FURTHER CONNECTION

We are not fighting against these people because we hate them, but we are fighting these people because we love them and we're the only thing can save them now. We are fighting to save these people from their hate and from all the things that would be so bad against them. We want them to see the right way. Every night of my life that I lay down before I go to sleep, I pray for these people that despitefully use me.

FANNIE LOU HAMER (1917–77), "WE'RE ON OUR WAY"

MAKING THE CONNECTIONS

Choose one or two questions for reflection:

1. What connections have you noticed between this week's texts and other passages in Scripture?

2. What connections have you made between this week's texts and the world beyond Scripture?

3. Does either of this week's two commentary themes speak especially to your life or the life of the world around you right now?

4. What is God saying to your congregation in particular through this week's readings and commentaries?

_____

_____

_____

_____

_____

Sabbath Day

SCRIPTURE OF ASSURANCE

For the message about the cross is foolishness to those who are perishing, but to us who are being saved it is the power of God. (1 Corinthians 1:18)

WEEKLY EXAMEN

- Take a quiet moment, seek out God's presence, and pray for the guidance of the Spirit.

- Consider the past week; recall specific moments and feelings that stand out to you.

- Choose one moment or feeling for deeper examination, thanksgiving, or repentance.

- Let go, breathe deeply, and invite Christ's love to surround and fill you in preparation for the week ahead.

- End with the Lord's Prayer.

The Week Leading Up to the
Eighth Sunday after the Epiphany

Isaiah 55:10–13

For as the rain and the snow come down from heaven,
  and do not return there until they have watered the earth,
making it bring forth and sprout,
  giving seed to the sower and bread to the eater,
so shall my word be that goes out from my mouth. (vv. 10–11a)

Psalm 92:1–4, 12–15

It is good to give thanks to the LORD,
  to sing praises to your name, O Most High;
to declare your steadfast love in the morning,
  and your faithfulness by night. (vv. 1–2)

1 Corinthians 15:51–58

The sting of death is sin, and the power of sin is the law. But thanks be to God, who gives us the victory through our Lord Jesus Christ. (vv. 56–57)

Luke 6:39–49

"Why do you call me 'Lord, Lord,' and do not do what I tell you?" (v. 46)

LECTIO DIVINA

Underline a word or phrase that especially grabs your attention. Pray from that word or phrase and ask God to help you connect to its particular invitation for you this week.

Themes from This Week's Writers

THEME 1: *Trust in God's Word*

Isaiah 55:10–13

[These] verses 10–13 indicate the utter reliability of God's word; it is as trustworthy as the natural cycle of water on the earth and the fertility it brings (v. 10). That cycle is entirely dependable, regular, virtually automatic.

BRENT A. STRAWN

Isaiah 55:10–13

Just as rain and snow reliably water the ground, transforming the earth, and creating the conditions for life, so too the word of God.

STACEY SIMPSON DUKE

Luke 6:39–49

It turns out that like homebuilders who choose good foundation stones, the better builders are not the people who talk a good game but, rather, the people who hear Jesus and do what he says.

WES AVRAM

THEME 2: *By Their Fruits, You Will Know Them*

Psalm 92:1–4, 12–15

The righteous flourish like a palm and grow like a cedar (Ps. 92:12). They are rooted and strong, nourished by their devotion and refreshed by God's faithfulness.

JOHN W. WURSTER

1 Corinthians 15:51–58

The project of living into resurrection hope and witnessing to Christ's victory over death—within history—requires vigilance against the sin of exclusion and a false trust in our own ability to safeguard against it.

MARÍA TERESA DÁVILA

Luke 6:39–49

We can claim anything. It is our fruit—what we do—that distinguishes us. Jesus is the master, the good tree, and his words are the good fruit, the treasure.

ROBERT F. DARDEN

WHAT IS THE HOLY SPIRIT SAYING TO YOU THIS WEEK?

_____

_____

_____

_____

_____

A SPIRITUAL PRACTICE FOR THIS WEEK

Make Paul's words about death your meditation this week: *Where, O death, is your victory? Where, O death, is your sting?* Write them out, say them aloud, sing them, draw and doodle them. What is the Spirit's invitation to you, in these words?

First Reading

Isaiah 55:10–13

So shall my word be that goes out from my mouth;
  it shall not return to me empty,
but it shall accomplish that which I purpose,
  and succeed in the thing for which I sent it. (v. 11)

REFLECTION

[The word of God] goes out from God to accomplish God's purpose, which is to transform us, and indeed the whole world, creating in us the conditions for life. When this life blooms within us, we, like the earth, yield fruit; we participate in God's purpose by passing the gift forward. The success of this work depends not on our efforts but on our yielding. Can we let go of our frantic attempts to contain and control what we have been given?

STACEY SIMPSON DUKE

RESPONSE

How do you try to contain and control what God has given you? How has this helped you? How has it hurt you, or those you love? What would it look like, in your life right now, to yield to God's power and God's gifts instead?

PRAYER

God, you send your word to me that it may sprout, grow, and produce fruit. Help me let go into your abundance and purpose today. Amen.

Canticle

Psalm 92:1–4, 12–15

The righteous flourish like the palm tree,
    and grow like a cedar in Lebanon.
They are planted in the house of the LORD;
    they flourish in the courts of our God. (vv. 12–13)

REFLECTION

Planting, growing, and bearing fruit are prominent motifs in the day's
readings from Isaiah and Luke. . . . The word of God is filled with
vitality and potential, eventually providing seeds to the sower, eventually
providing bread to the eater, eventually providing sustenance for the
journey, eventually providing shelter from stormy blasts, eventually
providing companionship through the valley of the shadow of the death.
What might God's nourishing word bring forth in our lives? What are
the areas in need of refreshment? Where is the parched ground desperate
for water?

JOHN W. WURSTER

RESPONSE

What is growing in your life right now? How are you "green and full of
sap"? What is still struggling to grow, needing water? What might God's
word be trying to nourish in you this week?

PRAYER

God, I declare your steadfast love and faithfulness today. Give me life so
that I may flourish in you. Amen.

Second Reading

1 Corinthians 15:51–58

The sting of death is sin, and the power of sin is the law. But thanks be to God, who gives us the victory through our Lord Jesus Christ. (vv. 56–57)

REFLECTION

Likewise, groups that have been at the receiving end of exclusion, oppression, and violence hear in the closing chapters of 1 Corinthians the promise of a wholeness and justice that is beyond the scope of human understanding, but that appears within history in Christ's victory over death. It is this hope that freed Cesar Chavez, Dietrich Bonhoeffer, Martin Luther King Jr., and others to proclaim victory over the deaths dealt wrongly and unjustly to so many. . . . Paul's mockery of death becomes a brazen invitation to life truly lived in resurrection hope.

MARÍA TERESA DÁVILA

RESPONSE

Where do you see resurrection hope most needed in your community or country right now? How is resurrection hope active or lacking in your own life? How, in Christ, can you make a mockery of death this week and put your trust in resurrection hope?

PRAYER

Thanks be to you, O God, that in Christ, death has been swallowed up. Show me how to put on immortality and to know that in you, my labors are not in vain. Amen.

Gospel

Luke 6:39–49

"That one is like a man building a house, who dug deeply and laid the foundation on rock; when a flood arose, the river burst against that house but could not shake it, because it had been well built." (v. 48)

REFLECTION

Saying something, but not really believing or living it, is sometimes called "lip service." . . . Verses 47–48 describe the dwelling place of the homeowner who hears and acts on the words of Jesus. This home is built on bedrock: solid, unmoving, able to weather life's storms and floods. In verse 49, the hapless homeowner who hears the words of Jesus but does not act on them instead builds a house on sand, a home that is washed away by the first heavy rain.

The proof, once again, is in the action.

ROBERT F. DARDEN

RESPONSE

What in the life of your church (or your life) is built on rock? What, would you say, is built only on sand? What will stand the test of time in Christ as rain and storms come, and what might be washed away? What is important about this?

PRAYER

Jesus, teach me to see the speck in my own eye, not the log in my neighbor's, that I may speak and act in love and build the house of my life on your rock. Amen.

Weekend Reflections

FURTHER CONNECTION

Nothing that is worth doing can be achieved in our lifetime; therefore we must be saved by hope. Nothing which is true or beautiful or good makes complete sense in any immediate context of history; therefore we must be saved by faith. Nothing we do, however virtuous, can be accomplished alone; therefore we must be saved by love. No virtuous act is quite as virtuous from the standpoint of our friend or foe as it is from our standpoint. Therefore we must be saved by the final form of love which is forgiveness.

REINHOLD NIEBUHR (1892–1971), *THE IRONY OF AMERICAN HISTORY*

MAKING THE CONNECTIONS

Choose one or two questions for reflection:

1. What connections have you noticed between this week's texts and other passages in Scripture?

2. What connections have you made between this week's texts and the world beyond Scripture?

3. Does either of this week's two commentary themes speak especially to your life or the life of the world around you right now?

4. What is God saying to your congregation in particular through this week's readings and commentaries?

_____

_____

_____

_____

_____

_____

Sabbath Day

SCRIPTURE OF ASSURANCE

Then Moses said to Aaron, "Say to the whole congregation of the Israelites, 'Draw near to the LORD, for he has heard your complaining.'" (Exodus 16:9)

WEEKLY EXAMEN

- Take a quiet moment, seek out God's presence, and pray for the guidance of the Spirit.

- Consider the past week; recall specific moments and feelings that stand out to you.

- Choose one moment or feeling for deeper examination, thanksgiving, or repentance.

- Let go, breathe deeply, and invite Christ's love to surround and fill you in preparation for the week ahead.

- End with the Lord's Prayer.

The Week Leading Up to the
Ninth Sunday
after the Epiphany

1 Kings 8:22–23, 41–43

Then Solomon stood before the altar of the LORD in the presence of all the assembly of Israel, and spread out his hands to heaven. (v. 22)

Psalm 96:1–9

Honor and majesty are before him;
  strength and beauty are in his sanctuary.

Ascribe to the LORD, O families of the peoples,
  ascribe to the LORD glory and strength.(vv. 6–7)

Galatians 1:1–12

Am I now seeking human approval, or God's approval? Or am I trying to please people? If I were still pleasing people, I would not be a servant of Christ. (v. 10)

Luke 7:1–10

When he heard about Jesus, he sent some Jewish elders to him, asking him to come and heal his slave. When they came to Jesus, they appealed to him earnestly, saying, "He is worthy of having you do this for him, for he loves our people, and it is he who built our synagogue for us." (vv. 3–5)

LECTIO DIVINA

Underline a word or phrase that especially grabs your attention. Pray from that word or phrase and ask God to help you connect to its particular invitation for you this week.

Themes from This Week's Writers

THEME 1: *Foreigners and Strangers Are Witnesses to God's Works*

1 Kings 8:22–23, 41–43

When the stranger comes to the temple, he or she will experience a God whose arms are outstretched, receptive, and embracing. They too will hear God's voice and experience God's presence.

JAMES H. EVANS JR.

1 Kings 8:22–23, 41–43

God hears even the prayers of those foreigners who may pray at the temple of Jerusalem (vv. 41–43). God's mercy toward the foreigner will be a witness to the reality of the presence of the Lord in the temple of Jerusalem.

PABLO A. JIMENEZ

Luke 7:1–10

Jesus is amazed that this Roman military leader is able to see what others have not yet perceived. . . . His own followers will refuse to see this truth until after the resurrection.

BRADLEY E. SCHMELING

THEME 2: *Foreigners and Strangers Are Blessed by God*

Psalm 96:1–9

The God of Israel is not exclusive, but rather yearns to gather all people. The God "above all gods," as Psalm 96:4b puts it, is the God who will also receive and welcome the foreigner, the stranger, and the outsider.

JOHN W. WURSTER

Galatians 1:1–12

In Paul's experience of his mission, Jew and Gentile alike received God's Holy Spirit; this was proof positive of God's adoption of each into God's family on the basis of God's gift (4:6–7).

DAVID A. DESILVA

Luke 7:1–10

This story effectively breaks the stereotype that all Gentiles are enemies of Israel, demonstrating how the blessings of God are meant to include the nations, which, as in this case, is through the agency of Israel's Messiah.

DIANE G. CHEN

WHAT IS THE HOLY SPIRIT SAYING TO YOU THIS WEEK?

_____

_____

_____

_____

_____

A SPIRITUAL PRACTICE FOR THIS WEEK

Seek to learn from the faithfulness and good works of "Gentiles" in your context. With prayer and holy curiosity, read and explore the website of a house of worship of a different faith. Perhaps visit (call ahead) or ask to share in a conversation with a person of that faith.

First Reading

1 Kings 8:22–23, 41–43

When a foreigner comes and prays toward this house, then hear in heaven your dwelling place, and do according to all that the foreigner calls to you, so that all the peoples of the earth may know your name and fear you, as do your people Israel, and so that they may know that your name has been invoked on this house that I have built. (vv. 42b–43)

REFLECTION

In these verses, Solomon petitions God on behalf of those who are not counted in the original covenant of God. Solomon sees this temple as more than a monument to the cultic solidarity of Israel. He affirms that "the foreigner," who is not ordinarily counted among the chosen ones, will come from a great distance, drawn by the name of the Almighty. Solomon begins to take on the role of the prophet who affirms that the reach and will of God transcend any narrow nationalistic interests.

JAMES H. EVANS JR.

RESPONSE

Make a list of countries that are especially strange, suspicious, or even distasteful to you. Pray for one of these countries today, asking God to hear the desires and sorrows of the leaders and people there. How does this feel?

PRAYER

O God, there is no God like you. Teach me to welcome strangers and foreigners to your love and your dwelling places, as you have welcomed me. Amen.

Canticle

Declare his glory among the nations,
  his marvelous works among all the peoples.
For great is the LORD, and greatly to be praised;
  he is to be revered above all gods. (vv. 3–4)

REFLECTION

All of these texts point homiletically to the width and breadth of the
kingdom of heaven. God's saving work is not limited to a particular place
or a particular people but, rather, is intended to spill over into all the
world. People are welcome across all sorts of boundaries and divisions.
Everyone with faith is included; no other qualification is necessary. Here
is an opportunity to proclaim the relentless inclusiveness of the gospel,
the love that keeps expanding, seeking out persons we might never
expect.

JOHN W. WURSTER

RESPONSE

Do we sometimes hoard the kingdom of heaven? What can that look
like? Who do you tend to exclude? Do you ever exclude yourself?
How is God inviting you this week to see the kingdom as a constantly
expanding place?

PRAYER

God, you are great and greatly to be praised. Help me to share your
works and glory among all people, and all the earth. Amen.

Second Reading

Galatians 1:1–12

I am astonished that you are so quickly deserting the one who called you in the grace of Christ and are turning to a different gospel—not that there is another gospel, but there are some who are confusing you and want to pervert the gospel of Christ. (vv. 6–7)

REFLECTION

Thank God the apostle Paul was not hesitant to pick a fight, a theological fight, a gospel fight, with those who followed him in the Galatian churches and reduced the gospel to pious platitudes and mindless aphorisms. . . . In an age in which the gospel of Jesus Christ is often diminished or obscured from pulpits, while a less challenging and more comfortable gospel is preached in its place, maybe preachers would do well to join the apostle Paul and pick a fight, a theological fight with those who preach pabulum at the cost of good and faithful theology.

GARY W. CHARLES

RESPONSE

What sort of pious platitudes drive you crazy? If you could pick a fight with some false or flavorless teachers in your church or community, what would it be over? What about the gospel must be heard today, at full strength, in your context?

PRAYER

O Jesus Christ, you gave us a gospel of love and justice. Give me strength and humility to fight for what is true and good, especially for the least of my brothers and sisters, in your name. Amen.

Gospel

Luke 7:1–10

"Lord, do not trouble yourself, for I am not worthy to have you come under my roof; therefore I did not presume to come to you. But only speak the word, and let my servant be healed." (vv. 6b–7)

REFLECTION

The centurion is an ambiguous figure. Representing the oppressive power of Rome, his loyalty resides with Caesar, but he addresses Jesus as Lord. Here is a generous patron of the Jewish people of Capernaum and the builder of their synagogue. . . . The city's patron becomes Jesus' client, and Jesus turns shame to honor by commending the centurion for his exemplary faith. This story effectively breaks the stereotype that all Gentiles are enemies of Israel, demonstrating how the blessings of God are meant to include the nations, which, as in this case, is through the agency of Israel's Messiah.

DIANE G. CHEN

RESPONSE

Read this passage and imagine yourself as the centurion, an outsider and hated oppressor approaching Jesus. Then, imagine yourself as a disciple, seeing an officer representing occupying forces ask Jesus for grace and receiving it. What feelings or experiences from your own life resonate?

PRAYER

Jesus, you welcome all people to come to you. Teach me to have faith. Speak your word, and I will be healed. Amen.

Weekend Reflections

FURTHER CONNECTION

Yitzak had survived the concentration camps. For many years he had lived, as it were, in a world of strangers. . . . [On a weeklong retreat, he] began to tell us of a walk he had taken on the beach the day before. In his mind, he had talked to God, asking God what all this was about. . . . He laughed. . . . "'I say to Him, 'God is it okay to luff strangers?' And God says, 'Yitzak, vat is dis strangers? You make strangers. I don't make strangers.'"

RACHEL NAOMI REMEN (1939–), KITCHEN TABLE WISDOM

MAKING THE CONNECTIONS

Choose one or two questions for reflection:

1. What connections have you noticed between this week's texts and other passages in Scripture?

2. What connections have you made between this week's texts and the world beyond Scripture?

3. Does either of this week's two commentary themes speak especially to your life or the life of the world around you right now?

4. What is God saying to your congregation in particular through this week's readings and commentaries?

_____

_____

_____

_____

_____

_____

Sabbath Day

SCRIPTURE OF ASSURANCE

> I bow down toward your holy temple
>> and give thanks to your name for your steadfast love and your
>> faithfulness;
>> for you have exalted your name and your word
>> above everything.
> On the day I called, you answered me,
>> you increased my strength of soul. (Psalm 138:2–3)

WEEKLY EXAMEN

- Take a quiet moment, seek out God's presence, and pray for the guidance of the Spirit.

- Consider the past week; recall specific moments and feelings that stand out to you.

- Choose one moment or feeling for deeper examination, thanksgiving, or repentance.

- Let go, breathe deeply, and invite Christ's love to surround and fill you in preparation for the week ahead.

- End with the Lord's Prayer.

The Week Leading Up to
Transfiguration Sunday

Exodus 34:29–35

Moses came down from Mount Sinai. As he came down from the mountain with the two tablets of the covenant in his hand, Moses did not know that the skin of his face shone because he had been talking with God. (v. 29)

Psalm 99

The LORD is king; let the peoples tremble!
He sits enthroned upon the cherubim; let the earth quake! (v. 1)

2 Corinthians 3:12–4:2

Since, then, we have such a hope, we act with great boldness, not like Moses, who put a veil over his face to keep the people of Israel from gazing at the end of the glory that was being set aside. (3:12–13)

Luke 9:28–36 (37–43a)

Now about eight days after these sayings Jesus took with him Peter and John and James, and went up on the mountain to pray. And while he was praying, the appearance of his face changed, and his clothes became dazzling white. (vv. 28–29)

LECTIO DIVINA

Underline a word or phrase that especially grabs your attention. Pray from that word or phrase and ask God to help you connect to its particular invitation for you this week.

Themes from This Week's Writers

THEME 1: *The Nature of God's Glory*

Exodus 34:29–35

While the people have in their experience seen God in the symbolic representation of the cloud or the pillar of fire, now they see God in the shining face of Moses. . . . The fact that he had been in the presence of God was obvious to others in a way that Moses did not immediately realize.

JAMES H. EVANS JR.

2 Corinthians 3:12–4:2

Now it is the "we" of the Christ followers who look upon God's glory in the face of Christ (cf. 3:18 and 4:6) and are changed as a result, not just because God's glory radiates from our faces, but because we ourselves are becoming ever more closely and fully a reflection of Christ's own character.

DAVID A. DESILVA

Luke 9:28–36 (37–43a)

Luke is the only Gospel writer who says that Jesus, Peter, James, and John go up the mountain *to pray*. The experience of transfiguration happens when these four create an intentional space for an encounter with the Divine.

BRADLEY E. SCHMELING

THEME 2: *Who Is Jesus?*

Psalm 99

On this holy mountain, Peter, James, and John get a glimpse of Jesus' future glory before he takes the journey to the cross.
The holiness of Jesus then is akin to the holiness of God.

KIMBERLY BRACKEN LONG

Luke 9:28–36 (37–43a)

The glow on Moses' face . . . was derived from or reflected off the glory of God. . . . Jesus' glory is the heavenly glory inherent in his divine identity, now revealed to those who believe in him.

DIANE G. CHEN

Luke 9:28–36 (37–43a)

The disciples are able to see the identity of Jesus, his face and his clothing transparent with glory, his person a thin place. It is grace to discover that the followers of Jesus, who so quickly fail, have an innate capacity to experience glory.

BRADLEY E. SCHMELING

WHAT IS THE HOLY SPIRIT SAYING TO YOU THIS WEEK?

_____

_____

_____

_____

_____

A SPIRITUAL PRACTICE FOR THIS WEEK

Begin to reflect on what your Lenten practice might be, whether giving something up, taking something on, fasts, almsgiving, changes or decorations in your home, or a book you will read. Ask the Holy Spirit to guide you. Find a balance between challenge and joy in whatever you choose.

First Reading

But whenever Moses went in before the LORD to speak with him, he would take the veil off, until he came out; and when he came out, and told the Israelites what he had been commanded, the Israelites would see the face of Moses, that the skin of his face was shining; and Moses would put the veil on his face again, until he went in to speak with him. (vv. 34–35)

REFLECTION

Most contemporary believers cannot relate to tablets of stone, shining faces, and veils that cover their leaders' faces. Furthermore, the text presents a dynamic that is utterly alien to most Christian churches: the affirmation that the leader or prophet enjoys a special relationship with God that manifests in a miraculous way. Although most parishioners expect their pastors to have a strong relationship with God, few view them with fear. Rather, most parishioners see them as empathetic, accessible, and friendly shepherds.

PABLO A. JIMENEZ

RESPONSE

Are you part of a congregation that expects its leader to have a particularly special relationship with God? How do you view the role of a pastor or priest in mediating or encouraging a relationship between God and people? What is important? What is not?

PRAYER

O God, you are always speaking to me, through others and to my own heart. Teach me to listen with a discerning spirit. Amen.

Canticle

Psalm 99

O LORD our God, you answered them;
    you were a forgiving God to them,
    but an avenger of their wrongdoings.
Extol the LORD our God,
    and worship at his holy mountain;
    for the LORD our God is holy. (vv. 8–9)

REFLECTION

The holiness of Jesus then is akin to the holiness of God. The psalmist points to the willingness of the God of justice to meet the people where they are, forgiving them for their failures to live up to God's commands. Similarly, Luke offers a vision of Jesus as he will one day be—glorious, victorious, reigning eternally with God—just before he turns his face to Jerusalem, where he will suffer and die for all people, in order to reconcile them with the God who insists on justice yet shows mercy.[1]

KIMBERLY BRACKEN LONG

RESPONSE

What does it mean that our powerful, almighty God is also merciful, suffering, and reconciling? Where do you see evidence of this in your own life or community this week? How do you reconcile these two in your own faith journey?

PRAYER

God, you are both forgiver and avenger. Uphold me and keep me in your ways, that I too may practice both mercy and justice. Amen.

---

1. J. Clinton McCann, "Psalms," in *New Interpreter's Bible* (Nashville: Abingdon Press, 1996), 4:1076.

Second Reading

2 Corinthians 3:12–4:2

And all of us, with unveiled faces, seeing the glory of the Lord as though reflected in a mirror, are being transformed into the same image from one degree of glory to another; for this comes from the Lord, the Spirit. (3:18)

REFLECTION

While this text looks back, sometimes in obscure ways, to Moses and the veil covering his face as he came down the mountain with the tablets of the law, ultimately the text points forward to the Spirit of God, who is engaged in transforming the world. In Christ, we "are being transformed into the same image from one degree of glory to another; for this comes from the Lord, the Spirit" (3:18). Simply put, God is not finished with us; in Christ, the Christian life is always a life of faith in progress.

GARY W. CHARLES

RESPONSE

When was a time you felt you were glowing with the presence of God? How have you seen the Spirit at work, lately, transforming a person or a community (or yourself) closer to glory? What is it like to think of transformation as a natural part of a life of faith?

PRAYER

Holy Spirit, in you I am being transformed from one degree of glory to another. Teach me not to lose heart. Amen.

Gospel

Luke 9:28–36 (37–43a)

On the next day, when they had come down from the mountain, a great crowd met him. Just then a man from the crowd shouted, "Teacher, I beg you to look at my son; he is my only child. Suddenly a spirit seizes him, and all at once he shrieks. It convulses him until he foams at the mouth; it mauls him and will scarcely leave him. I begged your disciples to cast it out, but they could not." (vv. 37–40)

REFLECTION

Can we truly understand the mystery of Christ's presence in our lives without engaging the work of healing and justice? Conversely, can we be sustained in our mission to be agents of liberation without being captured by the cloud of glory? Holding fast to this tensive relationship between mountain and valley allows us to be both restored and filled with renewed power, all without slipping into the clichés that often shape our off-the-mountain-into-the-valley, transfiguration-into-Lent approaches to this text. Our connections flow from mountain to valley for sure, but also from valley to mountain.

BRADLEY E. SCHMELING

RESPONSE

What is the tension in your own discipleship between the mountain and the valley? Where do you tend to spend more time? Why? Is God inviting you to reconsider the balance between these two somehow this week?

PRAYER

O God, you are full of glory and love. Lead me from mountain to valley and help me to live as your disciple. Amen.

Weekend Reflections

We live in a world where glory is possible, where light may break through at any moment. We believe in what we can see, but we believe more than that. Earth and flesh, comfort and sorrow, are terribly important to us, but they are not elemental. The world is not made out of them. The world is made out of light, which is straining against the skin of the world even as we speak. You never know when a face may begin to shine, including your own.

BARBARA BROWN TAYLOR (1951–), *BREAD OF ANGELS*

MAKING THE CONNECTIONS

Choose one or two questions for reflection:

1. What connections have you noticed between this week's texts and other passages in Scripture?

2. What connections have you made between this week's texts and the world beyond Scripture?

3. Does either of this week's two commentary themes speak especially to your life or the life of the world around you right now?

4. What is God saying to your congregation in particular through this week's readings and commentaries?

_____

_____

_____

_____

_____

Sabbath Day

SCRIPTURE OF ASSURANCE

Guard the good treasure entrusted to you, with the help of the Holy Spirit living in us. (2 Timothy 1:14)

WEEKLY EXAMEN

- Take a quiet moment, seek out God's presence, and pray for the guidance of the Spirit.

- Consider the past week; recall specific moments and feelings that stand out to you.

- Choose one moment or feeling for deeper examination, thanksgiving, or repentance.

- Let go, breathe deeply, and invite Christ's love to surround and fill you in preparation for the week ahead.

- End with the Lord's Prayer.

Ash Wednesday

Isaiah 58:1–12

Is not this the fast that I choose:
    to loose the bonds of injustice,
    to undo the thongs of the yoke,
to let the oppressed go free,
    and to break every yoke?
Is it not to share your bread with the hungry,
    and bring the homeless poor into your house;
when you see the naked, to cover them,
    and not to hide yourself from your own kin? (vv. 6–7)

Psalm 51:1–17

Create in me a clean heart, O God,
    and put a new and right spirit within me.
Do not cast me away from your presence,
    and do not take your holy spirit from me. (vv. 10–11)

2 Corinthians 5:20b–6:10

We entreat you on behalf of Christ, be reconciled to God. (v. 20b)

Matthew 6:1–6, 16–21

"But whenever you pray, go into your room and shut the door and pray to your Father who is in secret; and your Father who sees in secret will reward you." (v. 6)

Joel 2:1–2, 12–17

Yet even now, says the LORD,
    return to me with all your heart,
with fasting, with weeping, and with mourning;
    rend your hearts and not your clothing.
Return to the LORD, your God,
    for he is gracious and merciful,
slow to anger, and abounding in steadfast love,
    and relents from punishing. (vv. 12–13)

REFLECTIONS

Isaiah 58:1–12

In times of heightened conflict, anxiety can degrade the ethical and spiritual foundations on which a community has built its identity. The prophet in such times is called to help believers remember who they are.

CAROLYN J. SHARP

Joel 2:1–2, 12–17

At the same time, are we only called to individual, private acts of repentance, or are there important occasions when we need to gather as a community, to offer public corporate prayers of confession and repentance?

MARTHA L. MOORE-KEISH

Psalm 51:1–17

While not entirely clear, "willing spirit" may suggest generosity. In any case, the psalmist promises to turn outward (v. 13) and to become a witness to God's "righteousness" (v. 14, my trans.; NRSV "deliverance").

J. CLINTON MCCANN JR.

2 Corinthians 5:20b–6:10

Most people have probably heard that the vertical line points to our relationship with God while the horizontal line points us toward one another. Paul brings these two lines together in this text. Be reconciled to God. Be reconciled to one another.

BARBARA K. LUNDBLAD

Matthew 6:1–6, 16–21

Sometimes we give up something for Lent, maybe chocolate or alcohol, and we in effect "look dismal" and "disfigure our faces"—to ourselves, pitying or congratulating ourselves for such a noble sacrifice. Could it be cheerful, so we wash our face and look joyful, or actually know the joy of getting unattached or less attached to those treasures on earth?

JAMES C. HOWELL

RESPONSE

Choose one of these four quotes that particularly gets your attention and write or reflect on how God might be speaking to you, to your experience or questions about Ash Wednesday and Lent this year, or to this time in your life.

PRAYER

Have mercy on me and sustain in me a willing spirit, O God, as I begin this season of Lent. Amen.

The Week Leading Up to the
First Sunday in Lent

Deuteronomy 26:1–11

When you have come into the land that the LORD your God is giving you as an inheritance to possess, and you possess it, and settle in it, you shall take some of the first of all the fruit of the ground, which you harvest from the land that the LORD your God is giving you, and you shall put it in a basket and go to the place that the LORD your God will choose as a dwelling for his name. (vv. 1–2)

Psalm 91:1–2, 9–16

For he will command his angels concerning you
    to guard you in all your ways.
On their hands they will bear you up,
    so that you will not dash your foot against a stone. (vv. 11–12)

Romans 10:8b–13

"The word is near you,
    on your lips and in your heart"
(that is, the word of faith that we proclaim); because if you confess with your lips that Jesus is Lord and believe in your heart that God raised him from the dead, you will be saved. (vv. 8b–9)

Luke 4:1–13

Jesus answered him, "It is said, 'Do not put the Lord your God to the test.'" When the devil had finished every test, he departed from him until an opportune time. (vv. 12–13)

LECTIO DIVINA

Underline a word or phrase that especially grabs your attention. Pray from that word or phrase and ask God to help you connect to its particular invitation for you this week.

Themes from This Week's Writers

THEME 1: *Wandering in the Wilderness*

Deuteronomy 26:1–11

The modifier *'oved* may be translated as "wandering," but we should not imagine a purposeless traversing of terrain. The term could signify a journey or, alternatively, the nomadic or seminomadic movement of agriculturalists pasturing herds over great distances. Other meanings using that Hebrew root include losing one's way, going astray, and being a fugitive.

CAROLYN J. SHARP

Luke 4:1–13

This First Sunday in Lent is an invitation for Christians willingly to follow Jesus into the wilderness. Followers subject themselves to the kind of self-scrutiny and testing that unveils each person's deepest hopes as well as the darkest and most self-serving outcomes of their greatest capacities, gifts, and callings.

SHIVELY T. J. SMITH

Luke 4:1–13

How silly are we to think that if the Spirit leads, it will be to a smooth, comfortable, pleasant place. The Spirit that leads us led Jesus into peril.

JAMES C. HOWELL

THEME 2: *Hypocrisy and Humility*

Psalm 91:1–2, 9–16

As Albert Camus once suggested, it seems that some Christians are willing to ascend a cross, only to be seen from a greater distance! The things we give up for Lent can become sources of pride that call attention to ourselves, rather than practices of penitence and humility.

J. CLINTON McCANN JR.

Romans 10:8b–13

Heart (*kardia*) and lips/mouth (*stoma*) are connected. Heart is internal; lips and mouth are external. There must be congruence between the two. What we say with our lips should come from what we believe in our hearts.

BARBARA K. LUNDBLAD

Romans 10:8b–13

It is not enough to pay lip service, but neither is the sort of private and personal faith that never reaches the point of public confession adequate to the challenge of following Christ.

ANNA B. OLSON

WHAT IS THE HOLY SPIRIT SAYING TO YOU THIS WEEK?

_____

_____

_____

_____

A SPIRITUAL PRACTICE FOR THIS WEEK

Choose a particular way to fast on Ash Wednesday or another day this week. You might abstain from meat or alcohol, or skip lunch or dinner. Drink hot tea or water to calm a hungry stomach. Attend a service, spend time in prayer or spiritual reading, or take a quiet walk.

First Reading

Deuteronomy 26:1–11

"So now I bring the first of the fruit of the ground that you, O LORD, have given me." You shall set it down before the LORD your God and bow down before the LORD your God. Then you, together with the Levites and the aliens who reside among you, shall celebrate with all the bounty that the LORD your God has given to you and to your house. (vv. 10–11)

REFLECTION

For today it is natural to think it reasonable and responsible to give not the firstfruits of our labor—which we think of without qualification as *ours*—but to give from the excess of our wealth. . . . To give not from abundance but from firstfruits, by contrast, marks a radically contrary orientation, for it concretely acknowledges all we possess belongs first of all to God. Nothing is first of all *ours*. We give or possess only what we have already been given (Deut. 26:10).

WILLIAM GREENWAY

RESPONSE

Walk around your home and take in all that belongs to you. What is it like to say to yourself, "This all belongs to God, not to me"? How might this change how you view ownership, stewardship, or right use? What it is like to think about your cash giving, too, as giving what belongs to God, first?

PRAYER

Teach me, O Lord, to give to you from my firstfruits and to rejoice that all I possess belongs to you first. Amen.

Canticle

Psalm 91:1–2, 9–16

You who live in the shelter of the Most High,
  who abide in the shadow of the Almighty,
will say to the LORD, "My refuge and my fortress;
  my God, in whom I trust."
. . . .
Because you have made the LORD your refuge,
  the Most High your dwelling place,
no evil shall befall you,
  no scourge come near your tent. (vv. 1–2, 9–10)

REFLECTION

If there is a connection between Psalm 91:1–2, 9–16 and
Deuteronomy 26:1–11, the clue may be the Hebrew word translated
"dwelling place" (Ps. 91:9). . . . The exile represented a sort of renewed
landlessness, and Psalms 90–91 respond by suggesting that the true
home of the people of God is not the land; rather, it is God's own self.
The true assurance is to make "the Most High your dwelling place"
(Ps. 91:9).

J. CLINTON MCCANN JR.

RESPONSE

Sit in your home and write out or say to yourself, "I do not live here.
I live in the shelter of the Most High. My refuge, my fortress, my
dwelling place is not this place, but the living God." What do you hear
in these words today? What is reassuring? What is disturbing?

PRAYER

Almighty God, you are my refuge and my fortress, you are my dwelling
place, today and forever more. Amen.

Second Reading

Romans 10:8b–13

For there is no distinction between Jew and Greek; the same Lord is Lord of all and is generous to all who call on him. For, "Everyone who calls on the name of the Lord shall be saved." (vv. 12–13)

REFLECTION

When we claim a Lord who is not Caesar, what do we risk? What do we give up? Which principalities and powers have a claim on our allegiance? . . .

. . . Whatever our ideal political leader may look like, the call to confess one Lord takes Christians beyond the political divides of the moment, serving as a powerful reminder that no political leader can be our Messiah. This frees the church to speak directly to love for God and neighbor, to forgiveness and to the belovedness of all God's people, values with the potential to unite us when politics divides us.

ANNA B. OLSON

RESPONSE

Consider what powers and principalities, political movements, or leaders have a claim on your loyalty or gratitude at this time in your life. What does it mean to claim Christ above all these, to you?

PRAYER

Lord Jesus, you are the Messiah, the loving God of all people and generous to all who call on you, even me. Amen.

Gospel

Luke 4:1–13

Jesus, full of the Holy Spirit, returned from the Jordan and was led by the Spirit in the wilderness, where for forty days he was tempted by the devil. He ate nothing at all during those days, and when they were over, he was famished. (vv. 1–2)

REFLECTION

The wilderness is named as the site of John's prophetic preparation and witness (Luke 1:80; 3:2, 4; cf. 7:24). After the temptation, however, the wilderness becomes a space that Jesus traverses; and it is not the site of witness and prophecy. Rather, the wilderness becomes the site of Jesus' prayerful reprieves: "But he would withdraw to deserted places and pray" (Luke 5:16; cf. 4:42). The wilderness becomes a sanctuary for God's agent, providing an escape for rejuvenation and assurance.

SHIVELY T. J. SMITH

RESPONSE

Both John the Baptist and Jesus sought out the wilderness. The Israelites spent forty years there, wandering. What does wilderness mean to you? How might God be calling you to enter or return there this Lent?

PRAYER

Loving God, your Spirit leads us into the wilderness. Guide and sustain us, that we may find new life there in you. Amen.

Weekend Reflections

FURTHER CONNECTION

There are two equal and opposite errors into which our race can fall about the devils. One is to disbelieve in their existence. The other is to believe, and to feel an excessive and unhealthy interest in them.

C. S. LEWIS (1898–1963), *THE SCREWTAPE LETTERS*

MAKING THE CONNECTIONS

Choose one or two questions for reflection:

1. What connections have you noticed between this week's texts and other passages in Scripture?

2. What connections have you made between this week's texts and the world beyond Scripture?

3. Does either of this week's two commentary themes speak especially to your life or the life of the world around you right now?

4. What is God saying to your congregation in particular through this week's readings and commentaries?

MY CONNECTIONS

_____

_____

_____

_____

_____

_____

Sabbath Day

SCRIPTURE OF ASSURANCE

For surely I know the plans I have for you, says the LORD, plans for your welfare and not for harm, to give you a future with hope. (Jeremiah 29:11)

WEEKLY EXAMEN

- Take a quiet moment, seek out God's presence, and pray for the guidance of the Spirit.

- Consider the past week; recall specific moments and feelings that stand out to you.

- Choose one moment or feeling for deeper examination, thanksgiving, or repentance.

- Let go, breathe deeply, and invite Christ's love to surround and fill you in preparation for the week ahead.

- End with the Lord's Prayer.

The Week Leading Up to the
Second Sunday in Lent

Genesis 15:1–12, 17–18

And [Abram] believed the LORD; and the LORD reckoned it to him as righteousness. (v. 6)

Psalm 27

"Come," my heart says, "seek his face!"
Your face, LORD, do I seek. (v. 8)

Philippians 3:17–4:1

Therefore, my brothers and sisters, whom I love and long for, my joy and crown, stand firm in the Lord in this way, my beloved. (4:1)

Luke 13:31–35

[Jesus] said to them, "Go and tell that fox for me, 'Listen, I am casting out demons and performing cures today and tomorrow, and on the third day I finish my work.'" (v. 32)

LECTIO DIVINA

Underline a word or phrase that especially grabs your attention. Pray from that word or phrase and ask God to help you connect to its particular invitation for you this week.

Themes from This Week's Writers

THEME 1: *Hope and Endurance*

Genesis 15:1–12, 17–18

The Lord is able to fulfill the divine promise, no matter how morally reprehensible the patriarch has been, and no matter how hopeless the circumstance may appear.

CAROLYN J. SHARP

Psalm 27

Apparently, the psalmist continues to experience threat and opposition (see vv. 2–3, 6, 11–12), but his or her faith offers courage and strength to endure and to proceed toward the abundant life that God intends (v. 13).

J. CLINTON MCCANN JR.

Philippians 3:17–4:1

The Lenten call to repentance is inherently challenging. It is our grounding in God's love and the love of one another that provides freedom and safety for a life that must travel through and embrace humiliation.

ANNA B. OLSON

THEME 2: *"Our Citizenship Is in Heaven"*

Philippians 3:17–4:1

Paul wants the Philippians to do more than wait for heaven or pray for personal salvation. Instead Paul urges them to live now as though heaven is shaping their lives on earth.

BARBARA K. LUNDBLAD

Philippians 3:17–4:1

National belonging is among the sacrifices that may be demanded at the foot of the cross.

ANNA B. OLSON

Luke 13:31–35

In addition to practicing self-restraint, spiritual discipline, and moderation, Christians should seek opportunities to challenge the segments of society that harm innocent people who lobby for the justice and welfare of everyone.

SHIVELY T. J. SMITH

WHAT IS THE HOLY SPIRIT SAYING TO YOU THIS WEEK?

_____

_____

_____

_____

_____

A SPIRITUAL PRACTICE FOR THIS WEEK

Take a walk, and reflect or pray about Lenten hope and endurance. Look for a stick or rock that speaks to you. Put it in your house someplace you will see it, perhaps with a slip of paper that says, "Hope" or "The LORD is the stronghold of my life; of whom shall I be afraid?" (Psalm 27:1).

First Reading

Genesis 15:1–12, 17–18

On that day the LORD made a covenant with Abram, saying, "To your descendants I give this land, from the river of Egypt to the great river, the river Euphrates." (v. 18)

REFLECTION

The question of how to celebrate diversity in community without empowering sectarianism is vital. God's call to Abram addresses the dilemma by linking the blessing/affirmation of the particular to the benefit of all. That is, we rightly celebrate our families insofar as they are a blessing to all families, rightly celebrate our nation insofar as it is a blessing to all nations, and rightly celebrate our faith insofar as it is a blessing to people of all faiths.

WILLIAM GREENWAY

RESPONSE

What are some ways that your family is a blessing to all families? Your nation a blessing to all nations? Your faith a blessing to people of other faiths? Do you feel nudged by the Spirit to grow further in any of these?

PRAYER

O God, help me to see that all children are my descendants and all nations are my home. Amen.

Canticle

Psalm 27

The LORD is my light and my salvation;
  whom shall I fear?
The LORD is the stronghold of my life;
  of whom shall I be afraid? (v. 1)

REFLECTION

Psalm 27 begins by paralleling two affirmations about God with two
questions, "whom shall I fear?" and "of whom shall I be afraid?" . . .
    In any case, the trust that banishes fear is another connection
between Genesis 15 and Psalm 27. The first words spoken to Abraham
by the Lord in Genesis 15:1 are "Do not be afraid." Both Genesis 15
and Psalm 27 invite us at this point to consider that the opposite of faith
is not simply doubt. Rather, it is fear.

J. CLINTON MCCANN JR.

RESPONSE

Write "faith," "doubt," and "fear" as the titles of three lists, then write
down words or associations you make with each underneath—or draw
a picture of each, if you prefer. How are these three things at work right
now, in your own life and faith journey?

PRAYER

O God, you are the light and stronghold of my life; teach me not to be
afraid. Amen.

Second Reading

Philippians 3:17–4:1

But our citizenship is in heaven, and it is from there that we are expecting a Savior, the Lord Jesus Christ. (3:20)

REFLECTION

The Philippians may live in a Roman colony, often humiliated by imperial powers, but that is not their primary identity. They carry a different passport.

What passport do people carry on this Lenten journey? The journey to the cross is often portrayed as a journey of personal piety and prayer. Paul's Letter to the Philippians is a powerful reminder that following Jesus Christ is also a political journey. Our pledge of allegiance is to Christ above all earthly rulers. "Therefore, my brothers and sisters, . . . stand firm in the Lord" (4:1).

BARBARA K. LUNDBLAD

RESPONSE

What does your national identity or citizenship mean in your life right now? What about your Christian identity? What does it mean for you, at this time in your life and nation, that, "following Jesus Christ is also a political journey"?

PRAYER

Jesus Christ, my belonging and my citizenship are first in you. Amen.

Gospel

Luke 13:31–35

"Jerusalem, Jerusalem . . . How often have I desired to gather your children together as a hen gathers her brood under her wings, and you were not willing!" (v. 34)

REFLECTION

Solidarity with Jesus does not prop you up in a cheerful mood. We want to know, and to feel, the sorrows God feels. Even as we labor for good in the world, we should pause to grieve. Miroslav Volf, suggesting ways Christians might transform political life in America, has written, "Christian communities must learn how to work vigorously for the limited change that is possible, to mourn over persistent and seemingly ineradicable evils, and to celebrate the good wherever it happens."[1] It is the mourning we are most likely to miss.

JAMES C. HOWELL

RESPONSE

Jesus made lament a part of his spiritual and prophetic practice. What are some things you are grieving today, whether personally or for your community? Do you ever let yourself pause to feel grief? In what ways does it come out? What is a way you might grieve with God today?

PRAYER

Brother Jesus, teach me to lament with you and in you, over my own sorrows and over those of others. Amen.

---

1. Miroslav Volf, *A Public Faith: How Followers of Christ Should Serve the Public Good* (Grand Rapids: Brazos Press, 2011), 83.

Weekend Reflections

FURTHER CONNECTION

First, contemporary America is full of fear. And second, fear is not a Christian habit of mind. . . . We as Christians cannot think of Christ as isolated in space or time if we really do accept the authority of our own texts. Nor can we imagine that this life on earth is our only life, our primary life. As Christians we are to believe that we are to fear not the death of our bodies but the loss of our souls.

MARILYNNE ROBINSON (1943–), "FEAR"

MAKING THE CONNECTIONS

Choose one or two questions for reflection:

1. What connections have you noticed between this week's texts and other passages in Scripture?

2. What connections have you made between this week's texts and the world beyond Scripture?

3. Does either of this week's two commentary themes speak especially to your life or the life of the world around you right now?

4. What is God saying to your congregation in particular through this week's readings and commentaries?

MY CONNECTIONS

_____

_____

_____

_____

_____

Sabbath Day

SCRIPTURE OF ASSURANCE

Therefore, since it is by God's mercy that we are engaged in this ministry, we do not lose heart. (2 Corinthians 4:1)

WEEKLY EXAMEN

- Take a quiet moment, seek out God's presence, and pray for the guidance of the Spirit.

- Consider the past week; recall specific moments and feelings that stand out to you.

- Choose one moment or feeling for deeper examination, thanksgiving, or repentance.

- Let go, breathe deeply, and invite Christ's love to surround and fill you in preparation for the week ahead.

- End with the Lord's Prayer.

The Week Leading Up to the
Third Sunday in Lent

Isaiah 55:1–9

Why do you spend your money for that which is not bread,
    and your labor for that which does not satisfy?
Listen carefully to me, and eat what is good,
    and delight yourselves in rich food. (v. 2)

Psalm 63:1–8

Because your steadfast love is better than life,
    my lips will praise you.
So I will bless you as long as I live;
    I will lift up my hands and call on your name. (vv. 3–4)

1 Corinthians 10:1–13

No testing has overtaken you that is not common to everyone. God is faithful, and he will not let you be tested beyond your strength, but with the testing he will also provide the way out so that you may be able to endure it. (v. 13)

Luke 13:1–9

"So he said to the gardener, 'See here! For three years I have come looking for fruit on this fig tree, and still I find none. Cut it down! Why should it be wasting the soil?'" (v. 7)

LECTIO DIVINA

Underline a word or phrase that especially grabs your attention. Pray from that word or phrase and ask God to help you connect to its particular invitation for you this week.

Themes from This Week's Writers

THEME 1: *"Eat What Is Good"*

Isaiah 55:1–9

The bold exhortation embedded in verse 1's thrice-repeated imperative "come . . . come . . . come" is to choose well. Come to the water; come to the banquet; come and buy without money. Do not settle for costly things that provide little; take only what is good.

PATRICIA K. TULL

Isaiah 55:1–9

Sacrifice, fasting, penitence, and prayer are pathways to true abundance, spiritual abundance, God's abundance. God's abundance is found in a turn away from desire for worldly abundance.

DAVID A. DAVIS

Psalm 63:1–8

What is *truly* necessary for life as God intends it is God's own self. Actually, this is quite clear in the opening line of the psalm: "O God, you are my God, I seek you, my soul thirsts for you."

J. CLINTON MCCANN JR.

THEME 2: *What Is Repentance?*

1 Corinthians 10:1–13

These "warning" verses are reminiscent of a loving, worried parent who abandons concerns over intrinsic motivation and tries to scare their beloved child out of risky behavior by naming fearful, realistic, real-world consequences. We should guard against harmful misreading, while making clear how Paul's love for the Corinthians shines through in his warnings.

WILLIAM GREENWAY

Luke 13:1–9

The implication is that the one who truly repents will bear fruit, so that the dynamic, transformational character of true repentance is emphasized.

DENNIS E. SMITH

Luke 13:1–9

Repentance is often underplayed in the contemporary church. We may monotonously repeat a confession of sin in each Sunday's liturgy, but Jesus' insistence upon repentance seems to suggest an investment far greater than is common in our typical weekly confessions.

ADAM J. COPELAND

WHAT IS THE HOLY SPIRIT SAYING TO YOU THIS WEEK?

_____

_____

_____

_____

_____

A SPIRITUAL PRACTICE FOR THIS WEEK

Keep a simple fast for a day; perhaps from sugar, meat, dairy products, or alcohol. Then, read Isaiah 55:1–9 and reflect on spiritual "foods" in your life. How might God be inviting you to feast in ways that delight your soul, to eat what is good for the wholeness of yourself?

First Reading

Isaiah 55:1–9

Ho, everyone who thirsts,
  come to the waters;
and you that have no money,
  come, buy and eat!
Come, buy wine and milk
  without money and without price. (v. 1)

REFLECTION

A wonderful invitation. Only, at first blush it does not sound much like Lent.

The most meaningful and fulfilling Lenten journeys, however, include an encounter with God's abundant mercy, grace, and forgiveness. After the prophet strikes the vision of God's bounty so beautifully, the proclamation to follow turns to repentance, restoration, and life. The people in exile are called to turn away from the lure of a secure material future in Babylon and to seek after the lush spiritual reality offered in the sure and steadfast love of God.

DAVID A. DAVIS

RESPONSE

If your Lenten practice has been challenging or dull, reconsider what really matters to you this Lent and how you can tweak your practice to reflect this. If it has been challenging but fulfilling, what are you learning or experiencing this Lent as a result?

PRAYER

Loving God, teach me to eat what is good, to delight in the rich food of a life lived in you. Amen.

Canticle

Psalm 63:1–8

O God, you are my God, I seek you,
  my soul thirsts for you;
my flesh faints for you,
  as in a dry and weary land where there is no water. (v. 1)

REFLECTION

The NRSV regularly translates the Hebrew word involved as "soul," but
the word originally meant "throat" or "neck" (see Ps. 69:1, where the
NRSV translates it as "neck"). Apparently because everything necessary
for the sustenance of life—water, food, air—passes through the throat
or neck, the word came to mean something like "vitality, life," even
"appetite." In short, the issue is life, and what truly sustains life. . . .
  . . . What is *truly* necessary for life as God intends it is God's
own self.

J. CLINTON MCCANN JR.

RESPONSE

What is truly sustaining your life right now? How do you see God active
and alive in those things? How might God be offering God's own self
to you even more fully, at this time in your life? How might you open
yourself to receive what God is giving you?

PRAYER

God, you are my God and I am thirsty for you. Quench my soul in this
dry land with your grace and mercy. Amen.

Second Reading

1 Corinthians 10:1–13

Now these things occurred as examples for us, so that we might not desire evil as they did. Do not become idolaters as some of them did; as it is written, "The people sat down to eat and drink, and they rose up to play." (vv. 6–7)

REFLECTION

Entire industries exist that are devoted to the production of images that test one's convictions about everything from sexuality to consumption of goods to the blind acquisition of personal wealth. They can even obscure the path toward empathy and solidarity with those who simply cannot afford the way of life that many of these images represent. This is the contemporary experience of being enthralled to the "many gods and many lords" present in the marketplace. Though the forms of idolatry may be different from those at Corinth, the challenge to live faithfully in Christ still makes its claim on the church.

RICHARD F. WARD

RESPONSE

Reflect on a modern form of idolatry that has been getting a lot of your attention lately. How does it feed you? How does it deplete you? How might this be affecting your faith and self?

PRAYER

O God, you are faithful; strengthen me also to be faithful, to you and to things that give life. Save me from the worship and wrong use of that which idolizes or destroys. Amen.

Gospel

Luke 13:1–9

[Jesus] asked them, "Do you think that because these Galileans suffered in this way they were worse sinners than all other Galileans? No, I tell you; but unless you repent, you will all perish as they did." (vv. 2–3)

REFLECTION

Repentance is a vital theme in Luke. Terms for repentance occur in Luke and Acts more than twice as often as in all the other Gospels combined. The Greek *metanoia* means "to change one's mind." This is more than an intellectual change or passive concept. It signifies changing the focus of one's life, changing one's moral direction, a dynamic change in one's way of living. To repent is to live in a distinct and different way. Luke elucidates the full ramifications of repentance in Acts 26:20: "repent and turn to God and do deeds consistent with repentance."

DENNIS E. SMITH

RESPONSE

Which of Smith's various phrases redefining repentance speaks most to you this week? How might God be calling you not to perish, but to change, in this season of your life? In what way might repentance be life-giving for you this Lent?

PRAYER

Brother Jesus, lead me from pride to repentance; dig around me and put manure on me, that I may grow, bear fruit, and live in you. Amen.

Weekend Reflections

FURTHER CONNECTION

I once heard Father [James Otis Sargent] Huntington say that the
essence of immorality is the tendency to make an exception of one's
self and I would like to add that to consider one's self in any wise unlike
the rank and file of human life is to walk straight toward the pit of self-
righteousness.

JANE ADDAMS (1860–1935), "THE COLLEGE WOMAN
AND CHRISTIANITY"

MAKING THE CONNECTIONS

Choose one or two questions for reflection:

1. What connections have you noticed between this week's texts and
   other passages in Scripture?

2. What connections have you made between this week's texts and the
   world beyond Scripture?

3. Does either of this week's two commentary themes speak especially
   to your life or the life of the world around you right now?

4. What is God saying to your congregation in particular through this
   week's readings and commentaries?

_____

_____

_____

_____

_____

Sabbath Day

SCRIPTURE OF ASSURANCE

He said to me, Mortal, eat this scroll that I give you and fill your stomach with it. Then I ate it; and in my mouth it was as sweet as honey.

He said to me: Mortal, go to the house of Israel and speak my very words to them. (Ezekiel 3:3–4)

WEEKLY EXAMEN

- Take a quiet moment, seek out God's presence, and pray for the guidance of the Spirit.

- Consider the past week; recall specific moments and feelings that stand out to you.

- Choose one moment or feeling for deeper examination, thanksgiving, or repentance.

- Let go, breathe deeply, and invite Christ's love to surround and fill you in preparation for the week ahead.

- End with the Lord's Prayer.

The Week Leading Up to the
Fourth Sunday in Lent

Joshua 5:9–12

The LORD said to Joshua, "Today I have rolled away from you the disgrace of Egypt." (v. 9a)

Psalm 32

Happy are those whose transgression is forgiven,
   whose sin is covered.
Happy are those to whom the LORD imputes no iniquity,
   and in whose spirit there is no deceit. (vv. 1–2)

2 Corinthians 5:16–21

So if anyone is in Christ, there is a new creation: everything old has passed away; see, everything has become new! All this is from God, who reconciled us to himself through Christ, and has given us the ministry of reconciliation. (vv. 17–18)

Luke 15:1–3, 11b–32

And the Pharisees and the scribes were grumbling and saying, "This fellow welcomes sinners and eats with them." (v. 2)

LECTIO DIVINA

Underline a word or phrase that especially grabs your attention. Pray from that word or phrase and ask God to help you connect to its particular invitation for you this week.

Themes from This Week's Writers

THEME 1: *Return of the Prodigal*

Joshua 5:9–12

From being a people wandering through territory they do not possess, they have become a people treading on land portrayed as promised to them by God. They have crossed the Jordan River into the land, reenacting their exit from Egypt over the Red Sea.

PATRICIA K. TULL

Psalm 32

The psalmist, once silent before God, has been forgiven and now actively shares that blessed state by teaching and inspiring us. This theme of new life via God's grace appears in each of today's lections.

LEIGH CAMPBELL-TAYLOR

Luke 15:1–3, 11b–32

He does not show "tough love," lecture his son about his poor business decisions, or begin a squabble about his questionable spending habits. Instead, the father's welcome uncovers a love for human persons, not money and possessions.

ADAM J. COPELAND

THEME 2: *Rejoice in Reconciliation*

Joshua 5:9–12

The urgency of keeping the feast right there in Gilgal inaugurates new life in the land with an act of worship. It is a rite of remembering all that God has done and offering gratitude for the fulfillment of God's once and future promise.

DAVID A. DAVIS

2 Corinthians 5:16–21

This spirit of celebration suffuses today's reading, as a jubilant Paul urges us to embrace and celebrate the new life Jesus' fidelity opens to us.

WILLIAM GREENWAY

Luke 15:1–3, 11b–32

Exploring the joy in the heart of God, joy that arises when what has been cut off from divine blessing has been restored, brings us close to the center of this parable. Such great joy implies the resolution of deep anguish and excruciating heartbreak in God's self.

D. CAMERON MURCHISON

WHAT IS THE HOLY SPIRIT SAYING TO YOU THIS WEEK?

_____

_____

_____

_____

_____

A SPIRITUAL PRACTICE FOR THIS WEEK

Practice forgiveness for the everyday, irritating things that distract you from the big picture of God's purpose and love. (If you are hardest on yourself, practice forgiving yourself; if you are harder on others, practice forgiving others.) To remind you, each day write "FORGIVE" on a little piece of paper and set it in your shoe.

First Reading

Joshua 5:9–12

On the day after the passover, on that very day, they ate the produce of the land, unleavened cakes and parched grain. The manna ceased on the day they ate the produce of the land, and the Israelites no longer had manna; they ate the crops of the land of Canaan that year. (vv. 11–12)

REFLECTION

After decades of that daily bread coming from heaven and sustaining God's people in the wilderness, their nourishment was once again to come from the earth. Eating "the crops of the land of Canaan" (v. 12) implies a return to the rhythm and work of being stewards of the earth. As the manna ceases, God's people again share in the responsibilities of community, care, daily living. Other miracles of God will surely come, but once the people are inside the land of Canaan, the manna stops.

DAVID A. DAVIS

RESPONSE

Being reconciled with God, like the Israelites as they enter into Canaan, does not always mean life gets easier, but often that we are given more responsibility. This Lent, how might God be asking you to take more responsibility? For your life, your community, the earth, or the poor?

PRAYER

Lord God, you have supported me in the wilderness; teach me to tend my own crops, my life, and my community, that I may feed others. Amen.

Canticle

Psalm 32

While I kept silence, my body wasted away
through my groaning all day long.
. . . .
Then I acknowledged my sin to you,
and I did not hide my iniquity;
I said, "I will confess my transgressions to the Lord,"
and you forgave the guilt of my sin. (vv. 3, 5)

REFLECTION

The need for repentance does not require us to think of God as
punishing our silence by crushing us until we apologize. Rather,
verses 3–5 are an evocative description of how we feel when we strive to
live without God. Lent is a season designed for those who seek to repent
of this tendency and receive God's healing for sin-sick souls. . . .
. . . The psalmist, once silent before God, has been forgiven and
now actively shares that blessed state by teaching and inspiring us. This
theme of new life via God's grace appears in each of today's lections.

LEIGH CAMPBELL-TAYLOR

RESPONSE

How you can tell when you are "striving to live without God"? Make
a list of signs and symptoms this condition produces in you. Offer the
list as a prayer of confession, like the psalmist. Reread the whole of
Psalm 32, silently or aloud.

PRAYER

Loving God, I want to trust you, to not hide my iniquity and sins from
you, so that I may live in fullness and receive your forgiveness. Amen.

Second Reading

2 Corinthians 5:16–21

So we are ambassadors for Christ, since God is making his appeal through us; we entreat you on behalf of Christ, be reconciled to God. For our sake he made him to be sin who knew no sin, so that in him we might become the righteousness of God. (vv. 20–21)

REFLECTION

Paul understands himself to be an ambassador of this good news of God's plan for renewing creation. Why should the community live as if it were still a part of the old order, or relate to one another "according to the flesh," or understand themselves in terms of the worldly standards that they had come out from through their baptism? Why not appropriate and extend the gift of reconciliation that had been extended to them in the drama of God's redemption? In fact, Paul urges, why do you not become ambassadors and become reconciled among yourselves?

RICHARD F. WARD

RESPONSE

What kind of reconciliation might God be inviting you or your community to this season? How might you feel called to "be reconciled among yourselves," in your particular place and situation? How might you be called to be an ambassador, like Paul, of God's reconciliation this Lent?

PRAYER

In Christ, O God, you are reconciling the world to yourself; teach us, in Christ, to be reconciled to one another. Amen.

Gospel

Luke 15:1–3, 11b–32

"Then the father said to him, 'Son, you are always with me, and all that is mine is yours. But we had to celebrate and rejoice, because this brother of yours was dead and has come to life; he was lost and has been found.'" (vv. 31–32)

REFLECTION

Pharisees, older brothers, and solid church people like us need to be reminded that all those outsiders are not only God's children, but our sisters and brothers. When they are restored to the family, when they are found, a joyous celebration breaks out in the heart of God. Do we likewise rejoice?

. . . God's work is for a new creation in which all are reconciled to God, and God has entrusted precisely this ministry of reconciliation to the church. . . . We are summoned to the work of reconciliation, and above all we are encouraged to enter into its deep joy.

D. CAMERON MURCHISON

RESPONSE

We may think of reconciliation as painful or shameful rather than joyful. What is a reconciliation in your life you have avoided? What is a reconciliation your church or community may be avoiding? Is there a way to bring joy into these situations, rather than pain or shame?

PRAYER

Gracious God, enliven the joy of reconciliation in us, that we might choose to find and forgive one another. Amen.

Weekend Reflections

FURTHER CONNECTION

The question is not "How am I to find God?" but "How am I to let myself be found by him?" The question is not "How am I to know God?" but "How am I to let myself be known by God?" And, finally, the question is not "How am I to love God?" but "How am I to let myself be loved by God?" God is looking into the distance for me, trying to find me, and longing to bring me home.

HENRI J. M. NOUWEN (1932–96), *THE RETURN OF THE PRODIGAL SON*

MAKING THE CONNECTIONS

Choose one or two questions for reflection:

1. What connections have you noticed between this week's texts and other passages in Scripture?

2. What connections have you made between this week's texts and the world beyond Scripture?

3. Does either of this week's two commentary themes speak especially to your life or the life of the world around you right now?

4. What is God saying to your congregation in particular through this week's readings and commentaries?

Sabbath Day

SCRIPTURE OF ASSURANCE

So Moses cried out to the LORD, "What shall I do with this people? They are almost ready to stone me." (Exodus 17:4)

WEEKLY EXAMEN

- Take a quiet moment, seek out God's presence, and pray for the guidance of the Spirit.

- Consider the past week; recall specific moments and feelings that stand out to you.

- Choose one moment or feeling for deeper examination, thanksgiving, or repentance.

- Let go, breathe deeply, and invite Christ's love to surround and fill you in preparation for the week ahead.

- End with the Lord's Prayer.

The Week Leading Up to the
Fifth Sunday in Lent

Isaiah 43:16–21

I am about to do a new thing;
    now it springs forth, do you not perceive it?
I will make a way in the wilderness
    and rivers in the desert. (v. 19)

Psalm 126

The Lord has done great things for us,
    and we rejoiced.

Restore our fortunes, O Lord,
    like the watercourses in the Negeb. (vv. 3–4)

Philippians 3:4b–14

Beloved, I do not consider that I have made it my own; but this one thing I do: forgetting what lies behind and straining forward to what lies ahead, I press on toward the goal for the prize of the heavenly call of God in Christ Jesus. (vv. 13–14)

John 12:1–8

Six days before the Passover Jesus came to Bethany, the home of Lazarus, whom he had raised from the dead. There they gave a dinner for him. Martha served, and Lazarus was one of those at the table with him. Mary took a pound of costly perfume made of pure nard, anointed Jesus' feet, and wiped them with her hair. The house was filled with the fragrance of the perfume. (vv. 1–3)

LECTIO DIVINA

Underline a word or phrase that especially grabs your attention. Pray from that word or phrase and ask God to help you connect to its particular invitation for you this week.

Themes from This Week's Writers

THEME 1: *God Is Doing a New Thing*

Isaiah 43:16–21

With verse 16, the prophet discloses a theme underlying the prophet's work throughout: a dialogical call both to remember the past and to forget it—more precisely, to remember the grace of God's mighty deeds in the past while recognizing that new contexts call for the story line to take new forms. . . . God is doing a new thing, but what God is doing is continuous with all that has come before.

PATRICIA K. TULL

Psalm 126

"The psalmist stands with Isaiah, not looking to the past in hope of restoration to some old way of life, but living into God's new way of life. In our journey with God, we, with all the complexity of our history, are now being readied by Lent for Easter, which is the ultimate proof that God can be relied upon to do a glorious new thing.

LEIGH CAMPBELL-TAYLOR

Philippians 3:4b–14

What lies ahead is a cross, the symbol for how God has turned human wisdom upside down. Christ shares in our death in order to break the power that death has over us, and through resurrection we share in his risen life.

RICHARD F. WARD

THEME 2: *Faith Lives in the Present Moment*

Isaiah 43:16–21

The invocation of God's past action brings home the reality of and ongoing potential for God's present action. The God who made a way is the God who makes a way. Some moments in salvation history have life and breath for God's people in every generation. It is a sacred remembering that comes in the present.

DAVID A. DAVIS

Philippians 3:4b–14

This is Paul's realized eschatology, which is not about a future state in heaven, but about the power to see with eyes of faith in the present, even as, like Jesus, one lives directly in the face of death (v. 10).

WILLIAM GREENWAY

John 12:1–8

Instead of asking, "How can I save some time?" we are allowed to ask, "What is the saving God doing in this moment, and how can I be a part of it?" Mary discerned that the *kairos* of this moment was that Jesus was approaching his death, and her anointing of Jesus was how she participated in that moment.

ADAM J. COPELAND

WHAT IS THE HOLY SPIRIT SAYING TO YOU THIS WEEK?

_____

_____

_____

_____

_____

A SPIRITUAL PRACTICE FOR THIS WEEK

For a day or two, set your phone to alert you for two or three of the traditional times of prayer (morning, midday, evening, bedtime). Reflect on either "What saving thing is God doing in this moment, and how can I be a part of it?" or "God is doing a new thing; do I perceive it?" at each alert.

First Reading

Isaiah 43:16–21

Do not remember the former things,
  or consider the things of old.
I am about to do a new thing;
  now it springs forth, do you not perceive it? (vv. 18–19a)

REFLECTION

[This is] a dialogical call both to remember the past and to forget it—
more precisely, to remember the grace of God's mighty deeds in the past
while recognizing that new contexts call for the story line to take new
forms. Second Isaiah's arguments throughout have creatively recombined
elements of earlier Judean traditions. Under the prophet's hand the
terms shift—sometimes subtly, sometimes abruptly—so that while the
words sound familiar, they are being adapted for a new audience in
new circumstances. God is doing a new thing, but what God is doing is
continuous with all that has come before.

PATRICIA K. TULL

RESPONSE

What mighty deeds, story lines, or gifts of God have repeated through
your life or your church's thus far? What new thing is God doing that is
emerging right now? How is this new thing continuous with the past,
and how does it take the story in a new direction?

PRAYER

O God of new things, show me how to perceive what you have done
and what you are doing now in my life and in my community. Amen.

Canticle

Psalm 126

When the Lord restored the fortunes of Zion,
  we were like those who dream.
Then our mouth was filled with laughter,
  and our tongue with shouts of joy;
then it was said among the nations,
  "The Lord has done great things for them." (vv. 1–2)

REFLECTION

Although some interpreters are tempted to dismiss this dream state as a condition of drowsiness or grogginess, it is the same word used for famous dreams like those of Joseph. . . . That is not some sort of hazy lightheadedness. No, that is powerful God-blessed dreaming. Making use of that concept, one's approach to preaching today's Isaiah text would be to ponder how faithful people can "perceive" the "new thing" God is doing (Isa. 43:19). What could predispose us to notice this new and extravagant thing God is undertaking in our midst? Could the answer lie in being "like those who dream" (Ps. 126:1)?

LEIGH CAMPBELL-TAYLOR

RESPONSE

What do you think it could mean to be "like those who dream"? How would this compare to "those who reason," "those who plan," or "those who regret"? How could dreaming—perhaps even as a Lenten practice— help you perceive a new thing God is doing, in your life or your church?

PRAYER

Loving God, teach me to dream, to laugh, to shout, and to see your kingdom, alive around me. Amen.

Second Reading

Philippians 3:4b–14

I want to know Christ and the power of his resurrection and the sharing of his sufferings by becoming like him in his death, if somehow I may attain the resurrection from the dead.

Not that I have already obtained this or have already reached the goal; but I press on to make it my own, because Christ Jesus has made me his own. (vv. 10–12)

REFLECTION

This is Paul's realized eschatology, which is not about a future state in heaven, but about the power to see with eyes of faith in the present, even as, like Jesus, one lives directly in the face of death (v. 10). . . . In other words, while Christians may believe in and celebrate heaven, the goal of Christian spirituality is never heaven. The goal of Christian spirituality is one's own imitation/realization of *the spirit of Christ* celebrated in the *kenōsis* hymn, a spirit of compassion and sympathy, a spirit which leads to a life that remains faithful to loving action for others, even unto death.

WILLIAM GREENWAY

RESPONSE

This Lent, what does it mean for you to "see with eyes of faith in the present"? What role has the anticipation of heaven played in your spiritual life? How have you desired to imitate the spirit of Christ in your own life, here and now?

PRAYER

Christ Jesus, strengthen me to press on and to become like you, in death and resurrection, knowing you have made me your own. Amen.

Gospel

John 12:1–8

Jesus said, "Leave her alone. She bought it so that she might keep it for the day of my burial. You always have the poor with you, but you do not always have me." (vv. 7–8)

REFLECTION

The contrast between the needs of the poor and the extravagance of the ointment is a central theme of the story. . . . John makes clear that in contrast to Mary, who clearly discerns the exceptional, suffering servant character of the moment, Judas does not even truly believe the significant concern he voices but just wants the money for himself.

Jesus' response . . . should not be taken to imply that selfless care for the poor is not typically a high priority, especially since all the Gospels connect the death of Jesus to his solidarity with the poor and outcast (e.g., Mark 10:43–44).

DENNIS E. SMITH

RESPONSE

In this moment over dinner with Jesus, Mary and Judas have different concerns. Think about the past day or so in your own life: what concerns have been primary for you? What could it look like to increase your awareness of the presence of Christ in each present moment?

PRAYER

Jesus, teach us not to be afraid of your death, but to see you in all moments and places, especially in our neighbor and in the poor. Amen.

Weekend Reflections

FURTHER CONNECTION

Somewhere in my formative years, I made the mistake of telling the prioress that the reason I wanted to be excused from Matins and the evening curfew was because I had a term paper to write for a college class which I had no time to complete before that. She let her body sink back into her high-backed wooden chair from which point she could see me more piercingly, tapped her finger over her lips, and looked down at me over her glasses. "My dear child," she said slowly to make sure I didn't miss the important of the message, "we have all the time there is."

JOAN CHITTISTER (1936–), *WISDOM DISTILLED FROM THE DAILY*

MAKING THE CONNECTIONS

Choose one or two questions for reflection:

1. What connections have you noticed between this week's texts and other passages in Scripture?

2. What connections have you made between this week's texts and the world beyond Scripture?

3. Does either of this week's two commentary themes speak especially to your life or the life of the world around you right now?

4. What is God saying to your congregation in particular through this week's readings and commentaries?

_____

_____

_____

_____

_____

Sabbath Day

SCRIPTURE OF ASSURANCE

My soul clings to the dust;
  revive me according to your word.
When I told of my ways, you answered me;
  teach me your statutes.
Make me understand the way of your precepts,
  and I will meditate on your wondrous works. (Psalm 119:25–27)

WEEKLY EXAMEN

- Take a quiet moment, seek out God's presence, and pray for the guidance of the Spirit.

- Consider the past week; recall specific moments and feelings that stand out to you.

- Choose one moment or feeling for deeper examination, thanksgiving, or repentance.

- Let go, breathe deeply, and invite Christ's love to surround and fill you in preparation for the week ahead.

- End with the Lord's Prayer.

The Week Leading Up to
Palm/Passion Sunday

Luke 19:28–40

Some of the Pharisees in the crowd said to him, "Teacher, order your disciples to stop." He answered, "I tell you, if these were silent, the stones would shout out." (vv. 39–40)

Isaiah 50:4–9a

The Lord GOD helps me;
    therefore I have not been disgraced;
therefore I have set my face like flint,
    and I know that I shall not be put to shame;
    he who vindicates me is near. (vv. 7–8a)

Philippians 2:5–11

And being found in human form,
    he humbled himself
    and became obedient to the point of death—
    even death on a cross. (vv. 7b–8)

Luke 22:14–23:56

"Simon, Simon, listen! Satan has demanded to sift all of you like wheat, but I have prayed for you that your own faith may not fail; and you, when once you have turned back, strengthen your brothers." (22:31–32)

LECTIO DIVINA

Underline a word or phrase that especially grabs your attention. Pray from that word or phrase and ask God to help you connect to its particular invitation for you this week.

Themes from This Week's Writers

THEME 1: *The Suffering Servant*

Isaiah 50:4–9a

The exact identity of the Servant may not matter as much as the theology expressed in the four poems: God has called the Servant and poured out the divine spirit; the Servant ministers within the community of the displaced exiles; the Servant accepts the suffering caused by this ministry; the Servant reveals the divine will for justice among all nations.

CHARLES L. AARON JR.

Philippians 2:5–11

For example, to have the "same mind" as Christ, some should be challenged to be more self–giving, repenting of their pride. However, others need be encouraged to live with greater cognizance of how precious they are, resisting shame and self-denigration as those who have been exalted in Christ.

CYNTHIA L. RIGBY

Luke 22:14–23:56

Perhaps here more than anywhere else, Jesus' humanity and divinity are revealed in equal measure: he agonizes over his destiny, yet chooses God's will above his own.

PATRICK W. T. JOHNSON

THEME 2: *Bearing Witness*

Philippians 2:5–11

This early Christian hymn tells the story of the Christ event and our relation to it in a way that is consistent with the rhythm of baptism. Entering obediently into the water, we are emptied, with Christ Jesus; emerging from the water we are exalted to new life, joining hands with all people everywhere who confess Jesus Christ as Lord.

CYNTHIA L. RIGBY

Luke 19:28–40

Who is this man? That is a question we do well to ponder every day. Is he a prophet? A dedicated teacher? A storyteller? Whether we have spent a lifetime in the church, or are new to the faith, Jesus is always asking us, as he asked his disciples, "Who do you say that I am?" (Luke 9:20).

LUCY LIND HOGAN

Luke 23:1–49

A danger in Luke's narrative, as in the other Gospels, is for us blithely to lay blame for Jesus' crucifixion at the feet of the Jewish leaders and Jewish people. The preacher could use Luke's ambiguous "they" to bring *us* into the shouting crowd and to place *us* with those who lead Jesus away. If we think this whole tragic scene is about the sins of *other* people, we have missed the point.

PATRICK W. T. JOHNSON

WHAT IS THE HOLY SPIRIT SAYING TO YOU THIS WEEK?

_____

_____

_____

_____

_____

A SPIRITUAL PRACTICE FOR THIS WEEK

Next week—Holy Week—was historically a time of dread for Jews because it was so common a time for Christians to commit violence against them. Find a synagogue nearby, even if it is miles away, and pray for the congregation this week. Send them a note, if you feel so moved.

Liturgy of Palms

Psalm 118:1–2, 19–29

Open to me the gates of righteousness,
   that I may enter through them
   and give thanks to the LORD.

This is the gate of the LORD;
   the righteous shall enter through it. (vv. 19–20)

REFLECTION

These verses contain space; they make room for a story that is still
unfolding. Specific acts of praise are named and invited, to be sure. . . .
But there is space in the language and in the images for what is to come.
The open gates invite us through, and beyond will be both death and
life. A rejected stone will become our firm foundation, though we may
not know how. What is to come will indeed be the Lord's doing; we
cannot always imagine just how marvelous it will be.

ERIC WALL

RESPONSE

What kind of room is in you for this chapter of Christian story this
year? Do you see space for yourself in the language and images of the
psalm? How do you plan to be part of Christ's passion story this week,
if you are able?

PRAYER

O Lord, make me your witness; show me how to follow you through the
gates and into Jerusalem in this holiest of weeks. Amen.

First Reading

Isaiah 50:4–9a

The Lord God has opened my ear,
    and I was not rebellious,
    I did not turn backward.
I gave my back to those who struck me,
    and my cheeks to those who pulled out the beard;
I did not hide my face
    from insult and spitting. (vv. 5–6)

REFLECTION

[There is] a plurality of holy possibilities: the traditional Christian
identification of the Servant with Jesus drives us forward into the
passion narrative of Luke and the ecclesial challenge of Philippians to
seek to emulate the mind of Christ; the identification of the Servant
with the prophet reminds us there is a time to stand defiantly against the
wicked and to confess our anguish to God; the communal identification
of the Servant with Israel presses the Christian community to consider
its actions in the face of societal pressure to maintain the status quo.

DAVID G. GARBER JR.

RESPONSE

Which face of the Suffering Servant speaks most to what you, your
church, or your community is facing right now? Is there a call to imitate
Christ, to lament and defy the wicked, or, as a community, to help
redeem the world? How might God be speaking to your situation, in
this prophecy?

PRAYER

Brother Jesus, open my ears to the servanthood you call me to, and help
me not to turn backward or hide my face. Amen.

Second Reading

Philippians 2:5–11

Let the same mind be in you that was in Christ Jesus,
who, though he was in the form of God,
    did not regard equality with God
    as something to be exploited,
but emptied himself,
    taking the form of a slave. (vv. 5–7a)

REFLECTION

Sometimes the language of suffering and emptying can be misunderstood. Christians are not called to endure the merciless suffering of abuse under the idea that we are called to be obedient and to suffer. This passage is about finding ways to love ourselves and others in generous and merciful ways, not about self-denigration or having our capacity to love destroyed by the cruelty of an oppressor. This is not Jesus' message to us. Further sacrifice is no longer needed.

SHANELL T. SMITH

RESPONSE

What does it mean to you, this year, that God emptied Godself to be closer to us in Jesus? That God did not exploit God's power, but gave it away? This Holy Week, what does this mean for you?

PRAYER

Form, O Lord, the same mind in me that was in Jesus Christ: a mind of love, generosity, and mercy. Amen.

Palm Gospel

Luke 19:28–40

As they were untying the colt, its owners asked them, "Why are you untying the colt?" They said, "The Lord needs it." Then they brought it to Jesus; and after throwing their cloaks on the colt, they set Jesus on it. (vv. 33–34)

REFLECTION

Luke's listeners quite possibly had experienced other royal processions. Their community may have been conquered. They would have watched as the conqueror moved into the city to hymns and shouts. . . . Luke's king is a different kind of leader. Jesus rides not on a horse, a symbol of authority. Rather, he mounts a donkey, a symbol of humility. He comes in peace and in the name of the God who has sent him to live among people and to show people the loving face of God.

LUCY LIND HOGAN

RESPONSE

Imagine in detail (or draw) what it would be like to witness a conquering king parade through a community, in the past or present. Now, imagine a parade that is just fun; for instance, for Independence Day or a team victory. Then, imagine the procession of Jesus: how is it similar? different?

PRAYER

Lord Jesus, you rode up into Jerusalem and toward your death on the back of an untamed colt. Show me how to walk beside you, this week and all my life. Amen.

Passion Gospel

Luke 23:1–49

It was now about noon, and darkness came over the whole land until three in the afternoon, while the sun's light failed; and the curtain of the temple was torn in two. Then Jesus, crying with a loud voice, said, "Father, into your hands I commend my spirit." Having said this, he breathed his last. (vv. 44–46)

REFLECTION

Now the power of darkness is at its peak. Jesus, however, is at peace. Luke gives us no cry of dereliction, but draws on Psalm 31 as Jesus entrusts himself to God. Following his death, we hear a final declaration of innocence, this time from a Roman centurion who thereby "glorifies God." Luke concludes the scene at the cross with the women from Galilee looking on. Unlike the crowds, who beat their breasts, they are not gawking. They are *bearing witness*, painting a third portrait of discipleship, as those who follow Jesus attend to him with love.

PATRICK W. T. JOHNSON

RESPONSE

Bearing witness to Christ may sound passive, but it is something more than simply being an onlooker or gawker. Look up the word "witness" and reflect on its meanings. What could the Holy Spirit be saying to you this Holy Week through this word?

PRAYER

O God, we stand at a distance, watching these things take place, bearing witness with you and one another. Amen.

Weekend Reflections

FURTHER CONNECTION

The cross and the lynching tree interpret each other. Both were public spectacles, shameful events, instruments of punishment reserved for the most despised people in society. . . . The crowd's shout "Crucify him!" (Mk 15:14) anticipated the white mob's shout "Lynch him!" Jesus' agonizing final cry of abandonment from the cross, "My God, my God, why have you forsaken me?" (Mk 15:34), was similar to the lynched victim Sam Hose's awful scream as he drew his last breath, "Oh, my God! Oh, Jesus."

JAMES H. CONE (1938–2018), *THE CROSS AND THE LYNCHING TREE*

MAKING THE CONNECTIONS

Choose one or two questions for reflection:

1. What connections have you noticed between this week's texts and other passages in Scripture?

2. What connections have you made between this week's texts and the world beyond Scripture?

3. Does either of this week's two commentary themes speak especially to your life or the life of the world around you right now?

4. What is God saying to your congregation in particular through this week's readings and commentaries?

_____

_____

_____

_____

_____

_____

Sabbath Day

SCRIPTURE OF ASSURANCE

> O send out your light and your truth;
>   let them lead me;
> let them bring me to your holy hill
>   and to your dwelling. (Psalm 43:3)

WEEKLY EXAMEN

- Take a quiet moment, seek out God's presence, and pray for the guidance of the Spirit.

- Consider the past week; recall specific moments and feelings that stand out to you.

- Choose one moment or feeling for deeper examination, thanksgiving, or repentance.

- Let go, breathe deeply, and invite Christ's love to surround and fill you in preparation for the week ahead.

- End with the Lord's Prayer.

Holy Thursday

Exodus 12:1–4 (5–10), 11–14

The blood shall be a sign for you on the houses where you live: when I see the blood, I will pass over you, and no plague shall destroy you when I strike the land of Egypt. (v. 13)

Psalm 116:1–2, 12–19

I love the LORD, because he has heard
  my voice and my supplications.
Because he inclined his ear to me,
  therefore I will call on him as long as I live. (vv. 1–2)

1 Corinthians 11:23–26

And when he had given thanks, he broke it and said, "This is my body that is for you. Do this in remembrance of me." (v. 24)

John 13:1–17, 31b–35

"So if I, your Lord and Teacher, have washed your feet, you also ought to wash one another's feet. For I have set you an example, that you also should do as I have done to you." (vv. 14–15)

REFLECTIONS

Exodus 12:1–4 (5–10), 11–14

In both Testaments the act of violence resulted in healing, redemption, and blessing. No passage of Scripture explains the violence necessary for salvation in a way that resolves all of the tension and answers the agonizing questions. The reader can only affirm that God's ultimate purpose was reconciliation and salvation.

CHARLES L. AARON JR.

Psalm 116:1–2, 12–19

Whenever Israel called, the Lord God heard and answered. Our pleas for mercy are heeded; God hears. God makes and keeps the promises of covenant, even as Jesus gives a new commandment and calls for new actions—the washing of feet, the sharing of a eucharistic meal. By sharing in a sacramental meal, Jesus indicates his participation in our afflictions.

JOSEPH A. DONNELLA II

1 Corinthians 11:23–26

What exactly does Jesus want us to remember by way of this shared meal? Certainly he wants us to remember his death on our behalf. However, the preacher might note that Jesus says, "Do this in remembrance *of me*," not "Do this, so you will not forget what I have done for you." Could it be that Jesus wants us to remember not only *what he did* for us but, also, *that he is* for us?

CYNTHIA L. RIGBY

John 13:1–17, 31b–35

If Jesus' signs express his divinity, the *kinds* of signs—healings and feeding of the five thousand—express his great care and love for others. It is the passionate, self-giving love behind the signs that John wants to underscore for the community. This lesson, here expressed through the only foot washing account in the Gospels, takes up the majority of John 13 and is, therefore, telling.

ZAIDA MALDONADO PÉREZ

RESPONSE

Choose one of these four quotes that particularly gets your attention and write or reflect on how God might be speaking to you, to your experience or questions about Holy Week this year, or to this time in your life.

PRAYER

O Jesus, you offer me yourself in gifts of bread, wine, washed feet, and even your precious death. Show me how to offer myself to you, too. Amen.

Good Friday

Isaiah 52:13–53:12

He was despised and rejected by others;
  a man of suffering and acquainted with infirmity;
and as one from whom others hide their faces
  he was despised, and we held him of no account. (53:3)

Psalm 22

O my God, I cry by day, but you do not answer;
  and by night, but find no rest. (v. 2)

Hebrews 10:16–25 and Hebrews 4:14–16; 5:7–9

For we do not have a high priest who is unable to sympathize with our weaknesses, but we have one who in every respect has been tested as we are, yet without sin. Let us therefore approach the throne of grace with boldness, so that we may receive mercy and find grace to help in time of need. (4:15–16)

John 18:1–19:42

Jesus answered, "My kingdom is not from this world. If my kingdom were from this world, my followers would be fighting to keep me from being handed over to the Jews. But as it is, my kingdom is not from here." (18:36)

REFLECTIONS

Isaiah 52:13–53:12

By suffering alongside the least of these, the church can participate in Christ's work. Instead of perpetuating suffering and alienation, we might read Isaiah 52:13–53:12 as a call to stand in solidarity with the least of these in our own era.

DAVID G. GARBER JR.

Psalm 22

The emotions that accompany sheer and utter abandonment can shake us to the core. Yet the tone of suffering is disrupted as the sufferer moves beyond lament to thanksgiving. . . . What is sacrificial in this regard is the giving of one's self in pursuit of a better, godlier, more human way of being.

JOSEPH A. DONNELLA II

Hebrews 10:16–25 and Hebrews 4:14–16; 5:7–9

Good Friday invites Christians to reflect on Jesus' ministry that includes his unique priesthood and his subsequent death. It argues that Jesus has made a way for Christians to be bold and unwavering in their faith during times of suffering, encouraging believers to take courage from the high priest who gave his life for the world.

SHANELL T. SMITH

John 18:1–19:42

As John tells the passion story, Jesus goes about his business quite calmly and deliberately, to the extent that from his perspective there really does not seem to be much either frightening or sad about it (no "agony in the garden" here!). He is the calm center of things. The drama of the story lies in the way other characters interact with him.

IAN A. MCFARLAND

RESPONSE

Choose one of these four quotes that particularly gets your attention and write or reflect on how God might be speaking to you, to your experience or questions about Holy Week this year, or to this time in your life.

PRAYER

Jesus, remember me when you come into your kingdom. Amen.

The Week Leading Up to
Easter Day/Resurrection
of the Lord

Isaiah 65:17–25

For I am about to create new heavens
　　and a new earth;
the former things shall not be remembered
　　or come to mind. (v. 17)

1 Corinthians 15:19–26

For he must reign until he has put all his enemies under his feet. The last
enemy to be destroyed is death. (vv. 25–26)

John 20:1–18

[The angels] said to her, "Woman, why are you weeping?" She said to them,
"They have taken away my Lord, and I do not know where they have laid
him." (v. 13)

Luke 24:1–12

The women were terrified and bowed their faces to the ground, but the men
said to them, "Why do you look for the living among the dead? He is not
here, but has risen." (v. 5)

LECTIO DIVINA

Underline a word or phrase that especially grabs your attention. Pray
from that word or phrase and ask God to help you connect to its
particular invitation for you this week.

Themes from This Week's Writers

THEME 1: *A New Heaven and a New Earth*

Isaiah 65:17–25

"Imagine a just world, a joy-filled world, a realm of peace," God says. Preachers and congregants alike shout, "Yes! I can imagine that!" Preachers and congregants alike whisper, "Impossible."

CATHY CALDWELL HOOP

Acts 10:34–43

Clearly Luke wants us to understand that the resurrection of Jesus Christ is an event of cosmic significance: the very structures of the universe, as well as the socially constructed "givens," what we have always assumed to be true, are all to be rethought and reimagined in light of the exciting new events triggered by God's work in Christ.

A. KATHERINE GRIEB

1 Corinthians 15:19–26

Thus the resurrection remains the defining act of God on our behalf and must resound through our proclamation. In response, we live in the knowledge that, no matter what we encounter in life, God in Christ will have the last word, even victory over "the last enemy" (v. 26), death.

BEVERLY ZINK-SAWYER

THEME 2: *Jesus Lives*

Psalm 118:1–2, 14–24

Can we know redemption when it feels as if we are in the grips of desolation? Can hope endure despite the grave? Easter proclaims, "Yes!" Why? Because Jesus lives.

JOSEPH A. DONNELLA II

John 20:1–18

Yet Jesus has not returned to stay. If Mary had thought that by finding the body of Jesus she could somehow hold on to him, she now discovers that even though Jesus is alive, he has not returned to life as before.

MARIANNE MEYE THOMPSON

John 20:1–18

We too want to encounter the living Stranger who calls each of us by name.

AMY PLANTINGA PAUW

WHAT IS THE HOLY SPIRIT SAYING TO YOU THIS WEEK?

_____

_____

_____

_____

_____

A SPIRITUAL PRACTICE FOR THIS WEEK

This week, strive to be as present to the readings and services of Holy Week as you can. Consider fasting in some way on Good Friday; abstain from meat or alcohol, or skip lunch or dinner entirely. Drink hot tea or water to ease a hungry stomach.

First Reading

Isaiah 65:17–25

But be glad and rejoice forever
    in what I am creating;
for I am about to create Jerusalem as a joy,
    and its people as a delight.
I will rejoice in Jerusalem,
    and delight in my people;
no more shall the sound of weeping be heard in it,
    or the cry of distress. (vv. 18–19)

REFLECTION

The church's appeal to our text from Isaiah is made possible by an interpretive move that morphs *the destruction and restoration of Jerusalem* into *the crucifixion and resurrection of Jesus*, without losing any of the "this-worldly" socioeconomic political accent of the old text. The "new Jerusalem" becomes, in Christian interpretation, the risen Christ and the new world of well-being that he makes possible and over which he governs. In the Gospel reading the Easter reality of Jesus can no more be explained than can be the new Jerusalem of Isaiah, which defies all conventional political wisdom.

WALTER BRUEGGEMANN

RESPONSE

Imagine your own city, town, or congregation restored and transformed like the new Jerusalem. What wonders of beauty, justice, and love would you like to dream about? How might this be a way, not to despair at what is missing, but to imagine in new ways the "Easter reality of Jesus"?

PRAYER

Risen Christ, you are the new world in which we live. Help me to see the new reality you are creating. Amen.

Canticle

Psalm 118:1–2, 14–24

I shall not die, but I shall live,
    and recount the deeds of the LORD.
The LORD has punished me severely,
    but he did not give me over to death. (vv. 17–18)

REFLECTION

Do we fear what death has come to mean in our culture? Are we afraid
that no one will remember us, or care that we ever existed? Resurrection
opens us to see life and death in a different guise, to experience life in a
new condition of life with God. We declare that what Jesus experiences,
we will experience. Our hoped-for future with God is made possible by
what happens to Jesus in life, death, and resurrection. . . .

Life is more than a steadfast rush toward death's emptiness and
nothingness.

JOSEPH A. DONNELLA II

RESPONSE

How do you picture death? What do you fear about it? What do you
believe, or strive to believe, about life after death, in light of Jesus'
resurrection? What does it mean to you that "what Jesus experiences,
we will experience"?

PRAYER

O God, I thank you for becoming my salvation. Your steadfast love
endures forever. Amen.

Second Reading

Acts 10:34–43

Then Peter began to speak to them: "I truly understand that God shows no partiality, but in every nation anyone who fears him and does what is right is acceptable to him." (vv. 34–35)

REFLECTION

Peter is *petros* or rock. . . .

The image of a rock does not easily lend itself to being something that can change, and being faithful against insurmountable challenges can seem like pushing against a boulder. We see, however, in Peter, that we too can change, and we believe that which we once thought impossible. In Peter's case, the message he hears is that Gentiles are also loved by God. This was a powerful new story in which old perceptions and norms were challenged and even removed. Ultimately, Jesus' resurrection left all the disciples ready for new paradigms of possibilities.

MICHAEL BATTLE

RESPONSE

Throughout his life and work, Peter struggled with the new story being revealed in Jesus. What does it mean for you that one of Jesus' most prominent disciples struggled to change his mind? Is there a way in which Christ is calling you, too, this Easter, to change your mind?

PRAYER

Gracious God, you sent your son, Jesus Christ, to be Lord of all. Show me, like Peter, how to believe what I may have once believed impossible. Amen.

Second Reading

1 Corinthians 15:19–26

But in fact Christ has been raised from the dead, the first fruits of those who have died. For since death came through a human being, the resurrection of the dead has also come through a human being; for as all die in Adam, so all will be made alive in Christ. (vv. 20–22)

REFLECTION

On Easter, twenty-first-century worshipers proclaim, fervently or perfunctorily, "Christ is risen; he is risen indeed!" However, if asked whether they believe that *their* dead bodies will be raised, many would respond with puzzlement, doubt, or denial. . . .

The inclusive resurrection of Christ and human bodies affirms the goodness of creation. Bodily life is not a lower form of existence, to be disdained or discarded. The obvious question, now as then, is, "How are the dead raised? With what kind of body do they come?" (15:35). A "spiritual body," says Paul. Not a bodiless spirit, but a transformed body. Easter gospel!

JOSEPH D. SMALL

RESPONSE

How is your body "you"? Not "you"? How is your body a delight? A trial? What does it mean to you that bodily life continues, somehow, beyond death via a "spiritual body" or "transformed body" in Christ? For your own body? For the bodies of those you love?

PRAYER

Jesus Christ, teach me to hope in you, not only in this life and this body, but in and through resurrection, yours and mine. Amen.

Gospel

John 20:1–18

Jesus said to her, "Woman, why are you weeping? Whom are you looking for?" Supposing him to be the gardener, she said to him, "Sir, if you have carried him away, tell me where you have laid him, and I will take him away." (v. 15)

REFLECTION

Like Mary returning to the tomb when others went back home, many people come to church on Easter morning not sure what they are looking for. They come weighed down with grief and disappointment, hungry for hope. Even those who come to church confident and joyful are still learning what it means to believe in Jesus' name and claim their identity as children of God (John 1:12). We are all, like Mary, somewhere between grief and joy, somewhere between despair and faith. . . . The good news of Easter is that these encounters continue.

AMY PLANTINGA PAUW

RESPONSE

How are you feeling, as Easter Sunday draws near? Where are you between grief and joy, despair and faith? What you are looking for, returning again to the empty tomb?

PRAYER

Brother Jesus, guide me to your empty tomb, meet me where I am, and help me, in you, to find what I am seeking. Amen.

Gospel

Luke 24:1–12

But on the first day of the week, at early dawn, they came to the tomb, taking the spices that they had prepared. They found the stone rolled away from the tomb, but when they went in, they did not find the body. While they were perplexed about this, suddenly two men in dazzling clothes stood beside them. (vv. 1–4)

REFLECTION

From the patriarchs and prophets of the Old Testament to the disciples and apostles of the New Testament to those of us who are part of the Christian community today, perplexity in reaction to the amazing work of God is not uncommon. Indeed, this is a text that reveals a pattern of disorientation (as the women encounter the empty tomb), orientation (as they receive the message of Jesus' resurrection from the two men), and reorientation (as they respond to the good news of the resurrection by sharing the message with others). This pattern reflects the transformative work of God within and among us.

BEVERLY ZINK-SAWYER

RESPONSE

What transforming work might God be doing within you this Easter season? Within your community or congregation? What has been clear? What has been disorienting or perplexing? What reorientation do you seek?

PRAYER

O Christ, transform my lack of understanding into wonder and my confusion into joy. Amen.

Weekend Reflections

FURTHER CONNECTION

The history of the church tells us that we must identify the God of the resurrection with the God of the cross. To put it differently, the resurrection must be experienced in and through the cross just as the cross must be seen in the light of the resurrection. The fact is that the resurrection has not made the cross superfluous. This is a historical reality the church has to accept. The church, together with the world as a whole, continues to bear the pain and agony of the cross in the midst of the resurrection.

CHOAN-SENG SONG (1929–), *THIRD-EYE THEOLOGY*

MAKING THE CONNECTIONS

Choose one or two questions for reflection:

1. What connections have you noticed between this week's texts and other passages in Scripture?

2. What connections have you made between this week's texts and the world beyond Scripture?

3. Does either of this week's two commentary themes speak especially to your life or the life of the world around you right now?

4. What is God saying to your congregation in particular through this week's readings and commentaries?

_____

_____

_____

_____

_____

Sabbath Day

SCRIPTURE OF ASSURANCE

From now on, let no one make trouble for me; for I carry the marks of Jesus branded on my body.

May the grace of our Lord Jesus Christ be with your spirit, brothers and sisters. Amen. (Galatians 6:17–18)

WEEKLY EXAMEN

- Take a quiet moment, seek out God's presence, and pray for the guidance of the Spirit.

- Consider the past week; recall specific moments and feelings that stand out to you.

- Choose one moment or feeling for deeper examination, thanksgiving, or repentance.

- Let go, breathe deeply, and invite Christ's love to surround and fill you in preparation for the week ahead.

- End with the Lord's Prayer.

The Week Leading Up to the
Second Sunday of Easter

Acts 5:27–32

But Peter and the apostles answered, "We must obey God rather than any human authority." (v. 29)

Psalm 118:14–29

The stone that the builders rejected
　　has become the chief cornerstone.
This is the LORD's doing;
　　it is marvelous in our eyes. (vv. 22–23)

Revelation 1:4–8

Look! He is coming with the clouds;
　　every eye will see him,
even those who pierced him;
　　and on his account all the tribes of the earth will wail.
So it is to be. Amen. (v. 7)

John 20:19–31

After he said this, he showed them his hands and his side. Then the disciples rejoiced when they saw the Lord. Jesus said to them again, "Peace be with you. As the Father has sent me, so I send you." (v. 20–21)

LECTIO DIVINA

Underline a word or phrase that especially grabs your attention. Pray from that word or phrase and ask God to help you connect to its particular invitation for you this week.

Themes from This Week's Writers

THEME 1: *Speak Out, Do Not Be Silent*

Acts 5:27–32

This testimony contradicts the claims of empire in the same way in which the apostolic witness in our text contradicted the old order, refusing to be silenced.

WALTER BRUEGGEMANN

Acts 5:27–32

Look for the apostles in your midst whose voices have been muffled, if not silenced. Look for the apostles who name difficult realities. Their perceptive vision may encourage your congregation to practice an even deeper love of neighbor.

CATHY CALDWELL HOOP

Psalm 150 and Psalm 118:14–29

The praise and worship of God is a universal instruction. We join our voices to the chorus of creation, singing *hallelujah*, praise to God.

MARCI AULD GLASS

THEME 2: *Confess Christ, Crucified*

Revelation 1:4–8

If our concept of heaven is really a subtext or euphemism in which we retreat from a suffering world in order to enjoy our own spoils of war, then we are not following Jesus.

MICHAEL BATTLE

John 20:19–31

[This passage] is a guide for being an Easter community where the wounds of crucifixion are not denied, where the continuing reality of death and failure and trauma is not covered up, where our lament finds a communal home alongside our joy.

AMY PLANTINGA PAUW

John 20:19–31

Although Thomas is frequently called a doubter, Jesus does not invite him to stop doubting. Rather, Jesus invites Thomas to turn from being unbelieving (Greek *apistos*) to believing (*pistos*), that is, to put his trust in Jesus.

MARIANNE MEYE THOMPSON

WHAT IS THE HOLY SPIRIT SAYING TO YOU THIS WEEK?

_____

_____

_____

_____

_____

A SPIRITUAL PRACTICE FOR THIS WEEK

Celebrate the end of Lenten fasting and do some feasting this week. What does "feasting" mean to you this year? Choose celebration and fun all week, however that may look to you. You might buy flowers, wear bright colors, or enjoy a fun food.

First Reading

Acts 5:27–32

When they had brought them, they had them stand before the council. The high priest questioned them, saying, "We gave you strict orders not to teach in this name, yet here you have filled Jerusalem with your teaching and you are determined to bring this man's blood on us." (vv. 27–28)

REFLECTION

There is something that often precedes persecution: the silencing of the voice. In keeping with the theme of the apostles as civilly disobedient, a possible trajectory for preaching includes the voices in your congregation, in your community, in our nation, or in our world that are being silenced. Just as the religious leaders of Peter's day believed they were doing the right thing to attempt to silence Jesus' followers, we often silence voices that disturb us. Stories of oppression and exploitation clamor for our attention.

CATHY CALDWELL HOOP

RESPONSE

What stories of exploitation or oppression are hardest for you to listen to in your own community? Who are the apostles in your midst, trying to call attention to disturbing realities and being silenced? What is God trying to say to you or your community about Easter and resurrection, through them?

PRAYER

O God, strengthen us to speak and to invite others to speak, so that we may love and listen as we teach in your name. Amen.

Canticle

Psalm 150

Praise the LORD!
Praise God in his sanctuary;
  praise him in his mighty firmament!
Praise him for his mighty deeds;
  praise him according to his surpassing greatness! (vv. 1–2)

REFLECTION

If the human vocation is to praise God while we have breath, what does praise look like in an era when fewer and fewer people are gathering to join their voices in worship? . . . in a postmodern, post-Christendom, postdenominational world?

The passage from Acts 5 shows Peter and the apostles living out their vocation of praise by speaking and teaching about God, even after being instructed to be silent by the authorities. How do we see our vocation of praise play out in our lives? Does it lead us to speak and teach about God? Does it get us brought before the authorities?

MARCI AULD GLASS

RESPONSE

Make a list of ways you express praise to God in your own life—even if they are unconventional ways. Are any of them ways you speak out or teach about God, even without words? Would any get you brought before the authorities?

PRAYER

Mighty God, teach us to praise you in ways that might get us in trouble, for the sake of your love and your people. Amen.

Second Reading

Revelation 1:4–8

"I am the Alpha and the Omega," says the Lord God, who is and who was and who is to come, the Almighty. (v. 8)

REFLECTION

It may be that we imagine God as being far away because we cannot imagine God being on a suffering earth.

Although we have many questions about heaven and have difficulty talking about it, there is good news. We long so much for a different world from this one because the desire for a perfect world becomes the proper reaction to God's act in the crucified Christ. In other words, through the birth, life, death, and resurrection of Christ, God shows us that there is no once-removed reality between God and this earth.

MICHAEL BATTLE

RESPONSE

In what ways does God feel far away or removed from the world in your own spiritual life right now? How could God's suffering, as the crucified Christ and as "Alpha and Omega," be good news for you? To your community?

PRAYER

Gracious God, you are eternal and ever-present, and yet you came to be with us in Jesus and to suffer with us. Show me today how close you are to me. Amen.

Gospel

John 20:19–31

When it was evening on that day, the first day of the week, and the doors of the house where the disciples had met were locked for fear of the Jews, Jesus came and stood among them and said, "Peace be with you." After he said this, he showed them his hands and his side. Then the disciples rejoiced when they saw the Lord. (vv. 19–20)

REFLECTION

We might wish that Jesus' resurrection would erase the troubles of our past and catapult us into a wholly new future. In this fantasy, the Easter crowds at church would keep coming back week after week, and our own faith and witness would be fearless and exemplary, bearing none of the scars of our past failings and enmities. Instead, we look more like the disciples, our lives a mixture of fear and joy, doubt and faith.

AMY PLANTINGA PAUW

RESPONSE

What is a fantasy you have about what your spiritual life could or should look like? In what ways is your spiritual life affected by fear and doubt? What does it feel like to hear Jesus' peace extended to you today, regardless?

PRAYER

Jesus, help me receive your greeting of peace, just as I am, and to rejoice in your resurrection even with your scars intact. Amen.

Weekend Reflections

What people don't realize is how much religion costs. They think faith is a big electric blanket, when of course, it is the cross. It is much harder to believe than not to believe. If you feel you can't believe, you must at least do this: keep an open mind. Keep it open toward faith, keep wanting it, keep asking for it, and leave the rest to God.

FLANNERY O'CONNOR (1925–64), 1959 LETTER

MAKING THE CONNECTIONS

Choose one or two questions for reflection:

1. What connections have you noticed between this week's texts and other passages in Scripture?

2. What connections have you made between this week's texts and the world beyond Scripture?

3. Does either of this week's two commentary themes speak especially to your life or the life of the world around you right now?

4. What is God saying to your congregation in particular through this week's readings and commentaries?

_____

_____

_____

_____

_____

Sabbath Day

SCRIPTURE OF ASSURANCE

I will give thanks to you, O Lord, among the peoples;
I will sing praises to you among the nations.
For your steadfast love is as high as the heavens;
your faithfulness extends to the clouds. (Psalm 57:9–10)

WEEKLY EXAMEN

- Take a quiet moment, seek out God's presence, and pray for the guidance of the Spirit.

- Consider the past week; recall specific moments and feelings that stand out to you.

- Choose one moment or feeling for deeper examination, thanksgiving, or repentance.

- Let go, breathe deeply, and invite Christ's love to surround and fill you in preparation for the week ahead.

- End with the Lord's Prayer.

The Week Leading Up to the
Third Sunday of Easter

Acts 9:1–6 (7–20)

He fell to the ground and heard a voice saying to him, "Saul, Saul, why do you persecute me?" He asked, "Who are you, Lord?" The reply came, "I am Jesus, whom you are persecuting." (vv. 4–5)

Psalm 30

O Lord my God, I cried to you for help,
 and you have healed me.
O Lord, you brought up my soul from Sheol,
 restored me to life from among those gone down to the Pit.
 (vv. 2–3)

Revelation 5:11–14

And the four living creatures said, "Amen!" And the elders fell down and worshiped. (v. 14)

John 21:1–19

When they had finished breakfast, Jesus said to Simon Peter, "Simon son of John, do you love me more than these?" He said to him, "Yes, Lord; you know that I love you." Jesus said to him, "Feed my lambs." (v. 15)

LECTIO DIVINA

Underline a word or phrase that especially grabs your attention. Pray from that word or phrase and ask God to help you connect to its particular invitation for you this week.

Themes from This Week's Writers

THEME 1: *Changed by Encounter with the Risen Christ*

Acts 9:1–6 (7–20)

Thus, with both Saul and Ananias, the direct witness of Jesus' lordly presence occupies the drama of the narrative. It is the presence of Jesus that makes all things new for both men.

WALTER BRUEGGEMANN

Revelation 5:11–14

Just when we are looking for a lion king or perhaps the boxer Rocky having laid low all opponents, we are shown instead "a Lamb standing as if it had been slaughtered" (v. 6), John's paradoxical description of the crucified and risen Messiah Jesus.

A. KATHERINE GRIEB

John 21:1–19

The risen Jesus forces Peter to confront his past, but he does not leave him there. Instead, he gives Peter another way to make his love manifest: he invites Peter to put his faith into action.

AMY PLANTINGA PAUW

THEME 2: *Forgiven, Then Called to Be Disciples*

Acts 9:1–6 (7–20)

God redeemed Saul, gave him a new name, and placed him on a new path. This same mercy is accessible to each of us, and to our corporate communities.

CATHY CALDWELL HOOP

Psalm 30

Even as he embraces the new movement of Jesus' followers, the Hebrew traditions and culture of his past continue to inform his identity. In Saul's life, much like Psalm 30, the mourning and the dancing, the Hebrew and Greek identities, exist together, and he offers praise to God through it all.

MARCI AULD GLASS

John 21:1–19

The last words that Jesus speaks to Peter—and to any of the disciples—in this Gospel are the invitation "Follow me!" (21:19, 22). These are also among the first words spoken to any of the disciples (1:43).

MARIANNE MEYE THOMPSON

WHAT IS THE HOLY SPIRIT SAYING TO YOU THIS WEEK?

_____

_____

_____

_____

_____

A SPIRITUAL PRACTICE FOR THIS WEEK

Search online for photos and videos of lambs. Then, imagine a lamb on a throne. After you stop laughing, draw this image, or write a paragraph or poem describing it. Reflect on what God might be inviting you to understand, even with humor, about Jesus, power, glory, and resurrection.

First Reading

Acts 9:1–6 (7–20)

But Ananias answered, "Lord, I have heard from many about this man, how much evil he has done to your saints in Jerusalem; and here he has authority from the chief priests to bind all who invoke your name." (vv. 13–14)

REFLECTION

Of course Jesus is going to love and forgive the bumbling Peter (the companion Gospel text, John 21). Peter made a rather embarrassing mistake, but he was not trying to *kill* anyone! We all stumble on our faith journeys, and are glad for God to forgive Peter. Saul's rescue, on the other hand, is so outrageous that it can only be the work of a foolishly forgiving God. . . .

. . . This same mercy is accessible to each of us, and to our corporate communities. The Easter miracle proves that God loves and forgives friends, betrayers, doubters, skeptics . . . even God's own enemies.

CATHY CALDWELL HOOP

RESPONSE

How do you understand the outrageousness of Saul's rescue? Have you ever had an experience of a "foolishly forgiving God"? Is there a sin you worry that God can never rescue you from? How can forgiveness transform a person?

PRAYER

God of mercy, you love your friends, but also your betrayers, doubters, skeptics, and enemies. Forgive me my sins and teach me this mercy. Amen.

Canticle

Psalm 30

"Hear, O LORD, and be gracious to me!
O LORD, be my helper!"

You have turned my mourning into dancing;
you have taken off my sackcloth
and clothed me with joy,
so that my soul may praise you and not be silent. (vv. 10–12a)

REFLECTION

In Psalm 30, past deliverance leads to hope and faith in future
deliverance. . . . In claiming that "weeping may linger for the night, but
joy comes with the morning" (v. 5), the psalmist is not telling people
to get over their grief before their grief is done with them, but reminds
them that grief will not be with them forever. God turned the psalmist's
"mourning into dancing" (v. 11), and such deliverance is the focus of
our prayers and hopes.

MARCI AULD GLASS

RESPONSE

Paul and Peter each spent time in grief and isolation. This time became
a crucial part of God's call to them, and even turned into joy. How has
this been true in your own life? How has this been true, even, this week?
How does this psalm speak to you?

PRAYER

O Lord, my helper, hear me, then turn my grief into dancing that I may
praise you. Amen.

Second Reading

Revelation 5:11–14

Worthy is the Lamb that was slaughtered
to receive power and wealth and wisdom and might
and honor and glory and blessing! (v. 12b)

REFLECTION

This passage suggests that the most powerful beast is a Lamb, and that
should strike the reader as strange. . . . No one in heaven and earth has
power comparable to this Lamb. Ferocious-looking monsters, sing to
a Lamb.

John's vision here includes a disconcerting image of the Lamb saving
us. What power does a lamb have to save anyone? It cannot even save
itself. In many sacrificial rituals, the lamb is the chief victim. How can
the victim save the perpetrator?

MICHAEL BATTLE

RESPONSE

Make a list of the traits of a lamb. Does a lamb have anything
resembling power? How can a victim save anyone, much less the
perpetrator? What could it mean that the power of Christ's resurrection
is shown here in a lamb?

PRAYER

Lamb of God, save me and preserve me through your power, honor,
glory, and blessing. Amen.

Gospel

John 21:1–19

Jesus said to them, "Come and have breakfast." Now none of the disciples dared to ask him, "Who are you?" because they knew it was the Lord. Jesus came and took the bread and gave it to them, and did the same with the fish. (vv. 12–13)

REFLECTION

Scripture is where, by the power of the Spirit, we meet Jesus again and again. The texts of Scripture stabilize our access to the risen Jesus, assuring future generations that he can be present with them too. . . . The risen Christ always retains some of the strangeness of the original encounters with him (21:4, 12). Christ's presence is never wholly predictable, never under our control. Yet in Scripture, at the Table, and in the care of the suffering and vulnerable, we meet him still.

AMY PLANTINGA PAUW

RESPONSE

Do you feel you meet Jesus "again and again" in your own life? Or not? Or, are you unsure? What does it mean that the presence of the risen Christ is "strange" and "unpredictable"? What good news could be found in this?

PRAYER

Risen Christ, help me to recognize you in Scripture and my community, that you may be present with me and help me to feed your sheep. Amen.

Weekend Reflections

FURTHER CONNECTION

As all Christian leaders have been, are, and will be, Peter is imperfect. And as all good Christian leaders are, Peter is well aware of his imperfections. The disciples too know who they are getting as their leader. They will not need—or be tempted—to elevate Peter into some semi-divine figure; they have seen him at his worst. Jesus forgives Peter because he loves him, because he knows that his friend needs forgiveness to be free, and because he knows that the leader of his church will need to forgive others many times.

JAMES MARTIN, SJ (1960), *JESUS: A PILGRIMAGE*

MAKING THE CONNECTIONS

Choose one or two questions for reflection:

1. What connections have you noticed between this week's texts and other passages in Scripture?

2. What connections have you made between this week's texts and the world beyond Scripture?

3. Does either of this week's two commentary themes speak especially to your life or the life of the world around you right now?

4. What is God saying to your congregation in particular through this week's readings and commentaries?

MY CONNECTIONS

_____

_____

_____

_____

_____

Sabbath Day

SCRIPTURE OF ASSURANCE

> I have put my words in your mouth,
>   and hidden you in the shadow of my hand,
> stretching out the heavens
>   and laying the foundations of the earth,
>   and saying to Zion, "You are my people." (Isaiah 51:16)

WEEKLY EXAMEN

- Take a quiet moment, seek out God's presence, and pray for the guidance of the Spirit.

- Consider the past week; recall specific moments and feelings that stand out to you.

- Choose one moment or feeling for deeper examination, thanksgiving, or repentance.

- Let go, breathe deeply, and invite Christ's love to surround and fill you in preparation for the week ahead.

- End with the Lord's Prayer.

The Week Leading Up to the
Fourth Sunday of Easter

Acts 9:36–43

He turned to the body and said, "Tabitha, get up." Then she opened her eyes, and seeing Peter, she sat up. He gave her his hand and helped her up. Then calling the saints and widows, he showed her to be alive. (vv. 40b–41)

Psalm 23

Even though I walk through the darkest valley,
   I fear no evil;
for you are with me;
   your rod and your staff—
   they comfort me. (v. 4)

Revelation 7:9–17

I said to him, "Sir, you are the one that knows." Then he said to me, "These are they who have come out of the great ordeal; they have washed their robes and made them white in the blood of the Lamb." (v. 14)

John 10:22–30

"My sheep hear my voice. I know them, and they follow me. I give them eternal life, and they will never perish. No one will snatch them out of my hand." (vv. 27–28)

LECTIO DIVINA

Underline a word or phrase that especially grabs your attention. Pray from that word or phrase and ask God to help you connect to its particular invitation for you this week.

Themes from This Week's Writers

THEME 1: *Hope for New Life*

Acts 9:36–43

This is a story located in the Easter cycle of the church, not simply because death is defied and God's will for life prevails, but because Dorcas rises and her Easter life leads disciples—female and male—to attend to the ones who are most often neglected or forgotten by society, but never forgotten by God.

GARY W. CHARLES

Revelation 7:9–17

Claiming [resurrection] hope is important for us as believers two thousand years later, especially in this Easter season, as we consider how John's melodic vision in Revelation 7:9–17 continues to encourage our witness today.

RUTH FAITH SANTANA-GRACE

John 10:22–30

Then, while he has their attention, Jesus speaks about himself: he is the door of the sheep, and those who enter by him are promised abundant life (10:7). He is the Good Shepherd (v. 14), and those who know his voice belong to his fold and are promised eternal life.

MARK PRICE

THEME 2: *One Shepherd, Many Peoples*

Acts 9:36–43

Tabitha was known by two names, indicating that she was a person of mingled cultures, like many people in our world today. . . . Tabitha reminds Christians today that being a follower of Jesus includes selflessly demonstrating one's love and faith through action across cultural divides.

MARIANNE BLICKENSTAFF

Psalm 23

It would be a powerful invitation to proclaim we are invited to God's table, even as we are people whose relationships with others are fractured to the point of having/being enemies. God our shepherd prepares the feast at the Table, where our cup overflows, and where our enemies who betray us are invited to sit next to us.

MARCI AULD GLASS

Revelation 7:9–17

This is no vague melting-pot diversity. In their unity, the diverse peoples who follow the Lamb and sing hymns of praise retain their distinctive identities.

GREG CAREY

WHAT IS THE HOLY SPIRIT SAYING TO YOU THIS WEEK?

_____

_____

_____

_____

A SPIRITUAL PRACTICE FOR THIS WEEK

Notice the Tabithas in your community this week: women and men behind the scenes who serve the needy or work with their hands. Pray for them by name, send thank-you notes, or ask them about their ministry or the people they serve. Let them know they make a difference.

First Reading

Acts 9:36–43

So Peter got up and went with them; and when he arrived, they took him to the room upstairs. All the widows stood beside him, weeping and showing tunics and other clothing that Dorcas had made while she was with them. (v. 39)

REFLECTION

On the basis of other biblical stories of people being raised from death . . . we might conjecture that members of Tabitha's community hope Peter can restore her to life, but the story does not say they specifically ask for a miracle. Their purpose is to call attention to who she was and what she has done for them. Such love needs a witness.

Such a bold confirmation of community love has a tendency to spread outward to touch even more lives, until—like the Holy Spirit moving like wind and fire—it brings hope and sustenance to multitudes.

MARIANNE BLICKENSTAFF

RESPONSE

What traditions or customs for expressing gratitude or thanks have you seen in your congregation or community? Have you ever seen gratitude or mutual love bring new life to a person or community? How?

PRAYER

Loving God, show us how to be witnesses to one another's love and good works, in life and death. Amen.

Canticle

Psalm 23

He makes me lie down in green pastures;
he leads me beside still waters;
    he restores my soul. (vv. 2–3a)

REFLECTION

The Hebrew *nefesh* means "life breath," and while it is usually translated
as "soul," the phrase is stronger than "restores my soul" suggests. A nice,
hot bubble bath restores my soul. Without *nefesh*, humans are not alive.
Verse 3 is a description of divine CPR, where God brings us back to life.

The NRSV removed the familiar KJV refrain "though I walk through
the valley of the shadow of death" in verse 4 and replaced it with
"though I walk through the darkest valley." . . . But to walk through a
"darkest valley," one just needs a good flashlight. To walk through the
"valley of death's shadow," one wants God alongside.

MARCI AULD GLASS

RESPONSE

Reflect on the word *nefesh*: what is "life breath," for you? What is a
comparison from your own life of a "darkest valley" versus "a valley of
death's shadow"? What is it like to imagine God alongside you, not just
a "good flashlight"?

PRAYER

Shepherd God, walk with me through the valleys of death's shadow and
restore my life's breath; in you I will not falter. Amen.

Second Reading

Revelation 7:9–17

After this I looked, and there was a great multitude that no one could count, from every nation, from all tribes and peoples and languages, standing before the throne and before the Lamb, robed in white, with palm branches in their hands. They cried out in a loud voice, saying,

"Salvation belongs to our God who is seated on the throne,
and to the Lamb!" (vv. 9–10)

REFLECTION

The language of diversity—"from every nation, from all tribes and peoples and languages"—applies both to the Lamb's followers and to those who oppose them (10:11; 11:9; 13:7; 17:15). As much as Revelation values diversity, it recognizes that diversity does not guarantee virtue. This needs to be acknowledged. Nevertheless, Revelation imagines an ecumenical people of God in which diversity is valued and named rather than erased. The end of the story involves healing for the nations (22:2).

GREG CAREY

RESPONSE

In Revelation, all people are not the same, although they all wear the same robe. What does this mean? What does this say about the kingdom of God's future? Our present world? How is this a "healing for the nations"?

PRAYER

Lamb of God, we are blessed by our many differences, but we all belong to you. Amen.

Gospel

John 10:22–30

At that time the festival of the Dedication took place in Jerusalem. It was winter, and Jesus was walking in the temple, in the portico of Solomon. So the Jews gathered around him and said to him, "How long will you keep us in suspense? If you are the Messiah, tell us plainly." (vv. 22–24)

REFLECTION

The purification of the temple following its desecration was an act of community renewal. It was a recommitment by God's people to the reality of God's promised presence among them as symbolized in the physical structure of the dwelling place of the Lord. Imagine Jesus stopping by a column, anticipating the question to come. "If you are the Christ, tell us plainly" (John 10:24). What more apt place and time could there be for those first-century Jews to hear Jesus proclaim his identity than in this particular place of worship and during this specific time of worship?

MARK PRICE

RESPONSE

The temple, like the body of Jesus, was a physical dwelling place for God. How well does your church's physical space symbolize a dwelling place for God? What are its limitations? How does your church space invite you to encounter Jesus?

PRAYER

Jesus, you are God's dwelling place; shepherd me to find my rest and my salvation in you. Amen.

Weekend Reflections

FURTHER CONNECTION

Christians need other Christians who speak God's Word to them.
They need them again and again when they become uncertain and
disheartened because, living by their own resources, they cannot help
themselves without cheating themselves out of the truth. They need other
Christians as bearers and proclaimers of the divine word of salvation.
They need them solely for the sake of Jesus Christ. The Christ in their
own hearts is weaker than the Christ in the word of other Christians.
Their own hearts are uncertain; those of their brothers and sisters are sure.

DIETRICH BONHOEFFER (1906–45),
LIFE TOGETHER (MADE INCLUSIVE)

MAKING THE CONNECTIONS

Choose one or two questions for reflection:

1. What connections have you noticed between this week's texts and other passages in Scripture?

2. What connections have you made between this week's texts and the world beyond Scripture?

3. Does either of this week's two commentary themes speak especially to your life or the life of the world around you right now?

4. What is God saying to your congregation in particular through this week's readings and commentaries?

MY CONNECTIONS

_____

_____

_____

_____

Sabbath Day

SCRIPTURE OF ASSURANCE

And he said to them, "Go into all the world and proclaim the good news to the whole creation." (Mark 16:15)

WEEKLY EXAMEN

- Take a quiet moment, seek out God's presence, and pray for the guidance of the Spirit.

- Consider the past week; recall specific moments and feelings that stand out to you.

- Choose one moment or feeling for deeper examination, thanksgiving, or repentance.

- Let go, breathe deeply, and invite Christ's love to surround and fill you in preparation for the week ahead.

- End with the Lord's Prayer.

The Week Leading Up to the
Fifth Sunday of Easter

Acts 11:1–18

"If then God gave them the same gift that he gave us when we believed in the Lord Jesus Christ, who was I that I could hinder God?" When they heard this, they were silenced. And they praised God, saying, "Then God has given even to the Gentiles the repentance that leads to life." (vv. 17–18)

Psalm 148

Kings of the earth and all peoples,
    princes and all rulers of the earth!
Young men and women alike,
    old and young together! (vv. 11–12)

Revelation 21:1–6

And I heard a loud voice from the throne saying,
    "See, the home of God is among mortals.
    He will dwell with them;
    they will be his peoples,
    and God himself will be with them." (v. 3)

John 13:31–35

"I give you a new commandment, that you love one another. Just as I have loved you, you also should love one another. By this everyone will know that you are my disciples, if you have love for one another." (vv. 34–35)

LECTIO DIVINA

Underline a word or phrase that especially grabs your attention. Pray from that word or phrase and ask God to help you connect to its particular invitation for you this week.

Themes from This Week's Writers

THEME 1: *What God Has Made Clean*

Acts 11:1–18

Peter had to rethink the importance of certain requirements for holiness that he had held dear all his life, traditions that his ancestors had practiced for centuries, practices that had distinguished Israel as the people of God. The Gentiles were receiving the Holy Spirit quite apart from the traditional ways.

MARIANNE BLICKENSTAFF

Acts 11:1–18

It is one thing for faithful Jews who follow Jesus, like Peter and Paul, to baptize Gentiles; it is quite another for them to defy purity traditions by sitting at table with the uncircumcised.

GARY W. CHARLES

Psalm 148

Psalm 148 calls us to take our place alongside the creeping things we may call unclean, the fire that burns and destroys, and even the foreign kings and princes, leaving room for the idea that someday God, who alone is exalted, may see fit to welcome the stranger to our table and *the* Table.

MARCI AULD GLASS

THEME 2: *Love One Another*

Psalm 148

Plenty of stories in the Hebrew Bible reflect how Israel saw a divine command to vanquish their foes in order to claim their land. Even more stories in Scripture, however, speak of the ever-expanding reach of God's steadfast love and mercy.

MARCI AULD GLASS

Revelation 21:1–6

This new heaven and earth are embodied in the form of a holy city. . . . God chooses to redeem the city as the place of new life and resurrection hope. This is a compelling reminder and call to the church today, prompting the church to reinvest our resources in these populated and complex centers of human engagement.

RUTH FAITH SANTANA-GRACE

John 13:31–35

In the Gospel, Jesus' death, though imposed upon him, becomes a gift essential to the transformation of his followers into a community defined by mutual love. . . . Jesus' physical departure (in the death, resurrection, and ascension) is the necessary impetus for his disciples to form a new community based on an understanding of what Jesus said in his life and what he did in his death—the embodiment of the love command.

MARK PRICE

WHAT IS THE HOLY SPIRIT SAYING TO YOU THIS WEEK?

_____

_____

_____

_____

_____

A SPIRITUAL PRACTICE FOR THIS WEEK

Try a restaurant or takeout meal outside your comfort zone; buy a food that is new and strange to you from a grocery store; or let a friend introduce you to something you never thought you would try. Give thanks and eat, then reread Acts 11:1–18 and reflect on your experience.

First Reading

Acts 11:1–18

Then Peter began to explain it to them, step by step, saying, "I was in the city of Joppa praying, and in a trance I saw a vision. There was something like a large sheet coming down from heaven, being lowered by its four corners; and it came close to me." (vv. 4–5)

REFLECTION

The canon is replete with divine visions, and the spiritual health of God's people is a direct result of how they attend to these visions from God. . . .

. . . Surely the church should read each of these visions with caution. Taking these visions from God seriously could shake the church from trying to hinder the movement of God by its obsession with what has always been and open it up to celebrate what it can become by the power of the Holy Spirit.

GARY W. CHARLES

RESPONSE

Is there a vision that you know you would be afraid to see, of the future of the church? Is there a vision you have had already that you have been avoiding? What might the power of the Holy Spirit be calling your congregation to open itself to in this season?

PRAYER

Holy Spirit, send forth your power that we may see beyond what we thought was unclean and impossible. Amen.

Canticle

Psalm 148

Praise him, sun and moon;
    praise him, all you shining stars!
Praise him, you highest heavens,
    and you waters above the heavens!
. . . .
Praise the LORD from the earth,
    you sea monsters and all deeps,
fire and hail, snow and frost,
    stormy wind fulfilling his command! (vv. 3–4, 7–8)

REFLECTION

Humanity is adept at pretending we are kind of a big deal. Perhaps we even forget just who it was that spun the whirling planets and set the stars in their courses. The psalmist does not forget: "Let them praise the name of the LORD, for his name alone is exalted; his glory is above earth and heaven" (v. 13). Only God's name is exalted. Only God's glory is above earth and heaven. Psalm 148 is a corrective to human hubris and self-importance. We matter. We are not all that matters.

MARCI AULD GLASS

RESPONSE

Write "We matter" and "We are not all that matters" at the top of a piece of paper. Write or offer a prayer of praise to God for each.

PRAYER

Wondrous God, you created all things and you created me; teach me humility and teach me praise. Amen.

Second Reading

Revelation 21:1–6

And the one who was seated on the throne said, "See, I am making all things new." Also he said, "Write this, for these words are trustworthy and true." (v. 5)

REFLECTION

God takes what has been—the old earth—and transforms it. God does not destroy it. John's vision of the end times threads together the biblical narrative affirming the heart of a God whose goal has always been to redeem a broken relationship. The vision of a new heaven and new earth (Rev. 21:1) descending from heaven reaffirms God's commitment to redeeming creation. . . . It is in this transformed place that God will dwell with the creatures (v. 3), thereby inviting us to see ourselves as part of this vision.

RUTH FAITH SANTANA-GRACE

RESPONSE

What does it mean to you that we do not need to fear that anything will be destroyed but only transformed? What are you most afraid of losing? If you imagine yourself as part of God's transformed creation, what do you see?

PRAYER

Redeemer God, you are making all things new; help me to let go and trust in you. Amen.

Gospel

John 13:31–35

Little children, I am with you only a little longer. You will look for me; and as I said to the Jews so now I say to you, "Where I am going, you cannot come." (v. 33)

REFLECTION

The kind of love that Jesus has demonstrated and is calling his disciples to imitate ("love one another as I have loved you") is also new in the kind of love Jesus has shown to them. . . . This radical act of hospitality, the washing of his disciples' feet, demonstrates Jesus' profound love for his followers, even for those who would betray him. Jesus waits until after the foot washing to send Judas away, including Judas in the act of love Jesus shows to his disciples.

CAROLYN B. HELSEL

RESPONSE

Try to imagine yourself in the place of Jesus, washing Judas's feet. What do you think or feel? Next, imagine being Judas. What do you think or feel? What does it mean to love one another, here? What does it mean to let Jesus love us? And our enemies?

PRAYER

Risen Christ, where you have gone, we cannot come, but teach us to love one another as you love us. Amen.

Weekend Reflections

For I know that love is ultimately the only answer to mankind's problems. . . . I'm not talking about emotional bosh when I talk about love, I'm talking about a strong, demanding love. And I have seen too much hate. I've seen too much hate . . . to want to hate myself, because every time I see it, I know that it does something to their faces and their personalities and I say to myself that hate is too great a burden to bear.

MARTIN LUTHER KING JR. (1929–68),
"WHERE DO WE GO FROM HERE?"

MAKING THE CONNECTIONS

Choose one or two questions for reflection:

1. What connections have you noticed between this week's texts and other passages in Scripture?

2. What connections have you made between this week's texts and the world beyond Scripture?

3. Does either of this week's two commentary themes speak especially to your life or the life of the world around you right now?

4. What is God saying to your congregation in particular through this week's readings and commentaries?

MY CONNECTIONS

_____

_____

_____

_____

_____

_____

Sabbath Day

SCRIPTURE OF ASSURANCE

Stand in the gate of the LORD's house, and proclaim there this word, and say, Hear the word of the LORD, all you people of Judah, you that enter these gates to worship the LORD. Thus says the LORD of hosts, the God of Israel: Amend your ways and your doings, and let me dwell with you in this place. (Jeremiah 7:2–3)

WEEKLY EXAMEN

- Take a quiet moment, seek out God's presence, and pray for the guidance of the Spirit.

- Consider the past week; recall specific moments and feelings that stand out to you.

- Choose one moment or feeling for deeper examination, thanksgiving, or repentance.

- Let go, breathe deeply, and invite Christ's love to surround and fill you in preparation for the week ahead.

- End with the Lord's Prayer.

The Week Leading Up to the
Sixth Sunday of Easter

Acts 16:9–15

When [Lydia] and her household were baptized, she urged us, saying, "If you have judged me to be faithful to the Lord, come and stay at my home." And she prevailed upon us. (v. 15)

Psalm 67

Let the peoples praise you, O God;
    let all the peoples praise you. (v. 3)

Revelation 21:10; 22–22:5

Its gates will never be shut by day—and there will be no night there. People will bring into it the glory and the honor of the nations. (21:25–26)

John 14:23–29

Jesus answered him, "Those who love me will keep my word, and my Father will love them, and we will come to them and make our home with them." (v. 23)

LECTIO DIVINA

Underline a word or phrase that especially grabs your attention. Pray from that word or phrase and ask God to help you connect to its particular invitation for you this week.

Themes from This Week's Writers

THEME 1: *Hospitality That Risks and Transforms*

Acts 16:9–15

[Lydia's] hospitality is insistent and expansive, marks of those who go down into the transforming, healing waters of baptism.

GARY W. CHARLES

Revelation 21:10; 22–22:5

This is a vision of confidence and inclusion. God's abiding presence in the new city means the gates never need to be shut (21:22–27).

GREG CAREY

John 14:23–29

Jesus not only brings believers into God's house, but Jesus turns believers into a home for God.

CAROLYN B. HELSEL

THEME 2: *Do Not Let Your Hearts Be Afraid*

Acts 16:9–15

[Paul] does not stop to weigh the risks. He approaches Lydia and her people with an open heart, trusting that God will break down the boundaries.

MARIANNE BLICKENSTAFF

John 14:23–29

Jesus encourages his disciples to be at peace, to not let their hearts be troubled. This is a mysterious peace, in that Jesus distinguishes it from that of the world.

CAROLYN B. HELSEL

John 14:23–29

To those of us who wring our hands watching the evening news or weep for our children's future after they have gone to bed, Jesus reminds us that he is not leaving us alone. . . . Yes, the peace of Christ is just what we need, and just what we have.

MARK PRICE

WHAT IS THE HOLY SPIRIT SAYING TO YOU THIS WEEK?

_____

_____

_____

_____

_____

A SPIRITUAL PRACTICE FOR THIS WEEK

Make praise your spiritual discipline this week. Write the word "praise" on your daily to-do list, draw or journal your praise, and speak, pray, or sing the words "Praise God" as often as you can.

First Reading

Acts 16:9–15

On the sabbath day we went outside the gate by the river, where we supposed there was a place of prayer; and we sat down and spoke to the women who had gathered there. A certain woman named Lydia, a worshiper of God, was listening to us; she was from the city of Thyatira and a dealer in purple cloth. The Lord opened her heart to listen eagerly to what was said by Paul. (vv. 13–14)

REFLECTION

The detail that God was the one who opened Lydia's heart is an important reminder that it is God who inspires faith through the workings of the Holy Spirit. Paul and his entourage preach the good news, but the opening of hearts is God's doing. We sometimes need to be reminded of this when we talk about "our" ministry. When we become discouraged, we can remember with gratitude and trust that it is the Holy Spirit's power, not ours, that opens hearts.

MARIANNE BLICKENSTAFF

RESPONSE

What does it mean if it is God—not us—who inspires faith and opens hearts? What does this mean for your planning, successes, and failures at ministry or service in your congregation? What invitation do you hear for yourself or your congregation in this?

PRAYER

Lord God, you are doing more than I can ask or imagine in me and in spite of me; help me to let go so you can work through me to open hearts and preach good news. Amen.

Canticle

Psalm 67

May God be gracious to us and bless us
  and make his face to shine upon us,
that your way may be known upon earth,
  your saving power among all nations. (vv. 1–2)

REFLECTION

The psalm echoes the Aaronic blessing in Numbers 6:24–26 and invokes
the biblical image of the face of God. In their poetic descriptions of
God, the Psalms repeatedly speak of God's face, as if a benevolent God,
in looking at us and really seeing us in our need, will send blessing. As
Christians, we have seen that face most clearly in the body of the man
Jesus. As we are gathered for worship, the body of Christ is around
us, and we marvel to recognize in our fellow worshipers the face of a
merciful God.

GAIL RAMSHAW

RESPONSE

What is it like to imagine God's face, as Jesus or in some other way,
seeing and welcoming you? Write a description of what you envision.
Then, how do you recognize the face of God in others? Today, try to
offer this face of God yourself to the people you encounter.

PRAYER

Gracious God, bless me and make your face to shine upon me that
I may shine your love upon others. Amen.

Second Reading

Revelation 21:10; 22–22:5

I saw no temple in the city, for its temple is the Lord God the Almighty and the Lamb. And the city has no need of sun or moon to shine on it, for the glory of God is its light, and its lamp is the Lamb. (21:22–23)

REFLECTION

First, there is no physical temple in this new Jerusalem that John envisions. . . .

The significance and relevance of contemporary temples are being challenged today as many church buildings have become peripheral to the neighborhoods in which they exist. . . . This growing reality compels us to consider what to do with unsustainable buildings as we seek to embody a relevant witness of hope and mission. It is an opportunity compelling us to consider options for new and creative spaces in which to welcome believers and nonbelievers alike, places where God, not bricks, is at the center.

RUTH FAITH SANTANA-GRACE

RESPONSE

What would your church be like without a permanent building? Imagine the losses, but also the opportunities. What would end? What could continue? What might emerge? Or, if your congregation already functions without its own building, how has that affected the meaning and practice of "church" for you?

PRAYER

Lamb of God, you are our true temple and the light of the city of God; may all people and nations walk in this light. Amen.

Gospel

John 14:23–29

"But the Advocate, the Holy Spirit, whom the Father will send in my name, will teach you everything, and remind you of all that I have said to you. Peace I leave with you; my peace I give to you. I do not give to you as the world gives. Do not let your hearts be troubled, and do not let them be afraid." (vv. 26–27)

REFLECTION

The more we allow our lives to be shaped by fear, the easier it becomes to value being safe over being faithful. If, however, we presume that our lives are shaped by the promised presence of the Holy Spirit, then we will be busy fulfilling an earlier promise of Jesus: doing "the works I do and, in fact . . . greater works than these" (John 14:12). If we love Jesus most—even more than those things that make us feel safe and comfortable—then we will keep his commandments (v. 15).

MARK PRICE

RESPONSE

What are some ways your life is shaped by your fears? What does it look in your context to value "being safe over being faithful"? What would it look like for you or your community to trust the Holy Spirit as your safety? What does it mean to love Jesus more than what feels safe and comfortable?

PRAYER

Risen Jesus, give me your peace and help me not to be troubled or afraid. Amen.

Weekend Reflections

FURTHER CONNECTION

Knowing the risk of giving, now try the even greater risk of receiving. Learn to be a generous receiver. Somebody wants to love you; think of that. Let down the barriers, open the doors, remove the inhibitions, let him in. Somebody less worthy of you wants you to accept him or her. Try it. Open your hand to receive what someone else is prepared to give to you. The old spiritual fathers used to say that we get so little from God because we are prepared to accept so little from God. Open your hands that you may be prepared to receive what is there for you. Open your hands, and open your hearts to the abundance that is waiting to fill them both.

PETER J. GOMES (1942–2011), *STRENGTH FOR THE JOURNEY*

MAKING THE CONNECTIONS

Choose one or two questions for reflection:

1. What connections have you noticed between this week's texts and other passages in Scripture?

2. What connections have you made between this week's texts and the world beyond Scripture?

3. Does either of this week's two commentary themes speak especially to your life or the life of the world around you right now?

4. What is God saying to your congregation in particular through this week's readings and commentaries?

MY CONNECTIONS

_____

_____

_____

_____

_____

Sabbath Day

SCRIPTURE OF ASSURANCE

He asked, "Do you understand what you are reading?" He replied, "How can I, unless someone guides me?" And he invited Philip to get in and sit beside him. (Acts 8:30b–31)

WEEKLY EXAMEN

- Take a quiet moment, seek out God's presence, and pray for the guidance of the Spirit.

- Consider the past week; recall specific moments and feelings that stand out to you.

- Choose one moment or feeling for deeper examination, thanksgiving, or repentance.

- Let go, breathe deeply, and invite Christ's love to surround and fill you in preparation for the week ahead.

- End with the Lord's Prayer.

Ascension of the Lord

Acts 1:1–11

But you will receive power when the Holy Spirit has come upon you; and you will be my witnesses in Jerusalem, in all Judea and Samaria, and to the ends of the earth. (v. 8)

Psalm 47 and Psalm 93

Sing praises to God, sing praises;
    sing praises to our King, sing praises. (47:6)
The LORD is king, he is robed in majesty;
    the LORD is robed, he is girded with strength. (93:1a)

Ephesians 1:15–23

And he has put all things under his feet and has made him the head over all things for the church, which is his body, the fullness of him who fills all in all. (vv. 22–23)

Luke 24:44–53

While he was blessing them, he withdrew from them and was carried up into heaven. And they worshiped him, and returned to Jerusalem with great joy; and they were continually in the temple blessing God. (vv. 51–53)

REFLECTIONS

Acts 1:1–11

Though power is a basic necessity not only for life but also for justice, its negative connotations may discourage the preacher from engaging this centerpiece of good news in the text. Power is coming, Jesus tells the church—Holy Spirit power. This is good news to a church called to follow Jesus into the fray. The world does not have a monopoly on power. God traffics in it as well.

ANDREW FOSTER CONNORS

Psalm 47 or Psalm 93

In recent decades, the metaphor of divine kingship has indeed been moderated, surrounded by other metaphors, but it is here on Ascension Day, when we praise Christ enthroned as the sovereign power of our lives. Americans claim the populace as sovereign; popular culture claims the self to be sovereign; Christians proclaim Christ as sovereign.

GAIL RAMSHAW

Ephesians 1:15–23

[Paul's] exhortations are to a subversive way of life that is anything but triumphant. God triumphs over the evil powers corrupting God's good world in the death of Christ, which is paradoxical: God wins by losing. Paul experiences Christ's triumph by preaching as a shamed prisoner (3:2–13).

TIMOTHY GOMBIS

Luke 24:44–53

Though Jesus physically withdraws from his followers (24:51), these dramatic actions attending his ascension certify a persisting spiritual connection between Lord and disciples, God and people, heaven and earth, rooted in practices of joyous worship and gracious blessing.

F. SCOTT SPENCER

RESPONSE

Choose one of these four quotes that particularly gets your attention and write or reflect on how God might be speaking to you, to your experience or questions about Christ's resurrection or ascension, or to this time in your life.

PRAYER

O Jesus Christ, you have gone from the earth but are with me and go before me. Fill me with your power and blessing that I might be your witness and disciple. Amen.

The Week Leading Up to the
Seventh Sunday of Easter

Acts 16:16–34

The jailer called for lights, and rushing in, he fell down trembling before Paul and Silas. Then he brought them outside and said, "Sirs, what must I do to be saved?" They answered, "Believe on the Lord Jesus, and you will be saved, you and your household." (vv. 29–31)

Psalm 97

Light dawns for the righteous,
 and joy for the upright in heart.
Rejoice in the Lord, O you righteous,
 and give thanks to his holy name! (vv. 11–12)

Revelation 22:12–14, 16–17, 20–21

It is I, Jesus, who sent my angel to you with this testimony for the churches. I am the root and the descendant of David, the bright morning star. (v. 16)

John 17:20–26

"Righteous Father, the world does not know you, but I know you; and these know that you have sent me. I made your name known to them, and I will make it known, so that the love with which you have loved me may be in them, and I in them." (vv. 25–26)

LECTIO DIVINA

Underline a word or phrase that especially grabs your attention. Pray from that word or phrase and ask God to help you connect to its particular invitation for you this week.

Themes from This Week's Writers

THEME 1: *God's Kingdom vs. the Kingdom of Empire*

Acts 16:16–34

The gospel makes clear the folly of imperial systems. The gospel does not tear down empires; it merely shows how empires are already teetering at the edge of destruction.

ERIC D. BARRETO

Acts 16:16–34

We are encouraged to get in trouble with the world, trusting that God will magnify our imperfect actions toward more perfect ends. In fact, every time disciples in the book of Acts challenge powers and suffer as a result, the church seems to add to its numbers.

ANDREW FOSTER CONNORS

Revelation 22:12–14, 16–17, 20–21

The resurrection of Christ is, by definition, an apocalyptic event. . . . It meant that Caesar was not Lord and that the Roman culture of excess, domination, and idolatry was doomed and, therefore, was not to be imitated by the churches but, on the contrary, was to be resisted.

SHARYN DOWD

THEME 2: *We Are God's Extended Family*

Acts 16:16–34

The power of Jesus' presence is such that entire households are drawn into God's grace by the Spirit. Faith in Luke–Acts is far more communal and collective than it is individualistic.

ERIC D. BARRETO

John 17:20–26

The extended family of God is ever extending, ever longing, ever praying for newly enlightened, beloved, and believing members.

F. SCOTT SPENCER

John 17:20–26

The passage invites us into a lived experience of the tenderness of God and deeper communion with the church that rests in the mutual knowledge and love between God and Jesus.

PHILIP BROWNING HELSEL

WHAT IS THE HOLY SPIRIT SAYING TO YOU THIS WEEK?

_____

_____

_____

_____

_____

A SPIRITUAL PRACTICE FOR THIS WEEK

Do some research and find out what prison is closest to your home. Learn more: Is it publicly or privately operated? How many people live and work there? This week, pray for this prison and its prisoners, staff, and warden. Consider writing a letter to your legislator on its behalf.

First Reading

Acts 16:16–34

While she followed Paul and us, she would cry out, "These men are slaves of the Most High God, who proclaim to you a way of salvation." She kept doing this for many days. But Paul, very much annoyed, turned and said to the spirit, "I order you in the name of Jesus Christ to come out of her." And it came out that very hour. (vv. 17–18)

REFLECTION

Paul's impulsive act is troubling and exciting. It is troubling to concede the church can be rash in its exercise of power with less than pure motivations. It is also exciting to see what God seems to do with this kind of power, even when unleashed in less than strategic ways. . . .

. . . Public conflict is the arena where the gospel thrives the most, where powers and principalities are exposed for their malicious intent or hypocrisy, thereby setting the stage for God's alternative. The church that gets itself in trouble with powerful forces finds the gospel message much easier to preach.

ANDREW FOSTER CONNORS

RESPONSE

What is your comfort level with public conflict? What about your congregation's comfort level? What kind of conflict might God be calling you or your congregation to engage as part of preaching the gospel?

PRAYER

God of power, teach me and my congregation to be troublemakers in your name, that through conflict we may preach the gospel. Amen.

Canticle

Psalm 97

All worshipers of images are put to shame,
    those who make their boast in worthless idols;
    all gods bow down before him.
. . . .
For you, O Lord, are most high over all the earth;
    you are exalted far above all gods. (vv. 7, 9)

REFLECTION

Despite our theological claim of monotheism, many Christians find
themselves willing to grant that other deities, or at least other names
of the unknowable divine, are quite alive, but that as Christians, we
are called to proclaim the triune God as the one God over all. What is
the meaning in our mouths in Sunday worship of the psalmist's talk of
"other gods"? Do we think of these gods as genuine objects of devotion,
or merely as "worthless idols" (v. 7)?

GAIL RAMSHAW

RESPONSE

Do you believe in "other names of the unknowable divine"? Had you
noticed before that Scripture mentions other gods? What does it mean
to you to speak these words in worship? Or to consider "idols" as other
objects of human worship—what would you include in that list?

PRAYER

Holy One, you are no image or idol, but the God beyond God; teach us
to find ourselves in your mystery and love. Amen.

Second Reading

Revelation 22:12–14, 16–17, 20–21

"See, I am coming soon; my reward is with me, to repay according to everyone's work. I am the Alpha and the Omega, the first and the last, the beginning and the end." (vv. 12–13)

REFLECTION

At the coming day of God's renewal of creation, there will indeed be a judgment when God rewards everyone according to their work—that is, according to the life they have lived. . . .

It is helpful to remind people that God is not looking for high performers or exceptionally heroic acts. Genuine Christian conduct consists in confessing sin, giving thanks to God for all things in Christ, and participating in the church in ways that take advantage of opportunities to serve and offer hospitality to the needy.

TIMOTHY GOMBIS

RESPONSE

What is it like to consider God rewarding us but also holding us accountable for our life? How might it feel scary? How might it feel freeing or redemptive? How does this list of "genuine Christian conduct" resonate with you? How might you add to or edit it?

PRAYER

Loving Jesus, you are my redeemer and my judge; give me courage to face my sins and to grow in your love. Amen.

Gospel

John 17:20–26

"The glory that you have given me I have given them, so that they may be one, as we are one, I in them and you in me, that they may become completely one, so that the world may know that you have sent me and have loved them even as you have loved me." (vv. 22–23)

REFLECTION

The breathtaking scope of Jesus' prayer for unity stretches in concentric circles as wide as the universe and as long as eternity, with the Father-Son bond of love forming both the dynamic core and the holistic circumference of this cosmic community . . .

. . . whom Jesus has faithfully made known to his disciples . . . in an invitational posture, welcoming, incorporating, "adopting" his believing "friends" (see 15:12–15) into the divine family circle, where their loving familiarity with the Father, Son, and one another may grow fuller and deeper.

F. SCOTT SPENCER

RESPONSE

Draw a picture that represents "the divine family circle," of the Trinity, the cosmos, and all people, as you imagine it. Incorporate some of the words of the Scripture passage, or the quote above, as you see fit. Pray as you draw and write.

PRAYER

Holy Trinity, show us how to be one as you are one, and to love one another as you have loved us. Amen.

Weekend Reflections

FURTHER CONNECTION

A sudden gale comes toward me from heaven,
and a melody drifts from the bamboo flute, plunging the world in gloom.
The black chrysanthemum opens its pure heart at the approach of night,
and the plum blossom, iron-boned in the frost, goes into bloom.

LIN ZHAO (1932–68), "BLOOD POEM ON SHIRT." ZHAO, A CHRISTIAN
CHINESE DISSIDENT IMPRISONED DURING THE CULTURAL
REVOLUTION, WROTE THIS POEM IN HER OWN BLOOD ON A
SHIRT BECAUSE SHE HAD NO OTHER WRITING MATERIALS.
AFTER EIGHT YEARS IN PRISON, SHE WAS EXECUTED.

MAKING THE CONNECTIONS

Choose one or two questions for reflection:

1. What connections have you noticed between this week's texts and other passages in Scripture?

2. What connections have you made between this week's texts and the world beyond Scripture?

3. Does either of this week's two commentary themes speak especially to your life or the life of the world around you right now?

4. What is God saying to your congregation in particular through this week's readings and commentaries?

_____

_____

_____

_____

_____

Sabbath Day

SCRIPTURE OF ASSURANCE

For no one can lay any foundation other than the one that has been laid; that foundation is Jesus Christ. (1 Corinthians 3:11)

WEEKLY EXAMEN

- Take a quiet moment, seek out God's presence, and pray for the guidance of the Spirit.

- Consider the past week; recall specific moments and feelings that stand out to you.

- Choose one moment or feeling for deeper examination, thanksgiving, or repentance.

- Let go, breathe deeply, and invite Christ's love to surround and fill you in preparation for the week ahead.

- End with the Lord's Prayer.

The Week Leading Up to the
Day of Pentecost

Genesis 11:1–9

Now the whole earth had one language and the same words. (v. 1)

Acts 2:1–21

Divided tongues, as of fire, appeared among them, and a tongue rested on each of them. All of them were filled with the Holy Spirit and began to speak in other languages, as the Spirit gave them ability. (vv. 3–4)

Romans 8:14–17

For all who are led by the Spirit of God are children of God. For you did not receive a spirit of slavery to fall back into fear, but you have received a spirit of adoption. (vv. 14–15a)

John 14:8–17 (25–27)

"But the Advocate, the Holy Spirit, whom the Father will send in my name, will teach you everything, and remind you of all that I have said to you." (v. 26)

LECTIO DIVINA

Underline a word or phrase that especially grabs your attention. Pray from that word or phrase and ask God to help you connect to its particular invitation for you this week.

Themes from This Week's Writers

THEME 1: *Diversity and Unity in Christ*

Genesis 11:1–9

Just as, in the tower of Babel, dialectical tensions are perceived of positive and negative renderings of both unity and diversity, so these same tensions are echoed in the story of Pentecost. Pentecost is not a story of diversity without difficulty. . . . Pentecost is not a story of unity without deep dislocation.

LEANNE VAN DYK

Acts 2:1–21

Jesus' ministry was wide-ranging and inclusive, as Luke's Gospel makes particularly clear with its attention to shepherds, foreigners, and even Roman soldiers who recognize Jesus' importance and power. Now those socially and economically disparate folk will come together to proclaim Christ crucified and risen.

SANDRA HACK POLASKI

Acts 2:1–21

The body of Christ is called to disrupt suspicion of difference by centering the good news in a way that prompts us to extend toward, not retreat from, people who are unlike ourselves.

STEPHANIE M. CRUMPTON

THEME 2: *The Holy Spirit*

Psalm 104:24–34, 35b

The Hebrew word of note here is *ruah*, which can be rendered in English as "spirit," "breath," or "wind." Recall that in Genesis 1:2, God's *ruah* swept over the waters of chaos: your Bible translation may cast this as spirit, or wind, or breath. Also, in this psalm, contemporary translations differ: God both takes away and sends forth either the divine spirit or breath.

GAIL RAMSHAW

Romans 8:14–17

The Spirit functions to assist the individual believer; for example, "the Spirit helps us in our weakness" by interceding for us (v. 26), but the primary role of the Spirit is the building up of the church, the body of Christ.

SANDRA HACK POLASKI

John 14:8–17 (25–27)

If they love him, they should demonstrate the same care, compassion, and concern to the people of God that he first showed them. . . . [Jesus] knows they are unable to do it on their own. He promises to send the Advocate who will give them the power to live out the faith with which they have been entrusted.

STEPHANIE M. CRUMPTON

WHAT IS THE HOLY SPIRIT SAYING TO YOU THIS WEEK?

_____

_____

_____

_____

_____

A SPIRITUAL PRACTICE FOR THIS WEEK

Celebrate Pentecost: wear red, buy or make wind chimes, fly a kite, blow bubbles, toast with a bubbly drink, sit with friends around a fire, learn to say "Peace be with you" in a new language, draw flames or doves in chalk on a sidewalk, driveway, or paper taped to your fridge.

First Reading

Genesis 11:1–9

So the LORD scattered them abroad from there over the face of all the earth, and they left off building the city. Therefore it was called Babel, because there the LORD confused the language of all the earth; and from there the LORD scattered them abroad over the face of all the earth. (vv. 8–9)

REFLECTION

Pentecost does not reverse the consequences of the tower, retreating to some imagined monolingual, monocultural ideal. Rather, ethnic, linguistic, and cultural differences are preserved, while the Holy Spirit serves, in Barreto's words, as a "binding agent," enabling each person to be understood in his or her own native tongue.[1] In the Babel account, fear is the binding agent that drives the building projects: fear of dispersal, of loss, of living with otherness. Both the Babel and the Pentecost accounts emphasize the power of human unity, without expecting human sameness, sending people out into the world to forge connections with those who are different from themselves.

CAMERON B. R. HOWARD

RESPONSE

What are ways—subtle or not—that people in your community expect one another to be "the same"? What would it look like for you to feel "understood in your own native tongue"? What is the good news of this gift of the Spirit—unity despite our differences—and how is it different from unity through sameness?

PRAYER

O God, even as we are scattered over the face of the earth you have made us each in your image; continue to draw us together by your Spirit. Amen.

1. Eric D. Barreto, "Negotiating Difference: Theology and Ethnicity in the Acts of the Apostles," *Word & World* 31, no. 2 (2011): 129–37.

Canticle

Psalm 104:24–34, 35b

When you hide your face, they are dismayed;
  when you take away their breath, they die
  and return to their dust.
When you send forth your spirit, they are created;
  and you renew the face of the ground. (vv. 29–30)

REFLECTION

God gives breath to all (v. 29), and when that breath is taken away, we revert to dust. As Christian funeral rites say it: "earth to earth, dust to dust." We are not little angels running around, but dust creatures of God's handiwork. In most translations of this psalm, verse 30 states that God sends forth the divine Spirit, and so all creatures are created. We in the church are to think of even the church as one of those creations, by which the very face of the ground is to be renewed.

GAIL RAMSHAW

RESPONSE

What does it mean to you to be created both of dust and of the Spirit? Does the gift of your breath feel linked to God's gift of the Holy Spirit? Stop and breathe with mindfulness for a while today and consider this connection.

PRAYER

Living God, send forth your Spirit and renew me, a creature of dust, and your church to serve your people. Amen.

Second Reading

Acts 2:1–21

And at this sound the crowd gathered and was bewildered, because each one heard them speaking in the native language of each. Amazed and astonished, they asked, "Are not all these who are speaking Galileans? And how is it that we hear, each of us, in our own native language?" (vv. 6–8)

REFLECTION

They could hear the good news of God for themselves. No one had to abandon the culture that gave them an identity in order to hear from God. God's word came that day in a way that expressed God's deep affirmation of diversity as a key ingredient in unity.

. . . In this moment it is diversity, not homogeneity, that brings this community of believers together. Difference is no longer an excuse for division or a justification for disparity.

STEPHANIE M. CRUMPTON

RESPONSE

Have you ever felt you had to abandon your culture to be part of a church or worship service? What could it mean that diversity is "a key ingredient in unity" for the work of God? How do you see this happening in your own community? Or thwarted?

PRAYER

Holy Spirit, teach us how to listen to one another, each in our own language, that we may hear unity in our diversity. Amen.

Gospel

John 14:8–17 (25–27)

And I will ask the Father, and he will give you another Advocate, to be with you forever. This is the Spirit of truth, whom the world cannot receive, because it neither sees him nor knows him. You know him, because he abides with you, and he will be in you. (vv. 16–17)

REFLECTION

The Greek word translated as "Spirit" and transliterated as *pneuma* also means "wind" or "breath" and points toward the *nature* of the Spirit: omnipresent and uncontrollable; felt or sensed rather than seen; inextricably connected with life itself. (Ancient Greek did not use initial capitals to distinguish between "Spirit" and "spirit."[2]) Jesus' description of the Spirit as Paraclete points to a *functional* definition, what the Spirit *does*: teach, help, advocate, intercede, and so on. Because the Paraclete is the Spirit of truth, it empowers the disciples to speak and act truthfully, even in the midst of opposition, temptation, and suffering.

SANDRA HACK POLASKI

RESPONSE

How do you feel the Spirit at work in your own congregation? In your own life? How might the Spirit be trying to push or surprise you in this time or season?

PRAYER

Holy Spirit, abide with me and be my comforter and advocate; teach me to speak the truth, to face opposition and suffering, and to sense your breath in all of life and creation. Amen.

---

2. During the time of composition of the New Testament, Greek was written in all capital letters (uncials), without punctuation or spaces (LIKETHIS). Around the end of the ninth century, scribes began using lower-case (minuscule) letters, and did not mark proper nouns with initial capitals.

Weekend Reflections

FURTHER CONNECTION

The conventional wisdom of the Tower of Babel story is that the collapse was a misfortune. That it was the distraction, or the weight of many languages that precipitated the tower's failed architecture. That one monolithic language would have expedited the building and heaven would have been reached. Whose heaven, she wonders? And what kind? Perhaps the achievement of Paradise was premature, a little hasty if no one could take the time to understand other languages, other views, other narratives period. Had they, the heaven they imagined might have been found at their feet. Complicated, demanding, yes, but a view of heaven as life; not heaven as post-life.

TONI MORRISON (1931–2019), NOBEL LECTURE

MAKING THE CONNECTIONS

Choose one or two questions for reflection:

1. What connections have you noticed between this week's texts and other passages in Scripture?

2. What connections have you made between this week's texts and the world beyond Scripture?

3. Does either of this week's two commentary themes speak especially to your life or the life of the world around you right now?

4. What is God saying to your congregation in particular through this week's readings and commentaries?

_____

_____

_____

_____

_____

_____

Sabbath Day

SCRIPTURE OF ASSURANCE

God said to me: O mortal, stand up on your feet, and I will speak with you. And when God spoke to me, a spirit entered into me and set me on my feet; and I heard God speaking to me. (Ezekiel 2:1–2)

WEEKLY EXAMEN

- Take a quiet moment, seek out God's presence, and pray for the guidance of the Spirit.

- Consider the past week; recall specific moments and feelings that stand out to you.

- Choose one moment or feeling for deeper examination, thanksgiving, or repentance.

- Let go, breathe deeply, and invite Christ's love to surround and fill you in preparation for the week ahead.

- End with the Lord's Prayer.

The Week Leading Up to
Trinity Sunday

Proverbs 8:1–4, 22–31

Does not wisdom call,
  and does not understanding raise her voice?

. . . .

The Lord created me at the beginning of his work,
  the first of his acts of long ago. (vv. 1, 22)

Psalm 8

When I look at your heavens, the work of your fingers,
  the moon and the stars that you have established;
what are human beings that you are mindful of them,
  mortals that you care for them? (vv. 3–4)

Romans 5:1–5

Therefore, since we are justified by faith, we have peace with God through
our Lord Jesus Christ, through whom we have obtained access to this grace
in which we stand; and we boast in our hope of sharing the glory of God.
(vv. 1–2)

John 16:12–15

"I still have many things to say to you, but you cannot bear them now." (v.
12)

LECTIO DIVINA

Underline a word or phrase that especially grabs your attention. Pray
from that word or phrase and ask God to help you connect to its
particular invitation for you this week.

Themes from This Week's Writers

THEME 1: *Nature of the Trinity*

Psalm 8

While Romans 5:1–5 points to God's reconciling work with humanity through Jesus Christ, and John 16:12–15 explains the work of the Holy Spirit as the Advocate, Psalm 8 connects to the first reading by praising God for the creation of all the creatures in the world, particularly human beings.

EUNJOO MARY KIM

Romans 5:1–5

Whatever Paul's language of God, Jesus Christ, Holy Spirit offers us on Trinity Sunday is not just about the internal doxology of the mysterious Godhead. It is also about the mystery of human communities, human realities of suffering, and gifts to humans of hope.

DAVID SCHNASA JACOBSEN

John 16:12–15

Perhaps we would best see this small reading from John 16 as one that offers a glimpse, a few small clues for grasping the triune nature of God. . . . Maybe what we find in this text is not an explanation of the Trinity, but a kind of recapitulation of the story the church year has been telling.

GEORGE R. HUNSBERGER

THEME 2: *Wonder and Joy in the Triune God*

Proverbs 8:1–4, 22–31

Pastoral leaders who name and nurture that deep disposition of delight and wonder can then also connect it to faithful action in the world. Wonder and witness are twin energies in the life of faith, both born of Wisdom who rejoices daily at the side of God.

LEANNE VAN DYK

Psalm 8

A reflection of Wisdom's joy and delight in God's work of creation can be heard in Psalm 8, which is the first hymn of praise in the book of Psalms.

EUNJOO MARY KIM

John 16:12–15

Perhaps Trinity Sunday can serve, positioned as it is in the church year just after Pentecost Sunday, to reprise the annual rhythm of advent/incarnation, cross/resurrection, and ascension/Pentecost, and fill us with wonder at the magnificence of the triune God's astounding action for the redemption of the world.

GEORGE R. HUNSBERGER

WHAT IS THE HOLY SPIRIT SAYING TO YOU THIS WEEK?

_____

_____

_____

_____

_____

A SPIRITUAL PRACTICE FOR THIS WEEK

Go out and sit in nature—or anywhere you can see some night sky—and read aloud either Psalm 8 or Proverbs 8:22–31. How do these words sound to you in this location? What does the passage seem to say to you about the Trinity?

First Reading

Proverbs 8:1–4, 22–31

When he established the heavens, I was there,
    when he drew a circle on the face of the deep,

. . . .

    then I was beside him, like a master worker;
and I was daily his delight,
    rejoicing before him always,
rejoicing in his inhabited world
    and delighting in the human race. (vv. 27, 30–31)

REFLECTION

While God created the earth, Wisdom was God's joyful companion.
Where the NRSV uses "master worker" in verse 30, an alternative (and,
in my evaluation, better) translation is "child." In other words, the
poem imagines the first take-your-daughter-to-work day, when God is
busy setting limits for the sea, and Wisdom is trailing along as a happy
observer, "rejoicing in his inhabited world and delighting in the human
race" (v. 31). To walk in the straight and righteous paths of Wisdom,
then, is to connect with this same primal joy.

CAMERON B. R. HOWARD

RESPONSE

Reflect on what it means for us that God created the world with joy.
What is the relationship of wisdom and joy, do you think? What about
in your own life?

PRAYER

God of Wisdom, you rejoice in all you have made; teach me to find joy
in your world, to seek wisdom in creation, and to delight in humankind.
Amen.

Canticle

Yet you have made them a little lower than God,
    and crowned them with glory and honor.
You have given them dominion over the works of your hands;
    you have put all things under their feet. (vv. 5–6)

REFLECTION

The poem says that the essential reason for us to praise God is that God
has created and cares for human beings. . . .

. . . [But how, when] not every human being is regarded as being "a
little lower than God" and crowned with "glory and honor"? . . .

Psalm 8, therefore, leads us to worship God the creator with joy and
delight in humility. It helps us remember who we are and what we are
required to do as God's precious creatures, and it invites us to praise
God for the continuous work of creation and recreation of all the world.

EUNJOO MARY KIM

RESPONSE

What does being "a little lower than God" as a human being mean to
you? What is the joy? What is the responsibility? How could praise
increase your humility? What about your accountability?

PRAYER

Holy Trinity, teach me joy and humility as a creature of your world and
a steward of the work of your hands. Amen.

Second Reading

Romans 5:1–5

And not only that, but we also boast in our sufferings, knowing that suffering produces endurance, and endurance produces character, and character produces hope, and hope does not disappoint us, because God's love has been poured into our hearts through the Holy Spirit that has been given to us. (vv. 3–5)

REFLECTION

Romans 5 bears only indirect witness to a way of thinking about God as Father, Son, and Holy Spirit. Yet at the same time, what are pictured here in starker relief are the relationships between God, Christ, and Holy Spirit, and the corresponding relationships in the church at Rome, to whom Paul writes. . . . These relational tensions and possibilities are what we should best juxtapose with the curious language of God, Jesus Christ, and Holy Spirit, . . . as close as first-century Paul gets to anything Trinitarian in Romans 5:1–5.

DAVID SCHNASA JACOBSEN

RESPONSE

What is your relationship to each of the persons of the Trinity? What relationships, past or present, with other groups or communities might be an influence on your relationship with the three persons of God?

PRAYER

Holy Trinity, your love has been poured into my heart through the Holy Spirit; help me to find a hope in suffering which will not disappoint me. Amen.

Gospel

John 16:12–15

"[The Spirit] will glorify me, because he will take what is mine and declare it to you. All that the Father has is mine. For this reason I said that he will take what is mine and declare it to you." (vv. 14–15)

REFLECTION

Jesus speaks about the Father as one other than himself, and likewise about the Spirit. Yet it is clear that the Father's things (his will, actions, and purposes . . .) have been given to Jesus, and the . . . Spirit will declare them to us, even after Jesus is no longer physically present to do so. What is made certain is that the three speak and act in the same vein, toward the same ends. . . .

Of course, that also leaves a lot unsaid. It takes more than an excerpt like this for the fullness of the doctrine to flower into view and settle into the church's consciousness.

GEORGE R. HUNSBERGER

RESPONSE

The Trinity is a mystery but that does not stop us from trying to explain it. Even Jesus is hard to follow here. In what ways do you long for certainty when it comes to theological terms and the nature of God? In what ways do you long for mystery, to leave things "unsaid"?

PRAYER

Holy Trinity, guide me into your truth and the things that are to come, that I may behold your mystery. Amen.

Weekend Reflections

FURTHER CONNECTION

It is commonly said that the Trinity is a mystery. And it certainly is. . . .
But it is not a mystery veiled in darkness in which we can only grope
and guess. It is a mystery in which we are given to understand that we
will never know all there is of God. . . . It is not a mystery that keeps
us in the dark, but a mystery in which we are taken by the hand and
gradually led into the light.

EUGENE PETERSON (1932–2018),
CHRIST PLAYS IN TEN THOUSAND PLACES

MAKING THE CONNECTIONS

Choose one or two questions for reflection:

1. What connections have you noticed between this week's texts and
   other passages in Scripture?

2. What connections have you made between this week's texts and the
   world beyond Scripture?

3. Does either of this week's two commentary themes speak especially
   to your life or the life of the world around you right now?

4. What is God saying to your congregation in particular through this
   week's readings and commentaries?

_____

_____

_____

_____

_____

_____

Sabbath Day

SCRIPTURE OF ASSURANCE

Do not worry about anything, but in everything by prayer and supplication with thanksgiving let your requests be made known to God. (Philippians 4:6)

WEEKLY EXAMEN

- Take a quiet moment, seek out God's presence, and pray for the guidance of the Spirit.

- Consider the past week; recall specific moments and feelings that stand out to you.

- Choose one moment or feeling for deeper examination, thanksgiving, or repentance.

- Let go, breathe deeply, and invite Christ's love to surround and fill you in preparation for the week ahead.

- End with the Lord's Prayer.

The Week Leading Up to
Proper 3

(Sunday between May 22 and May 28)

Isaiah 55:10–13

Instead of the thorn shall come up the cypress;
   instead of the brier shall come up the myrtle;
and it shall be to the LORD for a memorial,
   for an everlasting sign that shall not be cut off. (v. 13)

Psalm 92:1–4, 12–15

The LORD is upright;
   he is my rock, and there is no unrighteousness in him. (v. 15b)

1 Corinthians 15:51–58

Listen, I will tell you a mystery! We will not all die, but we will all be changed, in a moment, in the twinkling of an eye, at the last trumpet. For the trumpet will sound, and the dead will be raised imperishable, and we will be changed. (vv. 51–52)

Luke 6:39–49

"But the one who hears and does not act is like a man who built a house on the ground without a foundation. When the river burst against it, immediately it fell, and great was the ruin of that house." (v. 49)

LECTIO DIVINA

Underline a word or phrase that especially grabs your attention. Pray from that word or phrase and ask God to help you connect to its particular invitation for you this week.

Themes from This Week's Writers

THEME 1: *Build Your House on Rock*

Psalm 92:1–4, 12–15

The last strophe (vv. 12–15) reemphasizes that the righteous flourish like palm trees and the cedars of Lebanon, for God, who is upright, stands for them. The song ends with the praise of God as the rock of the righteous.

EUNJOO MARY KIM

Luke 6:39–49

When the inevitable floods come, when the inevitable troubles befall those who hear Jesus in the first century or in the twenty-first, those who have heard and followed will find their lives hold strong.

DAVID L. BARTLETT

Luke 6:39–49

These narratives caution against blind self-righteousness, separation of being from doing, and the catastrophe of building on a foundation other than Jesus' words and actions.

WM. LOYD ALLEN

THEME 2: *Transformation and Flourishing*

Isaiah 55:10–13

The Word, like rain, gives life amid a world broken in sin and injustice. The Word brings forth shade trees rather than brambles. The divine Word comes into creation to bring the full flourishing of creation. This flourishing itself, however, finds its ultimate end in God.

JOHN W. WRIGHT

1 Corinthians 15:51–58

The fact that our individual bodies are not shucked off and thrown away at the end of time illustrates something profound about God's love of our material world, which provides fodder for a fertile sermon topic on ecojustice and a divine desire for the salvation of our beautiful planet as well.

SUZANNE WOOLSTON BOSSERT

1 Corinthians 15:51–58

Paul's teaching on the mystery of the resurrection serves as a reminder to the church of Corinth and today of the great transformation and flourishing God has promised through the resurrection that will tie us all together yesterday, today, and forevermore.

BRIDGETT A. GREEN

WHAT IS THE HOLY SPIRIT SAYING TO YOU THIS WEEK?

_____

_____

_____

_____

_____

A SPIRITUAL PRACTICE FOR THIS WEEK

Write out Luke 6:41 on three small pieces of paper; keep one in your shoe and tape two to surfaces you often see (i.e., mirror, fridge, screens). Try to notice when you see a "speck" in another person and pray over your own "logs," with sincerity and, as needed, humor.

First Reading

Isaiah 55:10–13

So shall my word be that goes out from my mouth;
   it shall not return to me empty,
but it shall accomplish that which I purpose,
   and succeed in the thing for which I sent it. (v. 11)

REFLECTION

The Word, like rain, gives life amid a world broken in sin and injustice.
The Word brings forth shade trees rather than brambles. The divine
Word comes into creation to bring the full flourishing of creation. This
flourishing itself, however, finds its ultimate end in God. The divine
Word returns into the ultimate mystery of the divine mouth from which
it came forth.
   . . . This witness, the result of the coming of the Word of God, stands
forever and ever, a sign that God has not left us to ourselves.

JOHN W. WRIGHT

RESPONSE

How has God's Word brought you life and flourishing, lately? What
word from God are you still longing for? Spend some time with God
reflecting on this, offering thanksgiving or expressing longing.

PRAYER

O God, send forth your Word to me and all your people, that we may
accomplish your purpose for us. Amen.

Canticle

Psalm 92:1–4, 12–15

It is good to give thanks to the LORD,
  to sing praises to your name, O Most High;
to declare your steadfast love in the morning,
  and your faithfulness by night. (vv. 1–2)

REFLECTION

In this political and cultural situation, the observance of the Sabbath was a way of seeking God; it was a way to renew the identity of the Judeo-Babylonian community by remembering what God had done for them and hoping that God would have them return home. . . .
  . . . According to Psalm 92, the Sabbath day is not simply a weekly cycle of abstaining from work; it is the day of renewing the identity of believers by remembering the promise of the fulfillment of God's righteousness.

EUNJOO MARY KIM

RESPONSE

What about your identity in God needs to be renewed in this season of your life? Would observing some sort of practice of Sabbath help you to seek this? How might a practice of Sabbath, otherwise, allow you a way to seek and remember God more intentionally and regularly?

PRAYER

O Most High, it is good to declare your steadfast love in the morning and your faithfulness at night. Amen.

Second Reading

1 Corinthians 15:51–58

But thanks be to God, who gives us the victory through our Lord Jesus Christ. Therefore, my beloved, be steadfast, immovable, always excelling in the work of the Lord, because you know that in the Lord your labor is not in vain. (vv. 57–58)

REFLECTION

Are we modern Christians also afflicted at times by an inertia that comes from thinking that this earthly life is all there is (resurrection as metaphor), or that we are already saved though grace, end of story? . . . It is possible that many modern Christian communities today suffer from an *under*realized eschatology, focusing primarily on the present without much thought of something more. . . . This is the critical teaching that will help us live out a perfectly balanced eschatology— living fully in the present moment without discouragement because we are always moving onward toward a magnificent future.

SUZANNE WOOLSTON BOSSERT

RESPONSE

"Eschatology" is an intimidating word, but what we believe about the future defines our present. What does it mean to you to hear that, in Christ, we are promised a "magnificent future"? That death is not the end? That your present labors, by faith, are not in vain?

PRAYER

Thanks be to you, loving God, for the promise of a future in Christ, that my hope and labor will not be in vain. Amen.

Gospel

Luke 6:39–49

"No good tree bears bad fruit, nor again does a bad tree bear good fruit; for each tree is known by its own fruit. Figs are not gathered from thorns, nor are grapes picked from a bramble bush. The good person out of the good treasure of the heart produces good, and the evil person out of evil treasure produces evil; for it is out of the abundance of the heart that the mouth speaks." (vv. 43–45)

REFLECTION

In addition to comparing people to builders, in Luke 6:43–45, Jesus compares people to trees; good trees bear good fruit, evil trees evil fruit. . . . If you are seeking to be faithful, look to your integrity, your faithfulness, your trust in God. Good fruits will flow from good lives.

However, if you have noticed recently that you seem to sow discord, unhappiness, or thorns wherever you go, it may be time for radical tree surgery. . . .

. . . Put negatively, Jesus notices in Luke that sometimes human words, directed by more insidious purposes, sow weeds instead of flowers, discord instead of peace.

DAVID L. BARTLETT

RESPONSE

Reflect on a recent time that you used words to sow discord or unhappiness. Then, reflect on a time your words or actions brought forth fruit. What in your life needs more fertilizer? What needs "radical tree surgery"?

PRAYER

Loving God, create in me an abundant heart so that I might bear good fruit and my mouth speak love. Amen.

Weekend Reflections

FURTHER CONNECTION

My hope is built on nothing less
than Jesus' blood and righteousness;
I dare not trust the sweetest frame,
but wholly lean on Jesus' name.
On Christ, the solid rock, I stand;
all other ground is sinking sand,
all other ground is sinking sand.
When darkness veils his lovely face,
I rest on his unchanging grace;
in ev'ry high and stormy gale,
my anchor holds within the veil.

EDWARD MOTE (1797–1874), HYMN

MAKING THE CONNECTIONS

Choose one or two questions for reflection:

1. What connections have you noticed between this week's texts and other passages in Scripture?

2. What connections have you made between this week's texts and the world beyond Scripture?

3. Does either of this week's two commentary themes speak especially to your life or the life of the world around you right now?

4. What is God saying to your congregation in particular through this week's readings and commentaries?

_____

_____

_____

_____

_____

_____

Sabbath Day

SCRIPTURE OF ASSURANCE

> I was pushed hard, so that I was falling,
>> but the Lord helped me.
> The Lord is my strength and my might;
>> he has become my salvation. (Psalm 118:13–14)

WEEKLY EXAMEN

- Take a quiet moment, seek out God's presence, and pray for the guidance of the Spirit.

- Consider the past week; recall specific moments and feelings that stand out to you.

- Choose one moment or feeling for deeper examination, thanksgiving, or repentance.

- Let go, breathe deeply, and invite Christ's love to surround and fill you in preparation for the week ahead.

- End with the Lord's Prayer.

The Week Leading Up to
Proper 4
(Sunday between May 29 and June 4)

1 Kings 18:20–21 (22–29), 30–39

Elijah then came near to all the people, and said, "How long will you go limping with two different opinions? If the LORD is God, follow him; but if Baal, then follow him." The people did not answer him a word. (v. 21)

1 Kings 8:22–23, 41–43

Likewise when a foreigner, who is not of your people Israel, comes from a distant land because of your name—for they shall hear of your great name, your mighty hand, and your outstretched arm—when a foreigner comes and prays toward this house . . . (vv. 41–42)

Galatians 1:1–12

Paul an apostle—sent neither by human commission nor from human authorities, but through Jesus Christ and God the Father, who raised him from the dead—and all the members of God's family who are with me . . . (vv. 1–2a)

Luke 7:1–10

When Jesus heard this he was amazed at [the Roman centurion], and turning to the crowd that followed him, he said, "I tell you, not even in Israel have I found such faith." (v. 9)

LECTIO DIVINA

Underline a word or phrase that especially grabs your attention. Pray from that word or phrase and ask God to help you connect to its particular invitation for you this week.

Themes from This Week's Writers

THEME 1: *Welcoming Foreigners and Outsiders*

1 Kings 8:22–23, 41–43

The temple is a place of prayer for all people. The request to hear the prayer of the nonelect is a means of witness, so that non-Israelites might name the divine presence as the God of Israel, worshiped in the temple.

JOHN W. WRIGHT

Galatians 1:1–12

The degree of difficulty in this endeavor is steep for multiple reasons, not least of which was hodgepodge Galatian demographics. It was one thing to form gospel communities in the earliest days, when Jews preached to Jews, but when Gentiles were added to the mix, all the typical headaches of a start-up were compounded exponentially.

SUZANNE WOOLSTON BOSSERT

Luke 7:1–10

Here the centurion is an outsider because he is a Gentile, not a Jew— perhaps even more an outsider because he is a servant of the imperial power of Rome.

DAVID L. BARTLETT

THEME 2: *Who Has Authority to Speak for God?*

1 Kings 18:20–21 (22–29), 30–39

Here we see the terror in all our dialogues of hospitality and tolerance. . . .

. . . This is not a question of private faith. This is about public space, about which God and what rulers will rule. In the public arena, compassion and open doors are rare. In that place it is only power that matters.

LEWIS R. DONELSON

Galatians 1:1–12

Reasserting the truth and purity of God's message and of one's own authority is not a stance unique to Paul. He follows in a long scriptural tradition wherein God's appointed leaders must defend the prophetic message that has been preached, and the power of God behind it.

BRIDGETT A. GREEN

Luke 7:1–10

One of the most important is [Luke's] continuing claim that Jesus is a prophet. Prophets do not speak on their own authority; they speak the words God gives them to speak. They do not travel on their own authority; they go where God sends them. They do not heal on their own authority; they manifest the authority of the God who works through them.

DAVID L. BARTLETT

WHAT IS THE HOLY SPIRIT SAYING TO YOU THIS WEEK?

_____

_____

_____

_____

_____

A SPIRITUAL PRACTICE FOR THIS WEEK

Choose a writer, musician, or artist you do not know much about, who claims a community or ethnicity different from yours. Learn more about them and prayerfully interact with some of their work. What does this outsider to your experience reveal to you about God, life, or creation?

First Reading

1 Kings 8:22–23, 41–43

Then hear in heaven your dwelling place, and do according to all that the foreigner calls to you, so that all the peoples of the earth may know your name and fear you, as do your people Israel, and so that they may know that your name has been invoked on this house that I have built. (v. 43)

REFLECTION

These sentences open a small door out of the exclusiveness of this narrative. This is a political moment that recognizes that the God of Israel is Lord of all.

However, this opening is narrow and surrenders little. It is only the foreigner who submits to the claims of dominance of this temple who squeezes in this door. So it continues to be. We prefer to welcome only the foreigner, stranger, outsider who adopts our language and admits to our superiority. To enter our place, whether it be politics or theology, you must become us.

LEWIS R. DONELSON

RESPONSE

What is a time, recently, when you struggled to welcome or value a person who was a stranger or outsider to your way of life? What was threatening, do you think? What is another way you could see this person or a person like them?

PRAYER

Lord of all, teach me to welcome the stranger as you have welcomed me, that your house may be a house of prayer for all peoples. Amen.

Canticle

Psalm 96

For great is the LORD, and greatly to be praised;
  he is to be revered above all gods.
For all the gods of the peoples are idols,
  but the LORD made the heavens. (vv. 4–5)

REFLECTION

We often seek to design God to serve our purpose, especially when we are in such a desperate situation as the Israelites, who suffered from severe drought. Yet both texts from 1 Kings and Psalm 96 remind us that human-made gods are idols that are indifferent to people and powerless to get involved in their lives. . . .

. . . We need to discern whether the God we believe in is a domesticated god or the living God, who transcends our imagination, but is profoundly concerned with righteousness and truth for all the creatures in the world.

EUNJOO MARY KIM

RESPONSE

In what ways do you "domesticate" God, or "design God" to serve your own purpose or habits in your own spiritual life, do you think? What does imagining God as a "living God" mean for you and for God's call for your life right now?

PRAYER

O God of honor, majesty, strength, and beauty, you are no domesticated god or idol, but the living God; show me how to worship you in awe and wonder. Amen.

Second Reading

For I want you to know, brothers and sisters, that the gospel that was proclaimed by me is not of human origin; for I did not receive it from a human source, nor was I taught it, but I received it through a revelation of Jesus Christ. (vv. 11–12)

REFLECTION

Like Elijah in Israel, Paul must refute the false understanding of the power of God to save the people from the present evil age. He has to prove that his gospel of Jesus Christ is true and defend his authority as mediator, preacher, and teacher of the gospel. People believe a message true once they have confidence that the communicator is an authoritative source. Jesus does not have this problem. Convincing the people that he is a trusted source, Paul's task is to teach God's revelation of the true gospel of Jesus Christ and that its salvific power is unconditional.

BRIDGETT A. GREEN

RESPONSE

Many people are turned off by Christianity and churches because they do not see Christian leaders or people as trustworthy. Paul struggled with this, too. How might you or your congregation be called to reckon with "authority" or trustworthiness in the eyes of your local community?

PRAYER

O Jesus Christ, send me forth to your people with an authority that comes from your love, not from any human source. Amen.

Gospel

Luke 7:1–10

And Jesus went with them, but when he was not far from the house, the centurion sent friends to say to him, "Lord, do not trouble yourself, for I am not worthy to have you come under my roof; therefore I did not presume to come to you. But only speak the word, and let my servant be healed." (vv. 6–7)

REFLECTION

The missional church should take note of Jesus and the centurion's understanding of spiritual authority: it comes not from inherent self-worth, but from above. The centurion recognized that Jesus, like himself, was "a man set under authority" (v. 8) whose power came from above. It "amazed" Jesus that the centurion recognized and had faith in this hierarchy of power and authority invested in him (v. 9). The church's authority and power rise not from its own worthiness, but from God in Christ. The church is not the center; it is the sent.

WM. LOYD ALLEN

RESPONSE

How would you describe your church's authority or power? In what ways do you rely on human effort? In what ways do you see your worth and ministry as a gift from God? Is your church more likely to see itself as the sent, or the center?

PRAYER

Gracious Jesus, teach us that our worth as a congregation comes from you, not our own efforts; speak the word and we shall be healed. Amen.

Weekend Reflections

FURTHER CONNECTION

Diversity may be the hardest thing for a society to live with, and perhaps the most dangerous thing for a society to be without.

WILLIAM SLOANE COFFIN JR. (1924–2006),
THE HEART IS A LITTLE TO THE LEFT

MAKING THE CONNECTIONS

Choose one or two questions for reflection:

1. What connections have you noticed between this week's texts and other passages in Scripture?

2. What connections have you made between this week's texts and the world beyond Scripture?

3. Does either of this week's two commentary themes speak especially to your life or the life of the world around you right now?

4. What is God saying to your congregation in particular through this week's readings and commentaries?

MY CONNECTIONS

_____

_____

_____

_____

_____

_____

Sabbath Day

SCRIPTURE OF ASSURANCE

I pray that you may have the power to comprehend, with all the saints, what is the breadth and length and height and depth, and to know the love of Christ that surpasses knowledge, so that you may be filled with all the fullness of God. (Ephesians 3:18–19)

WEEKLY EXAMEN

- Take a quiet moment, seek out God's presence, and pray for the guidance of the Spirit.

- Consider the past week; recall specific moments and feelings that stand out to you.

- Choose one moment or feeling for deeper examination, thanksgiving, or repentance.

- Let go, breathe deeply, and invite Christ's love to surround and fill you in preparation for the week ahead.

- End with the Lord's Prayer.

The Week Leading Up to
Proper 5

(Sunday between June 5 and June 11)

1 Kings 17:8–16 (17–24)

She went and did as Elijah said, so that she as well as he and her household ate for many days. The jar of meal was not emptied, neither did the jug of oil fail, according to the word of the Lord that he spoke by Elijah. (vv. 15–16)

1 Kings 17:17-24

Elijah took the child, brought him down from the upper chamber into the house, and gave him to his mother; then Elijah said, "See, your son is alive." (v. 23)

Galatians 1:11–24

You have heard, no doubt, of my earlier life in Judaism. I was violently persecuting the church of God and was trying to destroy it. I advanced in Judaism beyond many among my people of the same age, for I was far more zealous for the traditions of my ancestors. (vv. 13–14)

Luke 7:11–17

When the Lord saw her, he had compassion for her and said to her, "Do not weep." Then he came forward and touched the bier, and the bearers stood still. And he said, "Young man, I say to you, rise!" (vv. 13–14)

LECTIO DIVINA

Underline a word or phrase that especially grabs your attention. Pray from that word or phrase and ask God to help you connect to its particular invitation for you this week.

Themes from This Week's Writers

THEME 1: *Compassion for Widows and Orphans*

1 Kings 17:8–16 (17–24) and 1 Kings 17:17–24

The drought indiscriminately impacts Elijah, the widow, and her son; the Lord's care indiscriminately sustains the Israelite prophet and the non-Israelite widow and her son.

JOHN W. WRIGHT

1 Kings 17:8–16 (17–24) and 1 Kings 17:17–24

All these stories build on the intensity of the tragedy of a widow, already bare and unprotected in the world, who is losing her only child. This story seems to have no purpose other than demonstrating God's compassion.

LEWIS R. DONELSON

Luke 7:11–17

Likewise, the church dare not let its eagerness to proclaim Jesus' power over death distract it from its mission to the living, some of whom may think themselves better off dead. Compassion for the dead man is not what motivates Jesus; a woman left bereft of any survival safety net in a patriarchal culture *is*.

WM. LOYD ALLEN

THEME 2: *Let Go of Human Law and Control*

Galatians 1:11–24

When he retells the story of his former life as a zealous Pharisee, Paul shows the Galatians that it would be easy, if not natural, for him to proclaim the gospel while observing the Torah, but salvation through Christ does not require work; it requires faith.

BRIDGETT A. GREEN

Galatians 1:11–24

Following in the footsteps of the notorious Saul, we moderns remain consistent in our propensity to challenge Christ's message of unconditional grace with our rigid opinions of what constitutes right action and right belief. Like a funhouse mirror refracting and multiplying the same image a thousand ways, we cannot seem to shake our human tendency and desire to control God.

SUZANNE WOOLSTON BOSSERT

Luke 7:11–17

No one at Nain asks Jesus to do anything. No faith is required for healing. None is asked for or mentioned. Jesus acts solely out of the gut-wrenching compassion he feels for the wailing widow.

WM. LOYD ALLEN

WHAT IS THE HOLY SPIRIT SAYING TO YOU THIS WEEK?

_____

_____

_____

_____

_____

A SPIRITUAL PRACTICE FOR THIS WEEK

Choose a story in the news that forecasts disaster. Using your prophetic imagination, envision an outcome of resurrection and new life, instead. Pray from your prophetic vision for the situation you chose. Strive to grow in faith that miracles are possible, but trust in God whether you witness a miracle or not.

First Reading

He cried out to the LORD, "O LORD my God, have you brought calamity even upon the widow with whom I am staying, by killing her son?" Then he stretched himself upon the child three times, and cried out to the LORD, "O LORD my God, let this child's life come into him again." The LORD listened to the voice of Elijah; the life of the child came into him again, and he revived. (vv. 20–22)

REFLECTION

This place is more the proper land of Baal than of the Lord. It is a curious command that becomes even more curious. The word of the Lord says, "I have commanded a widow there to feed you." A widow should be the last place to seek food in a drought. Elijah demands food from her. She affirms the absurdity of God's command, announcing that she has nothing and that she is about to fix her last meal for herself and her son. Then the miraculous power of God changes the story.

LEWIS R. DONELSON

RESPONSE

What would it mean to you, at this time in your life, to believe in the absurd and miraculous power of God to sustain you and those you love? How does that feel? How would you ask God to change your story, if you believed this was truly possible?

PRAYER

O God, let my jar of meal not be emptied or my jug of oil fail, that in you I may serve the needy and walk in the path you have called me to go. Amen.

Canticle

Psalm 30

By your favor, O LORD,
>you had established me as a strong mountain;
you hid your face;
>I was dismayed.

To you, O LORD, I cried,
and to the LORD I made supplication. (vv. 7–8)

REFLECTION

Despite her duress, or perhaps because of it, [the widow of Zarephath]
is willing to risk. Her generous act reveals an awareness of the limits of
human knowledge and control. . . . Verses 7–8 of Psalm 30 also reveal
the thinness of human knowledge and the shock of facing the limits
of one's control. The preacher might similarly emphasize the limits
of human knowledge and control and urge listeners to trust God. A
posture of trust often requires being willing to move beyond what we
know and face outcomes we cannot control.

DONYELLE MCCRAY

RESPONSE

What is a time you faced the limits of your own control? How were you
able to trust God through it? How were you not able? What in your life
right now might be requiring you, also, to let go and trust God beyond
what you know?

PRAYER

O Lord, hear me and be gracious to me; be my helper, that my soul may
praise you and not be silent. Amen.

Second Reading

Galatians 1:11–24

But when God, who had set me apart before I was born and called me through his grace, was pleased to reveal his Son to me, so that I might proclaim him among the Gentiles, I did not confer with any human being, nor did I go up to Jerusalem to those who were already apostles before me, but I went away at once into Arabia, and afterwards I returned to Damascus. (vv. 15–17)

REFLECTION

It might be fruitful to begin and end a sermon on Galatians 1:11–24 by acknowledging the role of surrender as both the struggle and triumph of faith. We have already noted the darker tendency of humans to temper or deny entirely the feeling of being out of control, by clinging to judgments about what might guarantee salvation and divine favor. . . . Divine nudges and directives often catapult recipients (Moses, Jesus, Paul, you, and me) into places of shadowy unknowing, which can manifest as lonely wilderness wandering as well as invigorating new adventures that elicit new passion and zeal.

SUZANNE WOOLSTON BOSSERT

RESPONSE

Make a list of words and phrases you associate with the word "surrender." In light of these, what does surrendering to faith or God mean to you? Does doing so threaten to bring you to "places of shadowy unknowing"? Could it lead to "new adventures"?

PRAYER

Loving Christ, call me through your grace and reveal yourself to me; teach me the struggle and triumph of surrender. Amen.

Gospel

Luke 7:11–17

The dead man sat up and began to speak, and Jesus gave him to his mother. Fear seized all of them; and they glorified God, saying, "A great prophet has risen among us!" and "God has looked favorably on his people!" (vv. 15–16)

REFLECTION

Remember that those who first heard Luke's Gospel already knew the rest of Jesus' story. . . . They know that the one who delivers life to the children and promises Paradise to the thief has himself been made victorious over death. . . . The goal of the story is also the ground of the story. The two bedazzling men tell the grieving women the good news, using exactly the same word Jesus used to bring life to the young man and the young woman, the same word that restored hope to Jairus and to the widow of Nain. "He has risen" (24:5).

DAVID L. BARTLETT

RESPONSE

What are you grieving in your life, or in your congregation, right now? How has death or dying touched you? How might Jesus be inviting you to "rise" now and walk, into new life through him?

PRAYER

Risen Christ, have compassion on me and help me to rise from grief and loss, as you also rose again from death and the tomb. Amen.

Weekend Reflections

The prophet engages in futuring fantasy. The prophet does not ask if the vision can be implemented, for questions of implementation are of no consequence until the vision can be imagined. The imagination must come before the implementation. Our culture is competent to implement almost anything and to imagine almost nothing. . . . It is the vocation of the prophet to keep alive the ministry of imagination, to keep on conjuring and proposing futures alternative to the single one the king wants to urge as the only thinkable one.

WALTER BRUEGGEMANN (1933–),
THE PROPHETIC IMAGINATION

MAKING THE CONNECTIONS

Choose one or two questions for reflection:

1. What connections have you noticed between this week's texts and other passages in Scripture?

2. What connections have you made between this week's texts and the world beyond Scripture?

3. Does either of this week's two commentary themes speak especially to your life or the life of the world around you right now?

4. What is God saying to your congregation in particular through this week's readings and commentaries?

MY CONNECTIONS

_____

_____

_____

_____

_____

_____

Sabbath Day

SCRIPTURE OF ASSURANCE

Do not quench the Spirit. Do not despise the words of prophets, but test everything; hold fast to what is good; abstain from every form of evil. (1 Thessalonians 5:19–22)

WEEKLY EXAMEN

- Take a quiet moment, seek out God's presence, and pray for the guidance of the Spirit.

- Consider the past week; recall specific moments and feelings that stand out to you.

- Choose one moment or feeling for deeper examination, thanksgiving, or repentance.

- Let go, breathe deeply, and invite Christ's love to surround and fill you in preparation for the week ahead.

- End with the Lord's Prayer.

The Week Leading Up to
Proper 6
(Sunday between June 12 and June 18)

1 Kings 21:1–10 (11–14), 15–21a

Ahab said to Elijah, "Have you found me, O my enemy?" He answered, "I have found you." (v. 20a)

2 Samuel 11:26–12:10, 13–15

Nathan said to David, "You are the man! . . . Why have you despised the word of the LORD, to do what is evil in his sight? You have struck down Uriah the Hittite with the sword, and have taken his wife to be your wife, and have killed him with the sword of the Ammonites." (12:7a, 9)

Galatians 2:15–21

I do not nullify the grace of God; for if justification comes through the law, then Christ died for nothing. (v. 21)

Luke 7:36–8:3

Now when the Pharisee who had invited him saw it, he said to himself, "If this man were a prophet, he would have known who and what kind of woman this is who is touching him—that she is a sinner." (7:39)

LECTIO DIVINA

Underline a word or phrase that especially grabs your attention. Pray from that word or phrase and ask God to help you connect to its particular invitation for you this week.

Themes from This Week's Writers

THEME 1: *Confronting Sin and Abuse of Power*

1 Kings 21:1–10 (11–14), 15–21a

The Scripture compels us to ask about the ways in which we are willing to sell ourselves or lose our moral center in order to possess what we think we deserve. Moreover, we are reminded of how often we allow others to do our moral dirty work so we can have what we desire.

C. MELISSA SNARR

1 Kings 21:1–10 (11–14), 15–21a and 2 Samuel 11:26–12:10, 13–15

In the current world, the abuse of power by rulers, governments, nation-states, and other formal power structures seems to be a never-ending reality. Yet in tandem with corrupt power we also discover a prophetic response that effects genuine social change. Similar to Elijah and Nathan, the prophetic message is not void of details; rather it embodies a critical awareness on how corrupt power is operating on both the macro and micro levels.

GREGORY L. CUÉLLAR

Galatians 2:15–21

The tension between sin and justification is healthy. It never allows Christians to take for granted our attitude and response to God's love for us. It is the antidote to presumption.

RENATA FURST

THEME 2: *Mercy and Accountability*

Psalm 32

There is good news in the reminder that God is the hope of the righteous as well as the wicked, merciful enough to lead a person from evil to moral purity.

DONYELLE MCCRAY

Luke 7:36–8:3

Preachers will need to decide whether to ask their congregation to identify with the woman in need of and receiving great forgiveness, or with the Pharisee who is a righteous person in need of less forgiveness but in need of having more mercy.

O. WESLEY ALLEN JR.

Luke 7:36–8:3

Jesus confronts Simon, the enemy, not out of contempt but out of love.

STEPHEN BOYD

WHAT IS THE HOLY SPIRIT SAYING TO YOU THIS WEEK?

_____

_____

_____

_____

_____

A SPIRITUAL PRACTICE FOR THIS WEEK

Consider the moral facades Ahab, David, and Simon wore; then draw, describe, or create a version of your own "moral mask." What can you learn about yourself? How would Jesus or a prophet call you to be accountable, behind this mask?

First Reading

1 Kings 21:1–10 (11–14), 15–21a or 2 Samuel 11:26–12:10, 13–15

[Elijah] answered, ". . . Because you have sold yourself to do what is evil in the sight of the LORD, I will bring disaster on you." (1 Kings 21:20b–21a)

But the thing that David had done displeased the LORD, and the LORD sent Nathan to David. He came to him, and said to him, "There were two men in a certain city, the one rich and the other poor." (2 Samuel 12:1)

REFLECTION

Preserving the moral facade, at all costs, is the costliest of sins, because it fundamentally assumes that we are beyond the gaze, accountability, and *redemption* of God.

This ultimate break from God is precisely when God sends prophets to poke holes in false morality and reminds us of the greater redemptive path. God's prophetic invitation may come in the form of Elijah's blunt confrontation or the subtler parabolic teaching of Nathan. The juxtaposition asks us to consider, as an ecclesial community and as individuals called to prophetic speech, what kind of word someone needs to hear to dissipate a moral mask.

C. MELISSA SNARR

RESPONSE

Consider your own "moral mask." What do you think you are protecting yourself from? In what ways are you hiding, or even harming, yourself? What is the "greater redemptive path" God might be calling you to? What about your church community?

PRAYER

O God of justice, lead me in your righteousness: send prophets into my life to speak your word and open my ears to listen, then teach me how to speak that word to others. Amen.

Canticle

Psalm 5:1–8

For you are not a God who delights in wickedness;
    evil will not sojourn with you.
The boastful will not stand before your eyes;
    you hate all evildoers.

. . . .

Lead me, O Lord, in your righteousness
    because of my enemies;
    make your way straight before me. (vv. 4–5, 8)

REFLECTION

God emerges as the omniscient judge who sees through corrupt schemes designed to conceal the murder of the innocent. Dramatic revelations and indictments reveal YHWH as the hope of the righteous and offer assurance that human suffering has a divine witness. Ultimately, this week's readings emphasize God's role as righteous judge and reader of human hearts.

DONYELLE MCCRAY

RESPONSE

Reflect on the image of God as witness to all evil acts and human suffering. Is this comforting or exasperating (since God does not stop all suffering)? Is it reassuring to you that God will judge, even if a human crime is never punished on earth? Or is this hard to grasp?

PRAYER

O God our judge, you are a witness to the sins and the suffering of all people; hear our cries and lead us in your righteousness. Amen.

Second Reading

Galatians 2:15–21

We ourselves are Jews by birth and not Gentile sinners; yet we know that a person is justified not by the works of the law but through faith in Jesus Christ. And we have come to believe in Christ Jesus, so that we might be justified by faith in Christ, and not by doing the works of the law, because no one will be justified by the works of the law. (vv. 15–16)

REFLECTION

The mystery of our personal and communal daily struggle with sin, while justified by faith in Christ Jesus, can make us better Christians. How does this help us? Ignorance, indifference, or insensitivity to the issues of personal or social sin or debt can undermine our perception of *our* need for forgiveness and justification in Christ, while being only too conscious of sin in others. This reading from Galatians is followed by Luke's Gospel, which depicts Simon the Pharisee, who is oblivious to his own sin (Luke 7:45–46) but apparently able to perceive sin in others.

RENATA FURST

RESPONSE

What sins are you especially good at noticing in others? What sins do you struggle with in yourself? How do you approach God's gift of forgiveness and grace in your life?

PRAYER

Jesus Christ, in your mercy, forgive us our sins as we forgive those who sin against us. Amen.

Gospel

Luke 7:36–8:3

Then turning toward the woman, [Jesus] said to Simon, "Do you see this woman? I entered your house; you gave me no water for my feet, but she has bathed my feet with her tears and dried them with her hair. . . . Therefore, I tell you, her sins, which were many, have been forgiven; hence she has shown great love. But the one to whom little is forgiven, loves little." (vv. 44, 47)

REFLECTION

Fred Craddock once remarked that the true measure of one's faith is not whom you are willing to feed, but whom you are willing to eat with. . . .
. . . The story in Luke is fraught with tensions: dinner guests who are really enemies, a hospitable host who is not really hospitable, and a woman known as a sinner who embodies the love and grace of the gospel. When Jesus is present, surprising transformations and experiences of healing are possible. Even a begrudging Simon, in opening his home and table to Jesus, moves into a new kind of space where unexpected things happen.

STEPHEN BOYD

RESPONSE

Think of a time when you took a risk by sharing a meal with someone. How did it feel? How did it change you, the other person, or your relationship? How is Communion a meal like this, for you or your congregation?

PRAYER

Jesus, be present at our table that love, mercy, and the unexpected might bring us closer to you and to one another. Amen.

Weekend Reflections

FURTHER CONNECTION

For me, forgiveness and compassion are always linked: how do we hold people accountable for wrongdoing and yet at the same time remain in touch with their humanity enough to believe in their capacity to be transformed?

BELL HOOKS (1952–), CONVERSATION WITH MAYA ANGELOU

MAKING THE CONNECTIONS

Choose one or two questions for reflection:

1. What connections have you noticed between this week's texts and other passages in Scripture?

2. What connections have you made between this week's texts and the world beyond Scripture?

3. Does either of this week's two commentary themes speak especially to your life or the life of the world around you right now?

4. What is God saying to your congregation in particular through this week's readings and commentaries?

MY CONNECTIONS

_____

_____

_____

_____

_____

_____

Sabbath Day

SCRIPTURE OF ASSURANCE

Speak to all the congregation of the people of Israel and say to them: You shall be holy, for I the LORD your God am holy. (Leviticus 19:2)

WEEKLY EXAMEN

- Take a quiet moment, seek out God's presence, and pray for the guidance of the Spirit.

- Consider the past week; recall specific moments and feelings that stand out to you.

- Choose one moment or feeling for deeper examination, thanksgiving, or repentance.

- Let go, breathe deeply, and invite Christ's love to surround and fill you in preparation for the week ahead.

- End with the Lord's Prayer.

The Week Leading Up to
Proper 7

(Sunday between June 19 and June 25)

1 Kings 19:1–4 (5–7), 8–15a

Then [Elijah] was afraid; he got up and fled for his life, and came to Beer-sheba, which belongs to Judah; he left his servant there. (v. 3)

Isaiah 65:1–9

I was ready to be sought out by those who did not ask,
  to be found by those who did not seek me.
I said, "Here I am, here I am,"
  to a nation that did not call on my name. (v. 1)

Galatians 3:23–29

There is no longer Jew or Greek, there is no longer slave or free, there is no longer male and female; for all of you are one in Christ Jesus. And if you belong to Christ, then you are Abraham's offspring, heirs according to the promise. (vv. 28–29)

Luke 8:26–39

As he stepped out on land, a man of the city who had demons met him. For a long time he had worn no clothes, and he did not live in a house but in the tombs. When he saw Jesus, he fell down before him and shouted at the top of his voice, "What have you to do with me, Jesus, Son of the Most High God?" (vv. 27–28a)

LECTIO DIVINA

Underline a word or phrase that especially grabs your attention. Pray from that word or phrase and ask God to help you connect to its particular invitation for you this week.

Themes from This Week's Writers

THEME 1: *God Is with You*

1 Kings 19:1–4 (5–7), 8–15a

Just as depression sets in, so does the healing care of God, which for
Elijah comes in the form of an angel. . . . Elijah's angel also serves as a
travel guide in the desert, providing him with life-giving care over the
next forty days and nights. With his strength restored, Elijah resumes his
prophetic call and receives a renewed mission.

GREGORY L. CUÉLLAR

1 Kings 19:1–4 (5–7), 8–15a and Isaiah 65:1–9

"You are not alone. I care for you. Now get back to it."

This may not be the most poetic summary of God's responses to
the laments of a refugee prophet and an exiled people, but the passages
before us contain this seemingly straightforward sentiment, even as
they invite reflection on rich themes of faithful relationship, divine
sustenance, and persistent mission.

C. MELISSA SNARR

Psalms 42 and 43

On one level, the psalmist is awash in sorrow and restless under its
waves. At the same time, the poet is mysteriously buoyed by God's
sustaining power.

DONYELLE MCCRAY

THEME 2: *Christ Crosses Boundaries*

Galatians 3:23–29

Paul's arguments about the law provide preachers an opportunity to
courageously examine, and disavow, cultural chauvinism. Cultural
chauvinism occurs when dominant social groups dismiss or devalue the
cultural histories and practices of minority groups.

BRAD R. BRAXTON

Galatians 3:23–29

People who live on the margins, as well as those who live in the center of society, need to see freedom from division as the work and gift of God. Galatians echoes the theme of Christ moving across social and ethnic borders found in today's Gospel reading.

RENATA FURST

Luke 8:26–39

Can we, can our churches, create gracious spaces where the wounded can come to be heard? Can we be honest about our own lives and the lives of others, while avoiding judgment? Can someone, like the man in our text, find healing through those willing to embody incarnational love?

STEPHEN BOYD

WHAT IS THE HOLY SPIRIT SAYING TO YOU THIS WEEK?

_____

_____

_____

_____

_____

A SPIRITUAL PRACTICE FOR THIS WEEK

Consider the social, racial, or class boundaries that mark your community. Map them: Where is the center? the margins? the wilderness? What lines cannot be crossed? How does your church participate in or resist these boundaries? Pray across the boundaries this week.

First Reading

1 Kings 19:1–4 (5–7), 8–15a

. . . and after the fire a sound of sheer silence. When Elijah heard it, he wrapped his face in his mantle and went out and stood at the entrance of the cave. Then there came a voice to him that said, "What are you doing here, Elijah?" . . . Then the Lord said to him, "Go, return on your way to the wilderness of Damascus." (vv. 12b–13, 15a)

REFLECTION

With a voice of missional realism, God asserts that Elijah is ready to return, in a verse not included at all in the Revised Common Lectionary (v. 18), and adds that he was *never actually alone* in this mission; there are *seven thousand* faithful who will be with him. In other words, you may think you are the last righteous one standing—but you have missed an entire faithful remnant already journeying on this mission. . . . At some point, your healing will be found again in your mission, alongside others who are walking your collective journey.

C. MELISSA SNARR

RESPONSE

Who do you consider your faithful companions on the journey, even when you are alone? What is your mission, would you say, at this time in your life? What kind of healing do you long for? How do all three of these things work together, or not, for you?

PRAYER

O God, you are with me on the journey, even through the wilderness; speak to me so I know I am not alone, even in silence. Amen.

Canticle

Why are you cast down, O my soul,
    and why are you disquieted within me?
Hope in God; for I shall again praise him,
    my help and my God. (43:5)

REFLECTION

Psalms 42 and 43 provide a series of ricocheting questions that offer
clues on Elijah's inner dialogue in the cave. First, there are the three
rounds of questions about sorrow, "Why are you cast down, O my
soul?" Interspersed among these questions are taunts from an enemy,
"Where is your God?" (42:3, 10), and questions directed at God, "Why
must I walk about mournfully because the enemy oppresses me?" (42:9;
43:2). The psalmist's deepest prayer is for an interruption that will usher
him out of his spiritual-psychological cavern. The miracle for Elijah is
that the internal dialogue is heard and interrupted.

DONYELLE MCCRAY

RESPONSE

What are harmful voices or taunts you hear in your own inner dialogue?
Compose a psalm of your own, of the questions and prayers you hear
in your "spiritual-psychological cavern." Pray for God's interruption of
your thoughts, that a voice of love prevails.

PRAYER

O God, I hope and trust in you; be my help and lead me from thirst
and disquiet to your living stream. Amen.

Second Reading

Galatians 3:23–29

As many of you as were baptized into Christ have clothed yourselves with Christ. There is no longer Jew or Greek, there is no longer slave or free, there is no longer male and female; for all of you are one in Christ Jesus. (vv. 27–28)

REFLECTION

Even "in Christ," there is social difference, but Christ abolishes the dominance of one over the other based on these differences. Jews should not dominate Gentiles; free persons should not dominate slaves; men should not dominate women. Christians should foster harmonious relationships characterized by mutuality and respect for social difference.

An analogy from music may be helpful. Harmony is the cooperative union of different voices. The various vocal parts must maintain their distinctiveness, even as they unite, if harmony is to exist.

BRAD R. BRAXTON

RESPONSE

What is the difference between unity and conformity? Is there an aspect of your personality or culture you have felt asked to leave behind in church? How could you or your congregation better seek "harmony" rather than uniformity as the goal of Christian life together?

PRAYER

O God, you made me and each of your children in your image; bind us together that we may all be one in Christ, but not be all the same. Amen.

Gospel

Luke 8:26–39

Those who had seen it told them how the one who had been possessed by demons had been healed. Then all the people of the surrounding country of the Gerasenes asked Jesus to leave them; for they were seized with great fear. So he got into the boat and returned. (vv. 36–37)

REFLECTION

Instead of expressing amazement, the crowds ask Jesus to leave (vv. 34–37). Like the demons, they recognize Jesus' power and are afraid. They prefer the demons they have normalized to the liberating power that is unknown. In a sense they have experienced Stockholm syndrome, in which hostages identify with the evil and destructive powers that kidnap them. . . . Asking a congregation to identify with the townsfolk and consider the ways they have accepted demonic forces in their midst, over against accepting God's liberating work in the world, offers preachers the opportunity to invite hearers into the liberating work of God's reign.

O. WESLEY ALLEN JR.

RESPONSE

Reflect on ways you identify with the townsfolk in this passage. What is a "demon" that you or your congregation may have normalized? How may you have asked Jesus to leave your neighborhood?

PRAYER

O Jesus, teach me to recognize your power and not be afraid, that I may be healed and changed by your love. Amen.

Weekend Reflections

FURTHER CONNECTION

God strengthen me to bear myself;
That heaviest weight of all to bear,
Inalienable weight of care.
All others are outside myself;
I lock my door and bar them out,
The turmoil, tedium, gad-about.
I lock my door upon myself,
And bar them out; but who shall wall
Self from myself, most loathed of all?

. . . .

Yet One there is can curb myself,
Can roll the strangling load from me,
Break off the yoke and set me free.

CHRISTINA ROSSETTI (1830–94), "WHO SHALL DELIVER ME?"

MAKING THE CONNECTIONS

Choose one or two questions for reflection:

1. What connections have you noticed between this week's texts and other passages in Scripture?

2. What connections have you made between this week's texts and the world beyond Scripture?

3. Does either of this week's two commentary themes speak especially to your life or the life of the world around you right now?

4. What is God saying to your congregation in particular through this week's readings and commentaries?

_____

_____

_____

_____

_____

_____

Sabbath Day

SCRIPTURE OF ASSURANCE

Love never ends. But as for prophecies, they will come to an end; as for tongues, they will cease; as for knowledge, it will come to an end. (1 Corinthians 13:8)

WEEKLY EXAMEN

- Take a quiet moment, seek out God's presence, and pray for the guidance of the Spirit.

- Consider the past week; recall specific moments and feelings that stand out to you.

- Choose one moment or feeling for deeper examination, thanksgiving, or repentance.

- Let go, breathe deeply, and invite Christ's love to surround and fill you in preparation for the week ahead.

- End with the Lord's Prayer.

The Week Leading Up to
Proper 8

(Sunday between June 26 and July 2)

2 Kings 2:1–2, 6–14

When they had crossed, Elijah said to Elisha, "Tell me what I may do for you, before I am taken from you." Elisha said, "Please let me inherit a double share of your spirit." (v. 9)

1 Kings 19:15–16, 19–21

So he set out from there, and found Elisha son of Shaphat, who was plowing. There were twelve yoke of oxen ahead of him, and he was with the twelfth. Elijah passed by him and threw his mantle over him. (v. 19)

Galatians 5:1, 13–25

For what the flesh desires is opposed to the Spirit, and what the Spirit desires is opposed to the flesh; for these are opposed to each other, to prevent you from doing what you want. (v. 17)

Luke 9:51–62

When the days drew near for [Jesus] to be taken up, he set his face to go to Jerusalem. And he sent messengers ahead of him. On their way they entered a village of the Samaritans to make ready for him; but they did not receive him, because his face was set toward Jerusalem. (vv. 51–53)

LECTIO DIVINA

> Underline a word or phrase that especially grabs your attention. Pray from that word or phrase and ask God to help you connect to its particular invitation for you this week.

Themes from This Week's Writers

THEME 1: *Taking Up the Mantle*

2 Kings 2:1–2, 6–14

In the transfer of prophetic leadership from Elijah to Elisha, the spirit (*ruach*) serves as a key ingredient to the well-being and authority of the succeeding prophet.

GREGORY L. CUÉLLAR

1 Kings 19:15–16, 19–21

Elisha invites us to consider how we could say yes to our deepest calling from God, whatever form that may take.

C. MELISSA SNARR

Luke 9:51–62

Jesus pushes whatever understanding of discipleship they had to a deeper level, and we are left to wonder how they responded to the call. This . . . becomes the open ending for us as well.

O. WESLEY ALLEN JR.

Luke 9:51–62

Because his disciples did not know what he would face in Jerusalem, Jesus prepared them both for the journey to Jerusalem and for continuing his ministry after he was gone.

STEPHEN BOYD

THEME 2: *Freedom from Law for Love*

Galatians 5:1, 13–25

Christian freedom is not unbridled but is manifested in a slavery to the welfare of one's neighbors (5:13). When communities fail to accentuate the primacy of love, a competitive, destructive impulse is unleashed, which consumes individuals and erodes communal bonds (vv. 14–15).

BRAD R. BRAXTON

Galatians 5:1, 13–25

What is the attraction of slavery? . . . Perhaps, for the Galatians, as for us, a yoke is a known pattern of behavior, "badges" that set us apart and give us a social identity, or a comfortable standard that neatly divides life into black and white. To live into the tension of freedom, we must embrace discomfort, messiness, and gray areas in relationships, worship, belief, and commitment.

RENATA FURST

WHAT IS THE HOLY SPIRIT SAYING TO YOU THIS WEEK?

_____

_____

_____

_____

_____

A SPIRITUAL PRACTICE FOR THIS WEEK

Try to follow some or all of the advice found in the verses by Wendell Berry in the Weekend Reflections this week. See what the Spirit nudges you toward. Perhaps add the poem as an event in your calendar each day, with a timed reminder, to prompt yourself.

First Reading

2 Kings 2:1–2, 6–14

He picked up the mantle of Elijah that had fallen from him, and went back and stood on the bank of the Jordan. He took the mantle of Elijah that had fallen from him, and struck the water, saying, "Where is the LORD, the God of Elijah?" When he had struck the water, the water was parted to the one side and to the other, and Elisha went over. (vv. 13–14)

REFLECTION

We may want to learn most deeply from this text by respecting its inscrutability. . . . This text may be most powerful when it illustrates how God ultimately operates beyond our narrow definitions and limited creativity in ways that consistently unsettle our routine sense of religious, social, and political practice. God's vision and salvific ends will exceed our expectations. We should hope that the awesome majesty of God lures us, in the name of love and redemption, beyond the constraints of what we think might be possible.

C. MELISSA SNARR

RESPONSE

Do Scripture passages like these unsettle you? Do they capture your imagination? How often are you able to believe that God's grace and vision will exceed your expectations? What do you wish was possible that right now seems impossible?

PRAYER

Holy One, you are the God who works wonders; I believe, help my unbelief. Amen.

Canticle

Psalm 16

Protect me, O God, for in you I take refuge.

You show me the path of life.
    In your presence there is fullness of joy;
    in your right hand are pleasures forevermore. (vv. 1, 11)

REFLECTION

When Jesus calls, "Follow me," one says, "Yes, but . . . let me go back to my family." Essentially, Jesus' response is that in following him there are no "buts"; if you have trust, like that of the psalmist, you will be confident that God will protect and provide, shelter and send you out.

Psalm 16 reveals two preaching avenues. The first is to preach that God is our refuge. . . . The second approach is to preach a call to trust and follow God into the world, on the path of life (v. 11), to a life of discipleship.

DONNA GIVER-JOHNSTON

RESPONSE

At this time in your life, do you need God most to be a refuge and shelter, or to call and lead you forward on the path of discipleship? Write a short prayer, and ask God for what you need.

PRAYER

O Jesus, teach me to trust and follow you that I may find fullness of life in your presence. Amen.

Second Reading

Galatians 5:1, 13–25

For you were called to freedom, brothers and sisters; only do not use your freedom as an opportunity for self-indulgence, but through love become slaves to one another. For the whole law is summed up in a single commandment, "You shall love your neighbor as yourself." (vv. 13–14)

REFLECTION

As the parent of any child transitioning into adult life knows, taking full responsibility for oneself is difficult. The joys of freedom can sometimes seem to be overwhelmed by the trials of responsibility. . . . This could explain the Galatians' hankering after the boundaries of the law. It may also explain the often outright rejection of preaching that calls an individual or community to maturity. People prefer the familiar boundaries of being a beloved child to the more challenging status of an adult who stands firm in the freedom for which "Christ has set us free."

RENATA FURST

RESPONSE

How might God be calling you or your community to a greater spiritual maturity? In what ways do you long to remain a beloved child? In what ways might there be greater freedom in Christ in growing toward "spiritual adulthood"?

PRAYER

Jesus Christ, you have set me free for joy and discipleship in loving my neighbor; give me grace to stand firm in you as an adult. Amen.

Gospel

Luke 9:51–62

As they were going along the road, someone said to him, "I will follow you wherever you go." And Jesus said to him, "Foxes have holes, and birds of the air have nests; but the Son of Man has nowhere to lay his head." (vv. 57–58)

REFLECTION

Jesus insists that the risk is necessary for the work of the kingdom.

. . . He knows the powers that aim to deter and defeat him. But he continues to bring good news to the poor, release to the captives, and freedom to the oppressed. With the disciples he bids us, "Follow me." Even in the face of inequity, racism, aggression, and violence, we turn our face toward him and follow, seeking to do the work of the kingdom, his work in the world.

STEPHEN BOYD

RESPONSE

How is your tolerance for risk? What are risks you are taking right now, in your life or as a congregation, that feel necessary for the work of the kingdom? Are there risks you have considered but have not taken yet?

PRAYER

O Jesus, Son of God, you found no place to lay your head here on earth; give me courage to follow you, even in risk and defeat, wherever you may go. Amen.

Weekend Reflections

FURTHER CONNECTION

So, friends, every day do something
that won't compute. Love the Lord.
Love the world. Work for nothing.
Take all that you have and be poor.
Love someone who does not deserve it.

WENDELL BERRY (1934–), "MANIFESTO:
THE MAD FARMER LIBERATION FRONT"

MAKING THE CONNECTIONS

Choose one or two questions for reflection:

1. What connections have you noticed between this week's texts and other passages in Scripture?

2. What connections have you made between this week's texts and the world beyond Scripture?

3. Does either of this week's two commentary themes speak especially to your life or the life of the world around you right now?

4. What is God saying to your congregation in particular through this week's readings and commentaries?

_____

_____

_____

_____

_____

_____

Sabbath Day

SCRIPTURE OF ASSURANCE

But avoid stupid controversies, genealogies, dissensions, and quarrels about the law, for they are unprofitable and worthless. (Titus 3:9)

WEEKLY EXAMEN

- Take a quiet moment, seek out God's presence, and pray for the guidance of the Spirit.

- Consider the past week; recall specific moments and feelings that stand out to you.

- Choose one moment or feeling for deeper examination, thanksgiving, or repentance.

- Let go, breathe deeply, and invite Christ's love to surround and fill you in preparation for the week ahead.

- End with the Lord's Prayer.

The Week Leading Up to
Proper 9
(Sunday between July 3 and July 9)

2 Kings 5:1–14

But his servants approached and said to him, "Father, if the prophet had commanded you to do something difficult, would you not have done it? How much more, when all he said to you was, 'Wash, and be clean'?" (v. 13)

Isaiah 66:10–14

As a mother comforts her child,
    so I will comfort you;
    you shall be comforted in Jerusalem. (v. 13)

Galatians 6:(1–6) 7–16

So then, whenever we have an opportunity, let us work for the good of all, and especially for those of the family of faith. (v. 10)

Luke 10:1–11, 16–20

The seventy returned with joy, saying, "Lord, in your name even the demons submit to us!" He said to them, "I watched Satan fall from heaven like a flash of lightning." (vv. 17–18)

LECTIO DIVINA

Underline a word or phrase that especially grabs your attention. Pray from that word or phrase and ask God to help you connect to its particular invitation for you this week.

Themes from This Week's Writers

THEME 1: *What Is God's Power Like?*

2 Kings 5:1–14

In this story, human power amounts to exceedingly little: neither the powerful commander nor the kings can do very much. Instead, God's power is found only by paying attention to lowly servants and an unimpressed prophet.

MATTHEW RICHARD SCHLIMM

Isaiah 66:10–14

The image of God dwelling once again in Jerusalem . . . now shifts in verse 13 from God as the sovereign one who dwells in Jerusalem and who will be worshiped by kings and nations, to God the compassionate one who, like a mother who comforts a child, will comfort the people in Jerusalem.

CAROL J. DEMPSEY, OP

Luke 10:1–11, 16–20

Apparently, God's power is already loose in the world. Proclamation of these texts should lead Christians to grapple with the ways God is already active among us, in judgment as well as redemption, and especially in those practices that make for peace.

STANLEY P. SAUNDERS

THEME 2: *The Risk and Gift of Welcoming All*

Galatians 6:(1–6) 7–16

It is not possible to avoid or ignore the unique and radical idea of inclusiveness that runs through this letter as Paul pastorally concludes: "let us not grow weary in doing what is right. . . . let us work for the good of all." In a time and context of religious tribalism, then and now, Paul loves that word "all": "*all* are one . . . work for the good of *all*."

JOHN M. BUCHANAN

Luke 10:1–11, 16–20

What kind of hospitality do we offer to the stranger, the outsider, the enemy? Do we go as colonizers or as peacemakers? What of ourselves are we prepared to give up in order to make peace?

STANLEY P. SAUNDERS

Luke 10:1–11, 16–20

Where have we said, "No, thank you, our town is fine the way it is" (v. 10)? While crying "Woe!" against the congregation seems ill-advised (vv. 12–15), it might be useful for preachers to cry, "Whoa!" to caution people about their inhospitality and instead invite them into a season of discernment about how God is calling them to live out the risky and joyful good news.

HIERALD E. OSORTO

WHAT IS THE HOLY SPIRIT SAYING TO YOU THIS WEEK?

_____

_____

_____

_____

_____

A SPIRITUAL PRACTICE FOR THIS WEEK

Notice how you "overpack" this week. Do you carry or prepare so much that trusting in the Spirit or your neighbor is hampered? Try to "underpack" in some ways this week—even to pack nothing, like the disciples—and see what happens.

First Reading

2 Kings 5:1–14

Naaman, commander of the army of the king of Aram, was a great man and in high favor with his master, because by him the LORD had given victory to Aram. The man, though a mighty warrior, suffered from leprosy. Now the Arameans on one of their raids had taken a young girl captive from the land of Israel, and she served Naaman's wife. She said to her mistress, "If only my lord were with the prophet who is in Samaria! He would cure him of his leprosy." (vv. 1–3)

REFLECTION

This story is about paradoxes of power. Nearly every verse makes some reference to the issue of who has status and authority. Almost every initial impression is turned on its head. The seemingly powerful end up dependent on the seemingly powerless. This text is thus perfect for sermons on the limits of human power, the importance of humility, and the God whose power can be found among the powerless.

MATTHEW RICHARD SCHLIMM

RESPONSE

What is God's power like? What was a time when you looked for the power of God in the wrong place? When have you experienced God's power among the powerless? Many people today cringe at the word "humility," but how would you define it, according to this story?

PRAYER

Gracious God, teach me humility and give me wisdom to look for your power among the powerless. Amen.

Canticle

Psalm 30

As for me, I said in my prosperity,
    "I shall never be moved."
By your favor, O LORD,
    you had established me as a strong mountain;
you hid your face;
    I was dismayed.

To you, O LORD, I cried,
    and to the LORD I made supplication. (30:6–8)

REFLECTION

One can interpret this psalm simplistically: pray long enough and God
will make everything all right. However, a more nuanced reading reveals
a deeper theological meaning. The psalmist has learned to give thanks in
times when God's presence is manifest and in times when the face of God
is hidden (v. 7), trusting that "weeping may linger for the night, but joy
comes with the morning" (v. 5). The psalmist testifies to the truth that
even when trouble comes, people can hope, pray, and praise. . . . Even in
times of distress, the psalmist finds joy and offers praise to God.

DONNA GIVER-JOHNSTON

RESPONSE

How do you relate to the psalmist? Does praise come easily to you? What
is a difficult or troubling situation you face right now? Try to write a
prayer or psalm of praise to God from the midst of distress.

PRAYER

O Lord my God, your anger is but for a moment but your favor is for
a lifetime; my weeping may linger for the night, but joy will come with
the morning. Amen.

Second Reading

Galatians 6:(1–6) 7–16

For neither circumcision nor uncircumcision is anything; but a new creation is everything! As for those who will follow this rule—peace be upon them, and mercy, and upon the Israel of God. (vv. 15–16)

REFLECTION

"Just Let the Circumcision Knife Slip" may not be the most acceptable title for Sunday's sermon, but would be the best summation of Paul's insistence on viewing faith from the inside out rather than the outside in. For all that we do in order to manifest outward signs of faith, be it through pious practices of prayer and devotion or engagement with God's world through acts of social justice, we encounter Paul's insistence on faith that dwells within. The preacher will help us encounter, again, faith that works through love.

LINDA MCKINNISH BRIDGES

RESPONSE

What practices in your life are most important to you right now as public signs of your faith? What does your faith look like on the inside, would you say? How do your outward practices support your inner faith? How do they distract?

PRAYER

O Christ, you have searched me and known me; teach me not to boast of anything but your cross, and that in you I have become a new creation. Amen.

Gospel

Luke 10:1–11, 16–20

"Go on your way. See, I am sending you out like lambs into the midst of wolves. Carry no purse, no bag, no sandals; and greet no one on the road. Whatever house you enter, first say, 'Peace to this house!'" (vv. 3–5)

REFLECTION

In commissioning seventy disciples, Jesus invites them—and us—into practices of risk. Risk traveling lightly. Risk rejection and welcome. Risk protest and proclaiming the good news of God's kingdom, which is coming near to every circumstance (Luke 10:9). This passage nurtures our capacity for risking. . . .

Jesus' instructions, "Carry no purse, no bag, no sandals" (v. 4), sound counterintuitive to many in our congregations. Should we not bring along extra, just in case? . . . Preachers may take this opportunity to explore how to undo understandings of the Christian journey that emphasize the individual and encourage overpacking.

HIERALD E. OSORTO

RESPONSE

How has God been inviting you to take risks in your Christian journey, recently? How might you be "overpacking"? How do you see yourself alone on the journey? How do you see yourself as part of a community on the journey?

PRAYER

Brother Jesus, send me out with peace and confidence on your way; show me I am not alone. Amen.

Weekend Reflections

FURTHER CONNECTION

This is what God's kingdom is like: a bunch of outcasts and oddballs gathered at a table, not because they are rich or worthy or good, but because they are hungry, because they said yes. And there's always room for more.

RACHEL HELD EVANS (1981–2019), *SEARCHING FOR SUNDAY*

MAKING THE CONNECTIONS

Choose one or two questions for reflection:

1. What connections have you noticed between this week's texts and other passages in Scripture?

2. What connections have you made between this week's texts and the world beyond Scripture?

3. Does either of this week's two commentary themes speak especially to your life or the life of the world around you right now?

4. What is God saying to your congregation in particular through this week's readings and commentaries?

MY CONNECTIONS

_____

_____

_____

_____

_____

_____

Sabbath Day

SCRIPTURE OF ASSURANCE

But speaking the truth in love, we must grow up in every way into him who is the head, into Christ, from whom the whole body, joined and knit together by every ligament with which it is equipped, as each part is working properly, promotes the body's growth in building itself up in love. (Ephesians 4:15–16)

WEEKLY EXAMEN

- Take a quiet moment, seek out God's presence, and pray for the guidance of the Spirit.

- Consider the past week; recall specific moments and feelings that stand out to you.

- Choose one moment or feeling for deeper examination, thanksgiving, or repentance.

- Let go, breathe deeply, and invite Christ's love to surround and fill you in preparation for the week ahead.

- End with the Lord's Prayer.

The Week Leading Up to
Proper 10

(Sunday between July 10 and July 16)

Amos 7:7–17

Then Amos answered Amaziah, "I am no prophet, nor a prophet's son; but I am a herdsman, and a dresser of sycamore trees, and the LORD took me from following the flock, and the LORD said to me, 'Go, prophesy to my people Israel.'" (vv. 14–15)

Deuteronomy 30:9–14

Surely, this commandment that I am commanding you today is not too hard for you, nor is it too far away. (v. 11)

Colossians 1:1–14

You have heard of this hope before in the word of the truth, the gospel that has come to you. Just as it is bearing fruit and growing in the whole world, so it has been bearing fruit among yourselves from the day you heard it and truly comprehended the grace of God. (vv. 5b–6)

Luke 10:25–37

And [Jesus] said to [the lawyer], "You have given the right answer; do this, and you will live."

But wanting to justify himself, he asked Jesus, "And who is my neighbor?" (vv. 28–29)

LECTIO DIVINA

Underline a word or phrase that especially grabs your attention. Pray from that word or phrase and ask God to help you connect to its particular invitation for you this week.

Themes from This Week's Writers

THEME 1: *Rise Up and Speak the Truth*

Amos 7:7–17

Bringing God's word to others is not easy: the opposition Amos faces makes this abundantly clear (Amos 7:10–17). Despite difficulties, the church is called to speak God's word to a world needing direction.

MATTHEW RICHARD SCHLIMM

Amos 7:7–17

The mission of the people of God is to advance such concerns by speaking truth to power locally, nationally, and globally, while living in a way that shows a fidelity to the word we teach and preach.

CAROL J. DEMPSEY, OP

Psalm 82

The psalmist's words can be a powerful prayer for God to "Rise up" and defeat the powers of evil, as well as a powerful plea for the people of God to "Rise up" and be the hands of Jesus on the earth, helping, healing, and bringing hope.

DONNA GIVER-JOHNSTON

THEME 2: *Love Is More Important Than Doctrine*

Colossians 1:1–14

The writer also wants believers to know that faithful discipleship is never a choice between correct theological beliefs or living a faithful, loving life with one's neighbors in the world. Both matter.

JOHN M. BUCHANAN

Luke 10:25–37

At the heart of all Christian practice is the dangerous impulse to reach out in compassion and genuine care, without regard for one's self-interest or even one's own salvation. Salvation is found not in building walls, but in joining arms with the enemy and the alien—notions directly contrary to current political tendencies.

STANLEY P. SAUNDERS

Luke 10:25–37

How will we allow ourselves to receive care from the person in the pews who disagrees with us most? That answer for many will center on Jesus and the good news of the kingdom he proclaims.

HIERALD E. OSORTO

WHAT IS THE HOLY SPIRIT SAYING TO YOU THIS WEEK?

_____

_____

_____

_____

_____

A SPIRITUAL PRACTICE FOR THIS WEEK

Practice hospitality to strangers this week in small, unexpected, but risky ways. Reach out to an unlikely stranger with some friendly conversation. Write a positive comment on an unfamiliar person's social media post. Send a thank-you or appreciative email or note to someone you do not really know.

First Reading

The LORD your God will make you abundantly prosperous in all your undertakings, in the fruit of your body, in the fruit of your livestock, and in the fruit of your soil. For the LORD will again take delight in prospering you, just as he delighted in prospering your ancestors. (v. 9)

REFLECTION

On the one hand, both Deuteronomy and prosperity theology say that good things come in this lifetime for those who obey God. . . . On the other hand, much of the health-and-wealth gospel today focuses on having the right mind-set, being optimistic, forgetting about the past, and trusting that God has good things in store for the future. . . . Deuteronomy, meanwhile, stresses remembering our past—including sinful mistakes (Deut. 1–4). It does not assume that everything will automatically turn out okay, especially when people lead wicked lives (28:15–68). . . . It teaches compassion toward the poor (15:7–11).

MATTHEW RICHARD SCHLIMM

RESPONSE

In what ways have you connected your good fortune to your good behavior or good attitude in this life? How does the message of Deuteronomy affirm or contradict what you believe makes a prosperous, faithful life?

PRAYER

O Lord, your word is already very near to my life, in my mouth and my heart; show me how to turn to you with all my heart and all my soul. Amen.

Canticle

To you, O Lord, I lift up my soul.
O my God, in you I trust;
    do not let me be put to shame;
    do not let my enemies exult over me.(vv. 1–2)

REFLECTION

With these texts, the preacher may proclaim a powerful word about the faithfulness of God in every time, from generation to generation. God's love and mercy have stood the test of time. . . .

. . . These readings invite the hearer to live in the tension between lament and praise, not as one without hope, but one who trusts that the God who has been faithful for generations will remember the covenant of steadfast love and mercy forever. So we respond with the psalmist, "O my God, in you I trust" (Ps. 25:2).

DONNA GIVER-JOHNSTON

RESPONSE

What does it mean to you to remember that God is faithful in every generation, despite terrible suffering? How do you live in the "tension between lament and praise" in your own life?

PRAYER

Ever-living God, lead me in your truth and teach me, for you are the God of my salvation; for you I wait all day long. Amen.

Second Reading

Colossians 1:1–14

For this reason, since the day we heard it, we have not ceased praying for you and asking that you may be filled with the knowledge of God's will in all spiritual wisdom and understanding, so that you may lead lives worthy of the Lord, fully pleasing to him, as you bear fruit in every good work and as you grow in the knowledge of God. (vv. 9–10)

REFLECTION

There are few words more comforting, more strengthening, and more empowering than "I am praying for you." . . . Perhaps we have heard those words as we encountered a particularly daunting challenge. They come from the heart, those words do, and there is something about them that is mysteriously powerful. Likewise, there are few words happier or more personally affirming than "I thank God for you." Those words are church language, the language of Christian love, and they carry and convey life both to those who hear them and to those who speak them.

JOHN M. BUCHANAN

RESPONSE

Why are these two phrases so powerful? How have they been powerful for you to hear from someone else? How have they been powerful for you to say to someone else? What is Paul teaching us about how to talk to each other, as Christians, do you think?

PRAYER

O God, with grace and peace I thank you today for these people . . . [*names*], that your word may grow and bear fruit in them, and also in me. Amen.

Gospel

Luke 10:25–37

"Which of these three, do you think, was a neighbor to the man who fell into the hands of the robbers?" He said, "The one who showed him mercy." Jesus said to him, "Go and do likewise." (vv. 36–37)

REFLECTION

The details demonstrate complete, relentless, boundless care. All this from a despised Samaritan, the enemy who has nothing to gain from this kind of care for an unknown victim. He demonstrates what it means to act as a neighbor and thus to fulfill the commandments.

This parable easily lends itself, first, to translation into more contemporary terms. The Samaritan could be an immigrant, an Arab, a released felon. Which enemy/neighbor seems most threatening and risky? . . . Salvation is found not in building walls, but in joining arms with the enemy and the alien—notions directly contrary to current political tendencies.

STANLEY P. SAUNDERS

RESPONSE

Which neighbor of yours feels most threatening and risky? What is a way, even if it sounds impossible, you or your congregation might join arms with them, care for them, or allow them to care for you—even if there is nothing to gain by doing so?

PRAYER

Jesus, teach me mercy so that I may know and love my neighbor as myself. Amen.

Weekend Reflections

FURTHER CONNECTION

"Who is my neighbor?" The neighbor was the Samaritan who approached the wounded man and made him his neighbor. The neighbor . . . is not he whom I find in my path, but rather he in whose path I place myself, he whom I approach and actively seek.

GUSTAVO GUTIÉRREZ (1928–), *A THEOLOGY OF LIBERATION*

MAKING THE CONNECTIONS

Choose one or two questions for reflection:

1. What connections have you noticed between this week's texts and other passages in Scripture?

2. What connections have you made between this week's texts and the world beyond Scripture?

3. Does either of this week's two commentary themes speak especially to your life or the life of the world around you right now?

4. What is God saying to your congregation in particular through this week's readings and commentaries?

MY CONNECTIONS

_____

_____

_____

_____

_____

_____

Sabbath Day

SCRIPTURE OF ASSURANCE

> But you, O Lord, are a shield around me,
>   my glory, and the one who lifts up my head. (Psalm 3:3)

WEEKLY EXAMEN

- Take a quiet moment, seek out God's presence, and pray for the guidance of the Spirit.

- Consider the past week; recall specific moments and feelings that stand out to you.

- Choose one moment or feeling for deeper examination, thanksgiving, or repentance.

- Let go, breathe deeply, and invite Christ's love to surround and fill you in preparation for the week ahead.

- End with the Lord's Prayer.

The Week Leading Up to
Proper 11
(Sunday between July 17 and July 23)

Amos 8:1–12

"The songs of the temple shall become wailings in that day,"
 says the Lord God;
"the dead bodies shall be many,
 cast out in every place. Be silent!" (v. 3)

Genesis 18:1–10a

The Lord appeared to Abraham by the oaks of Mamre, as he sat at the entrance of his tent in the heat of the day. He looked up and saw three men standing near him. When he saw them, he ran from the tent entrance to meet them, and bowed down to the ground. (vv. 1–2)

Colossians 1:15–28

For in him all the fullness of God was pleased to dwell, and through him God was pleased to reconcile to himself all things. (vv. 19–20a)

Luke 10:38–42

Now as they went on their way, Jesus entered a certain village, where a woman named Martha welcomed him into her home. She had a sister named Mary, who sat at the Lord's feet and listened to what he was saying. (vv. 38–39)

LECTIO DIVINA

Underline a word or phrase that especially grabs your attention. Pray from that word or phrase and ask God to help you connect to its particular invitation for you this week.

Themes from This Week's Writers

THEME 1: *Justice for the Poor*

Amos 8:1–12

Like Jesus' God (cf. Matt. 23:23), Amos's God is a God of justice—a God who sides with the poor when no one else comes to their aid (Ps. 12:5; Luke 6:24–25). This God refuses to do nothing while those in need suffer deeply.

MATTHEW RICHARD SCHLIMM

Amos 8:1–12

Amos's words call people everywhere to practice justice—to expose the injustices done to the poor and needy locally, nationally, and globally, and then take steps to eradicate such injustices. The practice of justice is an act and a virtue that hastens the reign of God.

CAROL J. DEMPSEY, OP

Psalm 52

The psalm uses vivid imagery for the disruptive chain reaction emanating from the deceitfulness of the powerful: slicing, devouring, snatching, tearing, uprooting. In both Amos and the psalm, bodies and landscapes are portrayed as violently riven.

BENJAMIN M. STEWART

THEME 2: *Welcome God in Our Midst*

Genesis 18:1–10a

The rationale for extending hospitality is multifaceted: first, the recognition that Jews and Christians alike share the same status of resident aliens and exiles (1 Pet. 1; 2:4–10), and second, in offering hospitality to another, one is offering it to Jesus (John 13:20).

CAROL J. DEMPSEY, OP

Colossians 1:15–28

If the reader has been perplexed by the preceding words of grand cosmic schemes, redeemer myths, and Hellenistic thought, the time has come to bring the message home to the reader narrowed down into a clear, succinct point: the vastness of this cosmic faith is lodged in the individual believer.

LINDA MCKINNISH BRIDGES

Luke 10:38–42

Together, Martha and Mary represent the alternative to those houses that do not welcome Jesus or his disciples (vv. 10–11, 12–15). In the house where Martha and Mary are in partnership, each bringing her "portion" to the table, God's kingdom draws near in both peace (v. 6) and power (vv. 9, 18–20).

STANLEY P. SAUNDERS

WHAT IS THE HOLY SPIRIT SAYING TO YOU THIS WEEK?

_____

_____

_____

_____

_____

A SPIRITUAL PRACTICE FOR THIS WEEK

Spend some time sitting still, like Mary. As little as thirty seconds is enough, but if you can, spend five minutes, ten minutes, or even thirty minutes, just listening. Listen to the world, listen for God or Jesus, listen to your body, listen to your soul. What do you notice?

First Reading

Amos 8:1–12

Hear this, you that trample on the needy,
  and bring to ruin the poor of the land,
saying, . . .
. . . .
"We will make the ephah small and the shekel great,
  and practice deceit with false balances,
buying the poor for silver
  and the needy for a pair of sandals,
  and selling the sweepings of the wheat." (vv. 4–6)

REFLECTION

God is angry because the poor and the needy are taken advantage of for economic gain (vv. 4, 6). The injustices are twofold: they are cheated out of money (v. 5), and they are made into bartered goods (v. 6). The text suggests that justice will be a corporate experience and not directed solely at the troublemakers. Looking at the text as a whole, and on a personal note, Amos shows us how power can be used abusively for self-serving purposes that deny others their legal rights and/or human dignity.

CAROL J. DEMPSEY, OP

RESPONSE

How do you see Amos's verses still speaking to this week's news? What are some ways that the goods you consume result from injustice or exploitation in the lives of others? What is one thing you could do to improve access to legal rights or dignity among your needy neighbors?

PRAYER

God of justice, may your anger spur me to witness and action on behalf of my poor and needy neighbors, that economic gain may be for all and not only a few. Amen.

Canticle

Psalm 15

O LORD, who may abide in your tent?
Who may dwell on your holy hill?

Those who walk blamelessly, and do what is right,
and speak the truth from their heart. (vv. 1–2)

REFLECTION

In response to the story of Abraham and Sarah's showing hospitality to strangers—"entertaining angels unawares," as the author of Hebrews puts it (Heb. 13:2)—we sing of the justice and righteousness required of those who would meet God face-to-face. Yet the song prepares us to be surprised by the gospel, where with Mary we are invited to rest, without works, before the face of God. Mary's rest before Jesus may bring preachers back to remember the final line of the psalm, perhaps with a sense of the countercultural resistance that such resting and immovability can involve.

BENJAMIN M. STEWART

RESPONSE

What is the relationship in your life or your congregation between work and rest? Is rest resisted in your community? How do you or might you use rest as a way to reconnect with God?

PRAYER

O God, show me how to abide in your tent and dwell on your holy hill, that I may trust in your steadfast love for ever and ever. Amen.

Second Reading

Colossians 1:15–28

To them God chose to make known how great among the Gentiles are the riches of the glory of this mystery, which is Christ in you, the hope of glory. It is he whom we proclaim, warning everyone and teaching everyone in all wisdom, so that we may present everyone mature in Christ. (vv. 27–28)

REFLECTION

The author of Colossians gives us this simple fact: Christ is *in* you, and that is the hope of glory. Preachers can help listeners know again the cosmic, vast glory of God, the ways that this glory is for the purpose of reconciliation, and how this vast glory with its reconciling character dwells in us, in each of us. . . . What would it mean to have persons of faith bearing the God-light in ruptured, broken, divided situations? What can it mean to us to see ourselves as ones who are to and do bear God's light in the world?

LINDA MCKINNISH BRIDGES

RESPONSE

Reflect on the presence of Christ's vast glory inside of you. Hold onto this image today as you find yourself in broken situations. What does it mean to see yourself as one who bears God's light into the world, instead of, say, using it only to defend or protect yourself?

PRAYER

O Christ, it is you I proclaim, and the riches of the glory of this mystery: that you dwell in me and all people. Amen.

Gospel

Luke 10:38–42

But Martha was distracted by her many tasks; so she came to him and asked, "Lord, do you not care that my sister has left me to do all the work by myself? Tell her then to help me." But the Lord answered her, "Martha, Martha, you are worried and distracted by many things; there is need of only one thing. Mary has chosen the better part, which will not be taken away from her." (vv. 40–42)

REFLECTION

Who among us has not been similarly distracted, worrying about details of the service project, the agenda for the meeting, the novelty of the sermon? Who among us has not on occasion opted for passive aggression on par with her complaint: "Lord, do you not care that my sister has left me to do all the work [i.e., to serve, to minister] by myself?" . . . Where have we diminished the role of various ministries to the chagrin of fellow disciples? When have we used those words ourselves to mask a deeper question: Do you truly see me?

HIERALD E. OSORTO

RESPONSE

What are some ways that you have felt invisible lately? Do you ever feel invisible to God? In what ways are you longing to be seen? What others in your life have you diminished, overlooked, or ignored, in turn, not truly seeing them either?

PRAYER

Gracious God, you see me and love me; help me not to be so distracted that I forget to see and love you in others. Amen.

Weekend Reflections

FURTHER CONNECTION

We shall not, we shall not be moved
We shall not, we shall not be moved
Like a tree that's planted by the water
We shall not be moved

We shall not, we shall not be moved
We shall not, we shall not be moved
We're fighting for our freedom
We shall not be moved

We shall not, we shall not be moved
We shall not, we shall not be moved
We're fighting for our children
We shall not be moved

AFRICAN AMERICAN SPIRITUAL, ADAPTED AS
CIVIL RIGHTS PROTEST SONG

MAKING THE CONNECTIONS

Choose one or two questions for reflection:

1. What connections have you noticed between this week's texts and other passages in Scripture?

2. What connections have you made between this week's texts and the world beyond Scripture?

3. Does either of this week's two commentary themes speak especially to your life or the life of the world around you right now?

4. What is God saying to your congregation in particular through this week's readings and commentaries?

_____

_____

_____

_____

_____

Sabbath Day

SCRIPTURE OF ASSURANCE

> I sought the LORD, and he answered me,
> and delivered me from all my fears.
> Look to him, and be radiant;
> so your faces shall never be ashamed. (Psalm 34:4–5)

WEEKLY EXAMEN

- Take a quiet moment, seek out God's presence, and pray for the guidance of the Spirit.

- Consider the past week; recall specific moments and feelings that stand out to you.

- Choose one moment or feeling for deeper examination, thanksgiving, or repentance.

- Let go, breathe deeply, and invite Christ's love to surround and fill you in preparation for the week ahead.

- End with the Lord's Prayer.

The Week Leading Up to
Proper 12
(Sunday between July 24 and July 30)

Hosea 1:2–10

Then the LORD said, "Name him Lo-ammi, for you are not my people and I am not your God." (v. 9)

Genesis 18:20–32

Far be it from you to do such a thing, to slay the righteous with the wicked, so that the righteous fare as the wicked! Far be that from you! Shall not the Judge of all the earth do what is just? (v. 25)

Colossians 2:6–15 (16–19)

God made you alive together with him, when he forgave us all our trespasses, erasing the record that stood against us with its legal demands. He set this aside, nailing it to the cross. He disarmed the rulers and authorities and made a public example of them, triumphing over them in it. (vv. 13b–15)

Luke 11:1–13

He was praying in a certain place, and after he had finished, one of his disciples said to him, "Lord, teach us to pray, as John taught his disciples." (v. 1)

LECTIO DIVINA

Underline a word or phrase that especially grabs your attention. Pray from that word or phrase and ask God to help you connect to its particular invitation for you this week.

Themes from This Week's Writers

THEME 1: *Where Is Good in the Midst of So Much Evil?*

Genesis 18:20–32

God does not *want* to destroy Sodom and Gomorrah. . . . As an agent of blessing, Abraham sought to prevent the destruction of the cities.

Abraham's actions can . . . remind us that the church's mission is to provide a blessing to others in an unrighteous and unjust time, when people are ensnared in a destructive culture.

RONALD J. ALLEN

Genesis 18:20–32

The church is called, in its prayer life, Sunday liturgy, and mission work, to ask God to reveal good in the midst of evil and preserve it. It does so assuming, in the Spirit of Christ, that the entire world is beloved and worth saving. It refuses to accept condemnation as the final word, seeking instead the merciful heart of God.

EMRYS TYLER

Colossians 2:6–15 (16–19)

Behind the code and its accusations are cosmic themes about "rulers and authorities," language that evokes spiritual cosmic battles that become institutionalized in systemic injustices, institutions, and injustices. Here we see the triumph of God in the grace of God revealed in Christ, creator, redeemer, and cosmic reconciler (v. 15).

SCOT MCKNIGHT

THEME 2: *Teach Us to Pray*

Genesis 18:20–32

In contrast to religious circles today that encourage people to be resigned to their perception of God's will, this passage authorizes wrestling openly with God.

RONALD J. ALLEN

Luke 11:1–13

If the Bible is a book of prayer, and the Lord's Prayer is a model of prayer, the question remains: Does God answer our prayers? Jesus' parable about neighbors in the middle of the night assures us that God indeed answers prayers.

R. ALAN CULPEPPER

Luke 11:1–13

As a general observation, though, note how short the Lord's Prayer is. This is true of Matthew's version, but Luke's version is shorter still. What does it mean that the heart of Christian prayer is this very small pile of words?

STEPHEN FARRIS

Luke 11:1–13

There is no guarantee in Luke that we will get what we ask for. . . . We may not even always sense the presence of the Holy Spirit. . . . The ultimate gift of prayer is, in the end, the Holy Spirit, God's own presence.

STEPHEN FARRIS

WHAT IS THE HOLY SPIRIT SAYING TO YOU THIS WEEK?

_____

_____

_____

_____

_____

A SPIRITUAL PRACTICE FOR THIS WEEK

Choose a place or community to pray for where you see persistent sins of greed, unfaithfulness, or fear. Look to find a sign of goodness that persists there, too, then, pray for the people of this place and that goodness. Use Psalm 85 or 138 in your prayers.

First Reading

Hosea 1:2–10 or Genesis 18:20–32

And the LORD said to him, "Name him Jezreel; for in a little while I will punish the house of Jehu for the blood of Jezreel, and I will put an end to the kingdom of the house of Israel. On that day I will break the bow of Israel in the valley of Jezreel." (Hosea 1:4–5)

Then Abraham came near and said, "Will you indeed sweep away the righteous with the wicked?" (Genesis 18:23)

REFLECTION

How do we reconcile divine love and compassion with such violent behavior on God's part? If God has the power to end injustice in a single stroke, and to invoke a world of complete blessing, why does God not do this? Other contemporary Christians believe that God's nature is unconditional love, so that God could not engage in violent punishment. Those who hold this perspective can still claim that sin leads to destruction. While God might not incinerate people, disobedience brings about social collapse. God does not have to destroy us. We destroy ourselves.

RONALD J. ALLEN

RESPONSE

Where have you seen injustice, over a long period of time, destroy a society? How is injustice currently destabilizing the community where you live? How do you reconcile God's love with violent descriptions like these passages?

PRAYER

God, you are full of love and full of righteous anger; teach us not to destroy ourselves, but to seek justice. Amen.

Canticle

Psalm 138

Though I walk in the midst of trouble,
    you preserve me against the wrath of my enemies;
you stretch out your hand,
    and your right hand delivers me.
The LORD will fulfill his purpose for me;
    your steadfast love, O LORD, endures forever.
Do not forsake the work of your hands. (vv. 7–8)

REFLECTION

With the image of humans as dust formed by God's hands, it is as if
God is being offered a reminder of the long arc of divine care for this
fragile and beloved creature: God's creation of the earth itself, God's
molding of the human creature from the dust and breathing into it
the breath of life, God's nurturance of human life among the other
flourishing creatures of earth. . . . The pleas from Abraham and the
psalmist imply that God will be moved to compassion by remembering
our earth-to-earth nature.

BENJAMIN M. STEWART

RESPONSE

When you pray and remind God of who you are, what does it mean, if
God knows everything? How does prayer shape your relationship with
God? Your relationship to the world?

PRAYER

Creator God, you made me from dust and the breath of life; when I call,
answer me, and increase my strength of soul. Amen.

Second Reading

Colossians 2:6–15 (16–19)

Therefore do not let anyone condemn you in matters of food and drink or of observing festivals, new moons, or sabbaths. These are only a shadow of what is to come, but the substance belongs to Christ. (vv. 16–17)

REFLECTION

Christ is our life. Christ's identity is our identity. Christ animates our existence. . . . Christ is God's beloved Son, and so we are God's beloved sons and daughters. His death to sin is our death to sin. His resurrection is our resurrection. His life is our life. His victory over the evil powers is our victory. If these realities are true, if we all share in the divine fullness of Christ's life and death, then we have no basis for ambitious competition with one another, for God can give no greater gift to his people than sharing in God's own life.

JOSHUA W. JIPP

RESPONSE

In what ways are you competitive with others? In what ways do you feel others judge you? Choose a phrase from the above reflection that most speaks to you today. How might it help you let go of feelings of comparison and envy?

PRAYER

Christ Jesus, you are my substance; help me continue to live my life in you—rooted and built up in you, that I may abound in thanksgiving. Amen.

Gospel

Luke 11:1–13

"Is there anyone among you who, if your child asks for a fish, will give a snake instead of a fish? Or if the child asks for an egg, will give a scorpion? If you then, who are evil, know how to give good gifts to your children, how much more will the heavenly Father give the Holy Spirit to those who ask him!" (vv. 11–13)

REFLECTION

This text uses three metaphors about questing: a beggar pleading, a seeker for wisdom searching, and a person knocking at a door (perhaps a homeless person seeking shelter—cf. Luke 13:24–25). Ask, seek, and knock; in each case, the desire is granted. Then Jesus advances a fourth metaphor—a child entreating a parent—and moves the argument from the lesser to the greater: if human beings know how to give to their children, how much more does God. The preacher may want to explore how these four metaphors suggest ways that prayers are answered.

R. ALAN CULPEPPER

RESPONSE

Reflect on these four metaphors for prayer. How do they differ? What feels familiar? Does one especially resemble you, today? Choose something significant to ask God for, in prayer, this week.

PRAYER

O God, teach us to pray, and to believe you are always doing all in your power to answer and to give us what we ask for. Amen.

Weekend Reflections

FURTHER CONNECTION

Imaginary evil is romantic and varied; real evil is gloomy, monotonous, barren, boring. Imaginary good is boring; real good is always new, marvelous, intoxicating.

SIMONE WEIL (1909–43), GRAVITY AND GRACE

MAKING THE CONNECTIONS

Choose one or two questions for reflection:

1. What connections have you noticed between this week's texts and other passages in Scripture?

2. What connections have you made between this week's texts and the world beyond Scripture?

3. Does either of this week's two commentary themes speak especially to your life or the life of the world around you right now?

4. What is God saying to your congregation in particular through this week's readings and commentaries?

MY CONNECTIONS

_____

_____

_____

_____

_____

_____

Sabbath Day

SCRIPTURE OF ASSURANCE

> When you pass through the waters, I will be with you;
>   and through the rivers, they shall not overwhelm you;
> when you walk through fire you shall not be burned,
>   and the flame shall not consume you. (Isaiah 43:2)

WEEKLY EXAMEN

- Take a quiet moment, seek out God's presence, and pray for the guidance of the Spirit.

- Consider the past week; recall specific moments and feelings that stand out to you.

- Choose one moment or feeling for deeper examination, thanksgiving, or repentance.

- Let go, breathe deeply, and invite Christ's love to surround and fill you in preparation for the week ahead.

- End with the Lord's Prayer.

The Week Leading Up to
Proper 13
(Sunday between July 31 and August 6)

Hosea 11:1–11

I will not execute my fierce anger;
  I will not again destroy Ephraim;
for I am God and no mortal,
  the Holy One in your midst,
  and I will not come in wrath. (v. 9)

Ecclesiastes 1:2, 12–14; 2:18–23

I hated all my toil in which I had toiled under the sun, seeing that I must leave it to those who come after me—and who knows whether they will be wise or foolish? (2:18–19a)

Colossians 3:1–11

Do not lie to one another, seeing that you have stripped off the old self with its practices and have clothed yourselves with the new self, which is being renewed in knowledge according to the image of its creator. (vv. 9–10)

Luke 12:13–21

"But God said to him, 'You fool! This very night your life is being demanded of you. And the things you have prepared, whose will they be?' So it is with those who store up treasures for themselves but are not rich toward God." (vv. 20–21)

LECTIO DIVINA

Underline a word or phrase that especially grabs your attention. Pray from that word or phrase and ask God to help you connect to its particular invitation for you this week.

Themes from This Week's Writers

THEME 1: *Called Back from Despair*

Hosea 11:1–11

Life is often anxious, alienated, and painful. While preachers can appropriately speak of God's love for individuals, the prophet has in mind God's fathomless love for Israel as community.

Despite the present raw, destructive fractiousness, God does not give up on human community as sphere for blessing. God seeks restoration.

RONALD J. ALLEN

Hosea 11:1–11

Unlike human judges and human parents, God will never give up on the children, no matter how bad things get.

EMRYS TYLER

Colossians 3:1–11

The Colossians have stripped off the "old self" and put on the "new self" (3:9b–10a). This is a self that transforms into Christlikeness (3:10b).

SCOT MCKNIGHT

THEME 2: *Wealth Will Not Save Us*

Ecclesiastes 1:2, 12–14; 2:18–23

Here the writer confesses to "hating" life's toil and to giving "the heart up to despair." Life is full of pain, and work is "a vexation." After death, the meaning of one's life vanishes like a vapor. Who knows whether those who inherit the results of one's labor will use it wisely or foolishly?

RONALD J. ALLEN

Luke 12:13–21

The challenge to live faithfully in this respect calls us to reexamine continually our lifestyle and financial choices, while participating in caring communities, providing for those in need, and persistently challenging societal structures that penalize the poor.

R. ALAN CULPEPPER

Luke 12:13–21

When the church is a sign of the kingdom, it will build not barns but a community with a different orientation than acquisition. It will be a community with a kingdom orientation.

STEPHEN FARRIS

WHAT IS THE HOLY SPIRIT SAYING TO YOU THIS WEEK?

_____

_____

_____

_____

_____

A SPIRITUAL PRACTICE FOR THIS WEEK

Choose one day this week to fast from purchasing anything or spend the whole week purchasing as little as possible; rely on what you already have or can get for free. Make a financial gift to a local food pantry or homeless shelter, a gift large enough to make you wince a bit.

First Reading

Ecclesiastes 1:2, 12–14; 2:18–23

What do mortals get from all the toil and strain with which they toil under the sun? For all their days are full of pain, and their work is a vexation; even at night their minds do not rest. This also is vanity. (2:22–23)

REFLECTION

The person and proclamation of Jesus Christ provide a helpful response to the cry of Ecclesiastes. Proclamation, praise, and prayer in worship answer feelings of despair with the promises of resurrection, the sovereignty of God, and the ability of the Spirit to grow good things, even where human ability withers and dies. So, Christians, receive the hope that not all toil is vanity if it is done with and for God (see Col. 3:23–24). . . . Christian life and worship lives in the tension between the tough experience of Ecclesiastes and the redemptive wisdom of Christ.

EMRYS TYLER

RESPONSE

Make a list of frustrated and cynical thoughts you have had lately. Title this list "Ecclesiastes." Then, under "Christ," list responses of hope and redemption that Jesus might say to you.

PRAYER

O Jesus, life is full of toil and pain; come and fill my heart with your wisdom and hope. Amen.

Canticle

Psalm 107:1–9, 43

Let them thank the LORD for his steadfast love,
> for his wonderful works to humankind.
For he satisfies the thirsty,
> and the hungry he fills with good things. (vv. 8–9)

REFLECTION

The saving action described in the psalm comes in response to the cry of the people in trouble. Worship this week may be in part a cry for deliverance from the deadly burdens of human acquisitiveness. In many of our congregations we are simultaneously trying to build additions to our barns—seeking greater material riches—even as we also suffer the environmental and social consequences of an economic system that privileges the wealthy. Seeking to transcend our compromised commitments and to be saved from their consequences, we sing our psalm to God.

BENJAMIN M. STEWART

RESPONSE

What "riches" or material things might you feel most hungry for, these days? What about your congregation? In what way does God fill you with good things already? In what way has God already satisfied your thirst?

PRAYER

Generous God, you want to satisfy my thirst and hunger; teach me gratitude and contentment in you. Amen.

Second Reading

Colossians 3:1–11

When Christ who is your life is revealed, then you also will be revealed with him in glory.

Put to death, therefore, whatever in you is earthly: fornication, impurity, passion, evil desire, and greed (which is idolatry). (vv. 4–5)

REFLECTION

The Colossians were marked by sexually immoral practices, behaviors that Paul seems to think are problematic because they are greedily preoccupied with the self rather than the other. Paul's demand that Christians reject these vices does not stem from a prudish, self-obsessed moralism. Rather, Paul understands that these vices lead to the destruction of community and stand against human flourishing. Those who are lying and are acting deceptively toward one another cannot participate in a community with trust, love, or humility. Those who are greedily consumed with acting out their sexual desires are not able to love and consider the good of others.

JOSHUA W. JIPP

RESPONSE

How much do you talk about sexual life or morality in terms of your faith or your church community? Or do you talk about sex and morality at all, with anybody? What would it mean to think of sexuality in terms of human flourishing rather than prudishness?

PRAYER

God of love, you created me for desire and delight; help me to turn my desires toward love and away from greed and deception, that Christ may be revealed in my body and soul. Amen.

Gospel

Luke 12:13–21

"And [the rich man] thought to himself, 'What should I do, for I have no place to store my crops?' Then he said, 'I will do this: I will pull down my barns and build larger ones, and there I will store all my grain and my goods. And I will say to my soul, Soul, you have ample goods laid up for many years; relax, eat, drink, be merry.'" (vv. 17–19)

REFLECTION

Notice four things about his thoughts: (1) the number of times "I" appears, (2) the number of times "my" appears, (3) the confident repetition of what he "will" do, and (4) that there is no mention of God. . . . He will store "all" his grain and goods, and then he fantasizes a life of ease, eating, drinking, and making merry (Isa. 22:12–14; Tob. 7:10–11; 1 Cor. 15:32). There is no one else in this picture except the rich man and his goods. . . . Could it be that his very possessions will demand his soul of him? Then whose will they be?

R. ALAN CULPEPPER

RESPONSE

When you think about your future, how do you picture yourself? How do you imagine your possessions? How do you imagine your loved ones? How do you imagine God in this picture?

PRAYER

God of abundance, help me to see the future defined by you and those I love, not by my goods, possessions, or income. Amen.

Weekend Reflections

FURTHER CONNECTION

Nada te turbe,	Let nothing disturb you,
nada te espante,	nothing frighten you,
Todo se pasa.	All things are passing.
Dios nose muda.	God never changes.
La paciencia todo alcanza.	Patience obtains all things.
Quien a Dios tiene	Whoever has God
nada le falta.	lacks nothing.
Solo Dios basta.	God is enough.

TERESA OF AVILA (1515–82), "NADA TE TURBE"

MAKING THE CONNECTIONS

Choose one or two questions for reflection:

1. What connections have you noticed between this week's texts and other passages in Scripture?

2. What connections have you made between this week's texts and the world beyond Scripture?

3. Does either of this week's two commentary themes speak especially to your life or the life of the world around you right now?

4. What is God saying to your congregation in particular through this week's readings and commentaries?

_____

_____

_____

_____

_____

Sabbath Day

SCRIPTURE OF ASSURANCE

Come to me, all you that are weary and are carrying heavy burdens, and I will give you rest. Take my yoke upon you, and learn from me; for I am gentle and humble in heart, and you will find rest for your souls. For my yoke is easy, and my burden is light. (Matthew 11:28–30)

WEEKLY EXAMEN

- Take a quiet moment, seek out God's presence, and pray for the guidance of the Spirit.

- Consider the past week; recall specific moments and feelings that stand out to you.

- Choose one moment or feeling for deeper examination, thanksgiving, or repentance.

- Let go, breathe deeply, and invite Christ's love to surround and fill you in preparation for the week ahead.

- End with the Lord's Prayer.

The Week Leading Up to
Proper 14
(Sunday between August 7 and August 13)

Isaiah 1:1, 10–20

When you stretch out your hands,
    I will hide my eyes from you;
even though you make many prayers,
    I will not listen;
    your hands are full of blood. (v. 15)

Genesis 15:1–6

And [Abram] believed the LORD; and the LORD reckoned it to him as righteousness. (v. 6)

Hebrews 11:1–3, 8–16

By faith we understand that the worlds were prepared by the word of God, so that what is seen was made from things that are not visible. (v. 3)

Luke 12:32–40

"But know this: if the owner of the house had known at what hour the thief was coming, he would not have let his house be broken into. You also must be ready, for the Son of Man is coming at an unexpected hour." (vv. 39–40)

LECTIO DIVINA

Underline a word or phrase that especially grabs your attention. Pray from that word or phrase and ask God to help you connect to its particular invitation for you this week.

Themes from This Week's Writers

THEME 1: *Faith Is the Assurance of Things Hoped For*

Genesis 15:1–6

Many congregations in historic denominations today are in diminishing circumstances and feel exiled. They are in danger of losing confidence in their ability to witness effectively. This text reminds them that God is faithful; blessing is possible, even in circumstances that seem unlikely.

RONALD J. ALLEN

Genesis 15:1–6

The reading from Genesis reminds us that trust is a crucial ingredient of life with God. God calls Abraham to trust a seemingly impossible promise. . . .

The family of God trusts in God's ability to fulfill promises, especially promises that elude reason or common experience.

EMRYS TYLER

Hebrews 11:1–3, 8–16

Faith is the settled conviction that the unseen God is real, and that while God remains hidden from our sight and our touch, this God continues to uphold this world and to commune with God's people.

JOSHUA W. JIPP

THEME 2: *Stay Alert to the Kingdom*

Psalm 33:12–22

The psalm, however, is not about human action at all. It is about God's creation and sustenance of the world, and the way God is at work to bring all of it to a good and righteous end.

ANGELA DIENHART HANCOCK

Luke 12:32–40

The first step in getting ready is to divest yourself of unnecessary baggage: sell what you have and give to the poor. . . . The reason to divest ourselves of material preoccupations is not . . . to be able to live freely and without worry; it is because where we put our treasure indicates ultimately where our hearts are.

R. ALAN CULPEPPER

Luke 12:32–40

Much of Luke 12 as a whole is about the imminence of something new. It is a challenge to live as if something new, the kingdom of God, is about to break into this world.

STEPHEN FARRIS

WHAT IS THE HOLY SPIRIT SAYING TO YOU THIS WEEK?

_____

_____

_____

_____

_____

A SPIRITUAL PRACTICE FOR THIS WEEK

Draw a personal faith family tree. Start with Abraham. You could also include other people of the Bible and Christian history, leaders or teachers from other traditions, favorite pastors and teachers, family, friends, or those who today are close companions on your faith journey.

First Reading

Genesis 15:1–6

He brought him outside and said, "Look toward heaven and count the stars, if you are able to count them." Then he said to him, "So shall your descendants be." And he believed the LORD; and the LORD reckoned it to him as righteousness. (vv. 5–6)

REFLECTION

All those holding faith in the God of Abraham, whether through Moses or Jesus Christ, are spiritual offspring of Abraham and Sarah. Reform Jewish synagogues and temples, Chinese house churches, Orthodox Jewish families in New York, Roman Catholic parishes in Peru, Syrian Christian dioceses—they all manifest the uncountable legacy Abraham was asked to imagine in the starry sky. . . . Doing so gives glory to the God who took the household of a single shepherd thousands of years ago and brought forth a people that continues to shape history with grace and mercy.

EMRYS TYLER

RESPONSE

Do you feel part of a spiritual family descended from Abraham? What is our shared inheritance from God with Jews, Christians, and Muslims? What do we still share today? Are there concrete ways you feel part of a shared spiritual household in your local community?

PRAYER

God of all, you made Abraham to be my ancestor, alongside so many of my sisters and brothers in faith; bring us together that we might continue to live from your righteousness and mercy. Amen.

Canticle

Psalm 33:12–22

Happy is the nation whose God is the LORD,
 the people whom he has chosen as his heritage.

The LORD looks down from heaven;
 he sees all humankind. (vv. 12–13)

REFLECTION

A search in Google Images for "Happy is the nation whose God is
the Lord" produces hundreds of results, many with verse 12b in the
foreground and an American flag waving away in the background. . . .
The psalm, however, is not about human action at all. It is about God's
creation and sustenance of the world, and the way God is at work to
bring all of it to a good and righteous end. . . . The psalmist sees beyond
the realpolitik of the fearful to the God who can deliver in ultimate,
unimaginable ways.

ANGELA DIENHART HANCOCK

RESPONSE

Make a list of forces and powers that protect you, your loved ones, and
your community. Then reflect on how God protects and sustains us,
perhaps not in the same ways. How is God "at work to bring all to a
good and righteous end," do you think?

PRAYER

O God of the nations, you look down from heaven and see all people in
the world you have made; sustain us and preserve us with your steadfast
love. Amen.

Second Reading

Hebrews 11:1–3, 8–16

If they had been thinking of the land that they had left behind, they would have had opportunity to return. But as it is, they desire a better country, that is, a heavenly one. Therefore God is not ashamed to be called their God; indeed, he has prepared a city for them. (vv. 15–16)

REFLECTION

We see a litany of names moving from Abel to Samuel and the prophets. Without names, we hear of "women" (v. 35) and an assortment of others (vv. 35b–38). Each of these died before receiving "what was promised." . . .

For Hebrews, then, living faithfully before God now entails looking to the fullness of God's kingdom in the future. Those who have faith now live with their eyes on the future kingdom, not by way of diminishing human and social realities in the present, but by seeing through today's realities to deeper and more lasting realities. That future gives perspective on how to live now.

SCOT MCKNIGHT

RESPONSE

When you look to the future and imagine God's kingdom, what do you see? Take some time to reflect. How does your life today reflect your belief? How could you align yourself even more with God's future?

PRAYER

God, I set out in this life, not quite knowing where I am going but seeking my homeland in you, walking by faith toward what I cannot yet see. Amen.

Gospel

"Be dressed for action and have your lamps lit; be like those who are waiting for their master to return from the wedding banquet, so that they may open the door for him as soon as he comes and knocks. Blessed are those slaves whom the master finds alert when he comes; truly I tell you, he will fasten his belt and have them sit down to eat, and he will come and serve them." (vv. 35–37)

REFLECTION

Here, upon his return, the master tightens his belt and serves the servants. That our master is one who takes on the form of a servant is good news. . . .

. . . the same as that of a *maître d'hôtel* in a fine restaurant, who says, "Right this way; the table's waiting." This ending to the metaphor of the return of the master, contrary to all social reality as it is, is also the introduction to the representation of the feast at which the master who gave his life for us will serve us bread and wine. The summons is, "Be prepared . . . to be served."

STEPHEN FARRIS

RESPONSE

What is it like to imagine that the second coming will not be a fiery war, but a vast feast? That Jesus will not wear a sword, but an apron? That Jesus, our savior and master, is also our great host and servant?

PRAYER

Gracious Jesus, you welcome us to your table; help me be alert and ready to accept your invitation, today and in the days to come. Amen.

Weekend Reflections

FURTHER CONNECTION

Faith is nothing more—but how much this is—than a motion of the soul toward God. It is not belief. Belief has objects—Christ was resurrected, God created the earth—faith does not. Even the motion of faith is mysterious and inexplicable: I say the soul moves "toward" God, but that is only the limitation of language. It may be God who moves, the soul that opens for him. Faith is faith in the soul. Faith is the word "faith" decaying into pure meaning.

CHRISTIAN WIMAN (1966–), *MY BRIGHT ABYSS*

MAKING THE CONNECTIONS

Choose one or two questions for reflection:

1. What connections have you noticed between this week's texts and other passages in Scripture?

2. What connections have you made between this week's texts and the world beyond Scripture?

3. Does either of this week's two commentary themes speak especially to your life or the life of the world around you right now?

4. What is God saying to your congregation in particular through this week's readings and commentaries?

_____

_____

_____

_____

_____

_____

Sabbath Day

SCRIPTURE OF ASSURANCE

For, "Everyone who calls on the name of the Lord shall be saved." (Romans 10:13)

WEEKLY EXAMEN

- Take a quiet moment, seek out God's presence, and pray for the guidance of the Spirit.

- Consider the past week; recall specific moments and feelings that stand out to you.

- Choose one moment or feeling for deeper examination, thanksgiving, or repentance.

- Let go, breathe deeply, and invite Christ's love to surround and fill you in preparation for the week ahead.

- End with the Lord's Prayer.

The Week Leading Up to
Proper 15
(Sunday between August 14 and August 20)

Isaiah 5:1–7

What more was there to do for my vineyard
  that I have not done in it?
When I expected it to yield grapes,
  why did it yield wild grapes? (v. 4)

Jeremiah 23:23–29

Is not my word like fire, says the LORD, and like a hammer that breaks a rock in pieces? (v. 29)

Hebrews 11:29–12:2

By faith the people passed through the Red Sea as if it were dry land, but when the Egyptians attempted to do so they were drowned. By faith the walls of Jericho fell after they had been encircled for seven days. (11:29–30)

Luke 12:49–56

"I came to bring fire to the earth, and how I wish it were already kindled! I have a baptism with which to be baptized, and what stress I am under until it is completed!" (vv. 49–50)

LECTIO DIVINA

Underline a word or phrase that especially grabs your attention. Pray from that word or phrase and ask God to help you connect to its particular invitation for you this week.

Themes from This Week's Writers

THEME 1: *God's Judgment Means That God Tells the Truth*

Isaiah 5:1–7 and Jeremiah 23:23–29

All of these passages are connected by the idea that God has expectations of us. God expects our trust. God has given us the blessings of the earth and of faith and the opportunity to have a relationship with a living God.

ELIZABETH C. LAROCCA-PITTS

Isaiah 5:1–7

The actions God promises—removing the hedge, breaking down the wall, ceasing to hoe or prune—are just God's way of seeing to it that Israel gets what it wants. The prophetic word assures us that God will not save us from the consequences of our own folly; often, this is judgment enough.

ROBERT A. RATCLIFF

Psalm 82

We can only ask for God's help in doing justice, reading the signs of the times, and speaking the truth—even "gods" do not get it right. . . . What are we asking, when we ask God to judge the world? To see it; to tell the truth about it; to make it right.

ANGELA DIENHART HANCOCK

THEME 2: *Not Peace, but Division*

Luke 12:49–56

Jesus problematizes the idea of peace and appears to yearn for something different, referencing the "stress" he feels as he anticipates a time of completion. . . .

. . . The message Jesus brings upsets order. It is meant to disquiet and disturb.

SALLY SMITH HOLT

Luke 12:49–56

The life [Jesus] is proposing will not be an easy one. Family members will be separated from each other as households experience division. Jesus' mission has become one of disturbing the orders we know, not merely bringing "peace."

ELIZABETH F. CALDWELL

Luke 12:49–56

Jesus is expecting more from them, the ones who have been listening to him, those who have seen him heal, perform miracles, confront authorities. His voice of prophetic urgency demands more than selective attentiveness if they are to be prepared for what he knows he is facing as he moves closer to Jerusalem.

ELIZABETH F. CALDWELL

WHAT IS THE HOLY SPIRIT SAYING TO YOU THIS WEEK?

_____

_____

_____

_____

_____

A SPIRITUAL PRACTICE FOR THIS WEEK

Sit, reflect, and pray with this difficult testimony from Jesus: I come not to bring peace, but division. What is peace and what is division, to Jesus? To you? To your community? Reflect on these two words, whether by journaling, making lists of related words, writing a poem, drawing or doodling.

First Reading

Am I a God near by, says the LORD, and not a God far off? Who can hide in secret places so that I cannot see them? says the LORD. Do I not fill heaven and earth? says the LORD. (vv. 23–24)

REFLECTION

The question is really a statement: we cannot put God in a box. This, it seems, was the mistake of the false prophets Jeremiah denounces in the passage. Their pleasing dreams contained only "the deceit of their own heart" (v. 26), rather than the hard truths Jeremiah knew the people needed to hear. The prophet reminds us that God will not be made a prop in some human stage play. . . .

. . . Only the God who *is* God is able to save us; no comfortable idol of our own making can do so.

ROBERT A. RATCLIFF

RESPONSE

How might have you, your community, or your community of origin put God into a box, or made God a prop for your own purposes instead of divine purposes? What "hard truths" might God be trying to communicate to you right now? What larger experience of God might set you free?

PRAYER

O Lord of creation, you are God both nearby and far off, you fill heaven and earth; teach me to hear your hard truths and to speak your word faithfully. Amen.

Canticle

Psalm 80:1–2, 8–19

Why then have you broken down its walls,
  so that all who pass along the way pluck its fruit?
The boar from the forest ravages it,
  and all that move in the field feed on it. (vv. 12–13)

REFLECTION

Maybe this is just what desperate people sound like. Not moxie, just panic.

. . . How do you get God to intervene? Remind God: you were such an excellent gardener, how energetically you made living space for us! Remember how gloriously we grew and spread and covered the land . . . ?

Now all of that has changed. The people know who is responsible when dreams go up in smoke. It is God who ruined everything: broke down the vineyard walls, invited the world to pillage, let the wild things devour. Why?

ANGELA DIENHART HANCOCK

RESPONSE

Reflect on a time you turned to God in desperation; or you may be feeling desperate now. How do you address God from this desperation? What hard truths might God be inviting you to face? What kind of answer do you hope for?

PRAYER

O God of hosts, stir up your might; come to save me and to save your people from desolation. Amen.

Second Reading

Hebrews 11:29–12:2

Therefore, since we are surrounded by so great a cloud of witnesses, let us also lay aside every weight and the sin that clings so closely, and let us run with perseverance the race that is set before us, looking to Jesus the pioneer and perfecter of our faith. (12:1–2a)

REFLECTION

[You] might reflect on how our time seems uniquely difficult and our challenges especially harrowing. Hebrews reminds us otherwise. It looks through a large lens and prompts us to remember the long arc of salvation history, inviting us to remember that we too have a place in the narrative. Reading about the heroes of the faith—biblical, ancient, or contemporary—is not merely an academic exercise or a form of religious entertainment; learning these sagas leads to a real-life response. . . . The sprint through Joshua, Judges, Samuel, and Kings culminates in Christ. Now we must run the race set before *us*.

JILL DUFFIELD

RESPONSE

How can you include yourself in God's salvation history? How have you already been part of God's plan and "the race set before us"? How do you see this race culminating in Christ?

PRAYER

O Jesus Christ, help me to run the race set before me, laying aside every weight and sin, and to see you and a great cloud of witnesses, before and alongside me. Amen.

Gospel

Luke 12:49–56

"Do you think that I have come to bring peace to the earth? No, I tell you, but rather division! From now on five in one household will be divided, three against two and two against three." (vv. 51–52)

REFLECTION

Keeping with the theme of upheaval present throughout the Gospel of Luke and found in Jesus' attention to the poor (e.g., 4:18; 16:19–31; 19:8–10) and even in stories of seating arrangements at banquets (14:7–24), duty-based relationships are being torn apart. This leaves broken families, but it also makes space for another kind of order to emerge; here we may find something beautiful growing out of and from the suffering that accompanies being broken. A new freedom is possible when obligations associated only with dutiful action are cast aside and thrown off.

SALLY SMITH HOLT

RESPONSE

What is valuable about having a sense of duty? What are liabilities? Why might Jesus have pushed against duty-based relationships? What are some duties or obligations in your own context that Jesus might ask to be broken or cast aside?

PRAYER

Jesus, show me how to interpret this present time, that I may not be afraid of upheaval, but know what relationships should be cast off and what obligations no longer serve you. Amen.

Weekend Reflections

FURTHER CONNECTION

Forgiving and being reconciled to our enemies or our loved ones are
not about pretending that things are other than they are. It is not
patting one another on the back and turning a blind eye to the wrong.
True reconciliation exposes the awfulness, the abuse, the pain, the
degradation, the truth. It could even sometimes make things worse. It
is a risky undertaking but in the end it is worthwhile, because in the
end dealing with the real situation helps to bring real healing. Spurious
reconciliation can bring only spurious healing.

DESMOND TUTU (1931–), *NO FUTURE WITHOUT FORGIVENESS*

MAKING THE CONNECTIONS

Choose one or two questions for reflection:

1. What connections have you noticed between this week's texts and
   other passages in Scripture?

2. What connections have you made between this week's texts and the
   world beyond Scripture?

3. Does either of this week's two commentary themes speak especially
   to your life or the life of the world around you right now?

4. What is God saying to your congregation in particular through this
   week's readings and commentaries?

_____

_____

_____

_____

_____

_____

Sabbath Day

SCRIPTURE OF ASSURANCE

God is faithful, and he will not let you be tested beyond your strength, but with the testing he will also provide the way out so that you may be able to endure it. (1 Corinthians 10:13b)

WEEKLY EXAMEN

- Take a quiet moment, seek out God's presence, and pray for the guidance of the Spirit.

- Consider the past week; recall specific moments and feelings that stand out to you.

- Choose one moment or feeling for deeper examination, thanksgiving, or repentance.

- Let go, breathe deeply, and invite Christ's love to surround and fill you in preparation for the week ahead.

- End with the Lord's Prayer.

The Week Leading Up to
Proper 16

(Sunday between August 21 and August 27)

Jeremiah 1:4–10

But the LORD said to me,
"Do not say, 'I am only a boy';
for you shall go to all to whom I send you,
and you shall speak whatever I command you." (v. 7)

Isaiah 58:9b–14

If you refrain from trampling the sabbath,
    from pursuing your own interests on my holy day;
if you call the sabbath a delight . . .
then you shall take delight in the LORD. (v. 13a, 14a)

Hebrews 12:18–29

Therefore, since we are receiving a kingdom that cannot be shaken, let us give thanks, by which we offer to God an acceptable worship with reverence and awe; for indeed our God is a consuming fire. (vv. 28–29)

Luke 13:10–17

But the leader of the synagogue, indignant because Jesus had cured on the sabbath, kept saying to the crowd, "There are six days on which work ought to be done; come on those days and be cured, and not on the sabbath day." (v. 14)

LECTIO DIVINA

Underline a word or phrase that especially grabs your attention. Pray from that word or phrase and ask God to help you connect to its particular invitation for you this week.

Themes from This Week's Writers

THEME 1: *What Is the Sabbath For?*

Isaiah 58:9b–14

They should not go out of their way to do purportedly "holy" things like fasting if they cannot do justice at the same time. God values justice and mercy more than such religious gestures, warns the prophet.

ELIZABETH C. LAROCCA-PITTS

Isaiah 58:9b–14

The prophet has nothing but scorn for such empty displays of religiosity. What good does a fast do us if all the while we quarrel, fight, and "strike with a wicked fist"?

ROBERT A. RATCLIFF

Luke 13:10–17

When Jesus heals her on the Sabbath, he comes under the immediate criticism of the leader of the synagogue for violation of Sabbath law, yet he has done so much more than this.

By transgressing several boundaries in his interaction with the bent-over woman, Jesus highlights that laws and rules are best interpreted through the lens of mercy.

SALLY SMITH HOLT

THEME 2: *God Sees and Calls Broken People*

Jeremiah 1:4–10

For every Isaiah saying, "Here am I, Lord, send me," there is at least one Moses saying, "Have you thought about my brother Aaron?" So often, the divine call is received not as a joy but as a burden.

ROBERT A. RATCLIFF

Luke 13:10–17

The woman does not ask to be healed. Jesus invites her to come to him. This woman, perhaps invisible to the community because of her illness and lack of status, is invited in by Jesus.

ELIZABETH F. CALDWELL

Luke 13:10–17

Jesus interacts with a woman, calling her over to an area of the synagogue that may have been reserved specifically for men. He also touches her, a woman, and one who has a disability and is bound by Satan. This closeness could render him unclean, but instead of letting the identity markers of the woman limit him, he accepts and works with and through each marker.

SALLY SMITH HOLT

WHAT IS THE HOLY SPIRIT SAYING TO YOU THIS WEEK?

_____

_____

_____

_____

_____

A SPIRITUAL PRACTICE FOR THIS WEEK

Pray for your congregation and its mission. What is God inviting you to consider for your church community in prayer through this week's readings? You might sit in the worship space for a while to pray, or use a photo or image from the church website or social media page.

First Reading

Jeremiah 1:4–10

"Do not be afraid of them,
for I am with you to deliver you,
says the LORD."

Then the LORD put out his hand and touched my mouth; and the LORD said to me,
"Now I have put my words in your mouth." (vv. 8–9)

REFLECTION

The readings this week from both Jeremiah and Luke pose a similar question. Will we claim the ministry God has given to us, whether or not we feel worthy or others consider us worthy? . . . Only those who are willing to take up the task, regardless of obstacles placed in the way, will fulfill the destiny God has for them. Humility is essential, but so also is courage. One must accept a gift from the hand of God before that gift can be shared with others. . . . No gift of God is meant only for the person to whom it is first given.

ELIZABETH C. LAROCCA-PITTS

RESPONSE

What new ministry, task, or gift might God be trying to offer you, in this season of your life? How might you feel unworthy of this invitation? What obstacles could be making you hesitate? How would this be a gift you would share with others? How would you grow?

PRAYER

Gracious God, help me to answer your call; help me not to be afraid, because you are with me to deliver me. Amen.

Canticle

Psalm 103:1–8

Bless the LORD, O my soul,
    and do not forget all his benefits—
who forgives all your iniquity,
    who heals all your diseases,
who redeems your life from the Pit,
    who crowns you with steadfast love and mercy. (vv. 2–4)

REFLECTION

In the second verse, the self urges itself to "bless the LORD" again, and not to lose track of all the things God does to promote well-being. . . . Some of the things named seem personal, and may be evidence that the writer of this psalm—like many who have loved it over the centuries—is recovering after a time of struggle or suffering. God's activities are wide-ranging: forgiving, healing, redeeming, satisfying, renewing, revealing, and making justice for those who need it most. All of this demonstrates that God is "abounding in steadfast love" (v. 8).

ANGELA DIENHART HANCOCK

RESPONSE

Place yourself alongside the psalmist, and reflect on an iniquity, disease, or Pit you are facing in your life right now. What glimpses of God's steadfast love and blessing have peeked through? For what might your soul bless the Lord this week?

PRAYER

Bless the Lord, O my soul, and all that is within me, because God redeems me and crowns me with steadfast love and mercy. Amen.

Second Reading

Hebrews 12:18–29

But you have come to Mount Zion and to the city of the living God, the heavenly Jerusalem, and to innumerable angels in festal gathering, and to the assembly of the firstborn who are enrolled in heaven, and to God the judge of all, and to the spirits of the righteous made perfect. (vv. 22–23)

REFLECTION

Jaded to the transcendent though many contemporary Christians may be, hunger for mystery has not abated. Miraculously, congregations do gather week after week for worship, perhaps not expecting much, but their real presence is a decision that communicates hope that another real presence will show up too. Why else come to worship in an age when other options abound and no cultural pressure compels attendance? . . . [Let us] discern what images, biblical and otherwise, will move their hearers to the edge of their seats in anticipation of experiencing God.

JILL DUFFIELD

RESPONSE

Do you hunger for mystery in your worship with your congregation? How are you fed by Sunday worship? How are you still longing?

PRAYER

God of glory, you invite me into your presence each day and in worship every Sunday; help me to find what I long for and my congregation to be a place where those who are looking to meet you may find you. Amen.

Gospel

Luke 13:10–17

"And ought not this woman, a daughter of Abraham whom Satan bound for eighteen long years, be set free from this bondage on the sabbath day?" When he said this, all his opponents were put to shame; and the entire crowd was rejoicing at all the wonderful things that he was doing. (vv. 16–17)

REFLECTION

Sabbath was a joyful day for remembering Israel's release from slavery in Egypt. Frances Taylor Gench writes that since freedom and liberation are at the heart of Sabbath worship, "the release of a captive woman, then, is a highly appropriate way to make the day holy, representing the very fulfillment, rather than a violation, of the sabbath."[1] Rather than viewing the story as Jesus' correcting the synagogue leader, see it as Jesus acting consistently within his tradition. In setting her free on the Sabbath, Jesus also sets free those who are there.

ELIZABETH F. CALDWELL

RESPONSE

How is your faith community a place where you feel set free? Is it also a place where you feel limited or constrained? Do you feel able, like Jesus, to invite people from the edges to come in, for healing and community?

PRAYER

Jesus, redeemer, liberate me and all those who are bound or captive, that we may be free and rejoice at all the wonderful things you are doing among us. Amen.

---

1. Frances Taylor Gench, *Back to the Well: Women's Encounters with Jesus in the Gospels* (Louisville, KY: Westminster John Knox, 2004), 89.

Weekend Reflections

FURTHER CONNECTION

Six days a week we wrestle with the world, wringing profit from the earth; on the Sabbath we especially care for the seed of eternity planted in the soul. The world has our hands, but our soul belongs to Someone Else. . . . The Sabbath as a day of rest, as a day of abstaining from toil, is not for the purpose of recovering one's lost strength and becoming fit for forthcoming labor. The Sabbath is a day for the sake of life.

ABRAHAM JOSHUA HESCHEL (1907–72), *THE SABBATH*

MAKING THE CONNECTIONS

Choose one or two questions for reflection:

1. What connections have you noticed between this week's texts and other passages in Scripture?

2. What connections have you made between this week's texts and the world beyond Scripture?

3. Does either of this week's two commentary themes speak especially to your life or the life of the world around you right now?

4. What is God saying to your congregation in particular through this week's readings and commentaries?

_____

_____

_____

_____

_____

_____

Sabbath Day

SCRIPTURE OF ASSURANCE

All this is from God, who reconciled us to himself through Christ, and has given us the ministry of reconciliation; that is, in Christ God was reconciling the world to himself, not counting their trespasses against them, and entrusting the message of reconciliation to us. (2 Corinthians 5:18–19)

WEEKLY EXAMEN

- Take a quiet moment, seek out God's presence, and pray for the guidance of the Spirit.

- Consider the past week; recall specific moments and feelings that stand out to you.

- Choose one moment or feeling for deeper examination, thanksgiving, or repentance.

- Let go, breathe deeply, and invite Christ's love to surround and fill you in preparation for the week ahead.

- End with the Lord's Prayer.

The Week Leading Up to
Proper 17

(Sunday between August 28 and September 3)

Jeremiah 2:4–13

For my people have committed two evils:
    they have forsaken me,
the fountain of living water,
    and dug out cisterns for themselves,
cracked cisterns
    that can hold no water. (v. 13)

Proverbs 25:6–7

Do not put yourself forward in the king's presence
    or stand in the place of the great;
for it is better to be told, "Come up here,"
    than to be put lower in the presence of a noble.

Hebrews 13:1–8, 15–16

Let mutual love continue. Do not neglect to show hospitality to strangers, for by doing that some have entertained angels without knowing it. (vv. 1–2)

Luke 14:1, 7–14

"For all who exalt themselves will be humbled, and those who humble themselves will be exalted." (v. 11)

LECTIO DIVINA

Underline a word or phrase that especially grabs your attention. Pray from that word or phrase and ask God to help you connect to its particular invitation for you this week.

Themes from This Week's Writers

THEME 1: *Chasing after Other Gods*

Jeremiah 2:4–13

God offers us fresh running water, yet we prefer to dig cracked and decaying holes in the ground to hold stagnant water. The contrast between the living God of Israel and the dead, dormant gods of the nations is clear to Jeremiah, and he seeks to make it clear to his contemporaries.

ELIZABETH C. LAROCCA-PITTS

Jeremiah 2:4–13

God's heart is broken by our choice of that which is less than God, because God's love for us is so steadfast. . . .

. . . Being in relationship with us means that God has become open to just that same heartbreak when we, through negligence or ill will, reject God and God's children.

ROBERT A. RATCLIFF

Luke 14:1, 7–14

In the world Jesus brings, social status and wealth are not the markers by which we judge ourselves and others, because these are not the markers that God utilizes to determine our importance. Those who are exalted in this world will not be in such positions under God's standards, and those who are humbled in this world will be exalted in a system that belongs to God and not to Rome.

SALLY SMITH HOLT

THEME 2: *God's Table Fellowship*

Hebrews 13:1–8, 15–16

In any case, "hospitality" to the stranger captures the writer's attention. Unlike the undeveloped imperative to "continue" sibling love (*philadelphia*), the love of strangers (*philoxenia*) is amplified by a reference to "entertaining angels" unknowingly. This likely points to Genesis 18:1–15. There, Abraham and Sarah receive three visitors at the oaks of Mamre, a narrative long regarded . . . as an appearance of the Trinity.

PAUL K. HOOKER

Luke 14:1, 7–14

Jesus invites diners to think about their table guest list, whom they include, whom they exclude, where the guests will sit—all important considerations if they are to live into a new communal social order that demonstrates how they remember his teaching, walk in his ways, and sit at table with strangers and friends.

ELIZABETH F. CALDWELL

Luke 14:1, 7–14

Luke's Jesus proclaims that individuals matter simply because all are included and invited to participate in the communal banquet offered by God. In both worlds, the illusions of worth based on wealth and social status distort what is truly significant according to the teachings of Jesus.

SALLY SMITH HOLT

WHAT IS THE HOLY SPIRIT SAYING TO YOU THIS WEEK?

_____

_____

_____

_____

_____

A SPIRITUAL PRACTICE FOR THIS WEEK

At your workplace, gym, local store, or on social media, engage meaningfully with one or two people whom most others avoid. On Sunday, engage in conversation after worship or at coffee hour with someone most other people find difficult.

First Reading

Jeremiah 2:4–13

Has a nation changed its gods,
  even though they are no gods?
But my people have changed their glory
  for something that does not profit. (v. 11)

REFLECTION

Anything can be a center of value, but for most of us the list is pretty standard: home, family, tribe, occupation, religion, nation. These values tell us who we are and what we are worth. . . . The problem here, of course, is that all of these realities are temporal, transitory, and thus bound to fail us. They are our idols; the faith we invest in them is rightfully reserved for that which is ultimate. Realizing this truth is what opens to us the possibility of a real and radical monotheism: devotion to the God who alone is worthy of that devotion.

ROBERT A. RATCLIFF

RESPONSE

Which two of the centers of value listed above are most powerful for you right now? Consider how these are "temporal, transitory, and thus bound to fail." How does God live within, yet beyond, these things, for you?

PRAYER

Loving God, you are a fountain of living water; help me to seek you, not idols or cracked cisterns, as the source of my life and value. Amen.

Canticle

Psalm 112

Praise the LORD!
   Happy are those who fear the LORD,
   who greatly delight in his commandments.
Their descendants will be mighty in the land;
   the generation of the upright will be blessed. (vv. 1–2)

REFLECTION

Psalm 112 . . . is written in acrostic, meaning in its case that each line begins with a successive letter of the Hebrew alphabet from beginning to end. It shares the wisdom of God from *aleph* to *tav* or what we in English would call from A to Z. . . .

In Psalm 112, the one who delights in God's commands receives divine favor that enables a merciful, generous, and joyful lifestyle in God, and models the sharing of God's generosity effortlessly and continuously. . . . What Psalm 112 describes is far more profound than prosperity, but economic justice established through personal piety to God.

GERALD C. LIU

RESPONSE

Create your own acrostic, from A to Z, perhaps also answering the question of Psalm 112: What does a joyful life in God look like?

PRAYER

O God, show me how to delight in your commandments, that I may find joy and seek for the well-being and prosperity of all your people. Amen.

Second Reading

Hebrews 13:1–8, 15–16

Keep your lives free from the love of money, and be content with what you have; for he has said, "I will never leave you or forsake you." So we can say with confidence,

> "The Lord is my helper;
> I will not be afraid.
> What can anyone do to me?" (vv. 5–6)

REFLECTION

Contemporary believers might quickly acknowledge that nothing good can come from adultery or the sexual exploitation of other human beings. The harder mandate to execute in our daily living may be the one regarding money. American consumerism relentlessly beats the drum of discontent. . . . Lift up the hopeful word that comes in the wake of these warnings and admonitions, the promise of Christ's never-failing presence and help. Release from relentless consuming comes as a gift of Jesus Christ, akin to the peace that passes understanding (John 14:27). Contentment is to be received as a gift, not sought out as one more thing to be acquired.

JILL DUFFIELD

RESPONSE

How is your own life being influenced or swayed by the love of money or stuff right now? In what ways do you long for a "release from relentless consuming"? What are you truly seeking, that consumerism might be distracting you from? What does "contentment" mean to you?

PRAYER

O God, you will never forsake me; help me to free my life from a love of money and to be content with what I have. Amen.

Gospel

Luke 14:1, 7–14

"But when you give a banquet, invite the poor, the crippled, the lame, and the blind. And you will be blessed, because they cannot repay you, for you will be repaid at the resurrection of the righteous." (vv. 13–14)

REFLECTION

What markers does Jesus determine are important for us to consider? In this passage, Luke's Jesus highlights humility as a virtue. In a social context where humiliation and shame are to be avoided, the idea of voluntarily humbling oneself is unusual. . . . Further, in a world that expects reciprocity, the virtue of giving freely without expectation is radical. Inviting the dispossessed, disabled, and marginalized to share a meal brings true honor and blessing, because these are the people who are unable to provide reciprocity. In short, the practice of inclusion and habit of extending hospitality are markers that matter to God.

SALLY SMITH HOLT

RESPONSE

What was a time where you gave something, and your gift was not reciprocated or acknowledged? What is it like to imagine doing this on purpose? What kind of hospitality or humility might God be inviting you or your congregation to offer, without expectation of reciprocity?

PRAYER

Generous God, you give without conditions; teach me how to be blessed by those who cannot repay me. Amen.

Weekend Reflections

FURTHER CONNECTION

Everybody worships. The only choice we get is *what* to worship. And an outstanding reason for choosing some sort of god or spiritual-type thing to worship . . . is that pretty much anything else you worship will eat you alive. If you worship money and things—if they are where you tap real meaning in life—then you will never have enough. . . . Worship your own body and beauty and sexual allure and you will always feel ugly, and when time and age start showing, you will die a million deaths before they finally plant you.

DAVID FOSTER WALLACE (1962–2008), THIS IS WATER

MAKING THE CONNECTIONS

Choose one or two questions for reflection:

1. What connections have you noticed between this week's texts and other passages in Scripture?

2. What connections have you made between this week's texts and the world beyond Scripture?

3. Does either of this week's two commentary themes speak especially to your life or the life of the world around you right now?

4. What is God saying to your congregation in particular through this week's readings and commentaries?

_____

_____

_____

_____

_____

Sabbath Day

SCRIPTURE OF ASSURANCE

Put away from you all bitterness and wrath and anger and wrangling and slander, together with all malice, and be kind to one another, tenderhearted, forgiving one another, as God in Christ has forgiven you. (Ephesians 4:31–32)

WEEKLY EXAMEN

- Take a quiet moment, seek out God's presence, and pray for the guidance of the Spirit.

- Consider the past week; recall specific moments and feelings that stand out to you.

- Choose one moment or feeling for deeper examination, thanksgiving, or repentance.

- Let go, breathe deeply, and invite Christ's love to surround and fill you in preparation for the week ahead.

- End with the Lord's Prayer.

The Week Leading Up to
Proper 18

(Sunday between September 4 and September 10)

Jeremiah 18:1–11

Can I not do with you, O house of Israel, just as this potter has done? says the LORD. Just like the clay in the potter's hand, so are you in my hand, O house of Israel. (v. 6)

Deuteronomy 30:15–20

I call heaven and earth to witness against you today that I have set before you life and death, blessings and curses. Choose life so that you and your descendants may live. (v. 19)

Philemon 1–21

Perhaps this is the reason he was separated from you for a while, so that you might have him back forever, no longer as a slave but more than a slave, a beloved brother—especially to me but how much more to you, both in the flesh and in the Lord. (vv. 15–16)

Luke 14:25–33

"Whoever does not carry the cross and follow me cannot be my disciple." (v. 27)

LECTIO DIVINA

Underline a word or phrase that especially grabs your attention. Pray from that word or phrase and ask God to help you connect to its particular invitation for you this week.

Themes from This Week's Writers

THEME 1: *God Reshapes and Transforms Us*

Jeremiah 18:1–11

The vessel spoils, so the potter reworks it. To this point, we hear a potential message of grace. If we head in the wrong direction, God has a way of reworking us into a vessel pleasing to the Lord.

JOSEPH J. CLIFFORD

Jeremiah 18:1–11

The smell of the clay reminds us of Genesis and the way God formed humanity from the dust of the earth. Seeing and feeling the supple texture of the clay, being told we are like this clay, helps us know in our hearts that we can still change and be transformed.

ALLIE UTLEY

Philemon 1–21

Paul's letter portrays a real-life, real-time story of the power of the gospel to unsettle and ultimately reset both our interpersonal relationships and our wider cultural and social systems.

MAGREY R. DEVEGA

THEME 2: *The Cost of Discipleship*

Deuteronomy 30:15–20

We can choose life, or we can choose death. Sometimes this choice is obvious. At other times, particularly in times and places of abundance, it becomes more difficult to choose between life and death.

ALLIE UTLEY

Luke 14:25–33

This "Way" is the path of discipleship for those who will follow Jesus. Following Jesus means walking after Jesus. For Luke, Jesus' command to follow him involves a daily self-denial. No human relationships must interfere with following Jesus on his way. This self-denial and following Jesus' Way mean "one no longer lives for oneself but for the Kingdom of God."[1]

DONALD K. MCKIM

Luke 14:25–33

The words of Jesus in this text seem so difficult and unrealistic that we are often tempted to soften them. The point is that they *were* and *are* challenging. If it is too easy and attractive to follow Jesus, maybe we do not fully understand Jesus or the gospel.

LYNN JAPINGA

WHAT IS THE HOLY SPIRIT SAYING TO YOU THIS WEEK?

_____

_____

_____

_____

_____

A SPIRITUAL PRACTICE FOR THIS WEEK

Using clay or foil, make a little sculpture of yourself; the clumsier, the better. Leave it where you can see it this week and let it help you pray for your vulnerability and God's desire to rework you in love. Perhaps pray from Psalm 139—or Jeremiah 18, if you are brave.

---

1. George Eldon Ladd, *A Theology of the New Testament*, rev. ed. (Grand Rapids: Eerdmans, 1993), 130.

First Reading

Jeremiah 18:1–11

"Come, go down to the potter's house, and there I will let you hear my words." So I went down to the potter's house, and there he was working at his wheel. The vessel he was making of clay was spoiled in the potter's hand, and he reworked it into another vessel, as seemed good to him. (vv. 2–4)

REFLECTION

Perhaps the key to understanding the text is *malleability*. While on the wheel, clay must remain malleable in the potter's hands. The clay's shape changes as the wheel turns. To use the Reformed mantra, it is "reformed and always being reformed" by the potter. In Jeremiah 19:1–11, the clay hardens into a jug that is shattered as a sign of God's judgment. What if that is what happens when we harden? When our shape becomes fixed, we leave little room for God's grace to reshape us.

JOSEPH J. CLIFFORD

RESPONSE

In what ways have you or your congregation's shape become fixed or hardened in this time of life? Does anything feel as though it is brittle, liable to shatter? What still feels malleable? How might God be trying to reform or reshape you or your congregation in this season?

PRAYER

O God, help me not to be hard or brittle, that I may be continually reshaped by your loving hands. Amen.

Canticle

Psalm 139:1–6, 13–18

O LORD, you have searched me and known me.
You know when I sit down and when I rise up;
  you discern my thoughts from far away.
You search out my path and my lying down,
  and are acquainted with all my ways.
Even before a word is on my tongue,
  O LORD, you know it completely. (vv. 1–4)

REFLECTION

The psalmist proclaims that the formation of God has deeper reasoning than our understanding. God knows him in every movement and aspiration, in every way (Ps. 139:1–4). Like the potter's hands, God cradles the psalmist, "You hem me in, behind and before, and lay your hand upon me" (v. 5). That holy touch overwhelms him. It is "too wonderful," and unattainably high. It feels both tender and terrifying. Yet abiding in the place of being stressed, torqued, molded, and massaged by God produces intimate and unstoppable euphoria in God.

GERALD C. LIU

RESPONSE

How have you experienced "God's holy touch" at work in your life? What words above speak most to your journey? How does it feel to hear that God knows you deeply and wants to love you, no matter what has come before?

PRAYER

O Lord, you have searched me and known me; help me to know you more, even as I am fully known in you. Amen.

Second Reading

Philemon 1–21

I am appealing to you for my child, Onesimus, whose father I have become during my imprisonment. Formerly he was useless to you, but now he is indeed useful both to you and to me. I am sending him, that is, my own heart, back to you. (vv. 10–12)

REFLECTION

The repetition of Paul's "appeal" to Philemon cues his introduction of Onesimus into the letter, not as his slave but as "my child," a convert to Christ. Paul's radical transformation of Onesimus is subsequently deepened by personifying him as "my own heart" (v. 12), a source of compassion to Paul, and then by averring that he is "no longer . . . a slave but . . . a beloved brother" (v. 16). While nothing is said of the circumstances that brought the two together in a Roman prison, Paul's purposeful resetting of Onesimus's public identity is strategic.

ROBERT W. WALL

RESPONSE

Make a list of names or identities that you have been given in your life; how have you felt about these? What are names or identities you have similarly assigned others: loved ones, friends, or coworkers? What about those less valued in your community? What do these names deny about the identity we all have in God?

PRAYER

O God, teach me to see and treat all people as beloved brothers and sisters, in the flesh and in Christ. Amen.

Gospel

Luke 14:25–33

"Whoever comes to me and does not hate father and mother, wife and children, brothers and sisters, yes, and even life itself, cannot be my disciple. Whoever does not carry the cross and follow me cannot be my disciple. . . . So therefore, none of you can become my disciple if you do not give up all your possessions." (vv. 26–27, 33)

REFLECTION

Jesus asks his followers, then and now, to do something so difficult that they will doubt their abilities. They are surprised to find that the challenge often brings out the best in them. . . . In the end it is not their hard work or sacrifice or obedience that matters. They are given the grace to do what is hard.

. . . We will never know what we are in for. We will never get it all right. We will never earn God's approval by what we give up—but we can trust in the grace of the one we follow.

LYNN JAPINGA

RESPONSE

What cross are you carrying? How has it hurt? What kind of grace has God given you to carry it? What has it taught you about yourself? Are you able to believe in the power of God's grace over obedience or hard work? Why or why not?

PRAYER

O Jesus Christ, give me grace to carry my cross and follow you, that I may truly be your disciple. Amen.

Weekend Reflections

FURTHER CONNECTION

To do for yourself the best that you have it in you to do—to grit your teeth and clench your fists in order to survive the world at its harshest and worst—is, by that very act, to be unable to let something be done for you and in you that is more wonderful still. The trouble with steeling yourself against the harshness of reality is that the same steel that secures your life against being destroyed secures your life also against being opened up and transformed.

FREDERICK BUECHNER (1926–), *THE SACRED JOURNEY*

MAKING THE CONNECTIONS

Choose one or two questions for reflection:

1. What connections have you noticed between this week's texts and other passages in Scripture?

2. What connections have you made between this week's texts and the world beyond Scripture?

3. Does either of this week's two commentary themes speak especially to your life or the life of the world around you right now?

4. What is God saying to your congregation in particular through this week's readings and commentaries?

_____

_____

_____

_____

_____

Sabbath Day

SCRIPTURE OF ASSURANCE

> Let me hear of your steadfast love in the morning,
> for in you I put my trust.
> Teach me the way I should go,
> for to you I lift up my soul. (Psalm 143:8)

WEEKLY EXAMEN

- Take a quiet moment, seek out God's presence, and pray for the guidance of the Spirit.

- Consider the past week; recall specific moments and feelings that stand out to you.

- Choose one moment or feeling for deeper examination, thanksgiving, or repentance.

- Let go, breathe deeply, and invite Christ's love to surround and fill you in preparation for the week ahead.

- End with the Lord's Prayer.

The Week Leading Up to
Proper 19
(Sunday between September 11 and September 17)

Jeremiah 4:11–12, 22–28

I looked, and lo, the fruitful land was a desert,
and all its cities were laid in ruins
before the LORD, before his fierce anger. (v. 26)

Exodus 32:7–14

"Turn from your fierce wrath; change your mind and do not bring disaster on your people." . . . And the LORD changed his mind about the disaster that he planned to bring on his people. (vv. 12b, 14)

1 Timothy 1:12–17

I am grateful to Christ Jesus our Lord, who has strengthened me, because he judged me faithful and appointed me to his service, even though I was formerly a blasphemer, a persecutor, and a man of violence. (vv. 12–13a)

Luke 15:1–10

"Or what woman having ten silver coins, if she loses one of them, does not light a lamp, sweep the house, and search carefully until she finds it?" (v. 8)

LECTIO DIVINA

Underline a word or phrase that especially grabs your attention. Pray from that word or phrase and ask God to help you connect to its particular invitation for you this week.

Themes from This Week's Writers

Jeremiah 4:11–12, 22–28 and Exodus 32:7–14

Jeremiah and Exodus offer two contrasts in how God's servants respond to a sinful people. . . . In both texts the people have rebelled against God. In both texts, God's wrath burns hot. In both, God has resolved to destroy the people as a consequence of their sin. Both texts involve repentance. In Jeremiah, the people face destruction because they refuse to repent. In Exodus, however, Moses calls *God* to repent.

JOSEPH J. CLIFFORD

Jeremiah 4:11–12, 22–28

Hearing this admonition, we may be tempted to turn from God, to run away. We can turn, instead, toward God and hear these words as a message of love and grace. We are like children and so God is like a parent. Parents have moments of frustration with children. Can we not acknowledge humbly that God must feel that way about God's children? God loves us so much that God anguishes over us.

ALLIE UTLEY

Psalm 51:1–10

With the psalmist, we know that no matter how angry God seems, God desires human redemption.

That knowledge has a long tradition.

GERALD C. LIU

THEME 2: *God Seeks the Lost*

1 Timothy 1:12–17

None of that message, though, deters the central conviction that Paul maintains, which is that despite the ugliness and messiness of life in the real world, God grants strength, mercy, and grace for even a sinner like himself.

MAGREY R. DEVEGA

Luke 15:1–10

The determination of the shepherd to find the lost sheep and the woman to find the lost coin is the determination of God, who, in Jesus Christ, has come "to seek out and to save the lost" (19:10). This is God's divine initiative. Salvation, reconciliation, forgiveness of sin, and peace with God come through what God has done for humanity in Christ, taking the initiative to do for humans what we cannot do for ourselves.

DONALD K. MCKIM

Luke 15:1–10

The real point of the story is to recognize that we are all the lost who need to be found. Even if we have been obedient sheep for decades, we were at one point found by God. God still seeks. When shame makes us wander away from others into isolation, God comes looking for us. When we fail or hurt someone or say the wrong thing, God comes looking for us.

LYNN JAPINGA

WHAT IS THE HOLY SPIRIT SAYING TO YOU THIS WEEK?

_____

_____

_____

_____

_____

A SPIRITUAL PRACTICE FOR THIS WEEK

Write a dire prophecy for your nation or local community, detailing sins against God, neighbor, the marginalized, and the earth itself. Afterward, write out a counterargument to God, like Moses' in Exodus 32, explaining why there is still hope and its people should be spared.

First Reading

Jeremiah 4:11–12, 22–28

For my people are foolish,
  they do not know me;
they are stupid children,
  they have no understanding.
They are skilled in doing evil,
  but do not know how to do good. (v. 22)

REFLECTION

It is difficult to hear and understand such harsh words from God: "my people are foolish, they do not know me; they are stupid children, they have no understanding" (v. 22). Hearing this admonition, we may be tempted to turn from God, to run away. We can turn, instead, toward God and hear these words as a message of love and grace. We are like children and so God is like a parent. Parents have moments of frustration with children. Can we not acknowledge humbly that God must feel that way about God's children? God loves us so much that God anguishes over us.

ALLIE UTLEY

RESPONSE

Imagine the face of a respected teacher or adult from your childhood whom you loved and you knew loved you. Imagine them saying these words. How does this change the voice of God in your understanding? How do you hear these words speaking to the life of your community today?

PRAYER

Loving God, come to my aid even when I am stupid and foolish, even when there is no good I seem able to do, that I may turn back to you, again and again. Amen.

Canticle

Psalm 14

Fools say in their hearts, "There is no God."
    They are corrupt, they do abominable deeds;
    there is no one who does good.

The LORD looks down from heaven on humankind
    to see if there are any who are wise,
    who seek after God. (vv. 1–2)

REFLECTION

In the face of widespread addiction, unconscionable violence, political
and ecological turmoil, and so many other maladies, traumas, and
transgressions in our lives, it becomes all too easy to lose sight of
who God is. Worse, we may want to give up on the very idea of God
altogether. . . . Yet we cannot permit ourselves to get carried away.

We can find spiritual stamina to sustain us through the nihilism of
disbelief by remembering that even God gets carried away. . . . God
spews vitriol that threatens to annihilate it all. Yet ultimately God desires
to redeem.

GERALD C. LIU

RESPONSE

What was a time you lost your temper, recently? What is it like to
imagine God having that reaction, and spewing vitriol? Do you ever
want to give up on the idea of God? How do you find balance between
anger and perseverance?

PRAYER

O God, you look to see if there are any who are wise and seek after you;
help me today to turn away from evil toward justice and wisdom. Amen.

Second Reading

The saying is sure and worthy of full acceptance, that Christ Jesus came into the world to save sinners—of whom I am the foremost. (v. 15)

REFLECTION

The catchphrase "this saying is sure and worthy of full acceptance" (v. 15a) is routinely used in the Pastoral Epistles (see 1 Tim. 1:15; 3:1; 4:9; 2 Tim. 2:11; Titus 3:8; cf. Titus 1:9) to introduce a distinctively Pauline formulation of God's way of salvation. In this instance, "Christ Jesus came into the world to save sinners" serves as a "creedal cameo"[1]—a memorable yet dense phrase that helps converts to Jesus conceptualize their experience of being initiated into Christian faith.

ROBERT W. WALL

RESPONSE

What is a creedal cameo for you? In other words, what piece of Scripture or other wisdom is "sure and worthy of full acceptance" for you? What role has this phrase played in the story of your own journey in the Christian faith?

PRAYER

Christ Jesus, you came into the world to save us all; help me, like Paul, to offer my gifts and your gospel to your world, despite my weaknesses and sins. Amen.

1. Raymond F. Collins, *I and II Timothy and Titus,* New Testament Library (Louisville, KY: Westminster John Knox, 2002), 43.

Gospel

Luke 15:1–10

"Just so, I tell you, there will be more joy in heaven over one sinner who repents than over ninety-nine righteous persons who need no repentance." (v. 7)

REFLECTION

These initial parables were told in the context of "tax collectors and sinners" coming to listen to Jesus (15:1). This upset the Pharisees and scribes who were "grumbling and saying, 'This fellow welcomes sinners and eats with them'" (15:2; cf. 5:30; 7:34). . . .

Jesus' parables counter this attitude and its restrictiveness. . . . God's purpose is to restore the lost. God's way of work is to seek and save through merciful love. These parables offer testimony to the depths of God's compassion and the width of God's concern.

DONALD K. MCKIM

RESPONSE

Think of a person you often judge; consider how you might feel compassion for this person. What does it mean if God's response to our sin is not judgment, but compassion? How can you have more compassion and mercy for yourself?

PRAYER

Jesus, you are always seeking those who are lost, even me; teach me not to judge but to repent, that I may eat and rejoice with you at your table. Amen.

Weekend Reflections

FURTHER CONNECTION

Every person should have two pockets. In one pocket should be a piece of paper saying: "I am only dust and ashes." When one is feeling too proud, reach into this pocket and take out this paper and read it. In the other pocket should be a piece of paper saying: "For my sake was the world created." When one is feeling disheartened and lowly, reach into this pocket and take this paper out and read it. We are each the joining of two worlds. We are fashioned from clay, but our spirit is the breath of Adonai.

RABBI SIMCHA BUNIM (1767–1827)

MAKING THE CONNECTIONS

Choose one or two questions for reflection:

1. What connections have you noticed between this week's texts and other passages in Scripture?

2. What connections have you made between this week's texts and the world beyond Scripture?

3. Does either of this week's two commentary themes speak especially to your life or the life of the world around you right now?

4. What is God saying to your congregation in particular through this week's readings and commentaries?

_____

_____

_____

_____

_____

Sabbath Day

SCRIPTURE OF ASSURANCE

> Strengthen the weak hands,
>   and make firm the feeble knees.
> Say to those who are of a fearful heart,
>   "Be strong, do not fear!
> Here is your God.
>   He will come with vengeance,
> with terrible recompense.
>   He will come and save you." (Isaiah 35:3–4)

WEEKLY EXAMEN

- Take a quiet moment, seek out God's presence, and pray for the guidance of the Spirit.

- Consider the past week; recall specific moments and feelings that stand out to you.

- Choose one moment or feeling for deeper examination, thanksgiving, or repentance.

- Let go, breathe deeply, and invite Christ's love to surround and fill you in preparation for the week ahead.

- End with the Lord's Prayer.

The Week Leading Up to
Proper 20

(Sunday between September 18 and September 24)

Jeremiah 8:18–9:1

O that my head were a spring of water,
    and my eyes a fountain of tears,
so that I might weep day and night
    for the slain of my poor people! (9:1)

Amos 8:4–7

Hear this, you that trample on the needy,
    and bring to ruin the poor of the land,
saying, "When will the new moon be over
    so that we may sell grain;
and the sabbath,
    so that we may offer wheat for sale?" (vv. 4–5a)

1 Timothy 2:1–7

First of all, then, I urge that supplications, prayers, intercessions, and thanks-givings be made for everyone. (v. 1)

Luke 16:1–13

"No slave can serve two masters; for a slave will either hate the one and love the other, or be devoted to the one and despise the other. You cannot serve God and wealth." (v. 13)

LECTIO DIVINA

Underline a word or phrase that especially grabs your attention. Pray from that word or phrase and ask God to help you connect to its particular invitation for you this week.

Themes from This Week's Writers

THEME 1: *Pray for Everyone*

1 Timothy 2:1–7

Paul's initial instruction to Timothy seeks to bring clarity to the theological motive and public manner of Christian worship. In this regard, prayer is introduced as the quintessential worship practice, and the community's prayers are for everyone (1 Tim. 2:1–2), because God's desire is to save everyone (vv. 3–7).

ROBERT W. WALL

1 Timothy 2:1–7

Paul does not view worship as a political practice, as though the church's mission is complicit in a program of social domestication. His motive is clearly theological. Prayers for rulers, whether emperor or president, are offered to God in prospect of their conversion to the truth and salvation from their sins.

ROBERT W. WALL

1 Timothy 2:1–7

The human tendency is to pray egotistically, praising God on the basis of what God has done for us, neglecting to be thankful, and offering petitions only for our own needs. The kind of prayer that Paul describes, however, is "for everyone." It is a prayer that pushes our perspectives beyond ourselves to include others, even those with whom we are in conflict.

MAGREY R. DEVEGA

THEME 2: *You Cannot Serve God and Wealth*

Amos 8:4–7

At the heart of their injustice lies a greed that is incapable of enjoying seasons of rest like the new moon and the Sabbath, but instead longs to get back to the pursuit of unrighteous gain. Given God's judgment on the consumerism of Amos's day, it is impossible to imagine the scope of judgment in our day.

JOSEPH J. CLIFFORD

Luke 16:1–13

As contemporary Christians, we all have to come to terms with our relationship to the wealth we have been given, in various forms. Our issues are not whether or not we will have any wealth, but in what ways the wealth we do have can serve the purposes of God's reign rather than be loved for what it brings to us.

DONALD K. MCKIM

Luke 16:1–13

Perhaps Jesus is advising his listeners *not* to idolize and emulate the shrewd master. The kingdom operates with different values. Wealth and resources are not primarily for personal benefit, but a way to care for the whole community. Wealth and resources should not be used to manipulate and earn favors to be called in later.

LYNN JAPINGA

WHAT IS THE HOLY SPIRIT SAYING TO YOU THIS WEEK?

_____

_____

_____

_____

_____

A SPIRITUAL PRACTICE FOR THIS WEEK

Pick a difficult person or difficult public leader to pray for each day this week. You might use this prayer: "May they have enough. May they love and be loved. May they know and be known by God."

First Reading

Jeremiah 8:18–9:1

For the hurt of my poor people I am hurt,
   I mourn, and dismay has taken hold of me.

Is there no balm in Gilead?
   Is there no physician there?
Why then has the health of my poor people
   not been restored? (8:21–22)

REFLECTION

While the temptation is to resolve the lament in some way, the text does not do this. . . . In fact, the third question implies that there must *not* be a balm in Gilead. . . . Instead, the prophet . . . stands with the people in that pain, waiting for a future as yet undisclosed. Such solidarity with those who suffer offers a profound witness and potential for faithful proclamation.

. . . Where is God in all this? Is there no balm in Gilead? Is there no physician there? Unresolved pain is a reality of life; this passage reflects this reality.

JOSEPH J. CLIFFORD

RESPONSE

Why is it so difficult to sit with someone in pain without giving them advice, looking for a lesson, or assuring them of a positive outcome? How has God spoken with love to your own unresolved pain?

PRAYER

O God, for the hurt of my poor people I am hurt; if there can be no balm or healing now, still be with us and console us. Amen.

Canticle

Who is like the LORD our God,
   who is seated on high,
who looks far down
   on the heavens and the earth?
He raises the poor from the dust,
   and lifts the needy from the ash heap,
to make them sit with princes,
   with the princes of his people. (vv. 5–8)

REFLECTION

Neither the oppressed nor the despicable are beyond YHWH's care.
Likewise, in a social hierarchy in which the status of women was deeply
rooted in childbearing, YHWH, who remains "seated," will "cause to
be seated" (*Hofal*) the childless woman. . . . The attribute of YHWH
that inspires endless praise, and endless wonder, is divine reversal of
estate. YHWH elevates the lowly. It is they who "sit" with YHWH. The
faithful answer to the rhetorical *"Who is like YHWH our God?"* (v. 5a) is,
as the inclusio framing this psalm indicates (vv. 1, 9), praise.

E. CARSON BRISSON

RESPONSE

Do you tend, more often, to find reasons to look down on others, or to
worry that they are looking down on you? How is the Spirit speaking
to you, today, through this image of God favoring the weak? Or, what
invitation might God be making to your congregation through this image?

PRAYER

O God, you raise the poor from dust and lift the lowly to the seats
of princes; from the rising of the sun to its setting your name is to be
praised. Amen.

Second Reading

1 Timothy 2:1–7

First of all, then, I urge that supplications, prayers, intercessions, and thanksgivings be made for everyone, for kings and all who are in high positions, so that we may lead a quiet and peaceable life in all godliness and dignity. (vv. 1–2)

REFLECTION

This kind of prayer sets the tone for the remainder of this passage. The rest of the text explores different ways that the worship of God and the affirmation of God's nature ought to transcend the kinds of divisions we experience in our individual relationships and society at large. His words echo the call of Jesus in the Beatitudes to pray for one's enemies and to bless those who curse one. There ought to be no room for bias or discrimination in the way a person prays. It surpasses all boundaries that would otherwise divide us.

MAGREY R. DEVEGA

RESPONSE

Today, pray for an authority in your life whom you might not otherwise think much about. What is it like to do this? What other forgotten leaders in your life or community might need prayer, whom you otherwise overlook or even dislike?

PRAYER

O Jesus Christ, teach me to pray; and teach me to pray for everyone, because you desire everyone to be saved and to come to the knowledge of your truth. Amen.

Gospel

Luke 16:1–13

"And his master commended the dishonest manager because he had acted shrewdly; for the children of this age are more shrewd in dealing with their own generation than are the children of light. And I tell you, make friends for yourselves by means of dishonest wealth so that when it is gone, they may welcome you into the eternal homes." (vv. 8–9)

REFLECTION

In effect, Jesus was saying, What if disciples who seek God's reign would exhibit the kind of intelligence and shrewdness of the cunning manager?

Should we too urge those who use their intellects and astuteness in their daily work to bring their same aptitudes to bear in living as disciples who serve the reign of God? Use the abilities you have to deal with your "own generation" (v. 8). . . .

. . . Will you live as "children of this age" or as "children of light"? Will you use your shrewdness to serve only yourself, or others?

DONALD K. MCKIM

RESPONSE

Have you ever been dishonest or used shrewd dealings to serve others or to benefit those outside your family or inner circle? Could you or your church community be more shrewd in your own life or ministry?

PRAYER

Christ of all people, show me how to be shrewd and cunning, that I might make friends and speak for your gospel, perhaps even by dishonest wealth. Amen.

Weekend Reflections

FURTHER CONNECTION

A real man or woman of prayer, then, should be a live wire, a link between God's grace and the world that needs it. In so far as you have given your lives to God, you have offered yourselves, without conditions, as transmitters of His saving and enabling love: and the will and love, the emotional drive, which you thus consecrate to God's purposes, can actually do work on supernatural levels for those for whom you are called upon to pray. One human spirit can, by its prayer and love, touch and change another human spirit; it can take a soul and lift it to the atmosphere of God.

EVELYN UNDERHILL (1875–1941), *LIFE AS PRAYER*

MAKING THE CONNECTIONS

Choose one or two questions for reflection:

1. What connections have you noticed between this week's texts and other passages in Scripture?

2. What connections have you made between this week's texts and the world beyond Scripture?

3. Does either of this week's two commentary themes speak especially to your life or the life of the world around you right now?

4. What is God saying to your congregation in particular through this week's readings and commentaries?

_____

_____

_____

_____

_____

_____

Sabbath Day

SCRIPTURE OF ASSURANCE

It is no longer I who live, but it is Christ who lives in me. And the life I now live in the flesh I live by faith in the Son of God, who loved me and gave himself for me. (Galatians 2:20)

WEEKLY EXAMEN

- Take a quiet moment, seek out God's presence, and pray for the guidance of the Spirit.

- Consider the past week; recall specific moments and feelings that stand out to you.

- Choose one moment or feeling for deeper examination, thanksgiving, or repentance.

- Let go, breathe deeply, and invite Christ's love to surround and fill you in preparation for the week ahead.

- End with the Lord's Prayer.

The Week Leading Up to
Proper 21
(Sunday between September 25 and October 1)

Jeremiah 32:1–3a, 6–15

Take these deeds, both this sealed deed of purchase and this open deed, and put them in an earthenware jar, in order that they may last for a long time. For thus says the LORD of hosts, the God of Israel: Houses and fields and vineyards shall again be bought in this land. (vv. 14b–15)

Amos 6:1a, 4–7

Alas for those who lie on beds of ivory,
    and lounge on their couches.
. . . .
Therefore they shall now be the first to go into exile,
    and the revelry of the loungers shall pass away. (vv. 4a, 7)

1 Timothy 6:6–19

As for those who in the present age are rich, command them not to be haughty, or to set their hopes on the uncertainty of riches, but rather on God who richly provides us with everything for our enjoyment. (v. 17)

Luke 16:19–31

"But Abraham said, 'Child, remember that during your lifetime you received your good things, and Lazarus in like manner evil things; but now he is comforted here, and you are in agony.'" (v. 25)

LECTIO DIVINA

Underline a word or phrase that especially grabs your attention. Pray from that word or phrase and ask God to help you connect to its particular invitation for you this week.

Themes from This Week's Writers

THEME 1: *Right Use of Wealth*

Jeremiah 32:1–3a, 6–15

Here we witness Jeremiah—at a time when the spirits of the people are at their very lowest—engaging in an energizing act of prophetic promise and hope.

What does it mean to "buy a field in Anathoth" in today's world?

LEONORA TUBBS TISDALE

1 Timothy 6:6–19

Paul is less concerned with how much a believer has than with the believer's focus: are we focused on God or gain? . . .

. . . The preacher could pair Paul's word with the Jeremiah text to emphasize the importance of stewardship. The point in both texts is not how much money people have, but if they are using it to the glory of God.

KEN EVERS-HOOD

1 Timothy 6:6–19

The church is called to resist hierarchies based on wealth and power and to embrace all those redeemed and gifted by the Spirit.

This means engaging in practices such as simplicity, welcoming the stranger, and charity and justice on behalf of the least in our midst.

DAVID F. WHITE

THEME 2: *Wealth Can Corrupt*

Amos 6:1a, 4–7

Complacency, opulence, and hedonism have inoculated the nation's elites against feeling sickened by the downfall of their nation. What are the consequences for such attitudes and behaviors? Their feasting will surely pass away, and they will be the "first to go into exile" (v. 7).

JARED E. ALCÁNTARA

Luke 16:19–31

Canonically speaking, the biblical witness speaks univocally about the dual, integrally related dangers wealth presents: the temptation to ignore neighbor, and the possibility of opening a chasm between ourselves and God by that inaction.

RICHARD W. VOELZ

Luke 16:19–31

We do know that the villain of the story is the man who possessed status, wealth, and power, but ignored the plight of the needy. His societal values left him so bereft that even in Hades, he does not understand the notions of compassion, equity, or justice.

NANCY LYNNE WESTFIELD

WHAT IS THE HOLY SPIRIT SAYING TO YOU THIS WEEK?

_____

_____

_____

_____

_____

A SPIRITUAL PRACTICE FOR THIS WEEK

Go to a luxury store, big-box store, or any site of consumerism nearby you, or just sit in your car in the parking lot, then study this week's readings from Amos and Luke. How is it to interact with these verses in this location? What do you notice?

First Reading

Jeremiah 32:1–3a, 6–15

Then my cousin Hanamel came to me in the court of the guard, in accordance with the word of the Lord, and said to me, "Buy my field that is at Anathoth in the land of Benjamin, for the right of possession and redemption is yours; buy it for yourself." Then I knew that this was the word of the Lord. (v. 8)

REFLECTION

He pays good money for land that will soon be worthless—both to him (given his imprisonment) and to his relatives (given the imminent fall of Judah). He engages in what, for the entire world, looks like an incredibly foolish act, and he does so in a very public manner.

Why this public sign-act from the prophet? . . .

What does it mean to "buy a field in Anathoth" in today's world?

LEONORA TUBBS TISDALE

RESPONSE

What is an example of what "buying a field in Anathoth" might look like in your own community or context? What would you purchase or what public sign might you enact as a crazy sign of hope and investment in God's future?

PRAYER

God of hope, the things you value seem worthless to so many; show me how to foolishly invest in your people and your promises. Amen.

Canticle

Psalm 91:1–6, 14–16

You who live in the shelter of the Most High,
    who abide in the shadow of the Almighty,
will say to the LORD, "My refuge and my fortress;
    my God, in whom I trust." (vv. 1–2)

REFLECTION

Psalm 91 . . . [addresses] in implied second person "the dwelling one"
(NRSV "You who live"), who enters the sanctuary of *Elyon* or *Shaddai*
(v. 1), . . . building from the familiar biblical metaphors of a protected
space for the afflicted or pursued, "refuge" (cf. Pss. 14:6, 46:1; 71:7;
94:22), to a more secure dwelling "fortress" (Pss. 31:3; 59:9, 17),
to a final and insurmountable declaration of the complete security
provided by "my God" (v. 2c). . . . The liturgical cry of verse 2 expresses
completely the core and unshakable identity of this "dweller" and
"abider."

E. CARSON BRISSON

RESPONSE

Make a list of places that feel like a secure dwelling place, refuge, or
fortress for you. Then create a psalm, prayer, or poem about dwelling in
God as one or more of these places.

PRAYER

O God, you are my shelter and refuge, my God, in whom I trust. Amen.

Second Reading

1 Timothy 6:6–19

Of course, there is great gain in godliness combined with contentment; for we brought nothing into the world, so that we can take nothing out of it. . . . But those who want to be rich fall into temptation and are trapped by many senseless and harmful desires that plunge people into ruin and destruction. (vv. 6–7, 9)

REFLECTION

The implication here is that simplicity is a secondary virtue that relies first on the faithfulness of God to provide what is needed. Trust in God's faithfulness is to be the secure foundation for our lives. . . . [Paul] states that those who love money—those having a disordered relationship with money—risk serious harm. He uses terms such as "pierced with pains," "ruin," and "destruction" to describe their fate. The "love" of money is a form of idolatry, an inordinate attachment to those things that are not worthy of love and cannot love us back.

DAVID F. WHITE

RESPONSE

What are some things you love that cannot love you back? How could this love harm you? How hard is it for you to believe that God's faithfulness and love will truly provide for you? How might you grow in this belief, during this season of your life?

PRAYER

Faithful God, protect me from senseless and harmful desires, that I may not fall into ruin or destruction, but be content in you. Amen.

Gospel

Luke 16:19–31

"'Besides all this, between you and us a great chasm has been fixed, so that those who might want to pass from here to you cannot do so, and no one can cross from there to us.'" (v. 26)

REFLECTION

The interconnectedness of our social existence is profound. Those with wealth are cautioned to end their isolation from the poor and to develop ways to work with and on behalf of the poor or risk torment.

This story is a chilling caution to those who place confidence in financial security over a life of service to neighbor. The parable teaches that divine judgment is concerned with our use of resources, wealth, and finances in this life, as these have consequences for the next life.

NANCY LYNNE WESTFIELD

RESPONSE

Reflect on ways that investing in the security of the poor is interconnected with your own security, in this life and the next. What are some ways you already share what you have? How might you feel the Spirit nudging you to do something more?

PRAYER

O Jesus, show me how to be comforted, not by luxury or riches, but by service and care for my neighbor. Amen.

Weekend Reflections

FURTHER CONNECTION

Rich people must criticize their own surroundings as a rich person: why they have wealth, and why there are so many poor people around them. If these people are rich Christians, they will find in this personal critique the beginning of their conversion: Why am I rich and why are there so many people who are hungry around me?

OSCAR ROMERO (1917–80), SERMON PREACHED
ON DECEMBER 16, 1979

MAKING THE CONNECTIONS

Choose one or two questions for reflection:

1. What connections have you noticed between this week's texts and other passages in Scripture?

2. What connections have you made between this week's texts and the world beyond Scripture?

3. Does either of this week's two commentary themes speak especially to your life or the life of the world around you right now?

4. What is God saying to your congregation in particular through this week's readings and commentaries?

_____

_____

_____

_____

_____

_____

Sabbath Day

SCRIPTURE OF ASSURANCE

For now we see in a mirror, dimly, but then we will see face to face. Now I know only in part; then I will know fully, even as I have been fully known. (1 Corinthians 13:12)

WEEKLY EXAMEN

- Take a quiet moment, seek out God's presence, and pray for the guidance of the Spirit.

- Consider the past week; recall specific moments and feelings that stand out to you.

- Choose one moment or feeling for deeper examination, thanksgiving, or repentance.

- Let go, breathe deeply, and invite Christ's love to surround and fill you in preparation for the week ahead.

- End with the Lord's Prayer.

The Week Leading Up to
Proper 22

(Sunday between October 2 and October 8)

Lamentations 1:1–6

Judah has gone into exile with suffering
    and hard servitude;
she lives now among the nations,
    and finds no resting place;
her pursuers have all overtaken her
    in the midst of her distress. (v. 3)

Habakkuk 1:1–4; 2:1–4

For there is still a vision for the appointed time;
    it speaks of the end, and does not lie.
If it seems to tarry, wait for it;
    it will surely come, it will not delay. (2:3)

2 Timothy 1:1–14

For this gospel I was appointed a herald and an apostle and a teacher, and
for this reason I suffer as I do. But I am not ashamed, for I know the one in
whom I have put my trust, and I am sure that he is able to guard until that
day what I have entrusted to him. (vv. 11–12)

Luke 17:5–10

The apostles said to the Lord, "Increase our faith!" (v. 5)

LECTIO DIVINA

Underline a word or phrase that especially grabs your attention. Pray
from that word or phrase and ask God to help you connect to its
particular invitation for you this week.

Themes from This Week's Writers

THEME 1: *O Lord, How Long Shall I Cry for Help?*

Habakkuk 1:1–4; 2:1–4

Habakkuk 1:1–4 asks two big questions and then laments the lack of answers: How long? and Why? (vv. 2–3). How long must I cry out for help to God with no revelation and no rescue? Why would a good God allow such violence and wickedness without doing anything?

JARED E. ALCÁNTARA

Habakkuk 1:1–4; 2:1–4

Faith in what? Faith in whom? The answers come a few verses earlier: faith in a vision that does not lie and faith in a God who answers our complaints. In the end, the promise comes to those who believe in a trustworthy revelation from God: "There is still a vision!"

JARED E. ALCÁNTARA

Lamentations 1:1–6

Beyond guilt, the writer is inviting hearers to own their shame. The reality is that we have done this to ourselves. This was a devastating admission for the "people of God." God's people are protected, special, and holy. Nothing bad can happen to God's people. This was the myth created by the priests.

DAN R. DICK

THEME 2: *Increase Our Faith!*

2 Timothy 1:1–14

Paul does not imagine himself or Timothy as fearless individuals, heroically choosing the faith as an expression of their free will. Rather, the faith summons them. This understanding of the faith as something that summons rather than something we heroically choose—so counter to our individualistic age—is worth preaching again and again today.

KEN EVERS-HOOD

Luke 17:5–10

In other words, Luke's Gospel accounts for how the fledgling church met the many challenges it was facing. A word on the power of what faith can accomplish, even to the point of absurdity, serves to encourage disciples of Jesus in the midst of challenge. . . . How significant it must have been—and indeed is—to repeat the promises of world–altering power for those living into the reign of God.

RICHARD W. VOELZ

Luke 17:5–10

In the mustard seed example and the slave illustration, Jesus' response to the demand for increased faith results in a double dose of scolding of the disciples. The gospel message is that even a little bit of faith is all that is needed to perform great ministry, miracles, exorcisms, and healings.

NANCY LYNNE WESTFIELD

WHAT IS THE HOLY SPIRIT SAYING TO YOU THIS WEEK?

_____

_____

_____

_____

_____

A SPIRITUAL PRACTICE FOR THIS WEEK

Use the disciples' words as your focus for prayer: Increase my faith. Write out the phrase on sticky notes and place where you will see them, use as a meditation mantra, or write out and illuminate the words as a drawing prayer. Where does the Spirit lead you?

First Reading

Lamentations 1:1–6 or Habakkuk 1:1–4; 2:1–4

The roads to Zion mourn,
    for no one comes to the festivals;
all her gates are desolate,
    her priests groan;
her young girls grieve,
    and her lot is bitter. (Lamentations 1:4)

REFLECTION

The cries of anguish in Habakkuk 1 and Lamentations 1 remind readers that, when faced with a choice between denying their tears and despairing in their tears, the prophets choose neither. Instead, they pray their tears. As Francis I. Andersen reminds us, "The freedom with which the prophet has the matter out with God shows how deep is the bond between them."[1] To lament is to bring one's agony before God, to trust that God is big enough to handle unanswered questions, and to hang on to hope that somehow a vision is still possible in the darkness.

JARED E. ALCÁNTARA

RESPONSE

"Pray your tears" by reflecting on or writing answers to one or more of these questions: What is an agony you face in your life? What is a lament on your heart? For what are you crying out for help? What vision in the darkness might God be offering you?

PRAYER

O God, how long shall I cry for help, and you will not listen? Help me to watch and wait to hear what you will say to me, my Lord and my God. Amen.

1. Francis I. Andersen, *Habakkuk,* Anchor Bible (New York: Doubleday, 2001), 109.

Canticle

Lamentations 3:19–26

My soul continually thinks of it
    and is bowed down within me.
But this I call to mind,
    and therefore I have hope:

The steadfast love of the LORD never ceases,
    his mercies never come to an end. (vv. 20–22)

REFLECTION

There is a "call to mind" (or "heart") that begins to allow hope. . . .
This is the wisdom waiting in the ruins to lead to a future. In an echo
of the "good" first pronounced over creation . . . and possible to see
only as shimmering hope in the fire of the moment (Lam. 2:3, 4), the
adjective "good" returns to the narrative and takes first position in the
next two clauses (Lam. 3:25, 26, also 27), evoking themes of wisdom,
not as a justification or explanation for loss, but nevertheless rising out
of that loss.

E. CARSON BRISSON

RESPONSE

What is something you have stopped hoping for? What is something
you have been afraid to hope for? What good might God be bringing
out of what now feels like only ruins and loss?

PRAYER

O God, my soul is bowed down within me; but with hope, I remember
that your steadfast love never ceases, that your mercies are new every
morning. Amen.

Second Reading

2 Timothy 1:1–14

Do not be ashamed, then, of the testimony about our Lord or of me his prisoner, but join with me in suffering for the gospel, relying on the power of God, who saved us and called us with a holy calling, not according to our works but according to his own purpose and grace. (vv. 8–9)

REFLECTION

Hope in the face of suffering . . . is a clear mark of the church. A church that avoids suffering is not comprehensible. In Christ's resurrection we are promised our own redemption. . . .

We live in an era that assumes that suffering of all sorts is both avoidable and to be avoided. Living a good life means denying death and suffering, our own and others. . . . Christians have long understood that our hearts do not become more loving apart from the friction involved in suffering on behalf of the stranger or God.

DAVID F. WHITE

RESPONSE

What are some ways you or your church have been able to be present to suffering or death? What are some ways you may have looked away? How is suffering—even death—part of "a good life" for you as a Christian, or for anyone who wants to grow in love?

PRAYER

Loving Christ, give me grace to suffer for the sake of love and your gospel; in you I put my trust. Amen.

Gospel

Luke 17:5–10

So you also, when you have done all that you were ordered to do, say, "We are worthless slaves; we have done only what we ought to have done!" (v. 10)

REFLECTION

In a story steeped in slave culture, Jesus indicts the disciples for expecting any reward, even the reward of increased faith. With this metaphor, Jesus teaches the disciples that the reward for ministry well done is simply the opportunity to do more work. . . . In the twenty-first century, the expectations for having done well are assumed to be instant gratification, feedback, praise, and reward through such social transactions as salary increases, bonus points in games, or cultural gestures of gratitude. What Jesus calls for, however, is a drastically countercultural virtue. Do not expect reward or praise.

NANCY LYNNE WESTFIELD

RESPONSE

How do you respond to praise? Do you love it? Squirm at it? What would it be like to never expect or receive praise? How can you know that God sees, affirms, and celebrates what you do, if there is no reward but "the opportunity to do more work"?

PRAYER

O Jesus, increase my faith; show me how to offer myself without any need of praise or reward. Amen.

Weekend Reflections

FURTHER CONNECTION

Train us, O Lord, to fling ourselves upon the impossible, for behind the impossible is your grace and your presence; we cannot fall into emptiness. The future is an enigma, our road is covered by mist, but we want to go on giving ourselves, because you continue hoping amid the night and weeping tears through a thousand human eyes.

LUÍS ESPINAL SJ (1932–80), *ORACIONES A QUEMARROPA*. ESPINAL, A POET, JOURNALIST, AND HUMAN RIGHTS ORGANIZER IN BOLIVIA WAS KIDNAPPED AND MURDERED BY A PARAMILITARY GROUP.

MAKING THE CONNECTIONS

Choose one or two questions for reflection:

1. What connections have you noticed between this week's texts and other passages in Scripture?

2. What connections have you made between this week's texts and the world beyond Scripture?

3. Does either of this week's two commentary themes speak especially to your life or the life of the world around you right now?

4. What is God saying to your congregation in particular through this week's readings and commentaries?

_____

_____

_____

_____

_____

Sabbath Day

SCRIPTURE OF ASSURANCE

> Show us your steadfast love, O LORD,
>   and grant us your salvation.
>
> Let me hear what God the LORD will speak,
>   for he will speak peace to his people,
>   to his faithful, to those who turn to him in their hearts.
>   (Psalm 85:7–8)

WEEKLY EXAMEN

- Take a quiet moment, seek out God's presence, and pray for the guidance of the Spirit.

- Consider the past week; recall specific moments and feelings that stand out to you.

- Choose one moment or feeling for deeper examination, thanksgiving, or repentance.

- Let go, breathe deeply, and invite Christ's love to surround and fill you in preparation for the week ahead.

- End with the Lord's Prayer.

The Week Leading Up to
Proper 23
(Sunday between October 9 and October 15)

Jeremiah 29:1, 4–7

But seek the welfare of the city where I have sent you into exile, and pray to the LORD on its behalf, for in its welfare you will find your welfare. (v. 7)

2 Kings 5:1–3, 7–15c

But [Naaman's] servants approached and said to him, "Father, if the prophet had commanded you to do something difficult, would you not have done it? How much more, when all he said to you was, 'Wash, and be clean'?" (v. 13)

2 Timothy 2:8–15

Do your best to present yourself to God as one approved by him, a worker who has no need to be ashamed, rightly explaining the word of truth. (v. 15)

Luke 17:11–19

Then one of them, when he saw that he was healed, turned back, praising God with a loud voice. He prostrated himself at Jesus' feet and thanked him. And he was a Samaritan. (vv. 15–16)

LECTIO DIVINA

Underline a word or phrase that especially grabs your attention. Pray from that word or phrase and ask God to help you connect to its particular invitation for you this week.

Themes from This Week's Writers

THEME 1: *Outsiders Recognize God's Truth First*

2 Kings 5:1–3, 7–15c

Notice that those who speak truth to him are his servants. It is they who convince him to change his mind. In order to be healed, Naaman must heed the counsel of so many that are beneath him: a servant girl, a backwoods prophet, and his own servants.

JARED E. ALCÁNTARA

2 Kings 5:1–3, 7–15c

This kind of pride believes that we are the only ones who truly see and understand. . . .

. . . As is so often the case, however, it is those on the margins who are able to detect with quicker clarity the divine truthfulness underneath Elisha's unfussy instructions.

SONG-MI SUZIE PARK

Luke 17:11–19

While those who live with Jesus go unknowing and unaware of Jesus' identity and power, the ones who are shunned most by the community recognize him. . . . [The lepers] were displaced vagabonds at the mercy of the environment and, often, cruel people. It is amazing that even in their pain, humiliation, and regrets, they recognize Jesus.

NANCY LYNNE WESTFIELD

THEME 2: *Jesus' Mission to Outsiders*

Luke 17:11–19

Luke's account in this story and elsewhere is provocative: Jesus' actions may scandalize those interested in guarding socioreligious boundaries. Nevertheless, Jesus acts with mercy toward outsiders, lauds their faith, eats at a variety of tables, and crosses a variety of boundaries.

RICHARD W. VOELZ

Luke 17:11–19

The good news of Jesus is that foreignness is included, incorporated, part of the whole; it is not ignored. The salvation and restoration for this foreign, Samaritan man was not in making him someone he is not. Rather, his healing restored him to his family as a Samaritan.

NANCY LYNNE WESTFIELD

2 Timothy 2:8–15

We live in a society of strangers, where interpersonal relationships are mediated by claims of formal rights against one another . . . [an] individualism hostile to self-giving love to which the gospel bears witness. . . . Into such a world, the church has a special role of rendering visible the truth of the cross—of suffering with others in the hope of the faithfulness of God to redeem.

DAVID F. WHITE

WHAT IS THE HOLY SPIRIT SAYING TO YOU THIS WEEK?

_____

_____

_____

_____

_____

A SPIRITUAL PRACTICE FOR THIS WEEK

Like Naaman and his servants or the disciples and the Samaritan leper, seek spiritual information, advice, or wisdom from a source you might normally dismiss as unthinkable, silly, or foreign to your experience. Use Psalm 111 as a companion prayer.

First Reading

Thus says the Lord of hosts, the God of Israel, to all the exiles whom I have sent into exile from Jerusalem to Babylon: Build houses and live in them; plant gardens and eat what they produce. (vv. 4–5)

REFLECTION

By telling a community that had been dispersed and displaced that it ought to try to live a good life, God is not simply requesting a lifestyle shift but a radical adjustment of their theology. By telling the exiled Israelites to build houses, go to work, marry, and pray for their new communities, God is, in fact, telling the Israelites to resist the allure of succumbing to their feelings of despair, dismay, depression, and numbness. To make the best of a bad situation. To try to move forward and survive.

Jeremiah, in essence, is calling on the exiled Israelites to sustain their faith in God.

SONG-MI SUZIE PARK

RESPONSE

What is a displacement or disappointment you or your congregation have faced recently? What have you grieved? What does faith look like in you now? How might God be calling you, now, to try to live a good life in your new situation?

PRAYER

O God, sustain my faith and my hope; help me to build, plant, and love where I live now, that in the welfare of this place, I will find my own welfare also. Amen.

Canticle

Psalm 111

Praise the LORD!
I will give thanks to the LORD with my whole heart,
in the company of the upright, in the congregation.
Great are the works of the LORD,
studied by all who delight in them. (vv. 1–2)

REFLECTION

Psalm 111 is presented as the prayer of a person who has been healed
of leprosy. Its primary point of reference is . . . the Aramean warrior
Naaman. . . . However, this psalm would serve equally well as the prayer
of the "tenth leper," the Samaritan who returned to thank Jesus. . . .
In both cases, the one praying is an outsider, a Gentile or a Samaritan
who has come to know and worship the Lord through the experience of
God's healing grace. . . .
. . . These Scriptures challenge us with their insistence that the best
examples of gratitude come from unexpected people and places.

DAVID GAMBRELL

RESPONSE

Reflect on an expression of gratitude or grace that you have witnessed
and admired in someone else. What might the Spirit be inviting you to
deepen in your own life and practice of gratitude?

PRAYER

O Lord, you are gracious and merciful; I give thanks to you with my
whole heart. Amen.

Second Reading

2 Timothy 2:8–15

If we have died with him, we will also live with him;
if we endure, we will also reign with him;
if we deny him, he will also deny us;
if we are faithless, he remains faithful—
for he cannot deny himself. (vv. 11b–13)

REFLECTION

"Okay, which is it, Paul? Denial or no denial? You can't have it both ways." Some may leap to the hope that the passage should be read in light of 2:13, arguing Christ will be faithful to us regardless of our faithfulness to him. Others . . . may choose to maintain the tension between Christ denying us and Christ remaining faithful, pairing grace and judgment in such a way as to show their mutual necessity. . . . In places like 2:25, Paul himself holds out hope even for seeming enemies of the gospel that, if corrected with gentleness, even they may return to the fold.

KEN EVERS-HOOD

RESPONSE

In what ways do you long for Christ's grace and faithfulness this week? Alternately, in what ways might you long for Christ's judgment and accountability? What might Jesus be inviting you to reflect about more deeply this week, here?

PRAYER

Jesus, I remember you, risen from the dead; help me to hold onto faith and endure through your faithfulness to me. Amen.

Gospel

Luke 17:11–19

As he entered a village, ten lepers approached him. Keeping their distance, they called out, saying, "Jesus, Master, have mercy on us!" (vv. 12–13)

REFLECTION

The suffering men recognize Jesus as he enters the village. . . . Perhaps the men recognized Jesus because one or two, before their illness, had been a member of one of the large crowds that gathered to hear Jesus' preaching and teaching. Perhaps, while begging on the outskirts of the village, they had heard gossip about a great healer who was traveling in the region. Maybe they recognized Jesus as an answer to prayer after long years of suffering, shame, and misery. It is important to Luke that Jesus be portrayed as recognized especially by those who are considered "other."

NANCY LYNNE WESTFIELD

RESPONSE

What was a time you recognized Jesus from a place of suffering in your own life? What is something you have learned about Jesus from someone else who was suffering? Why do you think it was important to Luke that Jesus be recognized especially by those who are "other"?

PRAYER

Jesus, Master, have mercy on me, that I might recognize you through the eyes of the stranger, and in my own pain and struggle. Amen.

Weekend Reflections

FURTHER CONNECTION

"This, Brother Leo, is what I understood: all lepers, cripples, sinners, if you kiss them on the mouth—"
He stopped, afraid to complete his thought.
"Enlighten me, Brother Francis, enlighten me, do not leave me in the dark."
Finally, after a long silence, he murmured with a shudder:
"All these, if you kiss them on the mouth—O God, forgive me for saying this—they all . . . become Christ."

NIKOS KAZANTZAKIS (1883–1957), *SAINT FRANCIS: A NOVEL*

MAKING THE CONNECTIONS

Choose one or two questions for reflection:

1. What connections have you noticed between this week's texts and other passages in Scripture?

2. What connections have you made between this week's texts and the world beyond Scripture?

3. Does either of this week's two commentary themes speak especially to your life or the life of the world around you right now?

4. What is God saying to your congregation in particular through this week's readings and commentaries?

_____

_____

_____

_____

_____

_____

Sabbath Day

SCRIPTURE OF ASSURANCE

> Blessed be the LORD,
> for he has heard the sound of my pleadings.
> The LORD is my strength and my shield;
> in him my heart trusts;
> so I am helped, and my heart exults,
> and with my song I give thanks to him. (Psalm 28:6–7)

WEEKLY EXAMEN

- Take a quiet moment, seek out God's presence, and pray for the guidance of the Spirit.

- Consider the past week; recall specific moments and feelings that stand out to you.

- Choose one moment or feeling for deeper examination, thanksgiving, or repentance.

- Let go, breathe deeply, and invite Christ's love to surround and fill you in preparation for the week ahead.

- End with the Lord's Prayer.

The Week Leading Up to
Proper 24

(Sunday between October 16 and October 22)

Jeremiah 31:27–34

I will put my law within them, and I will write it on their hearts; and I will be their God, and they shall be my people. (v. 33b)

Genesis 32:22–31

Then he said, "Let me go, for the day is breaking." But Jacob said, "I will not let you go, unless you bless me." (v. 26)

2 Timothy 3:14–4:5

All scripture is inspired by God and is useful for teaching, for reproof, for correction, and for training in righteousness. (3:16)

Luke 18:1–8

"And will not God grant justice to his chosen ones who cry to him day and night? Will he delay long in helping them?" (v. 7)

LECTIO DIVINA

Underline a word or phrase that especially grabs your attention. Pray from that word or phrase and ask God to help you connect to its particular invitation for you this week.

Themes from This Week's Writers

THEME 1: *Faithful Struggle*

Genesis 32:22–31

Somehow this wrestling lies at the heart of Jacob's vocation as Israel and therefore of his and Israel's experience of God's blessing.

. . . The God who has blessed Jacob is the very God who has opposed him—and left him with a limp. The limp and the blessing are inseparable.

TIM MEADOWCROFT

2 Timothy 3:14–4:5

Paul regards his persecutions as evidence of his faithfulness, and says flatly that it will be so for all followers of Christ.

. . . Paul is both teacher and example of how to behave as a true apostle in the face of inevitable persecution and suffering.

DAVID W. JOHNSON

Luke 18:1–8

Interestingly, to outmatch the powerful and unjust judge, the widow used the only weapon she possessed, namely, her audacious persistence.

VANTHANH NGUYEN, SVD

THEME 2: *The Letter and the Spirit of the Law*

Psalm 119:97–104

What does it mean to have such affection for the word of God—to know God's way "by heart" and to delight in the fulfillment of God's law? The Reformed theological tradition offers some insights for preachers considering these questions. John Calvin taught of "three uses of the law": as a mirror, a fence, and a guide.

DAVID GAMBRELL

Jeremiah 31:27–34

When the new covenant is realized, the need to teach God's ways (Deut. 11:20) becomes obsolete; the law given at Mount Sinai as intermediary is no longer required. . . . The knowledge of God written in the hearts arises from their experience of God's forgiving and not remembering their sins.

TIM MEADOWCROFT

2 Timothy 3:14–4:5

In the lectionary readings there is a tension between the letter and the Spirit. . . .

. . . There is no suggestion in the Timothy passage that attending to Scripture precluded being led by the Spirit. . . . It is easy to let the stress on conduct overwhelm the sense of the necessity of the Spirit's presence.

DAVID W. JOHNSON

WHAT IS THE HOLY SPIRIT SAYING TO YOU THIS WEEK?

_____

_____

_____

_____

_____

A SPIRITUAL PRACTICE FOR THIS WEEK

What is something you are longing for? Every day this week, like the persistent widow, pray and tell God what you desire. Be annoying about it: speak it out loud, write it out, complain, beg, and otherwise remind God constantly. How will God respond?

First Reading

Genesis 32:22–31

Jacob was left alone; and a man wrestled with him until daybreak. When the man saw that he did not prevail against Jacob, he struck him on the hip socket; and Jacob's hip was put out of joint as he wrestled with him. (vv. 24–25)

REFLECTION

Jacob pushes back and wrestles with God. He locks himself in a one-way battle for acceptance, determined not to relent until he wrests a blessing from one he sees as an opponent, but who actually is his strongest supporter.

We must admit we have wrestled with God and encountered God in deeply personal and life-changing ways—when yearning, fighting, clawing for an outcome different from the reality unfolding before us, when arguing that God's justice differs from our sense of fairness, when debating the advantages of advancing our will instead of God's will.

FAIRFAX F. FAIR

RESPONSE

What are you yearning, fighting, or clawing for, in this season of your life? How have you pushed back when God's will differs from your will? Is there a deep desire on your heart that you are willing to wrestle God for, to ask for God's blessing?

PRAYER

O God, I will wrestle with you, and not let you go, unless you bless me. Amen.

Canticle

Psalm 121

I lift up my eyes to the hills—
    from where will my help come?
My help comes from the LORD,
    who made heaven and earth. (vv. 1–2)

REFLECTION

As the widow exemplifies ceaseless prayer in the face of adversity, the psalm itself provides a model of such prayer. As the figure of the judge demonstrates the weakness and corruption of earthly authorities, the psalm directs us to trust in the almighty and eternal Creator of the cosmos. . . .

. . . From whom do we seek help in times of trouble? How do we pursue justice in a corrupt and callous world? The stories of Genesis 32 and Luke 18 suggest that God meets us in the struggle; the song of Psalm 121 promises that this is so.

DAVID GAMBRELL

RESPONSE

Read this psalm aloud or copy it out by hand, as a prayer. How is God meeting you in the struggle today, in this psalm? How is God inviting you to pursue justice, today?

PRAYER

Loving God, you will neither slumber nor sleep; you will keep my life and keep me from evil from this time on and forevermore. Amen.

Second Reading

2 Timothy 3:14–4:5

But as for you, continue in what you have learned and firmly believed, knowing from whom you learned it, and how from childhood you have known the sacred writings that are able to instruct you for salvation through faith in Christ Jesus. (3:14–15)

REFLECTION

For some faith traditions the Bible continues to be their final source. . . . For others the Bible is one of any number of sources they consult when seeking direction on how to live a life with purpose and meaning. . . .

For Paul, Scripture leads to a deep and profound faith in Jesus Christ. Though we may be inclined to get at that understanding of faith in Jesus Christ through different paths, if those paths lead to deeper faith and a solid commitment to Christ, then they should be regarded as viable and fitting paths to faith for contemporary times.

CLEOPHUS J. LARUE

RESPONSE

How would you describe your relationship with Scripture at this time in your life? How has it changed over time? What other texts, sources, or paths feed your relationship with Jesus or God?

PRAYER

Lord Jesus, I give you thanks for the sacred writings I have known, that instruct me in my faith and salvation in you; help me, still, to grow, learn, and believe. Amen.

Gospel

Luke 18:1–8

Then Jesus told them a parable about their need to pray always and not to lose heart. (v. 1)

REFLECTION

For Luke, it is *prayer with faith*, which is another name for persistence that will help overcome any injustice and wrong. . . . In Luke's view, prayer is the essential medium to strengthen faith and undo injustices and evil acts in the world. In Luke's Gospel, Jesus prays often. . . . He warns his disciples that it is only through prayer that they can overcome the trials that lie ahead (22:46). Consequently, the parable of the Unjust Judge and the Persistent Widow provides another lesson in the power of prayer that helps overcome all obstacles.

VANTHANH NGUYEN, SVD

RESPONSE

What kind of prayer most helps you feel close to God? (Formal? Informal? Alone? In a group? On the fly? On Sunday morning?) What does it mean, in your life now, that prayer might be an essential medium to strengthen faith? To overcome injustice?

PRAYER

O Jesus, teach me to pray; give me patience and persistence and help me not to lose heart, but to trust in your great love for me and all people. Amen.

Weekend Reflections

FURTHER CONNECTION

"What you promise when you are confirmed," said Julian's father, "is not that you will believe this forever. What you promise when you are confirmed is that that is the story you will wrestle with forever."

LAUREN F. WINNER (1976–), *STILL: NOTES ON A MID-FAITH CRISIS*

MAKING THE CONNECTIONS

Choose one or two questions for reflection:

1. What connections have you noticed between this week's texts and other passages in Scripture?

2. What connections have you made between this week's texts and the world beyond Scripture?

3. Does either of this week's two commentary themes speak especially to your life or the life of the world around you right now?

4. What is God saying to your congregation in particular through this week's readings and commentaries?

MY CONNECTIONS

_____

_____

_____

_____

_____

_____

Sabbath Day

SCRIPTURE OF ASSURANCE

"Ask, and it will be given you; search, and you will find; knock, and the door will be opened for you. For everyone who asks receives, and everyone who searches finds, and for everyone who knocks, the door will be opened." (Matthew 7:7–8)

WEEKLY EXAMEN

- Take a quiet moment, seek out God's presence, and pray for the guidance of the Spirit.

- Consider the past week; recall specific moments and feelings that stand out to you.

- Choose one moment or feeling for deeper examination, thanksgiving, or repentance.

- Let go, breathe deeply, and invite Christ's love to surround and fill you in preparation for the week ahead.

- End with the Lord's Prayer.

The Week Leading Up to
Proper 25
(Sunday between October 23 and October 29)

Joel 2:23–32

I will repay you for the years
    that the swarming locust has eaten,
the hopper, the destroyer, and the cutter,
    my great army, which I sent against you. (v. 25)

Jeremiah 14:7–10, 19–22

Although our iniquities testify against us,
    act, O Lord, for your name's sake;
our apostasies indeed are many,
    and we have sinned against you. (v. 7)

2 Timothy 4:6–8, 16–18

But the Lord stood by me and gave me strength, so that through me the message might be fully proclaimed and all the Gentiles might hear it. So I was rescued from the lion's mouth. (v. 17)

Luke 18:9–14

"The Pharisee, standing by himself, was praying thus, 'God, I thank you that I am not like other people: thieves, rogues, adulterers, or even like this tax collector.'" (v. 11)

LECTIO DIVINA

Underline a word or phrase that especially grabs your attention. Pray from that word or phrase and ask God to help you connect to its particular invitation for you this week.

Themes from This Week's Writers

THEME 1: *God Will Not Desert Us*

Joel 2:23–32

Though the drought and locust have stolen and stripped, God "will repay" the people for those lost years (2:25). The verb translated as "repay" stems from the same word group as the noun *shalom*, with its implication of wholeness and restoration. . . . The repayment of God means that the people will be secure, not only in their food supply (v. 26), but also in their identity as the covenant people of God (v. 27).

TIM MEADOWCROFT

Psalm 65

This appearance of Joel 2 (with its companion, Psalm 65) . . . helps us remember that God pours out the Spirit in all seasons, and on the whole earth—not just on the church or even the human race. Psalm 65 challenges us to broaden our horizons, to consider the universal scope of God's love for the world, including care for creation.

DAVID GAMBRELL

2 Timothy 4:6–8, 16–18

Today we are called to stand firm in that glorious conviction that, come what may, we are never left alone to fight this good fight on our own. Paul looks toward the end of his life with great confidence that the God who called him to this work will rescue him from every attack and save him for his heavenly kingdom (v. 18).

CLEOPHUS J. LARUE

Jeremiah 14:7–10, 19–22

We mirror Jeremiah's first hearers when we are blind to our complicity in the earth's devastation and the oppression of God's children, yet we persist in crying out to God for mercy.

FAIRFAX F. FAIR

Luke 18:9–14

While the Pharisee is confident of his own righteousness and therefore "gives thanks" that he is not like the rest, the tax collector sincerely confesses that he is a "sinner." . . .

There is little doubt about which of these men has lived a righteous life and which has not. Yet Jesus' evaluation in the parable turns the normal order of things upside down.

VANTHANH NGUYEN, SVD

Luke 18:9–14

The only realistic plea one can make to God is for mercy, not for acknowledgment of one's religious endeavors.

The parable's challenge in today's culture thus concerns the willingness of any—in the church or outside it—to face up to the truth of their part in structures of evil, and recognize the impossibility of evading that truth by concealing it beneath pious enthusiasm.

STEPHEN I. WRIGHT

WHAT IS THE HOLY SPIRIT SAYING TO YOU THIS WEEK?

_____

_____

_____

_____

_____

Pray the Jesus Prayer: *My Lord Jesus Christ, Son of God, have mercy on me, a sinner.* Pray silently or aloud. Match the phrases to your breath. Listen for what the Spirit may say to you about sin and God's mercy; or simply rest and trust in these ancient words.

First Reading

Have you completely rejected Judah?
  Does your heart loathe Zion?
Why have you struck us down
  so that there is no healing for us?
We look for peace, but find no good;
  for a time of healing, but there is terror instead. (v. 19)

REFLECTION

[Here] is a more explicit questioning of YHWH's disapproval along with a poignant longing for healing. . . . For the moment, though, this longing is met only by God's implacability. . . . Rather than restoration and healing, there is terror, a visceral fear. . . .

The challenge to preachers is to hold the unyielding silence of God with God's forgiveness and pouring out of the spirit anticipated by Joel. Part of the journey of faith is thus to be fortified by Peter's declaration from the book of Joel that "everyone who calls on the name of the Lord shall be saved."

TIM MEADOWCROFT

RESPONSE

Reflect on a time you felt God was silent or implacable; perhaps you feel this way now. How do the words of Jeremiah and the experience of Israel resonate with you today? What do you hear in the tension between God's silence and God's promise that the Spirit will pour out?

PRAYER

O Lord, you are in the midst of us and we are called by your name; do not forsake us. Amen.

Canticle

Psalm 84:1–7

Even the sparrow finds a home,
  and the swallow a nest for herself,
  where she may lay her young,
at your altars, O LORD of hosts,
  my King and my God. (v. 3)

REFLECTION

Psalm 84 might be understood as the prayer of the repentant tax
collector . . . [who] humbles himself before the Lord, confessing his sin
and calling on God's mercy. By contrast, this proud Pharisee praises his
own righteousness and pities his fellow worshipers. Which would stand
awe-struck in the temple, singing, "How lovely is your dwelling place"
(v. 1)? Which would say, "I would rather be a doorkeeper in the house
of my God" (v. 10)?

 . . . Psalm 84:1–7 expresses the wonder and gratitude of one who—
in spite of everything—has been invited to stand in the presence of the
Holy One.

DAVID GAMBRELL

RESPONSE

What is a place or sight that causes you to feel wonder and gratitude to
God? Choose a psalm verse that expresses your feeling and write it out
by hand. Doodle, decorate, or illuminate the phrase; or write a poem
from its words.

PRAYER

God of wonder, how lovely is your dwelling place! My heart and my
flesh sing for joy to you, the living God. Amen.

Second Reading

2 Timothy 4:6–8, 16–18

At my first defense no one came to my support, but all deserted me. May it not be counted against them! But the Lord stood by me and gave me strength, so that through me the message might be fully proclaimed and all the Gentiles might hear it. So I was rescued from the lion's mouth. (vv. 16–17)

REFLECTION

[Paul] has faced a trial alone and feels deserted. God, though, was with him. . . . Somehow Paul endured the trial, although 1 Timothy 1 suggests that he is still imprisoned in Rome, and it is clear throughout the epistle that he expects to be put to death very soon.

. . . His major concern is to prepare those who will come after him for their own ministry. In this context, "Timothy," who was undoubtedly a real person, also can symbolize any successor of Paul, from that day to this, who is undertaking service to the gospel.

DAVID W. JOHNSON

RESPONSE

In what ways might you, like Timothy, think of yourself as a successor of Paul? For example, in your many trials, passions and enthusiasms, boasting and imperfections, or love of Christ? How is Paul speaking to you, not just Timothy, in this letter?

PRAYER

O Christ, though I feel deserted or exhausted, stand by me and give me strength that, like Paul, I may proclaim your message of love and rejoice in you. Amen.

Gospel

Luke 18:9–14

He also told this parable to some who trusted in themselves that they were righteous and regarded others with contempt. . . . "For all who exalt themselves will be humbled, but all who humble themselves will be exalted." (vv. 9, 14b)

REFLECTION

The live-and-let-live mores of much of the world today may make it difficult to empathize with either the Pharisee or the tax collector. The Pharisee with his contemptuous dismissal of the less pious may seem a repugnant character. . . . The tax collector's self-abasement also seems excessive to those who value the need of self-esteem for human flourishing. It thus requires an effort on our part . . . as we penetrate beneath the surface of their postures in the temple to discover the attitudes that will, or will not, lead to liberating rightness with God today.

STEPHEN I. WRIGHT

RESPONSE

What are some ways you have veered toward self-righteousness, lately? Who do you enjoy looking down upon, at least sometimes? What could humility, as a liberating practice, look like for you this week?

PRAYER

Lord Jesus, you regarded no one with contempt; show me how to be humble and have mercy on me, a sinner. Amen.

Weekend Reflections

FURTHER CONNECTION

A brother committed a fault. A council was called, but Abba Moses refused to go. The priest sent him a message: "Come, for everyone is waiting for you." So, he took a leaking jug, filled it with water, and carried it with him. The others, seeing the trail of water behind him, asked, "What is this, Father?" He said, "My sins run out behind me, and I do not see them, and today I am coming to judge the sins of another." When they heard that they said no more to the brother but forgave him.

TRADITIONAL SAYING OF DESERT FATHERS AND
MOTHERS, FOURTH CENTURY CE

MAKING THE CONNECTIONS

Choose one or two questions for reflection:

1. What connections have you noticed between this week's texts and other passages in Scripture?

2. What connections have you made between this week's texts and the world beyond Scripture?

3. Does either of this week's two commentary themes speak especially to your life or the life of the world around you right now?

4. What is God saying to your congregation in particular through this week's readings and commentaries?

_____

_____

_____

_____

_____

Sabbath Day

SCRIPTURE OF ASSURANCE

Indeed, all who want to live a godly life in Christ Jesus will be persecuted. (2 Timothy 3:12)

WEEKLY EXAMEN

- Take a quiet moment, seek out God's presence, and pray for the guidance of the Spirit.

- Consider the past week; recall specific moments and feelings that stand out to you.

- Choose one moment or feeling for deeper examination, thanksgiving, or repentance.

- Let go, breathe deeply, and invite Christ's love to surround and fill you in preparation for the week ahead.

- End with the Lord's Prayer.

The Week Leading Up to
All Saints

(November 1 or the Sunday following)

Daniel 7:1–3, 15–18

I, Daniel, saw in my vision by night the four winds of heaven stirring up the great sea, and four great beasts came up out of the sea, different from one another. (vv. 2–3)

Psalm 149

For the LORD takes pleasure in his people;
    he adorns the humble with victory. (v. 4)

Ephesians 1:11–23

So that, with the eyes of your heart enlightened, you may know what is the hope to which he has called you, what are the riches of his glorious inheritance among the saints, and what is the immeasurable greatness of his power for us who believe, according to the working of his great power. (vv. 18–19)

Luke 6:20–31

"Blessed are you when people hate you, and when they exclude you, revile you, and defame you on account of the Son of Man. Rejoice in that day and leap for joy, for surely your reward is great in heaven; for that is what their ancestors did to the prophets." (vv. 22–23)

LECTIO DIVINA

Underline a word or phrase that especially grabs your attention. Pray from that word or phrase and ask God to help you connect to its particular invitation for you this week.

Themes from This Week's Writers

THEME 1: *What Is a Saint?*

Daniel 7:1–3, 15–18

Astonishingly, it is the saints who, in the face of chaotic geopolitical powers and of their own uncertainties and fears, are destined to rule from alongside the Ancient One in the throne room of heaven. As we celebrate All Saints' Day in the life of the church, they refer to those very saints whom we recall and among whom we number ourselves.

TIM MEADOWCROFT

Ephesians 1:11–23

While we may give thanks for the lives of particular individuals of ages past, we must also remember that God is glorified by the ordinary holy lives of believers in this and every age. Right now we are a part of God's heritage (1:11).

CLEOPHUS J. LARUE

Luke 6:20–31

In Paul's letters (e.g., Rom. 1:7; Eph. 1:1), "saints" is a common term for Christian believers. In the Gospels, the normal term for the followers of Jesus is "disciples"; here it is the disciples whom Jesus is addressing (Luke 6:20). The term "saints" echoes the OT notion of Israel as a "holy people," set apart by God for himself and his purposes, the object of God's freely bestowed love prior to any moral behavior.

STEPHEN I. WRIGHT

THEME 2: *Fulfillment of God's Kingdom*

Daniel 7:1–3, 15–18

All Saints points to a life beyond this world, a life where darkness is as light. This first of Daniel's visions provides an opportunity for the preacher to offer hope to the grieving and hope to the living in the proclamation of God's ultimate victory.

FAIRFAX F. FAIR

Ephesians 1:11–23

The eschatological element is clear; there is an age that has not yet come (v. 21) but is surely coming. The future redemption is more than a hope; it is a certainty, based on the "inheritance" that is guaranteed by the "seal of the Spirit."

DAVID W. JOHNSON

Luke 6:20–31

To those who are poor, hungry, weeping, and being persecuted for Christ belongs the kingdom of God, which for Luke is both a present reality and a future one. Consequently, the arrival of Jesus ushers in the presence of the reign of God and initiates a reversal of fortunes.

VANTHANH NGUYEN, SVD

WHAT IS THE HOLY SPIRIT SAYING TO YOU THIS WEEK?

_____

_____

_____

_____

_____

A SPIRITUAL PRACTICE FOR THIS WEEK

Set a table or altar in your home with pictures of saints who have gone before and who were spiritual teachers for you, whether traditional saints, family members, mentors, or other leaders in your life. Use as a focus for prayer this week.

First Reading

Daniel 7:1–3, 15–18

As for these four great beasts, four kings shall arise out of the earth. But the holy ones of the Most High shall receive the kingdom and possess the kingdom forever—forever and ever. (vv. 17–18)

REFLECTION

All Saints starts with the pain of loss in the remembrance of the deaths of those we love. Daniel's vision also begins in a place of great fear.

Many among us have a fear of the process of dying. Most of us push apocalyptic texts to the side. Similarly, our society pushes the dying to the margins, removed from our homes and other places of everyday life. This text transforms fear into hope. It gives us a powerful and reassuring vision of God's ultimate triumph over death and other challenges. All Saints points to a life beyond this world, a life where darkness is as light.

FAIRFAX F. FAIR

RESPONSE

How do you see death pushed to the margins in your community? How might Daniel's prophecies, despite their fantastic weirdness, echo your own fears, thoughts, or experiences of dying or losing someone you love? How do you imagine "a life beyond this world" and God's triumph over death?

PRAYER

Loving God, you promise to triumph over death, fear, and other great beasts; turn me toward hope and eternal life in you. Amen.

Canticle

Psalm 149

Let the high praises of God be in their throats
    and two-edged swords in their hands,
to execute vengeance on the nations
    and punishment on the peoples,
to bind their kings with fetters
    and their nobles with chains of iron,
to execute on them the judgment decreed.
    This is glory for all his faithful ones.
Praise the LORD! (vv. 6–9)

REFLECTION

Whatever the historical context, theological convictions, or literary intent
of the psalmist might have been, so-called religious violence is to be
condemned. On the other hand, we must not romanticize or spiritualize
the lives of the saints. Faithfulness to God *does* put us at odds with the
powers and principalities of the world, and *will* lead us into the fray—
figuratively speaking or otherwise. We believe that Christ *will* come again
to judge and rule the world, destroying the reign of sin and death forever.

DAVID GAMBRELL

RESPONSE

How does it affect your understanding of saints to imagine them
with two-edged swords? What kinds of saints do you imagine have
wielded such things? What would you confront or destroy in your own
community, if you could?

PRAYER

God of hosts, you call your saints to face the powers and principalities
of this world; give us courage not to turn away but, with Christ, to
confront injustice and abuse. Amen.

Second Reading

And he has put all things under his feet and has made him the head over all things for the church, which is his body, the fullness of him who fills all in all. (vv. 22–23)

REFLECTION

Those who have found unity in Christ Jesus and in the purposive acts of God do not fear this fast-approaching diverse world. Rather, we must celebrate it, for in this wonderful coming together of humanity from everywhere and everyplace we can see the furtherance of the redemptive purposes of God and praise God's name for the oneness found in Christ Jesus. Paul reminds us that regardless of race and ethnicity, Christians are members of the same body, a worldwide church, though we come into that body from different cultures.

CLEOPHUS J. LARUE

RESPONSE

What is it like to imagine the communion of saints as a crowd of halos of many ethnicities and cultures? What do you value about diversity in your own life or congregation? What do you value in your own ethnicity or culture as a part of the body of Christ?

PRAYER

Jesus Christ, you are the head of the church and we are your body; bless our fullness and diversity, even as you fill us, all in all, and make us one. Amen.

Gospel

Luke 6:20–31

"Blessed are you when people hate you, and when they exclude you, revile you, and defame you on account of the Son of Man. . . .

Woe to you when all speak well of you, for that is what their ancestors did to the false prophets.

But I say to you that listen, Love your enemies, do good to those who hate you." (vv. 22, 26–27)

REFLECTION

First, Christians are encouraged to live holy lives so that we too might be "blessed," like those countless holy women and men who have faithfully lived the teachings of Jesus and therefore are now truly blessed. Second, Christians are ambassadors of peace and reconciliation, even when we are maltreated and ridiculed. Finally, the Scripture reading and today's feast share an invitation to live a radical faith in God. It is a call from a life of self-absorption to holy simplicity, meekness, and charity.

VANTHANH NGUYEN, SVD

RESPONSE

What is one radical and impossible value or teaching in the blessings and woes of Luke that might be a nudge from God to you this week? How might these words be speaking to your life and journey toward radical faith? How do you feel called to be a saint?

PRAYER

Jesus, may these blessings and woes help me to do unto others as I would have them do unto me, under your mercy. Amen.

Weekend Reflections

FURTHER CONNECTION

Now it may not be obvious at first, but we actually have a day to remember crazy Christians. I think we call it All Saints' Day. It's not called "All the Same Day," it's called All Saints' Day, because the saints, though they were fallible and mortal and sinners like the rest of us, when push came to shove they marched to the beat of a different drummer. In their lifetimes, they made a difference for the kingdom of God.

MICHAEL B. CURRY (1953–), *CRAZY CHRISTIANS*

MAKING THE CONNECTIONS

Choose one or two questions for reflection:

1. What connections have you noticed between this week's texts and other passages in Scripture?

2. What connections have you made between this week's texts and the world beyond Scripture?

3. Does either of this week's two commentary themes speak especially to your life or the life of the world around you right now?

4. What is God saying to your congregation in particular through this week's readings and commentaries?

_____

_____

_____

_____

_____

_____

Sabbath Day

SCRIPTURE OF ASSURANCE

I have heard of your faith in the Lord Jesus and your love toward all the saints, and for this reason I do not cease to give thanks for you as I remember you in my prayers. (Ephesians 1:15–16)

WEEKLY EXAMEN

- Take a quiet moment, seek out God's presence, and pray for the guidance of the Spirit.

- Consider the past week; recall specific moments and feelings that stand out to you.

- Choose one moment or feeling for deeper examination, thanksgiving, or repentance.

- Let go, breathe deeply, and invite Christ's love to surround and fill you in preparation for the week ahead.

- End with the Lord's Prayer.

The Week Leading Up to
Proper 26

(Sunday between October 30 and November 5)

Habakkuk 1:1–4; 2:1–4

I will stand at my watchpost,
    and station myself on the rampart;
I will keep watch to see what he will say to me,
    and what he will answer concerning my complaint. (2:1)

Isaiah 1:10–18

Wash yourselves; make yourselves clean;
    remove the evil of your doings
    from before my eyes;
cease to do evil. (v. 16)

2 Thessalonians 1:1–4, 11–12

We must always give thanks to God for you, brothers and sisters, as is right, because your faith is growing abundantly, and the love of every one of you for one another is increasing. (v. 3)

Luke 19:1–10

When Jesus came to the place, he looked up and said to him, "Zacchaeus, hurry and come down; for I must stay at your house today." (v. 5)

LECTIO DIVINA

Underline a word or phrase that especially grabs your attention. Pray from that word or phrase and ask God to help you connect to its particular invitation for you this week.

Themes from This Week's Writers

THEME 1: *God Is the Savior, Not Us*

Habakkuk 1:1–4, 2:1–4

God wants Habakkuk and his community of runners to look—just look. To look at the proud, and see the proud clearly. If we see what the proud are, the text suggests, we will be able to see what the contrast to pride is: living not by running frantically from one (good) deed to the next, but instead living by faith, faith that God really will heal the world of all its violence at the end.

LAUREN F. WINNER

Psalm 119:137–144

Because the psalmist dwells in God's Word, trusting in God's future is an expression of faithfulness, even as the psalmist asks that God continually increase her or his understanding. The justice God promises is indeed on the way.

KIMBERLY BRACKEN LONG

Luke 19:1–10

Zacchaeus's story is not about what he does or does not do, but about what God is doing through Jesus. Jesus announces, "Today salvation has come to this house," because Jesus has invited himself into Zacchaeus's home. The plan is nothing less than God's design.

PATRICK J. WILLSON

THEME 2: *Cease to Do Evil, Learn to Do Good*

Isaiah 1:10–18

As Isaiah makes clear, true redemption comes only from justice (Isa. 1:27). . . .

. . . Jesus also preaches about the importance of justice. The story of Zacchaeus in Luke 19:1–10 offers an example of how an encounter with

Jesus moves a person to amend their wrongs and do right to those who he has harmed.

LYDIA HERNÁNDEZ-MARCIAL

2 Thessalonians 1:1–4, 11–12

Today's churches would do well to recover the robust sense of God's justice displayed in this chapter: recognition that God is like a "flaming fire" who aims to purify us will allow us to reclaim the drama and truth of the gospel.

EDITH M. HUMPHREY

Luke 19:1–10

Jesus' agenda is discipleship oriented. The Zacchaeus story is a useful picture for understanding what having wealth implies in the realm of faith. Zacchaeus, for example, is a saint when his story is juxtaposed with the parable of Lazarus the Rich Man (16:19–31) and the story of the rich ruler (18:18–25).

KENYATTA R. GILBERT

WHAT IS THE HOLY SPIRIT SAYING TO YOU THIS WEEK?

_____

_____

_____

_____

_____

A SPIRITUAL PRACTICE FOR THIS WEEK

Give a generous gift to a needy person or organization that cannot be repaid, anonymously if possible. For instance, give a wad of cash to a street musician or panhandler, drop off gift cards at a shelter, pay lunch debts at a school, or research how organizations can purchase and forgive medical debt.

First Reading

Habakkuk 1:1–4; 2:1–4

Then the LORD answered me and said:
Write the vision;
   make it plain on tablets,
   so that a runner may read it.
For there is still a vision for the appointed time;
   it speaks of the end, and does not lie.
If it seems to tarry, wait for it;
   it will surely come, it will not delay. (2:2–3)

REFLECTION

We are the runner. Everyone in our parish is the runner. Our colleagues and friends are the runner. Habakkuk tells us that the Lord wants this message to reach even us, in our busyness, in our dash through life.

What God proceeds to say is unsettling, especially for those of us who believe we can fix things, that the world can be made right through our constant action, our busyness. . . . Rather, it is God's action that this passage stresses. In the "appointed time," at "the end," God—*not we*—will set things right.

LAUREN F. WINNER

RESPONSE

How would you describe the "running" or busyness in your life? In your community? What messages from God about violence, injustice, or neighbors in need might you be dashing past? What do you hear for yourself this week in God's declaration that *God* will set things right, not humans?

PRAYER

O God, show me how to read your vision, even if I cannot stop running; teach me to trust in your actions and power, not just my own. Amen.

Canticle

Psalm 32:1–7

Then I acknowledged my sin to you,
  and I did not hide my iniquity;
I said, "I will confess my transgressions to the LORD,"
  and you forgave the guilt of my sin. (v. 5)

REFLECTION

The psalmist's experience . . . underscores the importance of not keeping silent about the burden of sin. The faithful worshiper speaks a confession to God, telling the truth about one's need for grace.

. . . Confession is not for the purpose of self-flagellation but rather to allow "streams of mercy never ceasing" to flow through the believer's life. Confession is always followed by forgiveness; telling the truth about our lives as individuals, as a community, and as a society allows the possibility of true repentance and makes room for the Holy Spirit to use us in the renewal of creation.

KIMBERLY BRACKEN LONG

RESPONSE

What is something in your life or your community's life that you have longed to confess or tell the truth about? If this made room in you or your community for the Spirit to "use you in the renewal of Creation," what might happen next?

PRAYER

God of grace, teach me to tell the truth about my life and confess to you; forgive the guilt of my sin and preserve me from trouble in the time of my distress. Amen.

Second Reading

2 Thessalonians 1:1–4, 11–12

Therefore we ourselves boast of you among the churches of God for your steadfastness and faith during all your persecutions and the afflictions that you are enduring.

. . . To this end we always pray for you, asking that our God will make you worthy of his call and will fulfill by his power every good resolve and work of faith. (vv. 4, 11)

REFLECTION

In an age of secularization and diminished religious affiliation, it is occasionally tempting to identify the contemporary church as a persecuted class; at the same time, of course, the history of the Western church abounds with a degree of political power unimaginable to the first-century audience of this letter, and any honest exegesis has to wrestle with the church's role not just as persecuted class but also as an agent of persecution itself. . . . The church as historical institution rarely fits the profile of victimhood necessary for this text to feel comfortable and heartwarming.

MATT GAVENTA

RESPONSE

What or who do you consider to be foes of your church community? How has your church been an agent of persecution, recently or in the past, especially of marginalized people? What kind of power or influence does your congregation have in your community, politically, economically, or socially?

PRAYER

O God, make us, your church, worthy of your call and fulfill by your power every good resolve and work of faith. Amen.

Gospel

Luke 19:1–10

[Zacchaeus] was trying to see who Jesus was, but on account of the crowd he could not, because he was short in stature. So he ran ahead and climbed a sycamore tree to see him, because he was going to pass that way. (vv. 3–4)

REFLECTION

For Luke, seeing Jesus *is* seeing God's salvation. This is what Zacchaeus wants to see. Jesus is salvation walking, and as Jesus enters Jericho, Zacchaeus climbs his sycamore. . . . The language of "trying to see" is phrased in terms of seeking, searching, and yearning. We may wonder at times what Jesus looked like, but Zacchaeus wants to see more than a face. He wants to see more than he can say, but he knows at least this much: it has to do with this Jesus entering Jericho.

PATRICK J. WILLSON

RESPONSE

Meditate on the phrase "Jesus is salvation walking"; you might create a poem or draw an image. Or reflect what you are trying to see, like Zacchaeus, in your journey with Christ right now.

PRAYER

O Jesus, show me how to see you, despite my limitations; may your salvation come to my house. Amen.

Weekend Reflections

FURTHER CONNECTION

There are two ways of being a prophet. One is to tell the enslaved that they can be free. It is the difficult path of Moses. The second is to tell those who think they are free that they are in fact enslaved. This is the even more difficult path of Jesus.

RICHARD ROHR (1943–), *FROM WILD MAN TO WISE MAN*

MAKING THE CONNECTIONS

Choose one or two questions for reflection:

1. What connections have you noticed between this week's texts and other passages in Scripture?

2. What connections have you made between this week's texts and the world beyond Scripture?

3. Does either of this week's two commentary themes speak especially to your life or the life of the world around you right now?

4. What is God saying to your congregation in particular through this week's readings and commentaries?

MY CONNECTIONS

_____

_____

_____

_____

_____

_____

Sabbath Day

He will transform the body of our humiliation that it may be conformed to the body of his glory, by the power that also enables him to make all things subject to himself. (Philippians 3:21)

WEEKLY EXAMEN

- Take a quiet moment, seek out God's presence, and pray for the guidance of the Spirit.

- Consider the past week; recall specific moments and feelings that stand out to you.

- Choose one moment or feeling for deeper examination, thanksgiving, or repentance.

- Let go, breathe deeply, and invite Christ's love to surround and fill you in preparation for the week ahead.

- End with the Lord's Prayer.

The Week Leading Up to
Proper 27
(Sunday between November 6 and November 12)

Haggai 1:15b–2:9

I am with you, says the LORD of hosts, according to the promise that I made you when you came out of Egypt. My spirit abides among you; do not fear. (2:4b–5)

Job 19:23–27a

And after my skin has been thus destroyed,
then in my flesh I shall see God. (v. 26)

2 Thessalonians 2:1–5, 13–17

As to the coming of our Lord Jesus Christ and our being gathered together to him, we beg you, brothers and sisters, not to be quickly shaken in mind or alarmed. (vv. 1–2a)

Luke 20:27–38

"But those who are considered worthy of a place in that age and in the resurrection from the dead neither marry nor are given in marriage. Indeed they cannot die anymore, because they are like angels and are children of God, being children of the resurrection." (vv. 35–36)

LECTIO DIVINA

Underline a word or phrase that especially grabs your attention. Pray from that word or phrase and ask God to help you connect to its particular invitation for you this week.

Themes from This Week's Writers

THEME 1: *Hope for the Future Reign of God*

Haggai 1:15b–2:9

Haggai's words affirm to a disappointed people with limited resources that God will provide necessary resources for the restoration of the temple to its former glory. Indeed, this construction will even surpass the original (2:9). The text uses eschatological language—that is, language referring to future times, to describe how God will indeed provide.

LYDIA HERNÁNDEZ-MARCIAL

Psalm 17:1–9

Job 19:23–27a and Psalm 17:1–9 do sound a tone of lament, but they also express deep confidence in God who redeems and restores. Even when worshipers voice their despair, they also profess their assurance in the coming reign of God. Even when we weep, we hope.

KIMBERLY BRACKEN LONG

2 Thessalonians 2:1–5, 13–17

Both speakers invite these anxious congregations to remember the old stories, to practice the well-worn liturgies, and to seek out the deep truths about who God's people are and who they are called to be. As personified by the words of the Lord on Haggai's lips, and as promised by the incarnate Truth proclaimed to this Thessalonian church, even when God's people forget the old stories, God's truth has a way of speaking for itself.

MATT GAVENTA

THEME 2: *Life after Death with God*

Job 19:23–27a

In the midst of these losses, Job's own future is disclosed to him: he can see his own corpse, decaying (Job 19:26). Yet surprisingly, this vision of

his death gives Job hope. At the end, he will see God (v. 26). We readers
see too; bodies molder, yet these bodies will also be resurrected.

LAUREN F. WINNER

Luke 20:27–38

We long to know more about what it means that to God "all of them are
alive," and we have our own questions about what life as "children of the
resurrection" might mean. It is not necessary for the preacher to answer
every question about the resurrection. It would be enough to enrich our
wonderings and point to their consummation in God.

PATRICK J. WILLSON

Luke 20:27–38

The afterlife is different from life on earth, Jesus explains. The world of
the present reality is not the only reality there is. The world to come into
which humans are resurrected from death is radically discontinuous with
a dying world.

KENYATTA R. GILBERT

WHAT IS THE HOLY SPIRIT SAYING TO YOU THIS WEEK?

_____

_____

_____

_____

_____

A SPIRITUAL PRACTICE FOR THIS WEEK

"Keep death always before your eyes," St. Benedict told his monks.
Find an image or replica of a skull to keep nearby this week, alongside
Job 19:25–27a. Reflect on your own death and the eventual loss of your
body, but also the continuation of your relationship with God.

First Reading

Haggai 1:15b–2:9

The silver is mine, and the gold is mine, says the LORD of hosts. The latter splendor of this house shall be greater than the former, says the LORD of hosts; and in this place I will give prosperity, says the LORD of hosts. (2:8–9)

REFLECTION

All of the wealth in the universe belongs to God, and all the power belongs to God. . . .

. . . We do not own anything, at least not in the typical sense of ownership. Sometimes, we get our hands on silver and gold, but we did not create the wealth and, per this passage, we do not dispose of it. Though it seems that we "have" silver or gold, we are only its caretakers. . . . Haggai invites us to give an account of what it means for us to "own" silver and gold, especially when, as Haggai states, everything ultimately belongs to the Lord (2:8).

LAUREN F. WINNER

RESPONSE

Reflect on this phrase: "I do not own anything." What is uncomfortable? What is freeing? What does it mean to you, in this season of your life, for God to call you the caretaker of what you own and earn, not the owner?

PRAYER

O Lord, all that exists belongs to you; your Spirit abides with me and I will not fear. Amen.

Canticle

Psalm 98

The LORD has made known his victory;
    he has revealed his vindication in the sight of the nations.
He has remembered his steadfast love and faithfulness
    to the house of Israel.
All the ends of the earth have seen
    the victory of our God. (vv. 2–3)

REFLECTION

This vision of the world as God intends it is cause for the church to praise as well, for Christians profess that the restoration of all creation has already been secured in Jesus Christ. Even though we continue to live in times of distress, we can look back and see how God has brought us this long way. Even while we continue to pray for wars to end and for justice to prevail, we can see where we are headed. Let the church praise God with the enthusiasm of the Psalms; let joy prevail, even in the face of hardship, for God's realm is on the way.

KIMBERLY BRACKEN LONG

RESPONSE

When you look back on your life, what signs of God's faithfulness stand out to you, today? In the life of your congregation? Your nation? How hard or easy is it for you to believe with hope that God's realm is on the way?

PRAYER

Steadfast God, remember your love and faithfulness to us and all the ends of the earth. Amen.

Second Reading

So then, brothers and sisters, stand firm and hold fast to the traditions that you were taught by us, either by word of mouth or by our letter. (v. 15)

REFLECTION

Paul uses the technical word for tradition (*paradosis*) that means "a gift given over." Alas, some translations will not use the word "tradition" in a positive sense . . . but substitute words like "teaching" wherever Paul approves of tradition. . . . As a result, generations of Christians have been predisposed to assess "tradition" as something foreign to biblical faith. Those who proclaim the Word might use this chapter as an antidote to this misapprehension that tradition is a dead thing that will bind rather than free Christians.

EDITH M. HUMPHREY

RESPONSE

Choose three church traditions to which you stand firm and hold fast. What is meaningful to you about each? Do you tend to enjoy tradition in your church or faith life, or to avoid it? What about it draws or repels you?

PRAYER

Lord Jesus Christ, you love us and through grace give us eternal comfort and good hope; comfort my heart and strengthen me in every good work and word. Amen.

Gospel

Luke 20:27–38

"And the fact that the dead are raised Moses himself showed, in the story about the bush, where he speaks of the Lord as the God of Abraham, the God of Isaac, and the God of Jacob. Now he is God not of the dead, but of the living; for to him all of them are alive." (vv. 37–38)

REFLECTION

Jesus seems to think that human relationships with the Creator matter beyond the grave. What this means sociopolitically is that bound up in life is the possibility of having a truly personal relationship with a God who transcends death itself. Empirical datum will never sufficiently verify what the heart of faith knows: that the God of Abraham, Isaac, Jacob, and Jesus honors our faith and promotes human flourishing, for the one with whom we have to do "is not God of the dead but of the living" (v. 38).

KENYATTA R. GILBERT

RESPONSE

We tend to focus on our relationship with God now, on earth. Today, spend some time meditating on your relationship with God beyond death. How does this feel? How might it lead you to a new understanding of God? Of yourself? Of others, the living or dead?

PRAYER

O Jesus, you reveal to me God, not of the dead but of the living; for to God, all are alive, both in this world and in the reign to come. Amen.

Weekend Reflections

I am not saying that we should love death, but rather that we should love
life so generously, without picking and choosing, that we automatically
include it (life's other half) in our love. This is what actually happens in
the great expansiveness of love, which cannot be stopped or constricted.
It is only because we exclude it that death becomes more and more
foreign to us and, ultimately, our enemy. It is conceivable that death is
infinitely closer to us than life itself. . . . What do we know of it?

RAINER MARIA RILKE (1875–1926), 1923 LETTER

MAKING THE CONNECTIONS

Choose one or two questions for reflection:

1. What connections have you noticed between this week's texts and
   other passages in Scripture?

2. What connections have you made between this week's texts and the
   world beyond Scripture?

3. Does either of this week's two commentary themes speak especially
   to your life or the life of the world around you right now?

4. What is God saying to your congregation in particular through this
   week's readings and commentaries?

_____

_____

_____

_____

_____

_____

Sabbath Day

SCRIPTURE OF ASSURANCE

But thanks be to God, who in Christ always leads us in triumphal procession, and through us spreads in every place the fragrance that comes from knowing him. (2 Corinthians 2:14)

WEEKLY EXAMEN

- Take a quiet moment, seek out God's presence, and pray for the guidance of the Spirit.

- Consider the past week; recall specific moments and feelings that stand out to you.

- Choose one moment or feeling for deeper examination, thanksgiving, or repentance.

- Let go, breathe deeply, and invite Christ's love to surround and fill you in preparation for the week ahead.

- End with the Lord's Prayer.

The Week Leading Up to
Proper 28
(Sunday between November 13 and November 19)

Isaiah 65:17–25

For I am about to create new heavens
    and a new earth;
the former things shall not be remembered
    or come to mind. (v. 17)

Malachi 4:1–2a

See, the day is coming, burning like an oven, when all the arrogant and all evildoers will be stubble. (v. 1a)

2 Thessalonians 3:6–13

And we did not eat anyone's bread without paying for it; but with toil and labor we worked night and day, so that we might not burden any of you. (v. 8)

Luke 21:5–19

"You will be hated by all because of my name. But not a hair of your head will perish. By your endurance you will gain your souls." (vv. 17–19)

LECTIO DIVINA

Underline a word or phrase that especially grabs your attention. Pray from that word or phrase and ask God to help you connect to its particular invitation for you this week.

Themes from This Week's Writers

THEME 1: *A New Heaven and a New Earth*

Malachi 4:1–2a

The sun of righteousness speaks of the breaking of a new dawn, of light shining in darkness. This same sun whose rays benevolently shine on the righteous, offering them warmth and comfort, also has the potential to fiercely burn down on the wicked.

L. JULIANA M. CLAASSENS

Isaiah 65:17–25

In offering assurances of an improved heaven and earth, Isaiah challenges the church to think about ways in which it can become cocreators in the fulfillment of this divine eschatological vision. It also challenges the people of God to consider how they have been apathetic toward and at points have even hindered the manifestation of this new divine order.

SONG-MI SUZIE PARK

2 Thessalonians 3:6–13

What Paul encourages in the concrete practices of the Christians in Thessalonica is foreshadowed in Isaiah's grand imagining of what God intends for the whole creation: communities of persons in which special advantage is not sought and communities of nature in which harm does not prevail.

D. CAMERON MURCHISON

THEME 2: *Endurance and Hope*

Isaiah 65:17–25 and Malachi 4:1–2a

Both these texts emerge out of a context of destruction and despair as the prophets . . . respectively envision a world in which there will be healing and salvation for their constituencies, who for a very long time have been living in a world marred by the effects of the violence and injustice enforced by one empire after another.

L. JULIANA M. CLAASSENS

Luke 21:5–19

What might bring terror should result instead in trust: Jesus said these things would happen. Therefore, though it appears as if God's plan and work has been undermined, it is not so. Despite the seeming signs of disaster, God is still in charge. God is faithful. The people, thus, should remain faithful to God.

PATRICK ODEN

Luke 21:5–19

A sermon that follows the words of Jesus might point to the witness of the church during the "time of the world" as displaying a particular ethic of disciplined love—for God and neighbor. This ascetic way of life nourishes and sustains the hope of a community whose vision is kept open by adoring praise of God.

MICHAEL PASQUARELLO III

WHAT IS THE HOLY SPIRIT SAYING TO YOU THIS WEEK?

_____

_____

_____

_____

_____

A SPIRITUAL PRACTICE FOR THIS WEEK

Watch an apocalyptic or dystopian movie or TV episode. How does it feel to see copious destruction and loss? Compare the story with the readings from Isaiah, Malachi, and Luke. What is similar? What is different? Where does the movie locate hope? What about the readings? What about you?

First Reading

Isaiah 65:17–25 or Malachi 4:1–2a

The wolf and the lamb shall feed together.

. . . .

They shall not hurt or destroy
on all my holy mountain,
says the Lord. (Isaiah 65:25)

The day that comes shall burn them up, says the Lord of hosts, so that it will leave them neither root nor branch. (Malachi 4:1b)

REFLECTION

This desire for recompense, especially from those who commit injustice—people who, as Malachi clarifies in 3:5, perjure and lie and oppress workers, widows, orphans, and immigrants—is understandable. Yet this desire for retribution is in direct contrast to the new world envisioned by Isaiah, in which weeping and hurt are abolished (Isa. 65:19, 25). Preachers will do well to explore the tension that emerges when Malachi 4:1–2a is juxtaposed to Isaiah 65: How can the people of God hate injustice and oppression without despising those who commit wrongdoing?

SONG-MI SUZIE PARK

RESPONSE

What is an injustice that really makes you angry? Do you ever wish for revenge or retribution on the perpetrators? What does it look like to fight injustice without hating your enemies? This week, how could you practice this?

PRAYER

O God, you are creating new heavens and a new earth; teach me to hate injustice, but not people. Amen.

Canticle

Isaiah 12 or Psalm 98

Sing praises to the Lord, for he has done gloriously;
　　let this be known in all the earth. (Isaiah 12:5)

Let the floods clap their hands;
　　let the hills sing together for joy
at the presence of the Lord, for he is coming
　　to judge the earth. (Psalm 98:8)

REFLECTION

In a time when oppressors grow stronger and genocide is part of the daily news, we must proclaim that a new day is coming. . . . To do so is not to resign ourselves to the evil of this day while we wait for the glory of the next. To preach and pray eschatologically—to sing of the day that is to come—is to reassure the people of God (and the world) of God's future, but it is also a call to action in the present.

KIMBERLY BRACKEN LONG

RESPONSE

What do you believe about God's kingdom, still to come? What is it like to reframe your perspective on the future from considering the next year or decade to considering the eschaton? How, for you or your community, might this result in a greater call to action in the present?

PRAYER

Ever-living God, surely you are my salvation; I will trust and will not be afraid. Amen.

Second Reading

2 Thessalonians 3:6–13

For we hear that some of you are living in idleness, mere busybodies, not doing any work. Now such persons we command and exhort in the Lord Jesus Christ to do their work quietly and to earn their own living. (vv. 11–12)

REFLECTION

Idleness appears problematic because it undermines the mutually supportive character of Christian community.

. . . Addressing "idlers" is part and parcel of maintaining the bonds of Christian love, just as are encouraging "the fainthearted" and helping "the weak." Overcoming idleness is not merely for instilling virtue in the individual inclined to it, but also for the sake of restoring the fullness of community. . . .

. . . Fundamentally [Paul] wants to ensure that no one takes advantage of the altruism of the Christian community, undermining generosity as a trustworthy bond of life together.

D. CAMERON MURCHISON

RESPONSE

Where is there more a tendency in your life: toward idleness or being a workaholic? Is one of these a pet peeve for you when you see it in others? How can you reframe this question, away from scolding or a virtue test, to a restoring of fullness of community, generosity, and trust?

PRAYER

Lord Jesus Christ, help me not to be weary in doing what is right, but to strive that all may work together for fullness of life and community in you. Amen.

Gospel

Luke 21:5–19

"When you hear of wars and insurrections, do not be terrified; for these things must take place first, but the end will not follow immediately. . . .

". . . I will give you words and a wisdom that none of your opponents will be able to withstand or contradict." (vv. 9, 15)

REFLECTION

The world seems to be getting worse and that is overwhelming. But our calling in God is to hope, and to trust that what we might see, what might very well be real, is not definitive for our hearts or our actions. We are to trust, and in trusting we are to live out with faithfulness the calling we have been given. We are to be careful, not be weighed down, as Jesus says in Luke 21:34. Redemption is indeed drawing near, but it takes eyes of faith to see and hearts of hope to trust.

PATRICK ODEN

RESPONSE

What is happening right now that is overwhelming for you, or even apocalyptic? How might God be inviting you to hope anyway, beyond what your eyes see? What does trust in Jesus Christ mean for you right now? How are you called to draw near to redemption?

PRAYER

Brother Jesus, I confess that sometimes I hear of wars and insurrections and I am terrified; please give me hope, that I may trust in you above all things. Amen.

Weekend Reflections

"But in the end, it's only a passing thing, this shadow. Even darkness must pass. A new day will come. And when the sun shines it will shine out the clearer. Those were the stories that stayed with you. That meant something, even if you were too small to understand why. But I think, Mr. Frodo, I do understand. I know now. Folk in those stories had lots of chances of turning back, only they didn't. They kept going, because they were holding on to something. That there is some good in this world, and it's worth fighting for."

SAMWISE GAMGEE, IN THE MOVIE *THE LORD OF THE RINGS:*
THE TWO TOWERS

MAKING THE CONNECTIONS

Choose one or two questions for reflection:

1. What connections have you noticed between this week's texts and other passages in Scripture?

2. What connections have you made between this week's texts and the world beyond Scripture?

3. Does either of this week's two commentary themes speak especially to your life or the life of the world around you right now?

4. What is God saying to your congregation in particular through this week's readings and commentaries?

_____

_____

_____

_____

_____

_____

Sabbath Day

SCRIPTURE OF ASSURANCE

> But I will hope continually,
>   and will praise you yet more and more.
> My mouth will tell of your righteous acts,
>   of your deeds of salvation all day long,
>   though their number is past my knowledge. (Psalm 71:14–15)

WEEKLY EXAMEN

- Take a quiet moment, seek out God's presence, and pray for the guidance of the Spirit.

- Consider the past week; recall specific moments and feelings that stand out to you.

- Choose one moment or feeling for deeper examination, thanksgiving, or repentance.

- Let go, breathe deeply, and invite Christ's love to surround and fill you in preparation for the week ahead.

- End with the Lord's Prayer.

The Week Leading Up to
Proper 29
(Reign of Christ)

Jeremiah 23:1–6

I will raise up shepherds over them who will shepherd them, and they shall not fear any longer, or be dismayed, nor shall any be missing, says the LORD. (v. 4)

Luke 1:68–79

"He has raised up a mighty savior for us
in the house of his servant David." (v. 69)

Colossians 1:11–20

For in him all the fullness of God was pleased to dwell, and through him God was pleased to reconcile to himself all things, whether on earth or in heaven, by making peace through the blood of his cross. (vv. 19–20)

Luke 23:33–43

The soldiers also mocked him, coming up and offering him sour wine, and saying, "If you are the King of the Jews, save yourself!" There was also an inscription over him, "This is the King of the Jews." (vv. 36–38)

LECTIO DIVINA

Underline a word or phrase that especially grabs your attention. Pray from that word or phrase and ask God to help you connect to its particular invitation for you this week.

Themes from This Week's Writers

THEME 1: *Shepherd Leadership*

Jeremiah 23:1–6

Jeremiah uses "shepherd" as a code word for a "leader"—someone responsible for the well-being of the flock. Indeed, ancient Near Eastern kings were often pictured with a shepherd's staff. Unsurprisingly, many of Israel's great leaders, such as Moses and David, were said to have been shepherds.

CARLTON J. "COBBIE" PALM

Jeremiah 23:1–6

In this time, God will raise up good leaders (shepherds) over God's people. These good shepherds are exemplified in the reference to the righteous king, a descendant, that is, a branch of the house of David who "shall reign as king and deal wisely, and shall execute justice and righteousness in the land" (v. 5).

L. JULIANA M. CLAASSENS

Luke 1:68–79

This canticle sings of what Jeremiah spoke of so long ago: the divine promise of a lasting and just king has at last been fulfilled. Jesus is that long-expected king for all of lost and fearful humanity, the king who will "deal wisely, and shall execute justice and righteousness in the land" (Jer. 23:5).

THOMAS G. LONG

THEME 2: *A Throne in the Shape of a Cross*

Colossians 1:11–20

The arc of prophecy stretches from the hope for the good shepherd and a righteous king to the actual appearance of the beloved Son in whom all things hold together.

. . . Both Luke and Colossians see God's reign accomplished in what humanly considered appears to be its opposite. The reign of God comes in the shape of a cross.

D. CAMERON MURCHISON

Luke 23:33–43

He exercised his divine authority with these words: "Father, forgive them; for they do not know what they are doing." This is the way God rules the world in the person and work of Jesus Christ. His throne is a wooden cross; his constituents are convicted sinners.

MICHAEL PASQUARELLO III

Luke 23:33–43

While others were willing to confess the lordship of Jesus in the midst of his ministry, only the criminal offers such a confession at the point at which Jesus and the systems of this world collide. . . .

. . . The criminal, who acknowledges his guilt, is comforted with the clemency of the king.

PATRICK ODEN

WHAT IS THE HOLY SPIRIT SAYING TO YOU THIS WEEK?

_____

_____

_____

_____

_____

A SPIRITUAL PRACTICE FOR THIS WEEK

As a focus for prayer, repeat the criminal's words: "Jesus, remember me when you come into your kingdom." Write out the phrase and put it in a shoe or wallet, hum or sing the Taizé chant, or journal about its meaning for you.

First Reading

Jeremiah 23:1–6

Woe to the shepherds who destroy and scatter the sheep of my pasture! says the LORD. (v. 1)

REFLECTION

Leaders . . . can lead us to safety and well-being, or they can lead us into alienation and despair. Indeed, the history of the world, including that of Israel, consisted of the terrible suffering and injustice that stemmed from bad leadership. . . .

God does not give up and has not given up on our capacity to help shepherd a better world that is in right relationship with God. The ultimate vision of God is to see our humanity step up and take leadership. Leadership of our own personal lives and destiny. Leadership in our families and communities. Leadership for our people and even our nation.

CARLTON J. "COBBIE" PALM

RESPONSE

Recall a time you saw bad leadership lead to suffering or injustice. What are the traits of this kind of leadership? What are traits that lead to well-being? How are you supporting or participating in good leadership in your own context? How might you be hindering or griping about leadership?

PRAYER

O God, raise up good shepherds over us so we shall not fear; and teach me, also, to help shepherd a better world, in right relationship with you. Amen.

Canticle

Psalm 46

He makes wars cease to the end of the earth;
  he breaks the bow, and shatters the spear;
  he burns the shields with fire.
"Be still, and know that I am God!" (vv. 9–10a)

REFLECTION

The world is shaking with violence, and the people are quaking with fear.
To these fears the psalmist says, "Do not be afraid; God's light is
breaking over us" (see v. 5). As for convulsions in the earth, God speaks
and the earth melts (see v. 6). As for warring nations, God "breaks the
bow and shatters the spear" (v. 9). "Be still, and know that I am God"
(v. 10) is best understood not as an invitation to quiet piety but as a
command to leave the battlefield: "Stop fighting . . . and know that I am
God" (TEV).

THOMAS G. LONG

RESPONSE

Reflect on "Be still, and know that I am God" as a command to leave
the battlefield. What is a fight that God might be asking you or your
congregation to relinquish? How has that fight drawn you away from
God's leadership or God's kingdom? What new energy might peace
bring?

PRAYER

God of hosts, teach me to be still and know you, that I may not fear or
make war but serve you and find refuge in you. Amen.

Second Reading

Colossians 1:11–20

He himself is before all things, and in him all things hold together. He is the head of the body, the church; he is the beginning, the firstborn from the dead, so that he might come to have first place in everything. (vv. 17–18)

REFLECTION

Christ is both creator and redeemer of this world. Some people may place their hope for humanity in governments, the United Nations, science, or other faith traditions. Paul, however, emphasizes that Christ "is before all things" (v. 17). All these human institutions are created, while Christ is eternal. As Christ is creator of all life, including human beings, he is also the redeemer. He is the beginning and the end, the Alpha and the Omega. In him all things will be restored and reconciled.

PHILIP WINGEIER-RAYO

RESPONSE

Choose one of the above words or phrases describing Jesus Christ, and rewrite it on a piece of paper. Write out other words or thoughts this inspires in you. What is Christ's invitation to you here?

PRAYER

O Christ, you are before all things, and in you all things hold together; in you all things will be restored and reconciled. Amen.

Gospel

Luke 23:33–43

Then he said, "Jesus, remember me when you come into your kingdom." He replied, "Truly I tell you, today you will be with me in Paradise." (vv. 42–43)

REFLECTION

In Jesus, divine power is vindicated in that it does not dominate, manipulate, or impose itself by force or violence, but serves by sharing itself. . . .

. . . God's divinity, as revealed in the humanity of Christ, does not consist in his ability to push things around, to impose the divine will and purpose from the security of detached, self-enclosed remoteness, or to sit in grandeur while the world carries out his demands. Far from being a neutral, impersonal force, distant and external to the world, God sends his glory into the world in the form of slavery, humiliation, suffering, and death on a cross.

MICHAEL PASQUARELLO III

RESPONSE

What is an image that comes to your mind when you reflect on power that serves by sharing itself in Jesus? What power or glory could there be in slavery, humiliation, suffering, and death on a cross? How does that contrast to power as grandeur, remoteness, distance, or detachment?

PRAYER

Jesus, you are my shepherd, savior, refuge, and king; remember me when you come into your kingdom. Amen.

Weekend Reflections

FURTHER CONNECTION

Really living like Christ will not mean reward, social recognition, and an assured income, but difficulties, discrimination, solitude, anxiety. Here, too, the basic experience of the cross applies: the wider we open our hearts to others, the more audibly we intervene against the injustice that rules over us, the more difficult our lives in the rich, unjust society will become.

DOROTHEE SOELLE (1929–2003), *THINKING ABOUT GOD*

MAKING THE CONNECTIONS

Choose one or two questions for reflection:

1. What connections have you noticed between this week's texts and other passages in Scripture?

2. What connections have you made between this week's texts and the world beyond Scripture?

3. Does either of this week's two commentary themes speak especially to your life or the life of the world around you right now?

4. What is God saying to your congregation in particular through this week's readings and commentaries?

_____

_____

_____

_____

_____

_____

Sabbath Day

SCRIPTURE OF ASSURANCE

"Peace I leave with you; my peace I give to you. I do not give to you as the world gives. Do not let your hearts be troubled, and do not let them be afraid." (John 14:27)

WEEKLY EXAMEN

- Take a quiet moment, seek out God's presence, and pray for the guidance of the Spirit.

- Consider the past week; recall specific moments and feelings that stand out to you.

- Choose one moment or feeling for deeper examination, thanksgiving, or repentance.

- Let go, breathe deeply, and invite Christ's love to surround and fill you in preparation for the week ahead.

- End with the Lord's Prayer.

Appendix
A Suggested Format for Small Groups

This book was designed to be used primarily by individuals but can also be the basis for shared study by a Bible study, a sermon group, or any small group. A group session can last one to two hours, depending on the size of the group and which options you choose. Feel free to experiment and tweak the suggestions to make a format that works for your group.

A group meeting on Sundays would easily match the rhythm of the weekly readings, but any day of the week can work. A group might choose to discuss the readings and passages of the past week or the upcoming week.

1. Opening
   Start in one or more of these ways:
   a. A minute of silence
   b. The sound of a singing bowl or bell
   c. An extemporaneous prayer
   d. Any other sign or mark of beginning
2. Introductions
   If introductions need to be made, invite each person to share:
   a. Their name
   b. A personal detail or two
   c. What brought them to join the group or why they keep coming back
3. Discussion Part 1
   Proceed in one or more of these ways:
   a. Discuss Themes from This Week's Writers. What theme resonates most? What commentary quotes stand out? How might the Spirit be speaking to your life or congregation?
   b. Discuss the Spiritual Practice: Who was able to try it? How did the Holy Spirit speak to you through this practice?
   c. Discuss the readings. Choose two or do all four. One person reads aloud the Scripture passage in its entirety from a Bible,

another reads aloud the commentary quote and the response questions, then all discuss. Close each discussion with that entry's prayer, said by one person or in unison.

4. Discussion Part 2

   Continue in one of these ways:

   a. Read aloud the Further Connection quote, then discuss intersections with the themes and Scripture from the past week, and any other outside connections you have noticed.

   b. Choose one or two of the questions from Making the Connections and discuss.

5. Closing

   Close in one or more of these ways:

   a. Invite each person to share one word that they are taking away from the gathering.

   b. Share briefly in the Weekly Examen (found in each Sabbath Day entry).

   c. Read aloud the Scripture quotes from the first page for next week.

   d. Ask one person to close the session with a prayer.

Sources of
Further Connections

Abba Moses. *See* Desert Fathers and Mothers

Addams, Jane. "The College Woman and Christianity." *Independent* 53, no. 2749 (August 8, 1901): 1853. *Lent 3*

African American spiritual. *See* Anonymous

Anonymous. "We Shall Not Be Moved." African American spiritual. Lyrics as heard in a recording by Mavis Staples in 2007. Track 3 on *We'll Never Turn Back*. ANTI- Records. *Proper 11*

Auden, W. H. *For the Time Being: A Christmas Oratorio*, 8. Princeton, NJ: Princeton University Press, 2013. First published 1944. *Christmas 1*

Berry, Wendell. "Manifesto: The Mad Farmer Liberation Front." In *The Country of Marriage: Poems*, 14. Berkeley: Counterpoint, 2013. First published 1971. *Proper 8*

Bolz-Weber, Nadia. Sermon for Epiphany 2, January 13, 2014. https://www.patheos.com/blogs/nadiabolzweber/2014/01/sermon-on-baptism-belovedness-and-how-god-is-like-a-duped-teacher/. *Baptism of the Lord*

Bonhoeffer, Dietrich. *Life Together*, translated by John W. Doberstein, 23. New York: Harper & Row, 1954. First published 1939. *Easter 4*

Brown, Brené. *The Gifts of Imperfection: Let Go of Who You Think You're Supposed to Be and Embrace Who You Are*, 80–81. Center City, MN: Hazelden, 2010. *Advent 3*

Browning, Elizabeth Barrett. *Aurora Leigh*. In *The Complete Poetical Works of Elizabeth Barrett Browning*, 372. Cutchogue, NY: Buccaneer Books, 1993. *Epiphany 5*

Brueggemann, Walter. *The Prophetic Imagination*, 40. 40th anniv. ed. Minneapolis: Fortress Press, 2018. *Proper 5*

Buechner, Frederick. *The Sacred Journey: A Memoir of Early Days*, 46. New York: Harper Collins, 1982. *Proper 18*

Bunim, Rabbi Simcha. In *Tales of the Hasidim: Later Masters*, edited by Martin Buber, 249–50. New York: Schocken, 1978. *Proper 19*

Chittister, Joan. *Wisdom Distilled from the Daily: Living the Rule of St. Benedict Today*, 75. New York: Harper, 1991. *Lent 5*

Coffin, William Sloane, Jr. *The Heart Is a Little to the Left: Essays on Public Morality*, 69–70. Hanover, NH: University Press of New England, 1999. *Proper 4*

Cone, James H. *The Cross and the Lynching Tree,* 161. New York: Orbis, 2011. *Palm/Passion Sunday*

Curry, Michael B. *Crazy Christians: A Call to Follow Jesus,* 5. New York: Church Publishing, 2013. *All Saints' Day*

Desert Fathers and Mothers. Traditional sayings (4th century). *Proper 25*

Espinal, Luís, SJ. *Oraciones a quemarropa,* 69. Lima: CEP, 1982. Quoted in Gustavo Gutiérrez, *On Job: God-Talk and the Suffering of the Innocent,* 91–92. Maryknoll, NY: Orbis, 2005. *Proper 22*

Evans, Rachel Held. *Searching for Sunday: Loving, Leaving, and Finding the Church,* 148. Nashville: Nelson Books, 2015. *Proper 9*

Francis. "The First Sign of Mercy." Sermon given June 8, 2016. Translation from https://aleteia.org/2016/06/08/pope-francis-the-christian-life-is -like-the-story-of-two-lovers/. Original at http://www.im.va/content /gdm/en/francesco/catechesi/2016-06-08Vaticanva.html. *Epiphany 2*

Francis of Assisi. Traditionally attributed. *Epiphany 6*

Gomes, Peter J. *Strength for the Journey: Biblical Wisdom for Daily Living,* 255. San Francisco: HarperCollins, 2003. *Easter 6*

Gutiérrez, Gustavo. *A Theology of Liberation: History, Politics, and Salvation,* 198. New York: Orbis, 1972. *Proper 10*

Hamer, Fannie Lou. "We're On Our Way." Speech at a civil rights meeting in Indianola, Mississippi, September 1964. https://teachingamerican history.org/library/document/were-on-our-way/. *Epiphany 7*

Heschel, Abraham Joshua. *The Sabbath,* 13–14. New York: Farrar, Straus & Giroux, 2005. First published 1951. *Proper 16*

hooks, bell. "'There's No Place to Go But Up'—bell hooks and Maya Ange-lou in Conversation." By Melvin McLeod. *Shambhala Sun* (now *Lion's Roar*), January 1998. https://www.lionsroar.com/theres-no-place-to-go -but-up/. *Proper 6*

Hurston, Zora Neale. *Their Eyes Were Watching God,* 150–51. New York: Harper & Row, 1990. First published 1937. *Advent 2*

Jackson, Peter, with Fran Walsh, Philippa Boyens, and Stephen Sinclair. *The Lord of the Rings: The Two Towers.* 2002. Movie based on the books by J. R. R. Tolkien. *Proper 28*

John of the Cross. "Del verbo divino." Translated by Heidi Haverkamp. *Advent 4*

Kazantzakis, Nikos. *Saint Francis: A Novel,* translated by P. A. Bien, 96. New York: Simon & Schuster, 1962. *Proper 23*

King, Martin Luther, Jr. "Where Do We Go from Here?" Speech to the Southern Christian Leadership Conference, Atlanta, August 16, 1967.

In *The Radical King*, edited by Cornel West, 175. Boston: Beacon Press, 2015. *Easter 5*

Lewis, C. S. *The Screwtape Letters*, ix. New York: HarperCollins, 1996. First published 1942. *Lent 1*

Lian Xi. *See* Lin Zhao

Lin Zhao. "Blood Poem on Shirt." In *Blood Letters: The Untold Story of Lin Zhao, A Martyr in Mao's China,* by Lian Xi, 91. New York: Basic Books, 2018. *Easter 7*

Martin, James, SJ. *Jesus: A Pilgrimage*, 449. New York: HarperCollins, 2014. *Easter 3*

Merton, Thomas. "The Measure of Charity." In *No Man Is an Island*, 168. New York: Harcourt Brace, 1955. *Epiphany 4*

Morrison, Toni. Nobel Lecture, December 7, 1993. https://www.nobelprize .org/prizes/literature/1993/morrison/lecture/. *Day of Pentecost*

Moses, Abba. *See* Desert Fathers and Mothers

Mote, Edward. "My Hope Is Built on Nothing Less." In *Glory to God*, 353. Louisville, KY: Westminster John Knox, 2013. *Proper 3*

Niebuhr, Reinhold. *The Irony of American History*, 63. New York: Scribner, 1952. *Epiphany 8*

Nouwen, Henri J. M. *The Return of the Prodigal Son: A Story of Homecoming*, 106. New York: Doubleday, 1994. *Lent 4*

O'Connor, Flannery. "Letter to Louise Abbot," 1959. In *The Habit of Being: Letters of Flannery O'Connor*, edited by Sally Fitzgerald, 354. New York: Vintage, 1980. *Easter 2*

Peterson, Eugene. *Christ Plays in Ten Thousand Places: A Conversation in Spiritual Theology*, 306. Grand Rapids: Eerdmans, 2005. *Trinity Sunday*

Pope Francis. *See* Francis

Remen, Rachel Naomi. *Kitchen Table Wisdom: Stories That Heal*, 155–56. New York: Riverhead Books, 1996. *Epiphany 9*

Rilke, Rainer Maria. "Letter to Countess Margot Sizzo-Noris-Crouy," 1923. In *A Year with Rilke: Daily Readings from the Best of Rainer Maria Rilke*, edited and translated by Joanna Macy and Anita Barrows, 87. New York: HarperOne, 2009. *Proper 27*

Robinson, Marilynne. "Fear." *New York Review of Books*, September 2015. https://www.nybooks.com/articles/2015/09/24/marilynne-robinson -fear/. *Lent 2*

Rohr, Richard. *From Wild Man to Wise Man: Reflections on Male Spirituality*, 41. Cincinnati: Franciscan Media, 2005. *Proper 26*

Romero, Oscar. Sermon preached December 16, 1979. In *Through the Year with Oscar Romero: Daily Meditations*, translated by Irene B. Hodgson, 133. Cincinnati: Franciscan Media, 2015. *Proper 21*

Rossetti, Christina. "Who Shall Deliver Me?" In *The Argosy*, 1:288. London: Strahan & Co., 1866. *Proper 7*

Rutledge, Fleming. *Advent: The Once and Future Coming of Jesus Christ*, 23. Grand Rapids: Eerdmans, 2018. *Advent 1*

Soelle, Dorothee. *Thinking about God: An Introduction to Theology*, 133. London: SCM Press, 1990. *Proper 29*

Song, Choan-Seng. *Third-Eye Theology*, 198–99. Rev. ed. New York: Orbis, 1991. *Easter Day/Resurrection of the Lord*

Taylor, Barbara Brown. *Bread of Angels*, 7. Cambridge, MA: Cowley, 1997. *Transfiguration Sunday*

Teresa of Avila. "Nada Te Turbe." Poem found after her death in her breviary, in her own handwriting. Translation by Heidi Haverkamp. *Proper 13*

Teresa of Calcutta. *The Love of Christ: Spiritual Counsels*, edited by G. Gorree and Jean Barbier, 8. San Francisco: Harper & Row, 1982. *Epiphany 3*

Thurman, Howard. *The Inward Journey*, 29. Richmond, IN: Friends United Press, 1971. *Christmas 2*

Tolkien, J. R. R. *See* Jackson, Peter

Tutu, Desmond. *No Future without Forgiveness*, 270. New York: Doubleday, 2000. *Proper 15*

Underhill, Evelyn. *Life as Prayer and Other Writings*, edited by Lucy Menzies, 55. New York: Morehouse, 1991. *Proper 20*

Wallace, David Foster. *This Is Water*, 100–106. From his 2005 commencement speech at Kenyon College. New York: Little, Brown, 2009. *Proper 17*

Weil, Simone. *Gravity and Grace*, translated by Arthur Wills, 120. Lincoln: University of Nebraska Press, 1997. *Proper 12*

Wiman, Christian. *My Bright Abyss*, 139. New York: Farrar, Straus & Giroux, 2013. *Proper 14*

Winner, Lauren F. *Still: Notes on a Mid-Faith Crisis*, 172. New York: HarperOne, 2012. *Proper 24*

Xi, Lian. *See* Lin Zhao

Zhao, Lin. *See* Lin Zhao

Contributors

Numbers in italics are page numbers on which each contributor's reflections can be found.

CHARLES L. AARON JR., Co-Director of the Intern Program, Associate Professor of Supervised Ministry, Perkins School of Theology, Dallas, TX; *208, 217.* MARK ABBOTT, Pastor, Community United Methodist Church, DeBary, FL; *103, 107, 114.* KLAUS-PETER ADAM, Associate Professor of Old Testament, Lutheran School of Theology at Chicago, Chicago, IL; *71, 74.* JARED E. ALCÁNTARA, Associate Professor of Preaching, Truett Theological Seminary, Waco, TX; *472, 481, 483, 490.* O. WESLEY ALLEN JR., Lois Craddock Perkins Professor of Homiletics, Perkins School of Theology at Southern Methodist University, Dallas, TX; *336, 349, 353.* RONALD J. ALLEN, Professor of Preaching and Gospels and Letters, Christian Theological Seminary, Indianapolis, IN; *39, 44, 48, 389, 392, 399, 408.* WM. LOYD ALLEN, Professor of Church History and Spiritual Formation, McAfee School of Theology, Mercer University, Atlanta, GA; *308, 322, 326, 327.* WES AVRAM, Senior Pastor, Pinnacle Presbyterian Church, Scottsdale, AZ; *113, 124, 132.*

ERIC D. BARRETO, Weyerhaeuser Associate Professor of New Testament, Princeton Theological Seminary, Princeton, NJ; *281.* DAVID L. BARTLETT†, Professor of New Testament Emeritus, Columbia Theological Seminary, Decatur, GA; *308, 313, 317, 318, 331.* MICHAEL BATTLE, Herbert Thompson Professor of Church and Society, and Director of the Desmond Tutu Center, General Theological Seminary, New York, NY; *226, 233, 237, 246.* RHODORA E. BEATON, Professor of Systematic Theology, Oblate School of Theology, San Antonio, TX; *96, 102, 106, 113, 117.* GLEN BELL, Senior Vice President of Development, Presbyterian Foundation, Jeffersonville, IN; *82.* MARIANNE BLICKENSTAFF, Managing Editor, *Interpretation: A Journal of Bible and Theology,* Union Presbyterian Seminary, Richmond, VA; *251, 253, 260, 269, 271.* SUZANNE WOOLSTON BOSSERT, Chaplain Volunteer for "Healing Paws" (canine therapy), Boston Medical Center; Boston Healthcare for the Homeless, Needham, MA; *309, 312, 317, 327, 330.* STEPHEN BOYD, John Allen Easley Professor of the Study of Religions, Wake Forest University, Department of the Study of Religions, Winston-Salem, NC; *336, 340, 345, 353, 358.* BRAD R. BRAXTON, Chief Diversity, Equity, and Inclusion Officer, St. Luke School, New York, NY; *344, 348, 354.* LINDA MCKINNISH BRIDGES, Director of Corporate and Foundation Relations, Office of Institutional Advancement, Salem College, Winston-Salem, NC; *366, 381, 384.* E. CARSON BRISSON, Associate Professor of Bible and Biblical Languages, Union Presbyterian Seminary, Charlotte, NC; *466, 475, 484.* MELISSA BROWNING†, Interim Director of Contextual Education and International Partnerships; Visiting Assistant

Professor of Contextual Education, Columbia Theological Seminary, Decatur, GA; *48, 50, 83, 85.* WALTER BRUEGGEMANN, William Marcellus McPheeters Professor Emeritus of Old Testament, Columbia Theological Seminary, Decatur GA; *224, 233, 242, 332.* JOHN M. BUCHANAN, Pastor Emeritus, Fourth Presbyterian Church; Former Editor/Publisher, *The Christian Century,* Chicago, IL; *362, 371, 375.*

ELIZABETH F. CALDWELL, Professor Emerita, McCormick Theological Seminary; Adjunct Faculty, Vanderbilt Divinity School, Nashville, TN; *418, 427, 431, 436.* CYNTHIA M. CAMPBELL, President Emerita, McCormick Theological Seminary; Retired Pastor, Highland Presbyterian Church, Louisville, KY; *3, 6, 12, 21, 25.* LEIGH CAMPBELL-TAYLOR, Pastor, Presbyterian Church (U.S.A.), Atlanta, GA; *190, 193, 199, 202.* GREG CAREY, Professor of New Testament, Lancaster Theological Seminary, Lancaster, PA; *252, 255, 269.* WARREN CARTER, LaDonna Kramer Meinders Professor of New Testament, Phillips Theological Seminary, Tulsa, OK; *82, 92, 102, 108.* GARY W. CHARLES, Pastor, Cove Presbyterian Church, Covesville, VA; *145, 155, 251, 260, 262, 269.* DIANE G. CHEN, Professor of New Testament, Palmer Theological Seminary of Eastern University, St. Davids, PA; *142, 146, 152.* L. JULIANA M. CLAASSENS, Professor of Old Testament and Head of Gender Unit, Faculty of Theology, Stellenbosch University, Stellenbosch, South Africa; *545, 554.* KIMBERLY L. CLAYTON, Interim Senior Pastor, Trinity Presbyterian Church, Atlanta, GA; *2, 5, 13, 15, 21, 24, 30, 33.* JOSEPH J. CLIFFORD, Pastor, Myers Park Presbyterian Church, Charlotte, NC; *444, 446, 453, 464, 465.* ANDREW FOSTER CONNORS, Senior Pastor, Brown Memorial Park Avenue Presbyterian Church, Baltimore, MD; *278, 281, 283.* ADAM J. COPELAND, Assistant Professor of Health Care Administration, Mayo Clinic College of Medicine and Science, Rochester, MN; *182, 190, 200.* SHANNON CRAIGO-SNELL, Professor of Theology, Louisville Presbyterian Theological Seminary, Louisville, KY; *71, 76, 83, 93.* STEPHANIE M. CRUMPTON, Assistant Professor of Practical Theology, McCormick Theological Seminary, Chicago, IL; *290, 291, 294.* GREGORY L. CUÉLLAR, Associate Professor of Old Testament, Austin Presbyterian Theological Seminary, Austin, TX; *390, 395, 400, 404, 409.* R. ALAN CULPEPPER, Dean Emeritus, McAfee School of Theology, Mercer University, Hartwell, GA; *390, 395, 400, 404, 409.*

ROBERT F. DARDEN, Professor of Journalism, Public Relations, and New Media, Baylor University, Waco, TX; *114, 119, 123, 128, 133, 137.* MARÍA TERESA DÁVILA, Visiting Associate Professor of Practice, Religious and Theological Studies, Merrimack College, North Andover, MA; *124, 133, 136.* DAVID A. DAVIS, Pastor, Nassau Presbyterian Church, Princeton, NJ; *181, 183, 190, 192, 200.* CAROL J. DEMPSEY, OP, Professor of Theology: Biblical Studies, Department of Theology, University of Portland, Portland, OR; *362, 371, 380, 382.* DAVID A. DESILVA, Trustees' Distinguished Professor of New Testament and Greek, Ashland Theological Seminary, Ashland, OH; *142, 151.* MAGREY R. DEVEGA, Senior Pastor, Hyde Park United Methodist Church, Tampa, FL; *444, 453, 463, 467.* DAN R. DICK, Assistant to the Bishop, Wisconsin Conference, United Methodist Church, Sun Prairie, WI; *481.* LEWIS R. DONELSON, Professor of New Testament, Austin Presbyterian Theological Seminary, Austin, TX; *317, 319, 326, 328.* JOSEPH A. DONNELLA II, Visiting

Professor of Worship, St. Mary's Ecumenical Institute, Baltimore, MD, and interim Pastor, St. Paul's Lutheran Church of Utica, Thurmont, MD; *210, 220, 222, 225.* SHARYN DOWD, Retired Pastor and Professor, Mableton, GA; *281.* JILL DUFFIELD, Senior Pastor, First Presbyterian Church, Greensboro, NC; *421, 430, 439.* PAUL SIMPSON DUKE, Co-Pastor, First Baptist Church of Ann Arbor, Ann Arbor, MI; *31, 35, 40.* STACEY SIMPSON DUKE, Co-Pastor, First Baptist Church of Ann Arbor, Ann Arbor, MI; *105, 123, 125, 132, 134.*

JAMES H. EVANS JR., President and Robert K. Davies Professor Emeritus of Systematic Theology, Colgate Rochester Crozer Divinity School, Rochester, NY; *141, 143, 151.* KEN EVERS-HOOD, Pastor, Tualatin Presbyterian Church, Tualatin, OR; *472, 481, 494.*

FAIRFAX F. FAIR, Pastor, First Presbyterian Church of Pasadena, Pasadena, TX; *501, 509, 519, 520.* STEPHEN FARRIS, Professor of Preaching Emeritus, Vancouver School of Theology; Dean Emeritus, St. Andrew's Hall; Visiting Professor of Preaching, University of Toronto, Etobicoke, Ontario; *390, 400, 409, 413.* RENATA FURST, Associate Professor of Scripture and Spirituality, Oblate School of Theology, San Antonio, TX; *335, 339, 345, 354, 357.*

DAVID GAMBRELL, Associate for Worship, Office of Theology and Worship, Presbyterian Mission Agency, Louisville, KY; *493, 499, 502, 508, 512, 521.* DAVID G. GARBER JR., Associate Professor of Old Testament and Hebrew, McAfee School of Theology, Mercer University, Atlanta, GA; *211, 219.* MATT GAVENTA, Senior Pastor, University Presbyterian Church, Austin, TX; *531, 536.* KENYATTA R. GILBERT, Professor of Homiletics, Howard University School of Divinity, Washington, DC; *528, 537, 541.* DONNA GIVER-JOHNSTON, Pastor, Community Presbyterian Church of Ben Avon, Pittsburgh, PA; *356, 365, 371, 374.* MARCI AULD GLASS, Pastor, Calvary Presbyterian Church, San Francisco, CA; *233, 236, 243, 245, 252, 254, 260, 263.* TIMOTHY GOMBIS, Professor of New Testament, Grand Rapids Theological Seminary, Grand Rapids, MI; *278, 285.* BRIDGETT A. GREEN, Assistant Professor of New Testament, Austin Presbyterian Theological Seminary, Austin, TX; *309, 318, 321, 326.* JOEL B. GREEN, Professor of New Testament Interpretation, Fuller Theological Seminary, Pasadena, CA; *2, 13, 17, 22.* WILLIAM GREENWAY, Professor of Philosophical Theology, Austin Presbyterian Theological Seminary, Austin, TX; *165, 174, 181, 191, 200, 213.* ALAN GREGORY, Principal, St. Augustine's College of Theology, West Malling, Kent, UK; *12, 14, 21, 31.* A. KATHERINE GRIEB, Director, Center for Anglican Communion Studies, Virginia Theological Seminary, Alexandria, VA; *222, 242.*

ANGELA DIENHART HANCOCK, Associate Professor of Homiletics and Worship, Pittsburgh Theological Seminary, Pittsburgh, PA; *408, 411, 417, 420, 429.* L. DANIEL HAWK, Professor of Old Testament and Hebrew, Ashland Theological Seminary, Ashland, OH; *3, 92, 113.* CAROLYN B. HELSEL, Associate Professor in the Blair Monie Distinguished Chair of Homiletics, Austin Presbyterian Theological Seminary, Austin,

TX; *261, 265, 269*. PHILIP BROWNING HELSEL, Assistant Professor in the Nancy Taylor Williamson Distinguished Chair in Pastoral Care, Austin Presbyterian Theological Seminary, Austin, TX; *282*. LYDIA HERNÁNDEZ-MARCIAL, Assistant Professor of Hebrew Bible, Wartburg Theological Seminary, Dubuque, IA; *528, 536*. LUCY LIND HOGAN, Hugh Latimer Elderdice Professor of Preaching and Worship, Wesley Theological Seminary, Washington, DC; *209, 213*. JOHN C. HOLBERT, Lois Craddock Perkins Professor Emeritus of Homiletics, Perkins School of Theology, Southern Methodist University, Dallas, TX; *39, 49, 52*. SALLY SMITH HOLT, Professor of Religion, Belmont University College of Theology and Christian Ministry, Nashville, TN; *417, 422, 426, 427, 435, 436, 440*. PAUL K. HOOKER, Associate Dean for Ministerial Formation and Advanced Studies, Austin Presbyterian Theological Seminary, Austin, TX; *436*. CATHY CALDWELL HOOP, Pastor, Grace Presbyterian Church, Tuscaloosa, AL; *222, 233, 235, 242, 244*. CAMERON B. R. HOWARD, Associate Professor of Old Testament, Luther Seminary, St. Paul, MN; *292, 301*. JAMES C. HOWELL, Senior Pastor, Myers Park United Methodist Church, Charlotte, NC; *161, 163, 177*. EDITH M. HUMPHREY, William F. Orr Professor of New Testament, Pittsburgh Theological Seminary, Pittsburgh, PA; *528, 540*. GEORGE R. HUNSBERGER, Professor Emeritus of Missiology, Western Theological Seminary, Holland, MI; *299, 300, 304*.

DAVID SCHNASA JACOBSEN, Professor of the Practice of Homiletics; Director of the Homiletical Theology Project, Boston University School of Theology, Boston, MA; *299, 303*. LYNN JAPINGA, Professor of Religion, Hope College, Holland, MI; *445, 449, 454, 464*. CYNTHIA A. JARVIS, Retired Minister/Head of Staff, The Presbyterian Church of Chestnut Hill, Philadelphia, PA; *72, 82, 87, 93, 97*. WILLIE JAMES JENNINGS, Associate Professor of Systematic Theology and Africana Studies, Yale Divinity School, New Haven, CT; *2, 7, 12, 26*. PABLO A. JIMENEZ, Associate Professor of Preaching; Associate Dean of the Latino and Global Ministries Program, Gordon Conwell Theological Seminary, South Hamilton, MA; *141, 153*. JOSHUA W. JIPP, Associate Professor of New Testament, Trinity Evangelical Divinity School, Deerfield, IL; *394, 403, 408*. DAVID W. JOHNSON, Associate Professor of Church History and Christian Spirituality, Austin Presbyterian Theological Seminary, Austin, TX; *499, 500, 513, 519*. PATRICK W. T. JOHNSON, Pastor, First Presbyterian Church, Asheville, NC; *208, 209, 214*. BETH FELKER JONES, Professor of Theology, Wheaton College, Wheaton, IL; *103, 114, 118*.

EUNJOO MARY KIM, Professor of Homiletics and Liturgics, Iliff School of Theology, Denver, CO; *299, 300, 302, 308, 311, 320*. STEVEN J. KRAFTCHICK, Professor Emeritus in the Practice of New Testament Interpretation, Candler School of Theology, Emory University, Atlanta, GA; *30*.

ELIZABETH C. LAROCCAPITTS, Senior Pastor, Saint Mark United Methodist Church, Atlanta, GA; *417, 426, 428, 435*. CLEOPHUS J. LARUE, Francis Landey Patton Professor of Homiletics, Princeton Theological Seminary, Princeton, NJ; *503, 508, 518, 522*. JOEL MARCUS LEMON, Associate Professor of Old Testament; Associate Director of the Graduate Division of Religion, Candler School of Theology, Emory University, Atlanta, GA; *48, 51, 57*. MICHAEL L. LINDVALL, Pastor Emeritus, The

Brick Presbyterian Church in the City of New York, New York, NY; *39, 43, 49, 53*. GERALD C. LIU, Assistant Professor of Worship and Preaching, Princeton Theological Seminary, Princeton, NJ; *438, 447, 453, 456*. KIMBERLY BRACKEN LONG, Editor, *Call to Worship*, Presbyterian Church (U.S.A.), Louisville, KY; *151, 154, 527, 530, 536, 539, 548*. THOMAS G. LONG, Bandy Professor Emeritus of Preaching, Candler School of Theology, Emory University, Atlanta, GA; *39, 41, 57, 60, 554, 557*. BARBARA K. LUNDBLAD, Joe R. Engle Professor of Preaching Emerita, Union Theological Seminary, New York, NY; *161, 164, 172, 176*.

ELLEN OTT MARSHALL, Associate Professor of Christian Ethics and Conflict Transformation, Candler School of Theology, Emory University, Atlanta, GA; *57, 61, 65*. J. CLINTON MCCANN JR., Evangelical Professor of Biblical Interpretation, Eden Theological Seminary, St. Louis, MO; *160, 163, 166, 172, 175, 181, 184*. DONYELLE MCCRAY, Assistant Professor of Homiletics, Yale Divinity School, New Haven, CT; *329, 335, 338, 344, 347*. IAN A. MCFARLAND, Robert W. Woodruff Professor of Theology, Candler School of Theology, Emory University, Atlanta, GA; *220*. DONALD K. MCKIM, Editor, Congregational Ministries Publishing, Presbyterian Church (U.S.A.), Germantown, TN; *4, 92, 95, 116, 445, 454, 458, 464, 468*. SCOT MCKNIGHT, Julius R. Mantey Professor of New Testament, Northern Seminary, Lisle, IL; *389, 399, 412*. TIM MEADOWCROFT, Senior Lecturer in Biblical Studies, Laidlaw College, Auckland, New Zealand; *499, 500, 508, 511, 518*. JAMES C. MILLER, Professor of Inductive Biblical Studies and New Testament, Asbury Theological Seminary, Florida Dunnam Campus, Orlando, FL; *123, 127*. BLAIR R. MONIE[†], Professor in The Louis H. and Katherine S. Zbinden Distinguished Chair of Pastoral Ministry and Leadership, Austin Presbyterian Theological Seminary, Austin, TX; *83, 88, 93, 98, 103*. MARTHA L. MOORE-KEISH, J. B. Green Professor of Theology, Columbia Theological Seminary, Decatur, GA; *160*. D. CAMERON MURCHISON, Professor Emeritus, Columbia Theological Seminary, Decatur, GA; *191, 193, 545, 549, 555*.

RODGER Y. NISHIOKA, Senior Associate Pastor; Director of Adult Educational Ministries, Village Presbyterian Church, Prairie Village, KS; *48*. VANTHANH NGUYEN, SVD, Professor of New Testament Studies, Catholic Theological Union, Chicago, IL; *499, 504, 509, 519, 523*.

PATRICK ODEN, Visiting Assistant Professor of Theology and Church History, Fuller Theological Seminary, Pasadena, CA; *546, 550, 555*. ANNA B. OLSON, Director of External Relations for Cristosal, an organization working to advance human rights in Central America; *164, 167, 172, 173*. HIERALD E. OSORTO, Executive Director for Student Equity and Belonging; Director, Office of Religious and Spiritual Life, Ithaca College, Ithaca, NY; *363, 367, 372, 385*.

CARLTON J. "COBBIE" PALM, Assistant Professor, Silliman University Divinity School, Negros Oriental, Philippines; *554, 556*. SONG-MI SUZIE PARK, Associate Professor of Old Testament, Austin Presbyterian Theological Seminary, Austin, TX; *490, 492, 545, 547*. JULIE FAITH PARKER, Associate Professor of Biblical Studies,

General Theological Seminary, New York, NY; *40.* MICHAEL PASQUARELLO III, Methodist Chair of Divinity, Director of the Robert Smith Jr. Preaching Institute, Beeson Divinity School, Samford University, Birmingham, AL; *546, 555, 559.* AMY PLANTINGA PAUW, Henry P. Mobley Jr. Professor of Doctrinal Theology, Louisville Presbyterian Theological Seminary, Louisville, KY; *223, 228, 234, 238, 242, 247.* AMY PEELER, Associate Professor of New Testament, Wheaton College, Wheaton, IL; Associate Rector of St. Mark's Episcopal Church, Geneva, IL; *31, 34, 42.* ZAIDA MALDONADO PÉREZ, Professor Emeritus of Church History and Theology, Asbury Theological Seminary, Florida Dunnam Campus, Orlando, FL; *218.* SANDRA HACK POLASKI, New Testament scholar and author, Richmond, VA; *290, 291, 295.* EMERSON B. POWERY, Professor of Biblical Studies, Messiah College, Mechanicsburg, PA; *61, 66, 72.* MARK PRICE, Pastor of Congregational Life, Christ United Methodist Church, Franklin, TN; *251, 256, 270, 274.*

GAIL RAMSHAW, Professor Emerita of Religion, La Salle University, Arlington, VA; *272, 278, 284, 291, 293.* ROBERT A. RATCLIFF, Editor-in-Chief, Westminster John Knox Press, Louisville, KY; *417, 419, 426, 435, 437.* CYNTHIA L. RIGBY, W. C. Brown Professor of Theology, Austin Presbyterian Theological Seminary, Austin, TX; *208, 218.*

RUTH FAITH SANTANA-GRACE, Executive Presbyter, Presbytery of Philadelphia, Philadelphia, PA; *251, 261, 264, 273.* STANLEY P. SAUNDERS, Associate Professor of New Testament, Columbia Theological Seminary, Decatur, GA; *362, 363, 372, 376, 381.* DAVID J. SCHLAFER, Independent Consultant in Preaching and Assisting Priest, Episcopal Church of the Redeemer, Bethesda, MD; *61, 63.* MATTHEW RICHARD SCHLIMM, Professor of Old Testament, University of Dubuque, Dubuque, IA; *362, 364, 371, 373, 380.* BRADLEY E. SCHMELING, Senior Pastor, Gloria Dei Lutheran Church, St. Paul, MN; *141, 151, 152, 156.* CAROLYN J. SHARP, Professor of Homiletics, Yale Divinity School, New Haven, CT; *160, 163, 172.* MATTHEW L. SKINNER, Professor of New Testament, Luther Seminary, St. Paul, MN; *57, 60, 71, 77.* JOSEPH D. SMALL, Retired, Office of Theology and Worship, Presbyterian Church (U.S.A.), Louisville, KY; *227.* DENNIS E. SMITH†, LaDonna Kramer Meinders Professor Emeritus of New Testament, Phillips Theological Seminary, Tulsa, OK; *182, 186, 204.* SHANELL T. SMITH, New Testament scholar and Founder and CEO of Shanell T. Smith Consulting, LLC, West Hartford, CT; *212, 220.* SHIVELY T. J. SMITH, Assistant Professor of New Testament, Boston University School of Theology, Boston, MA; *163, 168, 173.* DANIEL L. SMITH-CHRISTOPHER, Professor of Theological Studies (Old Testament), Director of New Zealand Study Programs, Loyola Marymount University, Los Angeles, CA; *12, 21, 23, 30, 32.* C. MELISSA SNARR, E. Rhodes and Leona B. Carpenter Associate Professor of Ethics and Society, Vanderbilt Divinity School, Nashville, TN; *335, 337, 344, 346, 353, 355.* F. SCOTT SPENCER, former Professor of Religion at Wingate University, Wingate, NC, and former Professor of New Testament and Biblical Interpretation at Baptist Theological Seminary at Richmond, Richmond, VA; *278, 282, 286.* BENJAMIN M. STEWART, Gordon A. Braatz Associate Professor of Worship; Director of Advanced Studies, Lutheran School of Theology at Chicago, Chicago, IL; *380, 383, 393, 402.* BRENT A. STRAWN, Professor of Old Testament,

Duke Divinity School, Durham, NC; *102, 123, 132*. JERRY L. SUMNEY, Professor of Biblical Studies, Lexington Theological Seminary, Lexington, KY; *60*.

MARIANNE MEYE THOMPSON, George Eldon Ladd Professor of New Testament, Fuller Theological Seminary, Pasadena, CA; *223, 234, 243*. LEONORA TUBBS TIS-DALE, Clement-Muehl Professor Emerita of Homiletics, Yale Divinity School, Durham, NC; *472, 474*. PATRICIA K. TULL, A. B. Rhodes Professor Emerita of Old Testament, Louisville Presbyterian Theological Seminary, Louisville, KY; *181, 190, 199, 201*. EMRYS TYLER, Teaching Elder and Co-Director, Sonlight Christian Camp, Pagosa Springs, CO; *389, 399, 401, 408, 410*.

ALLIE UTLEY, Fellow, Theology and Practice, Vanderbilt Divinity School, Nashville, TN; *444, 453, 455*.

LEANNE VAN DYK, President and Professor of Theology, Columbia Theological Seminary, Decatur, GA; *290, 299*. RICHARD W. VOELZ, Assistant Professor of Preaching and Worship, Union Presbyterian Seminary, Richmond, VA; *473, 482, 490*.

ERIC WALL, Assistant Professor of Sacred Music, and Dean of the Chapel, Austin Presbyterian Theological Seminary, Austin, TX; *210*. ROBERT W. WALL, Paul T. Walls Professor of Scripture and Wesleyan Studies, Seattle Pacific University and Seminary, School of Theology, Seattle, WA; *448, 457, 463*. RICHARD F. WARD, Visiting Professor of Preaching and Practical Theology, Phillips Theological Seminary, Tulsa, OK; *185, 194, 199*. THEODORE J. WARDLAW, President, Austin Presbyterian Theological Seminary, Austin, TX; *2, 16*. NANCY LYNNE WESTFIELD, Professor of Religious Education, Drew University Theological School, Madison, NJ; *473, 477, 482, 486, 490, 491, 495*. DAVID F. WHITE, C. Ellis and Nancy Gribble Nelson Professor of Christian Education, Professor in Methodist Studies, Austin Presbyterian Theological Seminary, Austin, TX; *472, 476, 485, 491*. KHALIA J. WILLIAMS, Assistant Dean of Worship and Music, Assistant Professor in the Practice of Worship, Candler School of Theology, Emory University, Atlanta, GA; *64, 72, 75, 86*. PATRICK J. WILLSON, Retired Pastor, Presbyterian Church (U.S.A.), Santa Fe, NM; *527, 532, 537*. PHILIP WINGEIER-RAYO, Academic Dean and Professor of Missiology and Methodist Studies, Wesley Theological Seminary, Washington, DC; *558*. LAUREN F. WINNER, Associate Professor of Christian Spirituality, Duke Divinity School, Durham, NC; *505, 527, 529, 537, 538*. JOHN W. WRIGHT, Independent Scholar, San Diego, CA; *308, 310, 317, 326*. STEPHEN I. WRIGHT, Vice Principal (Academic Director), Spurgeon's College, London, UK; *509, 514, 518*. JOHN W. WURSTER, Pastor/Head of Staff, Saint Philip Presbyterian Church, Houston, TX; *126, 132, 135, 141, 144*.

BEVERLY ZINK-SAWYER, Professor Emerita of Preaching and Worship, Union Presbyterian Seminary, Richmond, VA; *222, 229*.

Scripture Index

About the Editor

HEIDI HAVERKAMP is the author of *Advent in Narnia: Reflections for the Season* (Westminster John Knox, 2015) and *Holy Solitude: Lenten Reflections with Saints, Hermits, Prophets, and Rebels* (Westminster John Knox, 2017). Having often searched for robust devotional books that could hold her interest, she has tried to write some herself.